WEXFORD

A TOWN AND ITS LANDSCAPE

Billy Colfer

CORK UNIVERSITY PRESS

Irish Landscapes: Volume III
Wexford: A Town and its Landscape

General Editors:
F. H. A. Aalen
Kevin Whelan
Matthew Stout

First Published by
Cork University Press
Youngline Industrial Estate
Pouladuff Road
Togher
Cork
Ireland

British Library Cataloguing in Publication Data
A CIP catalogue record for this book is available from the British
Library.

ISBN 9 78185918 429 5

Colour Reproduction by Keystrokes, Dublin
Printed by Graphy Cems, Navarra, Spain

This publication has received support from the Heritage Council
under the 2008 Publications Grant Scheme.

CONTENTS

ACKNOWLEDGEMENTS

I first saw Wexford's spires and harbour from the front of St Peter's College when I arrived there as a boarder in the early 1950s. Having grown up surrounded by the sea in the Hook, I remember feeling glad that I had at least a view of the ocean. That was my usual perspective of the town during the next five years, apart from occasional excursions 'down town' when a family member or friend paid a visit and brought me out. On the first and last days of term, there was plenty of time to explore the Main Street due to the limited bus service to the Hook. Woolworths, with its huge array of knick-knacks and toys, was the big attraction. Occasionally, we were brought down to attend a music event during the Opera Festival or to watch a Shakespearean play by the Anew MacMaster repertory company in the Theatre Royal. On 'free days' we were brought on long walks to places of interest in the environs of the town. These excursions introduced us to Ferrycarrig, Trespan Rock, Ferrybank via the old 'barrel bridge', and Johnstown Castle. The routes seemed to be chosen carefully so as to avoid shops but the more adventurous usually found a way around this. Our main contact with the town was through the 'day boys' who, for a small commission, would smuggle in such delicacies as tipsy cakes and Cleeve's toffee, which were eagerly sought after by the always-hungry boarders.

After St Peter's, I departed for St Patrick's College in Dublin, thinking that I had shaken the dust of Wexford town off my feet. After two years' training, to my surprise, I was offered a job in St Brigid's National School in Roche's Road, which I was glad to accept as teaching posts were scarce in the early '60s. As newly-weds, when we lived in a flat in an historic bishop's house in High Street, at the top of Kayser's Lane, I gained a different Wexford experience by working back-stage in the Theatre Royal during the Opera Festival. After a few years in St Brigid's, I transferred to the C. B. S. and subsequently worked there for over thirty years. As a teacher of Wexford children, I began to get a new perspective on the town, the different areas, various families, even slight variations in accent. My interest in the town led me to join the Wexford Historical Society and to become acquainted with Dr George Hadden's work on the town, published in the first issues of the society's journal. As the school curriculum expanded, I began to introduce my classes to local studies and to take them on exploratory walks. This activity ignited my interest in the history of the town's development and I began to collect the material that ultimately led to this

publication, celebrating the evolution of one of Ireland's Viking towns. This study complements the *Atlas of the Irish Rural Landscape* and is the third of a series that will focus in detail on different regions in Ireland.

I must record my gratitude to many individuals, organisations, friends and family for their assistance in the preparation of this publication. The encouragement and support of my mentor and friend Professor Terry Barry, Trinity College Dublin, has been fundamental to my work. I wish to acknowledge the influence and encouragement of the Wexford Historical Society of which I am a long-time member. I acknowledge the support of County Manager, Eddie Breen, and Town Clerk, Pat Collins; I am grateful to Wexford County Librarian, Fionnuala Hanrahan, and her staff, particularly Celestine Rafferty, Jarlath Glynn and Gráinne Doran, for unfailing help and patience; also to the mayor and Borough Council for permission to use the town crest and the mayoral seal. I wish to acknowledge the assistance of staff in: the National Library of Ireland; the National Museum of Ireland, particularly Mary Cahill and Finbarr Connolly; Gregory O'Connor and Elizabeth McEvoy of the National Archives; the Royal Irish Academy, especially Siobhán O'Rafferty; the Royal Society of Antiquaries, particularly Colette Ellison; Julitta Clancy who compiled the index. Many individuals, who frequently double as valued friends, have helped in various ways: Hilary Murphy for generously sharing his vast knowledge of Wexford sources and families; Ned Culleton whose advice and experience have always been inspirational; Tom Williams for illustrations and informed comment; Bernard Browne who is always generous with his wide knowledge of sources and publications; Ian Doyle for suggestions on sources; Geraldine Stout for many stimulating discussions; borough engineer Eddie Taaffe; Martin McDonald of Wexford County Council; Eithne Scallan for images and contacts; Brendan Ennis of Kerlogue Enterprise Centre; Daithí and Mary Nevins for unfailing interest and encouragement. I wish to thank the many people who allowed illustrations to be reproduced or helped me to source images; these include Paddy Donovan, Chris Wilson for wildlife photographs, Ursula Sinnott of Wexford Festival Opera, Rikke Johanson of Roskilde Viking Ship Museum, Tim O'Neill, Fr Matt Glynn, Denise Murphy, Tomás Hayes, John Hayes, Oliver Doyle, Anna Kinsella, Fr Brendan Nolan, Tom and Teresa Wickham, Willie Murphy, Liam Lahiffe, Irene Elgee, an t-Ath.

Séamus de Vál, Frank Forde, Tony Reck, John Duffy, Brian Doyle, Peter Miller and Anne Marie Caulfield. A special appreciation for the encouragement, professionalism and friendship of the late Caroline Thomas.

I am fortunate in having the backing of two close friends in the preparation of this book: the assistance given by Kevin Whelan, Director of the Keough Naughton Notre Dame Centre, a generous supporter of my work over many years, has been invaluable; the expertise and technological prowess of Matthew Stout is evident in the design of the book and the preparation of maps. A special word of thanks to all my family members: Paul and Helen; Eoin, Jackie, Finn and Seán; Donal, Eamonn; Niall, Lisa and Grace, for support and patience during the necessarily selfish work on this project, with a particular note of appreciation to Eoin for his personal memoir. As always, my wife Noreen has given me unstinted encouragement and backing and we have enjoyed many leisurely outings together during the research for this publication.

Finally, I wish to thank my editors, F. H. A. Aalen, Matthew Stout and Kevin Whelan, and Cork University Press, for commissioning this book.

FROM THE EDITORS OF *IRISH LANDSCAPES*

The *Atlas of the Irish Rural Landscape* was conceived to heighten awareness of the cultural landscape. Beyond a superficial appreciation of 'scenery', the landscape rarely impinged on Irish national consciousness. Despite its centrality in our daily lives, its very ubiquity camouflaged it. The *Atlas* was designed to allow Irish people to see, rather than merely to look at, their landscape. It sought to enhance the legibility of the landscape, making the familiar exotic, lifting the lid off the present surface to show the buried layers underneath. Here was a 'deep Ireland' exhibiting a tenacious longevity beneath the seemingly overwhelming changes that had surged through it. Seen in this way, the cultural landscape acquired a historical resonance that heightened appreciation of its aesthetic allure.

The *Atlas* appeared in 1997 at the onset of the Tiger years, and its emphasis on the fragility of the rural landscape struck a chord at a moment of momentous transformation in Ireland. Irish people appreciated that a wider understanding of the landscape was needed to foster appropriate policies, and the intention of the *Atlas* was to emphasise that the landscape itself, not just a series of points in it, had to be recognised, understood and safeguarded as a central component of the national patrimony.

The *Atlas* team highlighted the dynamism of the landscape, and the richly cumulative ways in which it had evolved as a shared creation of myriad generations. The Irish landscape is the most democratic and pluralist of documents, bearing the residual imprints of diverse communities. One section of the *Atlas* comprised six short case-studies demonstrating that diversity across a series of regions – the Hook in Wexford, Lecale in Down, the Burren in Clare, the Bend of the Boyne in Meath, the Ring of Gullion in Armagh and Connemara in Galway. It was always our intention to expand these studies (and commission other) into full-length volumes, modelled on the *Atlas*. The warm reception of the original *Atlas* (reprinted six times) encouraged the series – inaugurated by Geraldine Stout's *Newgrange and the Bend of the Boyne* (2002) and Billy Colfer's *The Hook Peninsula* (2004).

These volumes on the Boyne and the Hook brilliantly displayed the thematic concerns of the original *Atlas*: the landscape as a reciprocal relationship between nature and culture; the variety of regional landscape as a reflection of cultural diversity; the challenge to the inherited landscape by increasingly pervasive forces for change; the appreciation of landscape as a dynamic force, and the need for change to be introduced in sympathy with the inherited grain of the landscape.

Billy Colfer's *Wexford* expands the series by taking a large town as its theme, while still replicating the landscape focus and thematic emphases of the series. Wexford town has a rich history, a varied archival record, and a powerful personality embedded in its tight streets. All this is carefully unpacked by Billy Colfer, as he painstakingly builds up the landscape layers that underpin the town, period by period, component by component. The emphasis is different from a conventional history because the author remains focused on helping the reader to understand how the landscape of the town is evolving, so that the whole is always greater than the sum of the parts. To achieve that understanding in this most cosmopolitan of towns, it is necessary to range far and wide – from the Viking north to the Mediterranean south, from privateers to navy commodores, from croppies to entrepreneurs.

The result is a magnificent treatment of the evolution of a town, understood not just as an abstract pattern of bricks and mortar, but as a real place where people lived and loved, shopped and traded, fell and rose, all the time creating through their accumulated efforts a rich communal fabric. Wexford town has its own distinctive setting on its shallow harbour, its own way of doing things, its own accent, its own inheritance of streets and buildings and spaces. Together, they create the town, whose story is so beautifully recorded here by Billy Colfer.

F. H. A. Aalen
Matthew Stout
Kevin Whelan

Dedicated to the extended Colfer and Walsh families

Loch Garman

Rína loch in loch-sa thess,
loch Garman na nglan-écess
cúan cróebach lethan nal-long,
óenach na nethar n-etromm.

Inad as ruitoles do ríg,
i comraic muir is mór-thír,
dún iar ndóichur indal as,
súairc Rosilad a senchas.

Chief lough of the southern loughs
Wexford of the celebrated sages
Its wide but winding harbour
The meeting place of slender ships.

A place fit for a king
Where sea and land meet
A stronghold after the idols were cast out
Whose history was happily heard.*

Eochaid Eolach Ua Cerin

12th-century Metrical Dindshenchas

Calligraphy by Tim O'Neill   Translation by Kevin Whelan

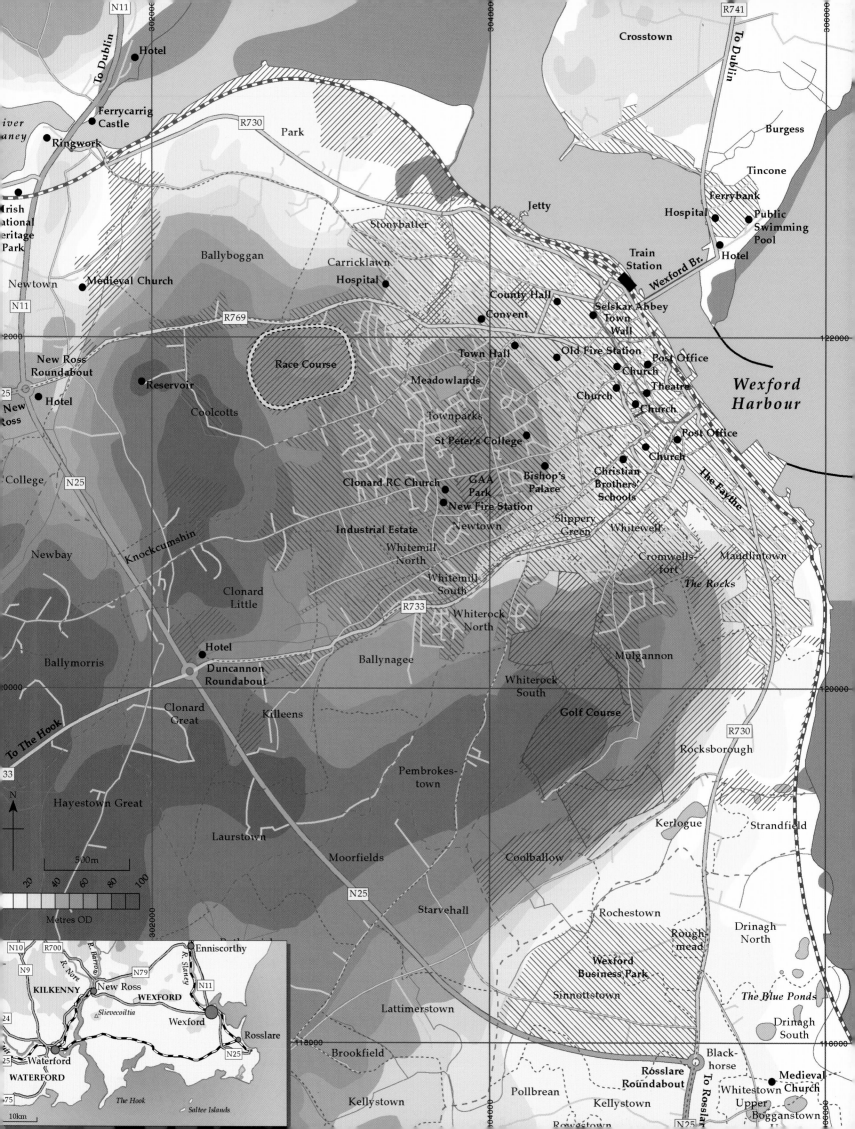

WEXFORD TOWN: INTRODUCTION

Wexford, located at the mouth of the Slaney, in the barony of Forth in south-east Ireland, is the principal town of the county to which it gives its name. The ready availability of an abundant food supply attracted settlement to the shores of the shallow estuary from earliest times. Known in Irish as Inbhear Sláine (the Slaney estuary), or Loch Garman, the harbour has been used as a gateway to south-east Ireland by successive waves of newcomers, including the Vikings (who gave it its present name), the Anglo-Normans and the English. The strategic nature of the estuary led to the town's foundation by Viking sea-rovers, but the shallow, barred nature of the harbour, and limited potential for navigation on 'the sandy Slaney',[1] hindered the town's growth. Historically, because of its location close to busy sea routes, Wexford has been of strategic importance, particularly in the medieval period. Only in the late nineteenth century, with the increasing draught of steamships, did the harbour finally lose out, giving way to the new port of Rosslare Harbour. A millennium of nautical involvement has had a marked impact on the evolution of the town and far-flung maritime influences contributed to its cultural identity.

Wexford's location on viable international trade routes inevitably influenced the town's growth. During the Viking period, links were established with other European ports. Following the taking of the town by the Anglo-Normans in the late twelfth century, protection was a priority as it provided a gateway to Britain for the recently arrived occupants. Security and administration requirements in the thirteenth century led to the strengthening of the Viking town wall and the construction of a castle. The granting of charters by the lords of Leinster in the medieval period established the fundamental matrix for subsequent social and infrastructural organisation, bestowing a cohesive character on the town's development and adding a new layer of occupants to the town and its hinterland.

Fig. 1 Wexford is located on the west shore of the Slaney estuary at the narrows between the inner and outer harbour. The ground climbs from the town to the 230m height of Forth Mountain to the south-west. For most of its existence, Wexford was confined to its walled medieval core and suburbs, with expansion taking place on land reclaimed from the harbour. During the last century, extensive growth has occurred, principally to the west.

In the mid seventeenth century, Wexford town, with the barony of Forth, had one of the highest densities of Old English family names in Ireland.[2] Similarly, the high ratio of English townland names with cultural elements is the product of this distinctive settlement history.

During the centuries following the arrival of the Anglo-Normans, Wexford enjoyed considerable status as an international port, despite endemic problems with the 'barred haven'. The town's success as a port was partly due to the policy of maintaining a fleet of small ships specifically designed to cope with the difficult harbour. This had the added advantage of facilitating trade with ports such as Bridgewater and Chester which had similar approaches. Early seventeenth-century Dutch charts containing instructions for navigating Wexford Harbour indicate the significance of the town as a port-of-call for European shipping. The fishing industry, based on the extramural suburb of the Faythe, was central to Wexford's prosperity and the town's fortunes ebbed and flowed with the unpredictable herring shoals.

The opening up of the New World and the Reformation transformed Ireland's international significance, resulting in changes to the political and religious landscapes. Subsequent to the introduction of the Penal Code, Wexford port spearheaded the transportation of young men to train as Counter-Reformation priests in the Irish colleges of continental Europe. When the Confederate Catholics rose in rebellion in 1641, Wexford was selected as their chief port because of its tactical location. The havoc wreaked by the town's fleet of privateer frigates on English shipping precipitated Cromwell's sack of the town in 1649, followed by the expulsion of the inhabitants and the confiscation of their property. This cataclysmic event intended, in theory at least, to create a tabula rasa, brought the town's medieval era to a bloody end and introduced an infusion of English settlers to inhabit the town. However, for pragmatic economic reasons, the new owners had no choice but to allow the former inhabitants to return as 'hewers of wood and drawers of water'. The Catholic merchants, whose expertise and continental contacts were essential to the town's prosperity, were also permitted to resume business, frequently as tenants in houses and premises which they previously owned. Although to some extent operating illegally, they emerged as a Catholic mercantile elite who fundamentally influenced the expansion of the town over the next two centuries . Until the early nineteenth century, the town was controlled politically by a minority Protestant ascendancy whose Georgian town houses brought a more formalised architectural style to Wexford's streets.

During the eighteenth century, Wexford ships travelled the sea lanes of the world and the fame of the town's mariners was widely acclaimed. Their skill was epitomised by Wexford man John Barry, hailed as the father of the American navy after their Revolution. By the end of the century, the town had become a primary centre of the corn trade, the many malt-stores in which barley was prepared for the breweries of Dublin creating a new element on the Wexford skyline. The first step towards major infrastructural innovation was the construction of bridges across the Slaney at Wexford and Ferrycarrig in the mid 1790s.

By the last decade of the century, the reverberations of revolutions in France and America, with their philosophy of liberty and equality, had reached Ireland. The establishment of the non-sectarian United Irishmen led inevitably to the Rebellion of 1798, mostly associated with county Wexford. Once again, because of the town's strategic significance, control of Wexford was hotly contested by both sides and for the third time in its history it was subjected to siege. Although taken by the rebel army and re-taken by the government forces, the town was fortunately not sacked, as on both occasions the occupying force left without offering any opposition. In the aftermath of the Rebellion, the business of the town returned to normal quite quickly. Early in the new century, industrial activity was given impetus by the creation of a new waterfront with a continuous quay. Extensive land reclamation in the south of the town facilitated the construction of new streets and a dockyard. The construction of a military road from Duncannon Fort to Wexford opened up a new road in the town along the

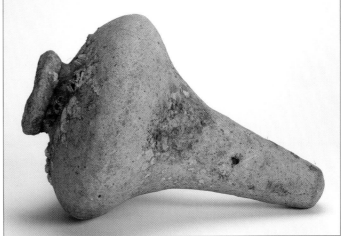

Fig. 2 Wexford's development was inextricably linked with its harbour and the sea. The town's significance as an international port is typified by this intact fifteenth-century Spanish oil jar brought up from the bottom of the harbour by a mussel dredger in the 1970s. The barnacle encrustation was caused by a long submersion in the sea.

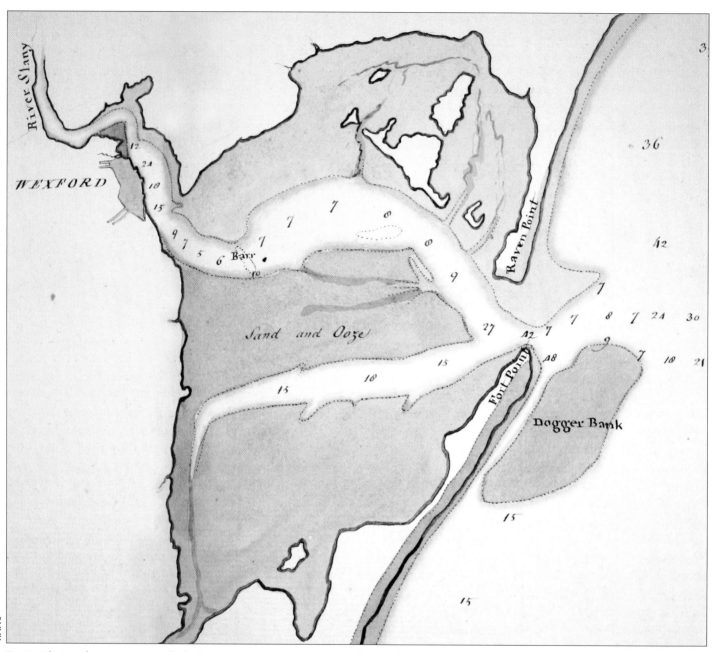

Fig. 3   The treacherous nature of the harbour led to frequent attempts to chart its shifting channels. This was made difficult by the baffling changes caused by wind and tide. This example from the 1770s illustrates the challenges presented by the bar at the narrow entrance and the fluctuating depth. During the last two centuries, the harbour has been changed radically by land reclamation to the north and south and the erosion of Rosslare point.

valley of the Bishopswater stream, which quickly became a focus for industrial development. In 1829, Wexford's political and social life was transformed by Catholic Emancipation, which allowed the Catholic business community to take control of the Corporation. This coincided with the emergence of powerful Catholic families who orchestrated a boom in shipping, business, industry and building over the next fifty years. The town's success inevitably attracted the railway, which, after arduous negotiations, was laid down along Wexford's quayfront in the 1880s, to connect with a proposed new port at Rosslare Harbour. As the relentless move towards bigger steamships gathered pace, the railway, although passing through the town on its way to Rosslare Harbour, effectively bypassed Wexford's barred estuary and ultimately hastened the demise of the port.

By the early twentieth century, the rapid growth which Wexford had experienced in the previous century had evaporated. In 1911, industrial production in the town was damaged by a bitter industrial confrontation between the recently unionised workers and the owners of the three iron works. The town remained largely aloof from the Easter rebellion of 1916, but was touched by the bitter civil war which followed the War of Independence. Wexford

Fig. 4   Until the early nineteenth century, Wexford's waterfront consisted of a series of jetties projecting into the harbour. The straight quayfront built at that time was extended late in the century to accommodate railway tracks. The recent extension was added to facilitate the main drainage scheme and to provide a successful waterfront amenity for the town. At present, the quay is used mostly by mussel dredgers and a small number of fishing boats.

shared in the European trauma of World War I during which many men from the town and district fought in the trenches. Towards the end of the war, the port's historically strategic location in relation to Irish Sea and Atlantic sea routes was again highlighted by the establishment of a U. S. Navy sea-plane base at Ferrybank, from which the seas off the south and east coast were patrolled in search of German submarines.

In the early years of the last century, apart from the development of land reclaimed from the harbour, Wexford's residential streets had not expanded beyond its medieval core and the extramural suburbs of the Faythe, John's Street and Slippery Green. Little changed until after World War II when the Corporation began to build housing estates on the periphery of the town. This trend accelerated exponentially during the second half of the twentieth century as private developers capitalised on an ever-increasing demand. Industry in Wexford experienced a similar pattern. As traditional industries encountered difficulties in the post-war period, the struggling town fell into a serious slump resulting in widespread emigration. This stagnant phase is well captured in Billy Roche's novel, *Tumbling down* and his *Wexford trilogy* of plays, and

also in Larry Kirwan's memoir, *Green suede shoes*. From the 1960s onwards, this situation has been gradually reversed, aided by the construction of a ringroad in the 1980s near which industrial estates were located, at Clonard, Drinagh and Kerlogue. Unlike the town's industrial recovery, Wexford no longer functions as a commercial cargo or ferry port. The harbour is used extensively by pleasure craft,[3] and, from a commercial perspective, its shallow mudflats host a thriving mussel industry.

In the thousand years since its foundation by the Vikings, Wexford has absorbed a succession of ethnic groups including Irish, Anglo-Normans (including English, French, Flemish and Welsh) and seventeenth-century English settlers. All of these have been absorbed into the town's melting-pot and have combined to give Wexford people their distinctive character, accent and personality. They have added to the fabric of the town over the centuries, collectively creating the modern Wexford. In the early years of the twenty-first century, Wexford, with the rest of Ireland, has been the destination for a new wave of arrivals from distant lands. In time, they will add their own chapters to the town's enduring story.

LOCATION AND ENVIRONMENT

Located on the northern periphery of the south county Wexford lowland plain, Wexford town is situated beside the Slaney estuary, at the eastern extremity of a ridge of high ground sloping from Forth Mountain, eight kilometres to the south-west. Landscape and environment fundamentally affected the growth of the town; the location beside a barred but strategic estuary and busy shipping lanes was of vital significance. Natural resources, on land and sea, influenced the site, nature and development of the town as well as the occupations and lifestyles of the inhabitants. The bedrock has been exploited as a valuable economic asset for building and other purposes. The soil, deposited over the rocks by glacial activity, has largely determined the quality of land and its potential for food production, which in turn inevitably impacted on subsequent settlement and society.

The Slaney rises in county Wicklow, entering county Wexford at Bunclody, before flowing diagonally across the county to enter the sea at Wexford Harbour.[1] The mouth of the Slaney consists of two sections, each with its own distinctive character. The inner estuary broadens out after the river has passed through the narrow glacial gorge at Ferrycarrig. Two small but significant streams enter this part of the estuary; the Sow from the north near Castlebridge and the Carrig river from the west just below Ferrycarrig. The water from the inner estuary is then confronted by another narrows before the force of the river is dissipated on the mudflats of the shallow outer harbour, created by the deposition of alluvial silt over the millennia, and augmented by sand eroded from the soft clay cliffs of the east coast. Unlike the inner harbour, the outer bay has undergone considerable change in historic times. This has been partly due to the impermanent nature of the north and south sandspits, which separate the harbour from the sea, and which are breached by a variable gap through which the river reaches the ocean. The silt still remaining in the river waters has added to the challenges of the tortuous harbour by forming a difficult bar outside the entrance. The two river narrows have been influential in the evolution of settlement around the estuary. The placenames Ferrycarrig and Ferrybank record the use of the narrows as ferry points. At the end of the eighteenth century, both were bridged and endure as bridging points to the present time.

Fig. 1   This aerial view, looking west from the harbour mouth, shows the town of Wexford at the centre of the picture, located just outside the river narrows between the inner and outer harbour at the mouth of the Slaney. The narrows, a traditional crossing-point, was bridged in 1794 and remains the location of the modern bridge. The extensive mudflats at the harbour mouth illustrate the challenging nature of the estuary for maritime activity. Rosslare sandspit is seen in the left foreground and the south slob is at centre-left. Between the two, the submerged banks of failed attempts at reclamation are visible. The shallow harbour with its extensive mudflats is now the centre of a thriving mussel industry.

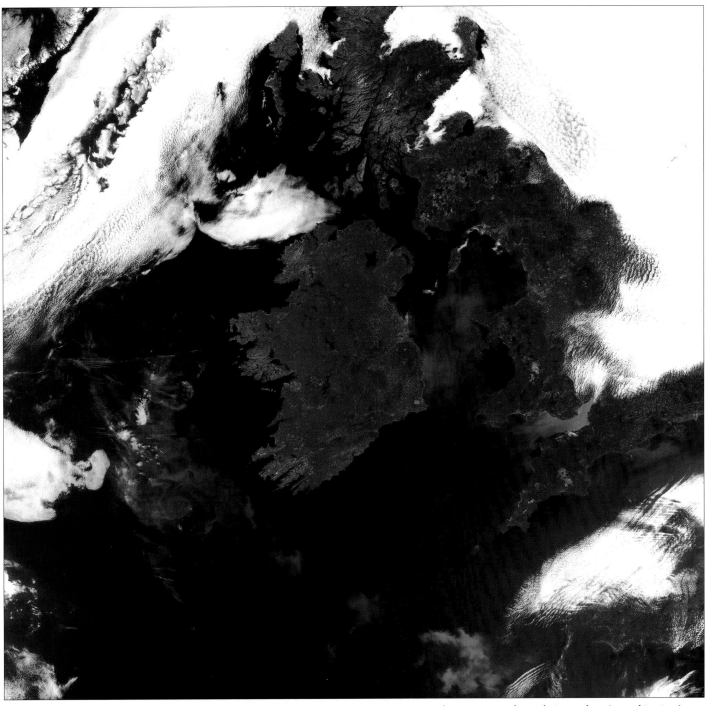

E.P.A.

Fig. 2   This satellite image illustrates Wexford's advantageous location as a port. Located at the entrance to the Irish Sea with its busy shipping lanes, it was strategically placed to trade with Britain and the continent. Despite endemic problems with a barred harbour, the town's locational advantages allowed it to operate as a busy port for many centuries. The advent of bigger steamships heralded the end of an era and although some of the smaller ships continued to cross the bar for a while, the port finally closed for commercial traffic in the mid twentieth century.

LOCATION

The Viking founders of the settlement that would eventually become Wexford town selected a site on the west bank of the outer harbour, just beyond the narrows. At this point, the river scoured out a deep channel close to the shore, making it a strategic location for the sea-faring inhabitants of the settlement. To the south-east, the marshy estuary of a small stream afforded protection as

well as providing a convenient beaching place for ships. Priority was given to the maritime advantages of the site as the topography was not conducive to settlement. The Viking encampment was situated on the shore-line, at the foot of a rocky slope which led to the high ground associated with the rough terrain of what is now called Forth Mountain, but known as Ard Lemnachta in the Celtic period.[2] South of the longphort, and the marshy

stream, a spur of this high ground terminates in rocky outcrops at Mulgannon and Kerlogue. The awkward slope, combined with the marshy valley to the south, hindered expansion, and, from the town's inception, encouraged reclamation from the shallow waters along the shore-line. Access to the hinterland was impeded by the difficult environment of Forth Mountain and the marshy estuary to the south. To the north-west, the deep glens of the Farnogue stream and the Carrig river presented further obstacles. As a result, roads from the town diverged south or north-west, skirting the high ground and fording the rivers at suitable points. These routes were linked by a road represented by the present John's Street and School Street.

Some of the town's placenames reflect the topography of the location: these include Rocksborough, Trespan Rock, Rocklands, Whiterock, Summerhill, Hill Street, Windmill Hill and Carrigeen (little rock). In the medieval core of the town, all of the streets slope down to the Main Street, particularly Bride Street, Peter's Street, Kayser's Lane and George's Street. Lanes and streets from the high central part of the Main Street fall sharply to what was the original shoreline; where this slope does not exist, the Main Street is still subject to occasional flooding, as the seawater reclaims what was formerly part of the harbour.

The site that became Wexford was selected in spite of locational disadvantages. The choice was primarily maritime, in spite of the treacherous navigational hazards off the south-east corner of Ireland and the tortuous harbour. The fact that the harbour, and ultimately the town, was given the descriptive name of Waesfiord – a broad, shallow bay – makes this point eloquently. On the plus side, the harbour offered deep-water anchorage close to the shore and limited access to the hinterland along the Slaney. The problems relating to navigation at a local level were compensated for by Wexford's advantageous position in the broader context of the Irish Sea trading network, and an unrivalled location in relation to Britain and the continent. In spite of endemic difficulties with a barred haven, this locational advantage sustained Wexford's status as a significant port until the early twentieth century and it is still being exploited by ferries from the modern port of Rosslare. Despite the awkward nature of the proto-urban site, it did offer certain attractions. Streams provided fresh water as well as power for mills and a plentiful supply of provisions was assured from the surrounding countryside and the rich waters of the harbour. More crucially, when the Vikings began to overwinter, the teeming wildfowl population on the mudflats, or slobs, provided an unlimited source of food. An account from 1682 describing the harbour as 'abundantly stored with wild fowl', would presumably have been valid for earlier centuries.[3]

GEOLOGY

Over a vast period of time, the area of south county Wexford has been the site of deep oceans, volcanoes, large rivers flowing through arid deserts, shallow tropical seas

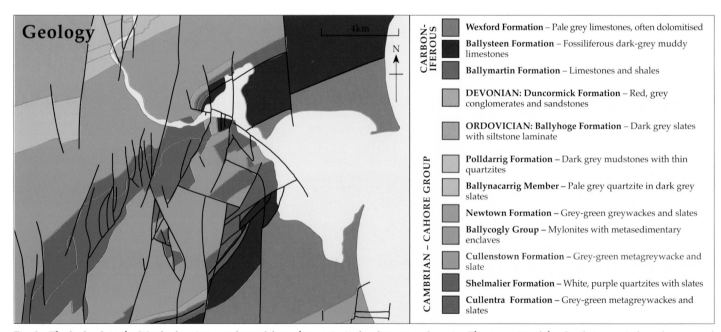

Fig. 3   The bedrock in the Wexford region was formed from three principal sedimentary deposits. These consist of the Cambrian period sandstones and siltstones with associated quartzites, best seen on the high ground of Forth Mountain, west of the town, where the rock was quarried in the recent past; a small deposit of Old Red Sandstone which has been quarried extensively and can be seen in some of the town's principal buildings; and the limestone deposits to the north and south of the harbour which have been exploited for commercial use at Kerlogue and Drinagh to the south-east of Wexford town.

Fig. 4 The siltstone and quartzite bedrock was quarried extensively at Carrigafoyle on Forth Mountain for many years. When the quarry closed down, the area was landscaped and the quarry site subsequenty flooded, creating a scenic lake with panoramic views of the surrounding countryside.

teeming with life and most recently frozen beneath glaciers. The rocks underlying the vicinity of Wexford town are primarily sedimentary in nature, deposited under the margins of an ocean which covered the region for millions of years.[4] Sedimentary rocks like sandstone and limestone are familiar as building materials such as cut stone and slates and as processed materials such as cement.

Greywacke Sandstones

The oldest rocks belong to the Cahore Group of the Cambrian period, deposited in a marine basin 570 to 510 million years ago by earthquake-generated currents which carried large quantities of sand and mud. These sedimentary rocks are principally represented in the Wexford town region by the Newtown, Cullentra and Cullenstown Formations, which are dominated by grey-green and occasionally purple or buff-coloured greywacke sandstones (grey or green sandstone or siltstone containing a high proportion of mud), metagreywackes (altered greywackes), and slates. The greywackes of these formations are interbedded with varying proportions of similarly coloured mudstones. A long section through the metagreywackes of the Cullentra Formation is exposed in a roadcut south of Ferrycarrig bridge. The greywacke succession was interrupted mid-way by the deposition of pure quartz sands (hard clear to white material) which

had been cleaned of muddy matter by the winnowing action of currents on a shallow marine shelf, forming the white and locally purple quartzites of the Shelmalier Formation. These quartzites have proved resistant to erosion and are exposed along the length of their outcrops. They have been quarried extensively, and on Forth Mountain the contact between the quartzite of the Shelmalier Formation and the underlying greywackes is exposed in the west wall of the Carrigfoyle quarry on

Fig. 5 South of Wexford town, in an area known as 'the rocks' in the townlands of Maudlintown, Rocksborough and Kerlogue, quartzite outcrops overlook the low-lying limestone to the south. This example, known as Maidentower, is just west of the Rosslare road.

Fig. 6   During the late nineteenth and early twentieth centuries, limestone was quarried at Drinagh, south of the town, near the water's edge, for use in the manufacture of cement in a factory equipped with the latest machinery. A series of flooded quarries in the vicinity are known as 'the blue ponds' because of the reflected colour of the grey-blue limestone. A tall chimney marks the ruins of the factory, now almost hidden in trees, a striking reminder of the extensive industry that was based on the limestone bedrock of the area. The proximity of the railway and the harbour provided convenient transport. The limestone was also burned in the kilns at nearby Kerlogue for sweetening land that was deficient in lime.

Shelmalier Commons. Outcrops of quartzite are also visible from the main road in the townlands of Maudlintown, Mulgannon, Rocksborough and Kerlogue, to the south of the town, and on the banks of the Slaney just north of Ferrycarrig bridge. The distinctive purple quartzite was used to construct a number of older buildings in Wexford town.

Old Red Sandstone

The Devonian period (410 to 355 million years ago) was a period of rapid erosion and deposition under semi-desert conditions in an area which had once been an ocean. This period saw the creation of red beds of locally derived pebble and cobble conglomerates, sandstones and mudstones. The beds of Old Red Sandstone survive only in separated outliers in south Wexford, where the entire succession of red conglomerates, sandstone and siltstone is well displayed along the west side of the Hook peninsula. The coarser-grained rock types represent river channels meandering over a floodplain, which in turn is indicated by the finer-grained siltstones and mudstones.[5] Old Red Sandstone rocks from the earliest Carboniferous period, known as the Duncormick Formation, are found in a narrow strip from Duncormick to Wexford town and

in an outlier at Park. Poorly exposed, the formation consists mostly of conglomerates with subsidiary siltstones, sandstones and mudstones.

Carboniferous Limestone

As the early Carboniferous sea (355 to 290 million years ago) gradually advanced northwards, successive depth-related sediments were laid down. This series, deposited

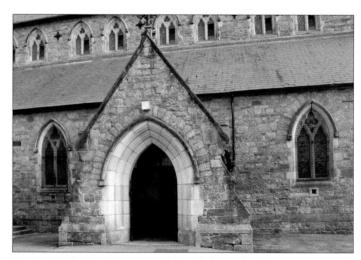

Fig. 7   Old Red Sandstone quarried at Park, north of the town, was used to build the twin churches at Bride Street and Rowe Street.

Fig. 8   This aerial perspective from the west shows the town perched between the outer and inner harbours. The dark area in the right middle-distance marks the wood on the Raven Point. The reclaimed area of the North Slob can be seen at right centre. Several building-sites chart the continued expansion of the town beyond its medieval core. The ring-road around the town, from Ferrycarrig to the Rosslare road, is at the bottom of the picture.

in deeper sub-tidal conditions, consists of interbedded dark-grey muddy limestones and calcareous shaley mudstones. In south county Wexford, limestone is found in the Hook peninsula and in a band running from Duncormick to Curracloe, forming the northern and southern shores of Wexford Harbour. The limestone underlying the Wexford town region is sub-divided into three formations.

The Ballymartin Formation   The Ballymartin Formation comprises a succession of interbedded dark-grey muddy limestones and calcareous mudstones. The presence of so much mud indicates that a land source, probably the Leinster Massif, was being eroded to supply the material.

The Ballysteen Formation   The lower part of the Ballysteen Formation consists of well bedded, relatively clean sand-grade limestones, passing gradually up into finer-grade and more muddy limestones. The formation represents carbonate sands and gravels produced primarily from the remains of crinoids[6] and fragments of other calcareous shellfish and corals which lived in the warm tropical shallow sea.

The Wexford Formation   The Ballysteen Formation is gradually overlain by the fine-grained limestone of the Wexford Formation, the topmost layers of which are rich in coral fossils. These limestones were laid down in shallow water conditions in an environment similar to the present day Persian Gulf.

The bedrock has been quarried for building and industrial purposes in several locations near the town. A quarry at Carrigfoyle on Forth Mountain which once produced quartzite aggregate is now closed. The floor of the disused quarry is flooded and the east side has been landscaped. The red and green slates, tightly folded with quartzite, which formed the east face, may still be seen. The west wall is formed by the quartzite of the Shelmalier Formation. South of the town, limestone was quarried extensively during the nineteenth century at Kerlogue, where it was burned to make lime and at Drinagh, where cement was manufactured. The site of the cement factory is marked by the survival of a tall chimney. The quarry holes, known as 'the blue ponds', are now flooded.

THE ICE AGE

About two million years ago, climate fluctuated between heat and cold, resulting in higher sea levels due to the melting of ice-caps during warm spells.[7] Evidence for these higher sea levels is provided by 'raised beaches' along the south Wexford coast. These consist of a layer of beach pebbles and sand occurring well above the height of present sea level. During cold periods, glaciers moved across the land, depositing a layer known as glacial drift, containing material ranging from large boulders to fine clay. Sand and gravel found in sand-pits is referred to as fluvioglacial because it was laid down by glacial melt-water. Glacial features in the Wexford town region are legacies of the most recent Quaternary events which ended 15,000 years ago. Ice advanced from the Irish Sea and covered the eastern and south-eastern part of county Wexford and deposited a level blanket of till over the underlying bedrock. A characteristic feature of these deposits is the presence of sea shells from the bottom of the Irish Sea in the gravel pits of the area. The most spectacular evidence of this incursion by ice from the Irish Sea is found in the Screen–Blackwater region to the north of Wexford Harbour. The ice transported vast quantities of sand and gravel from the sea bed and as the ice began to melt, this material was sorted into the layers which can be seen in sand-pits and coastal sections. When huge lumps of ice, which became buried beneath the sand, later melted, depressions known as 'kettle holes' were created. Many of these filled with water resulting in an undulating landscape of sandhills (known as 'kames') and small lakes or ponds. This distinctive region north of Wexford Harbour is one of the finest examples of 'kame and kettle' topography in Europe.

The Ice Age had a profound effect on the environment, rounding off hills and depositing glacial till which filled up depressions and smoothed off the landscape. Other Ice Age features included meltwater channels, particularly the spectacular example at Brownscastle and Mulmontry, just north of Taghmon. This feature was presumably created by the diversion of the Slaney when its original course was blocked by a glacier, across the county to Bannow Bay, along the present route of the river Corock and its tributary the Aughnagroagh.[8] The extensive silting of Bannow Bay, as well as a vast area of the off-shore sea bed, indicates that a huge volume of silt-laden water emptied into the bay at some period. The Slaney eventually established its present course by cutting a gorge through the soft siltstone rock at Ferrycarrig in order to reach the sea.[9] Following the dissolution of the ice sheets, the sea level, which had fallen by 100 metres, rose inexorably again, and the processes of coastal erosion and deposition began to sculpt the soft coastline. The vulnerable nature of the glacial till cliffs on

O.S.I.

Fig. 9   During the last Ice Age, a glacier moving in from the Irish Sea deposited a layer of sand and gravel on the area around Screen, north of Wexford Harbour. The action of the ice converted the deposit into low sand hills (kames) and hollows (kettles), many of them flooded. This unique landscape is one of the finest examples of Ice Age kame and kettle. The deposits can be seen in a number of sandpits where the commercial value of the sand is exploited.

Fig. 10   During the Ice Age, the Slaney was blocked by a glacier at Ferrycarrig, three kilometres up-stream from Wexford town. The force of the dammed water eventually cut a new channel through the soft rock, creating the gorge through which the river now flows. The Slaney originally ran through the low ground now occupied by the Irish National Heritage Park. The moraine formed by the ice still exists south of the park. The reed-bed at A marks the original course of the Slaney below Ferrycarrig. It is now occupied by a tributary flowing from Forth Mountain, known as the Carrig river.

by 100 metres, rose inexorably again, and the processes of coastal erosion and deposition began to sculpt the soft

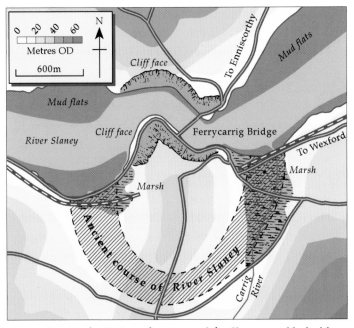

Fig. 11   During the Ice-Age, the course of the Slaney was blocked by a glacier, resulting in the re-routing of the river through the present gorge.

coastline. The vulnerable nature of the glacial till cliffs on Wexford's east coast contributed to the difficult nature of Wexford Harbour. As coastal erosion released material from the cliffs, it was deposited elsewhere, creating off-shore sandbanks, including the notorious bar at the entrance to the harbour. This slowed the exit of the river, encouraging the dropping of more silt in the estuary and the creation of the Rosslare and Raven sandspits. This on-going process creates a coastline that is hugely sensitive to human interference and the forces of nature.

SOILS

The most precious legacy of the Ice Age was the gift of the nutrient-rich material from which the soils were formed. Over time, climate, topography, vegetation and man impacting on these deposits have generated a complex soil pattern. The soils of the Wexford town region were formed from glacial drift emanating from the movement of glaciers from the Irish Sea and are mixed in quality.[10] The dominant soils in the area (the Rathangan Association, the Crosstown Complex and the Killinick Series), are generally well-drained, highly productive loams. The drainage of the sandy soils of the Screen Association, north of Wexford

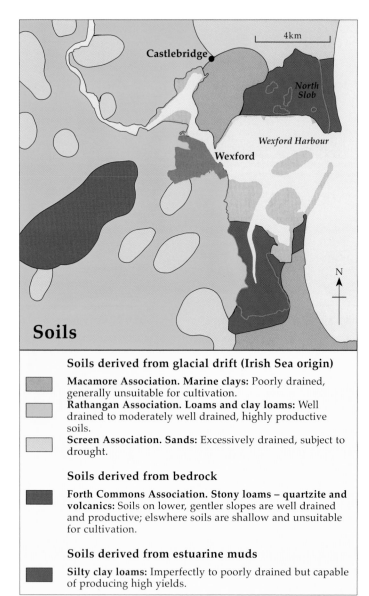

Soils

Soils derived from glacial drift (Irish Sea origin)

▨ **Macamore Association. Marine clays:** Poorly drained, generally unsuitable for cultivation.

▨ **Rathangan Association. Loams and clay loams:** Well drained to moderately well drained, highly productive soils.

▨ **Screen Association. Sands:** Excessively drained, subject to drought.

Soils derived from bedrock

▨ **Forth Commons Association. Stony loams – quartzite and volcanics:** Soils on lower, gentler slopes are well drained and productive; elswhere soils are shallow and unsuitable for cultivation.

Soils derived from estuarine muds

▨ **Silty clay loams:** Imperfectly to poorly drained but capable of producing high yields.

Fig. 12 The soils in the vicinity of Wexford, formed by Ice Age deposits, fall into eight categories with a mixed use range. Productivity has been improved by the use of fertiliser and machinery. North of Wexford's outer harbour, the coarse glacial sands of the Screen Association and the mixed deposits of the Macamore Association have a limited use-range. Elsewhere the land is generally productive apart from the Forth Commons Association which has a severely restricted use-range. The Wexford Slobs, reclaimed in the mid nineteenth century, are good for grass production and yield crops of wheat and barley under favourable conditions. Soil quality had a direct bearing on the region as settlers were attracted to the most productive soils.

Slob, are generally unsuitable for cultivation but are highly productive grassland soils. Excellent yields of wheat can be obtained in dry years. The productivity of soils has been improved greatly over the centuries by advances in technology and the application of fertilisers. The dangers of the excessive use of lime during the nineteenth century was expressed in the rhyme 'Lime and lime without manure/Makes both farm and farmer poor'. The soils in the hinterland of Wexford were of fundamental significance in the establishment of the settlement pattern in the region and in creating a support system which sustained the growth of the town.

WILDLIFE

Location and topography make Wexford Harbour and slobs a natural haven for birds migrating from Britain and the continent.[11] It is also a safe place for waders and wildfowl to feed, roost and breed. Features attractive to birds include the wide shallow harbour with extensive sandbars and mudbanks, protected by the sandspits of Rosslare and the Raven, the reedbeds of the slow-moving Slaney and large areas of reclaimed mudflats, traditionally known as slobs. More than 240 species of birds have been recorded in the harbour and slobs, including thousands of over-wintering ducks, geese and waders. The slobs are best known as the wintering place of 10,000 Greenland Whitefronted Geese, which represents one-third of the world population of the species! Historically, the presence

---

Solomon Richards' description of Wexford Harbour, 1682

The town and castle [of Wexford] *are washed on the north-east side by the mouth of the river Slaney, dilated into a pool of about six leagues in circumference, two necks of land from north and south pointing at each other over the harbour's mouth, without which lies the bar, at least a league at sea. This harbour or pool at the mouth of the river Slaney in Ireland, is abundantly stored with wild fowl, viz., teal, duck, wild swans, &c., but barnacle in multitudes, a fowl much bigger than a duck, but not so big as a goose, but as good meated as either. They are said by Gerrard and others, to breed, or rather to grow up trees (a gross mistake) but it is most certain that from the 21st day of August, on which day they come into the pool or harbour of Wexford, to the 21st May every year, they are in numbers wonderfull, but on the 21st day of May they do all leave it, going northwards by the sea, and in the opinion of many curious observers, they go to the Northern Isles of Scotland to breed, for on the 21st of August following, they do certainly return into the same pool or harbour of Wexford, bringing their young ones with them in numbers beyond expression. This relator, as he hath rode forward and backward betwixt Wexford and Dublin, hath often seen them at sea, coming a day or two after their departure, and for twenty years hath observed their not failing the time of going or coming, and also their swimming when the tide was with them, and their flying when the tide was against them, now and then resting themselves on the water.*

Brent Geese

Irish Hare

Little Egret

Emperor Dragonfly

Clouded Yellow Butterfly

Bee Orchid

Fig. 13 These pictures illustrate the vast number and variety of wildlife in Wexford Wildfowl Reserve, the Raven Nature Reserve, Wexford Harbour and the Wexford Slobs.

Red Squirrel

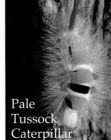
Pale Tussock Caterpillar

Peacock Butterfly

Atlantic Grey Seals

CHRISTOPHER J. WILSON

Fig. 14   In 1968, Wexford Wildfowl Reserve was established by the Department of Lands in association with the Irish Wildbird Conservancy (now IWC Birdwatch Ireland), primarily for the protection of Greenland Whitefronted Geese. The centre was opened officially in 1974. It was declared a Nature Reserve in 1981 and was extended in 1990. The North Slob and the Raven Wood are also designated as a Statutory Hare Reserve.

of such an abundant source of food in the harbour sustained settlement on its shores. A 1682 account described the arrival in the harbour, on 21 August, of the 'good meated' Barnacle geese in 'numbers beyond expression' and their departure on 21 May.[12] With such a tempting profusion of fish and fowl, it was inevitable that the community around the harbour would be steeped in the traditions of hunting and fishing. For generations, modern-day hunter-gatherers, living principally on Rosslare Burrow, used specialist techniques to harvest the mudflats and channels of the harbour. Mud boards, known as 'scooches', were attached to their feet to prevent sinking in the slimy ooze when searching for eels and shellfish. Fowlers operated at night in small, purpose built punts, fitted with fowling guns up to ten feet long. This activity demanded an intimate knowledge of the harbour and the wildfowl, and required great skill in handling the punt and the massive gun simultaneously.[13]

In 1968, 270 acres of the North Slob were purchased and the Wexford Wildfowl Reserve was established by the Department of Lands, in association with the Irish Wildbird Conservancy (now IWC Birdwatch Ireland). The finance was contributed by the World Wildlife Fund (now Worldwide Fund for Nature) and Messrs Arthur

Guinness. The centre was opened officially in 1974 and was declared a Nature Reserve in 1981 under the 1976 Wildlife Act. A further 207 acres was purchased in 1990 by the Office of Public Works in conjunction with the Irish Wildbird Conservancy. Although established primarily to create the proper conditions for the feeding and protection

ROBERT JOBSON

Fig. 15   Fowling depended on an inherited sense of the harbour and of the movement of the birds. The skillful wild-fowlers from north of the harbour who took part in the Rebellion of 1798 were immortalised in ballad by the lines 'What's the news, what's the news, oh my bold Shelmaliers, with your long-barrelled gun from the sea'.

CHRISTOPHER J. WILSON

Fig. 16   This picture captures the impressive sight of thousands of Greenland Whitefronted Geese leaving the North Slob in the late evening, heading towards Forth Mountain in the background before turning to head out to roost for the night on the sandbanks in Wexford Harbour.

of the Greenland Whitefronted Geese, in 1989 the North Slob, with the Raven Wood, was designated as a Statutory Hare Reserve. The Wildfowl Reserve draws 25,000 visitors annually. The combination of slob and harbour mudflats offers an attractive habitat. The reserve has proved to be a major attraction during the winter months when the arrival of the geese is a spectacular sight for nature lovers. It also adds a sense of natural splendour close to the town.

PRE-VIKING SETTLEMENT

A growing focus on the value of heritage has led to a deeper awareness of the intrinsic value of archaeological monuments as vital cultural elements of Irish life. An understanding of early settlement and society in the environs of Wexford Harbour depends on the survival of archaeological remains and the recovery of objects of historical significance. While every site is vital, an analysis of their distribution adds greatly to an appreciation of past societies. In spite of the advantages offered by the harbour as a gateway, as well as a source of food for incoming groups, the hinterland has surprisingly few surviving monuments from the prehistoric era. Over the past millennium, the productive soils of the region have been subjected to intensive cultivation and the scarcity of surviving sites may be due to removal by improving landowners. This scenario is strongly supported by an examination of ringforts in the region. As the pace of development accelerates, the archaeological record becomes ever more vulnerable and there is a risk that sites may be removed without investigation. Priority should be given to the conservation of monuments, as they provide crucial testimony to the changing lifestyles of previous generations.

The town of Wexford is located on the western shore of a broad shallow bay at the mouth of the Slaney where the river narrows between an outer and inner harbour. Because of shifting sands and land reclamation, the shape of the estuary has varied over the centuries. This is due in part to the impermanent nature of the long, narrow sandspits of the Raven and Rosslare to the north and south of the harbour's entrance. Archaeological discoveries, although sparse, help to build up an impression of pre-urban settlement around the shores of what is now known as Wexford Harbour. The plentiful food supply available in the bay, as well as its importance as a routeway, would inevitably have attracted settlement to its shores in prehistoric times.

As a strategic access point and routeway, as well as a source of abundant food, the shores of the estuary were a desirable settlement location. Flint implements dating from *c.* 5,000 to 3,000 B. C., found along the east coast of the county, are an indication of Mesolithic activity. These early people were drawn to the Slaney estuary and valley. Evidence for their presence around the river mouth, in the form of middens, was destroyed by natural and man-made changes. The harbour area continued as a focus for settlement in the Early Christian era.

N. M. I.

Fig. 1   The 1990 discovery of a gold hoard at Ballinesker on the east coast north of the harbour provides significant evidence for late Bronze Age activity in the vicinity of Wexford. The objects consist of two dress fasteners, one gold bracelet, two 'boxes' and two disks. The 'boxes' and disks have been identified as ear spools. These high-status objects point to the presence of a sophisticated society during the early part of the first millennium B. C.

NEOLITHIC

The Neolithic, or New Stone Age, saw the arrival of the first farmers. Pollen analysis shows that woodland was being cleared on Forth Mountain *c.* 4,000 B. C., to make way for farming.[1] Another indication of land clearance and agricultural practice is the variety of stone axeheads that have been found in the county. These early farmers are represented by a scatter of stone and flint implements near the Slaney estuary. Their descendants were responsible, *c.* 2,500 B. C., for building the dolmen (portal tomb), at Ballybrittas on Bree Hill, twelve kilometres up-river, not far from the right bank of the Slaney.[2] The potential for the recovery of evidence for Neolithic activity was demonstrated in 2002 by an archaeological excavation at Kerlogue, two kilometres south of Wexford town. Ideally located to exploit the resources of the harbour, the site yielded evidence for long-term occupation, including a quantity of Neolithic pottery.[3]

NED CULLETON

Fig. 2   Neolithic stone axes, like these examples found at Boolavogue and now in Enniscorthy Castle Museum, were used by the first farmers to clear woodland. The reconstructed handle shows how the axe was used.

BRONZE AGE

Evidence for Bronze Age settlement, particularly to the west of the estuary, is more plentiful and varied. Early Bronze Age burials in stone boxes, known as 'cists', have been found at Forth Mountain and Bolabaun to the west of the Slaney; urn burials have been uncovered at Newtown, near Ferrycarrig, and at Windmill Hill, just outside Wexford town. Bronze Age artefacts have been discovered at Forth Mountain and Johnstown.[4] The site at Kerlogue also yielded pottery and evidence for a large circular house from the early and late Bronze Age.[5] Two ancient cooking sites, known as *fulachta fiadh*, at Hayestown and Johnstown, may have originated in the Bronze Age but this technique survived into the Middle Ages. This

Fig. 3   Situated five kilometres from the right bank of the Slaney, twelve kilometres up-river from Wexford, this well-preserved portal tomb, known as a dolmen, at Ballybrittas on the slopes of Bree Hill, provides evidence for the existence of a well-organised, sophisticated society along the Slaney valley in the Neolithic period. Due to recent inappropriate planting, this important dolmen is now obscured by vegetation.

method of cooking involved dropping heated stones into a water-filled trough until it was brought to the boil. The food was then placed in the water to cook, more hot stones being added to maintain the correct temperature. The shattered stones were thrown into a pile surrounding the

Fig. 4   The shape of Wexford harbour has changed significantly during the past millennium. Sixteenth-century maps like the one shown here (Mercator, 1595), indicate that the harbour was more open to the sea at that time. The Rosslare sandspit is shown to the south but the same emphasis is not given to the Raven sandspit to the north, perhaps because it had not developed to its modern extent. The Raven Point used to be known as Norderey, indicating that it was formerly an island (the name contains the Norse suffix –ey, meaning island; perhaps North Island).

NED CULLETON

Fig. 5   In 1894, this Bronze Age clay urn, known as a food vessel, was discovered on Forth Mountain, as the stones of a cairn were being removed to provide material for building the breakwater in Wexford Harbour.

trough on three sides, eventually creating the diagnostic crescentic mound of burnt stones by which these sites are identified. The most significant late Bronze Age find in the vicinity of Wexford was the 1990 discovery of a gold hoard at Ballinesker on the east coast near the northern shore of the harbour.[6] The seven objects, found as a result of site clearance, consist of two dress fasteners, one gold

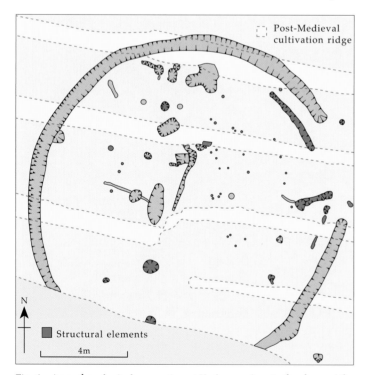

Post-Medieval cultivation ridge

N

Structural elements

4m

Fig. 6   An archaeological excavation at Kerlogue, close to the shore of the harbour, yielded Neolithic and Bronze Age artefacts as well as evidence for a circular Bronze Age house. These indications of long-term occupation could be attributed to the plentiful food supply in the harbour.

bracelet, two 'boxes' and two disks. The 'boxes' and disks are now restored and have been identified as spectacular ear spools, worn as personal ornaments. This has led to the identification of similar objects found elsewhere in Ireland, including four gold disks discovered in the late eighteenth century near Enniscorthy. These high-status objects point to the presence of a sophisticated hierarchical society in the region north of the estuary during the early part of the first millennium B. C. The presence of these Bronze Age gold artefacts in county Wexford may be related to gold deposits at Croghan Mountain on the Wexford/Wicklow border.[7]

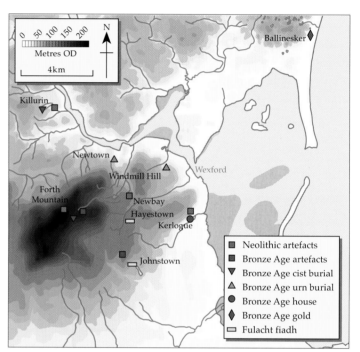

Metres OD

4km

N

Ballinesker

Killurin

Newtown

Windmill Hill

Wexford

Forth Mountain

Newbay

Hayestown

Kerlogue

Johnstown

■ Neolithic artefacts
■ Bronze Age artefacts
▼ Bronze Age cist burial
▲ Bronze Age urn burial
● Bronze Age house
◆ Bronze Age gold
▭ Fulacht fiadh

Fig. 7   The evidence for Neolithic and Bronze Age settlement in the hinterland of Wexford is distributed in the area west of the estuary. Pre-historic habitation sites close to the shoreline have been removed by extensive natural and man-made changes to the shape of the harbour.

IRON AGE

A Celtic Iron Age civilisation emerged in Europe in the middle of the first millennium B. C. and eventually extended from the Atlantic to the Black Sea.[8] This La Tène culture, so named after a site in Switzerland, dominated Europe until ultimately collapsing before the expanding Roman empire. Untouched by Rome, the Celts of Ireland and Britain flourished for many centuries longer. This period saw the emergence of small kingdoms in Ireland, defended by hilltop forts and linear earthworks. Towards the end of the Iron Age, the Irish Sea was a much-travelled highway, facilitating extensive contacts between communities on both sides. At the end of the first century A. D., the Roman historian Tacitus wrote of Ireland: 'The interior parts are little known, but through

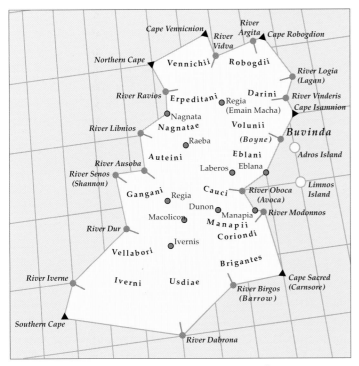

Fig. 8   The estuary of the Slaney did not feature on the second-century 'map' of the Greek cartographer, Ptolemy. Because of its significance from a maritime perspective, Carnsore Point is shown under the name Cape Sacred. The name of the barony of Bargy derives from the sept known as the Brigantes, shown in the south of the modern county Wexford.

commercial intercourse and the merchants there is better knowledge of the harbours and approaches.[9] In the mid-second century A. D., Ptolemy, a Greek cartographer living in Alexandria, compiled a list of known places in Ireland based on accounts of merchants and mariners. This 'map' identifies coastal promontory forts along the east coast of Ireland, some of which have recently produced evidence for Roman contacts.[10] A group known as the Menapii, recorded by Ptolemy in the general area of county Wicklow, was mistakenly associated with Loch Garman and, although the error was rectified, the erroneous association has persisted.[11]

Although evidence for Iron Age settlement in county Wexford is meagre, four coastal promontory forts associated with the period were located on the south Wexford coast.[12] Wexford Harbour, known as Loch Garman or Inbhear Sláine in the Celtic period, strategically located in relation to Britain and the continent, was presumably an important port of call on the Irish Sea trading route. There was a well-established link between south Wexford and Wales in the Early Christian period, which may account for the dedication of a holy well to St David of Wales near Oylegate.[13] An eleventh-century poem from the *Dindshenchas* describes Loch Garman as a busy, well-known venue for shipping. The 'ejection of idols' possibly refers to the triumph of Christianity over

paganism after the foundation of monasteries around the shores of the estuary during the Early Christian period.[14]

> Chief lough of the southern loughs
> Wexford of the celebrated sages
> Its wide but winding harbour
> The meeting place of slender ships.
>
> A place fit for a king
> Where sea and land meet
> A stronghold after the idols were cast out
> Whose history was happily heard.

EARLY CHRISTIAN SETTLEMENT

A combination of factors led to radical change in Irish society and landscape from the fifth century onwards. The advent of Christianity, leading to closer contact with the continent and the spread of technological innovations, were central to these changes. A substantial increase in pasture and arable farming, allied with the spread of a new type of plough and the horizontal mill, improved Irish food production, allowing an increase in population levels. This economic and demographic boom led to the construction of thousands of ringforts, enclosing single farmsteads involved in a predominantly pastoral economy, accompanied by complementary unenclosed settlement.[15] Crops were grown in irregular fields, some of which can still be identified. Ringforts are small circular enclosures, about 30m in diameter, usually consisting of an earthen bank and outer fosse which originally enclosed a house and farm buildings, and were used to protect the livestock in times of danger.[16] The vast majority of ringforts were constructed from the beginning of the seventh century to the end of the ninth century A. D. The ringfort is the most common archaeological feature in the Irish landscape, with at least 45,000 sites identified from various sources.[17]

By the beginning of the Early Christian period, about 400 A. D., the area now represented by county Wexford was controlled by a sept called the Uí Bairrche. They were replaced after several centuries by the Uí Chennselaig who gave their name to the kingdom which they ruled.[18] A number of septs who held minor kingdoms, or tuatha, in Uí Chennselaig, were dominated by the leading dynasty.[19] The Uí Bairrche and their allies the Fothairt occupied the two southern tuatha, to which they gave their name, now represented by the baronies of Bargy and Forth.[20] From the mythology associated with these Celtic groupings came the name of the river Sláine (Slaney) and the broad, shallow estuary of Loch Garman. Placenames containing the settlement-related elements 'Rath' (ringfort) and 'Baile'

C.U.C.A.P.

Fig. 9 Of twenty-seven recorded Early Christian ringforts in the Wexford region, only seven survive in various states of preservation. The rest have been identified from placename evidence or from aerial photography. This aerial view reveals a circular cropmark of an impressive bivallate ringfort at Kilmacree, five kilometres south-east of Wexford town.

(place) are also associated with the Early Christian era. A more substantial indication of settlement around Loch Garman in this period emerges from an analysis of the distribution of ringforts and church sites, the predominant settlement features in the Early Christian landscape.

Of twenty-seven ringforts recorded in the environs of Wexford Harbour, only seven survive above ground: the rest are identified from aerial photography or placename evidence.[21] As the removal of ringforts from the landscape has occurred since Norman times, these present an incomplete picture of the original pattern, but it is possible to make some general comments on their distribution. North of the harbour, ringforts are noticeably absent from the excessively drained kame and kettle area near the coast, which was not amenable to the cattle-based Celtic economy. Similarly, the rough terrain of Forth Mountain, west of Wexford town, was not attractive to ringfort dwellers.[22] The absence of ringforts in the immediate vicinity of the town could be due to their removal from burgal lands from medieval times onwards. The same applies to the lands of the borough of Carrig, situated three kilometres up-river in the townland of Newtown. If the lack of ringforts near Wexford can be attributed to the pressures of a high urban population, the density to the south of the town points to a substantial rural population in the pre-Norman period. This cluster is part of a concentration on the southern lowlands in the baronies of Forth and Bargy.[23]

Ecclesiastical centres

The most dramatic evidence for settlement around the shores of Loch Garman in the second half of the first millennium A. D., is the existence of at least fourteen Early Christian ecclesiastical foundations. The earliest and most famous of these was established in the fifth century by St Ibar (originally from the present county Down), said to have been a contemporary of St Patrick:[24]

> The light of bishop Ibar
> Who has smote every heresy's head
> A splendid flame over a sparkling wave
> In Becc-Eriu he departed.

There are strong indications that Uí Chennselaig was evangelised from Wales, independently of, and prior to, the Patrician mission.[25] The foundation, initially a school, was located on the small island of Begerin in the shallow northern part of Loch Garman. As contemplative places of peace and solitude, islands were frequently used as locations for early church sites. The monastery became famous and Ibar, who was also a bishop, was credited with converting many of the Irish to Christianity. He died

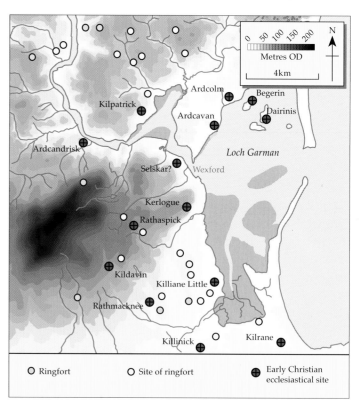

Fig. 10 The twenty-seven ringforts recorded in the Wexford hinterland are concentrated in two groupings. Both clusters are located on the better quality soils, one on the left bank of the Slaney, north of the town, and the other to the west of Wexford Harbour. Similarly, the fourteen Early Christian church sites are divided into two main groups: one on the islands and coast of the northern part of the estuary, the other associated with the ringforts west and south of the harbour.

Fig. 11   A cross-inscribed boulder and cross slab from Begerin church site, drawn by George Victor Du Noyer in the mid nineteenth century.

R. I. A.

Solomon Richards' account of Begerin, 1682

In this great pool or harbour is an island, called the Great Island. It is indeed, two islands, but being wadable from one to the other, they are accounted but one. There is also a lesser island, called Beg-Erin, in English 'Little Ireland'. In this island is a little chapel, and in that a wooden idol, in the shape of an old man, called St Iberian, from one Iberian, the patron saint of a church, the now chief in repair and in use in Wexford town. Which Iberian was (as he desired) buried in this island of Beg Erin. To him people go to worship, and in cases of controversies about debt, or otherwise, the parties go to this Island, where one swears before St Iberian, and the other is willingly concluded by his oath. Some idle fellows that love not wooden gods, have twice or thrice stolen away St Iberian, and cleft him and burned him, but still phoenix-like, another rises out of his ashes, and is placed there again, and the silly people are persuaded that it is restored by a miracle. And if the new one be the younger, the miracle is the greater. But there one is this day, and a living priest goes over now and then to fetch the silly people's offerings to keep them for St Iberian, no doubt on't.

c. 500 A. D. and was buried on Begerin. During the reclamation of the North Slob a wooden causeway was discovered between Begerin and the islands to the southeast. The monastery was in decline by the arrival of the Anglo-Normans in the late twelfth century. In the 1180s, the church and island of Begerin was granted to the Benedictine monks of St Nicholas, Exeter.[26]

Several other churches were established around the northern part of the estuary. St Caomhán's name survives in the placename Ardcavan, where he founded a church

WEXFORD COUNTY LIBRARY

Fig. 12   This bridge formerly connected Begerin Island (on the left) to the northern shore of the harbour. Forth Mountain and the spires of Wexford can be seen in the background. The 1949 drawing is by the late Mai McElroy, distinguished Wexford artist and local historian.

Fig. 13 A decorated cross and boulder from the church site on the island of Begerin to the north of Wexford Harbour, recorded in the nineteenth century. The reverse of the cross is inscribed with a horse and rider.

Fig. 14 A bullán stone in the vicinity of Killiane church. Usually associated with Early Christian church sites, the original purpose of these hollowed-out basin stones remains enigmatic.

near the water's edge. He also had a foundation on Dairinis, an island in the harbour which cannot now be identified. North of Ardcavan, also near the shore, a church dedicated to St Colmcille was founded at Ardcolm. The surviving circular graveyard testifies to the site's Early Christian origins.[27] Other churches were located to the west of the southern part of the harbour, in the area of greatest ringfort density. The names of four, Killiane, Killinick, Kildavin and Killiloge (modern Kerlogue), contain the prefix 'Kill' (*cill*: a church or cell). Circular

graveyards at Killiane, Killinick, Kildavin and a bullán stone at Killiane are diagnostic of Early Christian origin. The name Rathaspick (*rath an easpaig*: the bishop's rath) also indicates the early origins of the church there.

A pre-Viking settlement existed where three land routes met at the áth cliath (ford of the wattles) of Dublin: an associated early ecclesiastical enclosure has been identified in the modern street layout.[28] A similar scenario can be postulated for Loch Garman. Extensive evidence for settlement on both sides of the estuary suggests that, in the

Fig. 15 The medieval parish church of Killiane is located near the shore of the estuary south of Wexford. Killiane was part of the liberties of the town. The church is at the centre of a circular enclosure, marked by the line of trees, indicating that it occupies the site of an Early Christian foundation.

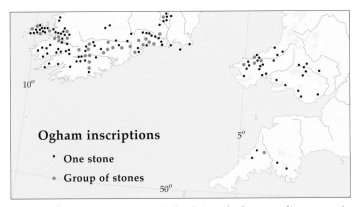

Fig. 16   The earliest writing in Ireland, inscribed on standing stones in an alphabet known as ogham, dates from about 300 A. D. and was used for several centuries. Ogham stones, often associated with Early Christian churches, are densest in southern Ireland and Wales, indicating contact between the two communities. Historically, the sea facilitated contact between the two regions. In the Early Christian period, monks from south Wales established foundations in south Wexford and in the late twelfth century the initial groups of Anglo-Normans to arrive in Ireland were recruited by Diarmait Mac Murchada in the Pembroke area. Many of the Welsh surnames that arrived at that time are now regarded as typical of county Wexford.

Early Christian period, approach roads converged on a ferry across the narrows between the inner and outer harbour (the site of the present bridge). As at Dublin, a semi-circular feature in the modern streetscape, generally regarded as a legacy of an Early Christian church enclosure, indicates that an Early Christian ecclesiastical foundation was located overlooking the ferry crossing, where the remains of Selskar Abbey now stand, with perhaps an adjacent pre-Viking proto-settlement. The foundation of the

RICHARD BOYLE

Fig. 17   A one metre high ogham stone at Cotts, Tacumshin in the south of the county, with an inscription deciphered as reading IARNI.

Augustinian priory of SS Peter and Paul at Selskar, after the arrival of the Anglo-Normans, is a further indication of an earlier church, as Irish monastic houses frequently adopted the Augustinian rule in the twelfth century.[29]

TOWNLANDS

The townland network provides the most pervasive landscape survival from the Gaelic era. Most townlands, many retaining their Irish names, pre-dated the arrival of the Anglo-Normans.[30] An analysis of townlands provides information on settlement patterns, relating in particular to the colonisation of the northern part of the barony of Forth by Anglo-Norman settlers in the late medieval period.[31] In the hinterland of Wexford, names such as Coolballow (*cúl bealach*: back road) and Coolree (*cúil fhraoigh*: heathery corner), convey topographical information. Others contain elements relating to former settlement activity: these include Bally (*baile*: place/home), Kil (*cill*: church) and Rath (*ráth*: ringfort). On the outskirts of Wexford, the large townland of Townparks with the small townlands to the immediate south, represent the historic corporation lands of the town.

Just south of Wexford town, a band of townlands with Irish names, in the parishes of Maudlintown and St Peter's running west on the high land leading to Forth Mountain, suggest that this marginal land was not attractive to the new medieval settlers and remained in the hands of the Irish. Some of the names reflect the nature of the topography; these include Rocksborough, Whiterock and Clonard (*cluain ard*: high meadow). The townlands in the parish of Carrig, bordering the Slaney to the west of Wexford, were associated with the failed medieval borough of Carrig, located in the townland of Newtown. The divisions in this parish are bigger, suggesting larger units of landholding and a more sparse settlement pattern. By contrast, the dense settlement on the rich land of the parish of Drinagh and part of Rathaspick, to the south, resulted in a complex of small townlands, many of them named after the medieval settler followed by the suffix 'town'. The parish of Killiane, on the other hand, was held by a free tenant of the borough of Wexford and was divided into five large townlands, four of them with Irish names.[32] Continuity of use is demonstrated in the case of the four rural parishes, all of which retained the Irish name of the original church centre.

Archaeological and historical evidence for ringforts and ecclesiastical centres indicates that the region around Loch Garman, in the tuatha of Fothairt, supported a considerable population towards the end of the first millennium, presumably attracted by the

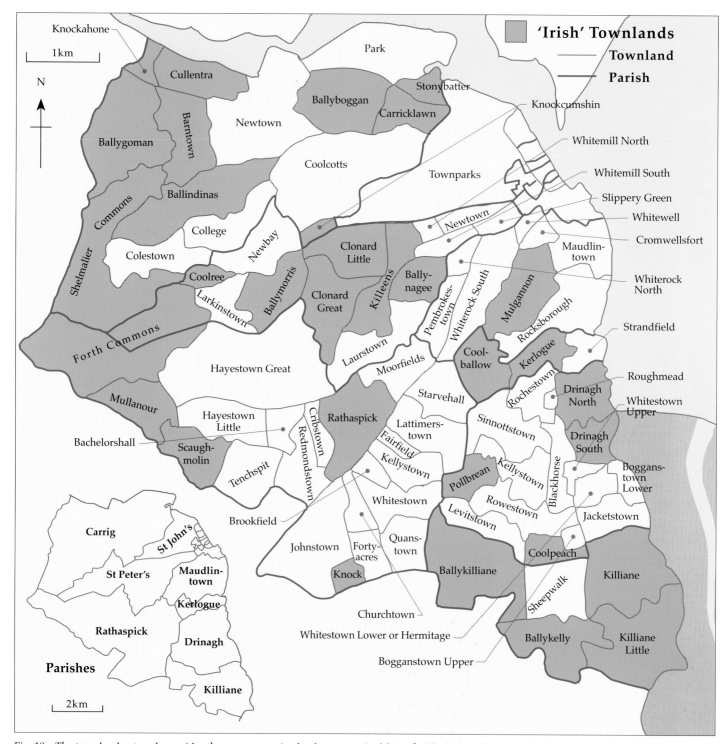

'Irish' Townlands
—— Townland
—— Parish

Fig. 18   The townland network provides the most pervasive landscape survival from the Gaelic era. Most townlands, many retaining their Irish names, pre-date the Anglo-Normans. An analysis of townlands provides information on settlement patterns, relating in particular to the colonisation of the barony of Forth by Anglo-Norman settlers in the late medieval period. The large townland of Townparks represents most of the liberties of the medieval town. A band of townlands with Irish names, running west on the high land leading to Forth Mountain, suggests that this marginal land was not attractive to English-speaking settlers and remained in the hands of the Irish. The dense settlement on the rich land to the south resulted in a complex of small townlands, many of them named after the original settler followed by the suffix 'town'. Continuity of use is demonstrated in the case of the four rural parishes, all of which retained the Irish name of the original church centre.

advantages afforded by the estuary and river. When the Scandinavian Vikings appeared off the south-east coast, they were quick to explore and exploit the estuary in their shallow-draught longships, eventually establishing a *longphort* or base on its shores which would evolve into the town of Wexford.

Carrig river

URBAN ORIGINS: THE VIKING ERA

For 300 years, beginning at the end of the eighth century, western Europe was subjected to attacks by roaming bands of sea-raiders from Scandinavia in search of plunder.[1] They were known by various names but are now generally described as Vikings (so called from their habit of lurking in the *vikr*, or inlets) or Norsemen, as those who reached Ireland were mainly from the region now known as Norway. The background to the Viking raids is obscure but it may have been related to the development of excellent shallow-draught sailing ships which brought the rest of Europe within easy reach of Scandinavian sailors. Monastic centres, with their concentrations of people, valuables and food, were irresistible targets, especially those situated near the coastline and on navigable rivers. Viking activity in Loch Garman was first recorded in 819 when the monastery on Begerin was attacked,[2] beginning an association with the harbour which was to last for four centuries. This was followed by raids on the monastery of Kilmokea on Inis Teimle (now Great Island) on the river Barrow about

820.[3] Raids on Taghmon and St Mullins are recorded for 824 and 825[4] and at the same period the Norse were defeated by Cairbre, king of Uí Chennselaig, aided by the community of Taghmon.[5] Further raids were reported on Ferns in 835 and 839.[6] In the 840s, the Vikings set up defended bases at Annagassan (in county Louth) and Dublin and for a while the raids intensified.

During the latter part of the century, the Vikings' focus switched to England, perhaps due to significant resistance by the Irish.[7] The first mention of a base in Uí Chennselaig was in 888 when the Norse of Port Lairge (Waterford), Loch Garman (Wexford Harbour) and St Mullins were defeated by the Irish.[8] A second wave of Viking raiding began in 914 with the advent of a great fleet in Waterford Harbour and, although vigorously resisted by the Irish, persisted until the middle of the century. From that point on, the Vikings made their heaviest impact on Ireland as traders and merchants from their port towns of Dublin, Wexford, Waterford, Cork and Limerick.[9]

Fig. 1   In 2007, a replica Viking longboat sailed from Roskilde to Dublin to mark the historical connection between Denmark and Ireland. The 30m ship, named *Sea Stallion from Glendalough,* was modelled on a wreck discovered in Roskilde fiord but built in Dublin in the mid eleventh century. Ships like this, ideally suited for navigating in shallow waters, frequented Waesfiord for several centuries duing the Middle Ages.

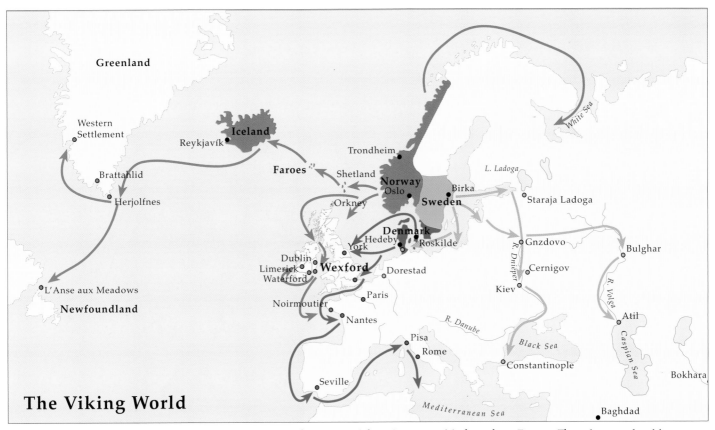

Greenland

Western
Settlement

Iceland

Reykjavík

Faroes

Shetland

Trondheim

L. Ladoga

White Sea

Brattahlid

Herjolfnes

Norway

Oslo

Birka

Staraja Ladoga

Orkney

Sweden

L'Anse aux Meadows

Newfoundland

Denmark

Hedeby

York

Roskilde

Gnzdovo

Bulghar

Dublin

Limerick

Waterford

Wexford

Dorestad

Cernigov

R. Dnieper

Kiev

R. Volga

Paris

Noirmoutier

Nantes

R. Danube

Atil

Caspian Sea

Pisa

Rome

Black Sea

Constantinople

Bokhara

Seville

Mediterranean Sea

Baghdad

The Viking World

Fig. 2   Because of their skill as navigators on river and sea, the impact of the Vikings was felt throughout Europe. They also completed long ocean voyages, reaching Iceland, Greenland and Newfoundland. Ireland's central location made it a crucial staging point for Atlantic voyages.

WAESFIORD: URBAN ORIGINS

It is not known at what stage the Norse *longphort*[10] at Loch Garman, first mentioned in 888, became a permanent base. It may have coincided with the establishment of a settlement at Waterford, shortly after the arrival of the great fleet in 912.[11] In 933 the foreigners of Loch Garman were again mentioned when they killed the son of Cairbre, lord of Uí Chennselaig, in a nocturnal raid[12] but no further references have been identified.

The Norse gave the descriptive name Waesfiord, a broad shallow bay, to the estuary at the mouth of the Slaney and the settlement became known by the same name.[13] The name may have derived from Ueigsford, possibly meaning 'the fiord of the water-logged land',[14] but the early adoption of the form Waesfiord makes it the more likely choice.[15] Waesfiord shares a common etymological origin with the Wash, a similar inlet on the east coast of England. The shallow-draught nature of their longships gave the Vikings a decisive advantage in dealing with the devious channel. Due to ever-shifting sands and nineteenth-century land reclamation, the modern harbour looks very different to the one that the Vikings frequented. The northern part contained several islands, most notably Begerin; the sand-dune area between

Curracloe and the Ravan Point was formerly known as Norderey,[16] (suffix–*ee*, an island, possibly north island), suggesting that a deep channel north of Begerin Island entered the sea at Curracloe.

The first temporary longphort established by the Vikings in Loch Garman was probably located on one of the islands, possibly Begerin which they used as a retreat after the arrival of the Anglo-Normans in the late twelfth century. Because of their defensive qualities, islands were frequently chosen as overwintering trading sites by the Norse raiders.[17] The exact location of the initial trading-base on the site of the town has not been identified but it may have been situated in a defensive position on the slope of a low promontory beside the harbour in the South Main Street/Bride Street area of the modern town. The promontory was insulated to the south by the marshy basin of a slow-moving stream; another stream flowed from the high ground 200 metres to the north. The estuaries of the streams created a deep pool, like the Dubh linn of Dublin, providing a suitable anchorage close to the shore. The inlet was subsequently included within the town ramparts, emphasising the importance of the deep pool. The pool's significance and location is marked by the Crescent Quay in the modern waterfront. The stream

*A bitter wind to-night. It tosses
the white hair of the Irish Sea. It will toss
the fierce raiders from Norway off their courses.
To-night I sleep in peace.*

(Translated by Seamus Heaney)

which flowed through the Norse settlement is also remembered in the name of Paul (originally Pole) Quay; a tidal inlet was commonly referred to as a 'pole' or 'pill'. The first bridge at Wexford was constructed over this inlet at a place still called Stonebridge. The stream, now known as the Bishopswater or Horse river, has been culverted and the low-lying marshy ground reclaimed, but periodic flooding occurs along its course, particularly at King Street and South Main Street. Topographically, the location was similar to Dublin and Waterford which were both situated where tributary streams entered the main river.[18] Sites associated with a tributary stream, protected by a marshy area and adjacent to a ferry-crossing, were typical of Viking settlements.[19]

As at Dublin,[20] the site at Loch Garman was overlooked by a ridge ten metres in height. The existence of a suitable ferry point on the Slaney and the convergence of several routeways could indicate the presence of an Early Christian ecclesiastical foundation, perhaps on the site of Selskar Abbey, where a semi-circular road feature may reflect the line of a monastic enclosure. In 1987 a crucial archaeological excavation at Bride Street, in the area between the two streams, uncovered sixteen medieval house sites, the earliest dating to the beginning of the eleventh century.[21] The property boundaries of the three earliest houses did not respect the lines of the modern

Fig. 4   This nineteenth-century map shows Wexford Harbour before the reclamation of the north and south slobs. The monastic centres on the islands in the north of the harbour were targeted by the Vikings.

streets, indicating that there were modifications to the layout of the early settlement. A smaller excavation at nearby Oyster Lane in 1974 revealed no evidence from the Viking period, possibly because it was nearer the shoreline and would have been utilised only after land reclamation.[22] As in the case of the earlier levels at Bride Street, the alignment of structural features at Oyster Lane did not conform to later boundary lines.

It is not possible at this stage to be precise about the morphology of the early Norse town. The earliest indications of its extent occur in the religious boundaries of the eleventh and twelfth centuries, by which time Scandinavian communities in Ireland had accepted Christianity and the addition of churches had impacted on the topography of the town.[23] The Norse towns established independent ecclesiastical structures, sending their bishops to Canterbury for consecration.[24] Unlike the later Anglo-Norman towns which were based on one large parish, the Norse towns favoured a complex system of small parishes, based on churches located both inside and outside the town wall.[25] An examination of 1841 O. S. maps reveals that parish boundaries followed the line of town defences in

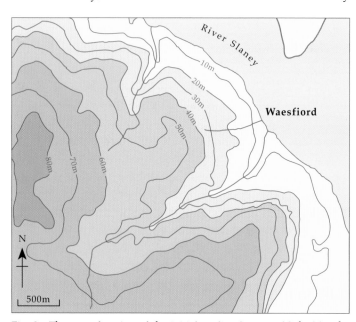

Fig. 3   The exact location of the initial trading-base established by the Vikings on the site of Wexford town has not been identified, but it may have been situated near the shore, on the slope of a low promontory in the South Main Street/Bride Street area. This site was protected to the south by the marshy valley of a slow-moving stream which provided a landing beach for shipping. The town subsequently spread along the shoreline and onto land reclaimed from the estuary.

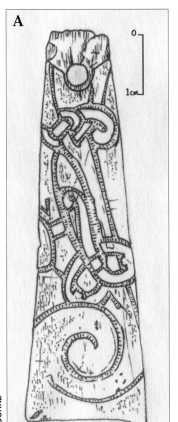

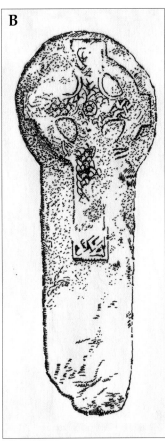

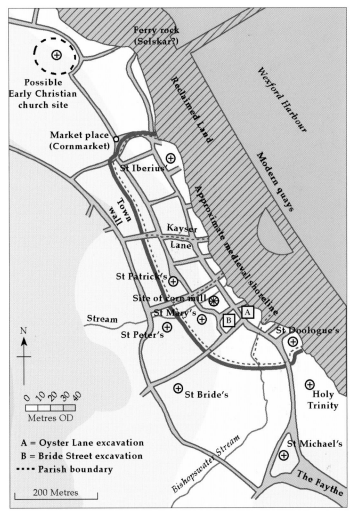

E. BOURKE

Fig. 5   (A) This bone pendant with Viking inter-lacing, dating to *c.* 1050, was found in 1988, with many other Viking artefacts, during an archaeological excavation at Bride Street in Wexford. (B) The Scandinavian influenced inter-lace on this cross (now in the National Museum) from the monastic site on Begerin Island suggests that the island was under the control of the Hiberno-Norse of Wexford. One of the churches in the town was dedicated to St Ibar, the founder of the monastery on the island. Following the arrival of the Anglo-Normans, some of the Norse took refuge on Begerin.

Fig. 6   This map shows the conjectural extent of twelfth-century Hiberno-Norse Wexford, based on pre-Anglo-Norman parishes. The town had four intra-mural parishes with four other churches outside the southern gates. There is some evidence for the existence of an Early Christian church on the site of Selskar Abbey. Extensive evidence for Viking occupation was found in an archaeological excavation at Bride Street (B).

subsequent to the foundation of the town suggests that ecclesiastical boundaries can be used as indicators of earlier urban development. There were five intramural parishes in the Anglo-Norman town of Wexford: St Doologue's, St Mary's, St Patrick's, St Iberius' and Selskar.[26] It is possible to speculate on how many of these were included within the rampart of the Norse town.

Starting in the south of the town, the smallest parish, St Doologue's, was bounded by the town wall and the stream which had been included within the defences. St Doologue's, or Olaf's, was a Norse dedication, also found in Dublin and Waterford.[27] The dedication of the neighbouring parish of St Mary's, bounded by the stream, the town wall and Peter's Street, was also pre-Norman[28] and the remains of Viking houses were excavated here.[29] The dedication of the next parish, St Patrick's, bounded by Peter's Street, the town wall and Kayser Lane, also has pre-Norman parallels.[30] It is unlikely that Kayser, the 'road to the quay' of the Viking town,[31] would have followed the

line of the town defences, indicating that the next parish, St Iberius, was also part of the Norse town. The Scandinavian-influenced decoration on a tenth-century cross-slab from Ibar's monastery on Begerin, now in the National Museum,[32] indicates a devotion to the saint and explains the dedication within the town. Cornmarket, the Bullring and Common Quay Street form the northern boundary of St Iberius parish and, presumably, this line marked the extent of the Norse town.

There is a marked change in the street pattern north of this point and the curved line of Cornmarket could follow the line of the Norse defences. This is supported by an eighteenth-century observation that 'the old wall of the town' ran down towards the sea near the Bullring.[33] If the Norse town consisted of these four parishes, the ramparts enclosed twenty-five statute acres (ten hectares), compared with fifty statute acres for Dublin (twenty hectares) and

Lane) and the principal thoroughfare of the town. This passed though the *faithche* (now the Faythe) just south of the town, through a southern and northern gate, to approach the ferry along a track by the foreshore, later known, after land reclamation, as Fore Street and Ferryboat Lane.[38] Another street ran parallel to it, higher up near the top of the slope. Formerly Back Street, this is now (for the most part) called High Street. There were three intersecting streets: Kayser's Lane, Peter Street and Bride Street. Narrow lanes ran down the incline from the main thoroughfare to the waterfront.

Four extramural pre-Norman churches associated with town gates on the southern side of the town may indicate the existence of suburbs.[39] The exact site of the church of the Holy Trinity is not known but it was described in 1684 as being 'near the castle' and is remembered in the name of Trinity Street.[40] Trinity well is shown near the seashore on the 1840 Ordnance Survey town plan. The approximate sites of St Bride's and St Peter's are known and their dedications survive as street names. The graveyard of St Michael's survives at Michael Street. All of these

Fig. 7 Kayser's Lane (the lane to the quay), originally leading from High Street to the shoreline, retains the Viking name relating to its original function. Forming the boundary between the parishes of St Patrick's and St Iberius', it must have been a central feature of the twelfth-century Hiberno-Norse town. At present, it crosses the Main Street and continues on, under an archway, towards the waterfront.

with fifty statute acres for Dublin (twenty hectares) and eighteen statute acres (seven hectares) for Waterford.[34]

Accepting this hypothesis, the market-place (modern Cornmarket) probably approached by a town gate, was situated just outside the town wall 200 metres from the conjectured monastic centre. Market-places were typically located to the east or south-east of monastic enclosures.[35] The connecting road, now Abbey Street, may have been the Market Street referred to in the thirteenth century.[36] The ferry landing, located at the point where the crossing was shortest, was situated to the north of the Norse town, making it accessible to the native Gaelic population. The area where it was situated was called Selskar, from the Norse *sker* meaning a rock.[37] A rock outcrop, one of several in the harbour, may have provided the base for the ferry quay. In time the name was also applied to the locality and the abbey. The ferry was approached by two roads, one from the monastic centre (now represented by Trimmer's

Fig. 8 A Viking Age timber pathway with remains of a post and wattle house wall exposed during the Bride Street excavation. The pathway was used to provide a dry walk-way as the lower levels were near sea-level. Ten levels of houses were recovered during the excavation; the seven upper levels were aligned with the modern street boundaries.

Fig. 9   This reconstruction of a Viking house at the Irish National Heritage Park, Ferrycarrig, is based on one of the house types found in the archaeological excavation at Bride Street. A sequence of sixteen houses, dating from *c.* 1000 to 1300, were recovered from the small site.

dedications were paralleled at Dublin, where they are regarded as pre-Norman.[41] Obviously the conjectured Norse town described here belongs to the twelfth century as the parochial system could not have developed until after the Norse were Christianised in the early eleventh century. Norse Wexford existed in this form for at least a century before the arrival of the Anglo-Normans.

NORSE RURAL SETTLEMENT

The Norse controlled considerable areas in the hinterlands of their towns and settled them with farming communities.[42] Archaeological findings in Dublin have shown that the town could not have existed without the produce of its rural hinterland, known as *Dyflinarskiri*, which provided vital supplies of food and raw materials. A discussion of this area uses archaeological and historical data, as well as place-name evidence, to assess its extent and significance.[43] The existence of a distinct Norse settlement in rural Wexford in the thirteenth century is known from an account of 'the rents, services and customs of the foreign Ostmen (Norse) of the county of Wexford'.[44] There was presumably a large rural Norse population

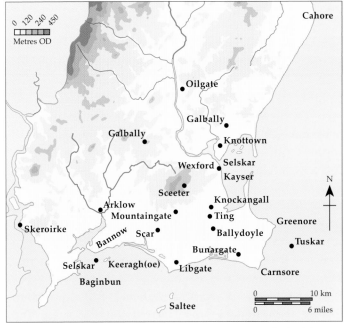

Fig. 10   Placenames of Norse provenance in county Wexford have a predominantly coastal orientation, reflecting the seafaring ethos of the Norse and their control of the littoral. Inland, the names are concentrated in the southern baronies of Forth and Bargy, a strong indication that this region was controlled by the Norse of Wexford town.

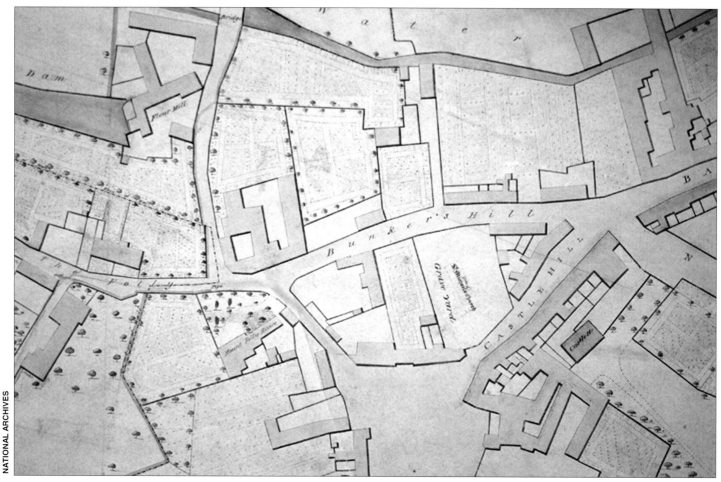

NATIONAL ARCHIVES

Fig. 11   The site of the Hiberno-Norse church of St Michael shown on the 1840 O. S. plan of Wexford, just outside the town wall to the south.

living in the barony of Forth (south of Wexford town), in the pre-Norman period, holding property 'by an early non-feudal land system'.[45] In the absence of historical sources, placenames of possible Scandinavian origin are valuable in assessing the extent of the area under Norse control. The townland index for the county and the half-inch O. S. sheets yield twenty-five names of Norse provenance.[46] These are predominantly in the south of the county with a concentration in the barony of Forth. A coastal concentration from Wexford around to Waterford indicates Norse control of the littoral between the two towns. The most crucial group of names from a settlement perspective is located in the heart of the barony of Forth, south of Wexford town. The townland of Ting[47] in the parish of Rathmacknee may refer to the presence of a rural Thingmount, or Norse assembly place.[48] The nearby Irish townland names of Knockangall and Ballydoyle are a further indication of Norse activity in this area. They contain the Irish element *gall*, a foreigner, which was commonly used in reference to Vikings,[49] as, for example, in the case of Fingal in county Dublin and Gaultier in county Waterford.[50] Knockangall (*Cnoc an Ghaill*), the hill

of the foreigner, and Ballydoyle (*Baile Dubgall*), the place of the black foreigner, while not linguistic borrowings from Scandinavia, have obvious Viking associations.[51] These placenames suggest that the Norse controlled the coastal area of southern Uí Chennselaig, particularly the barony of Forth, during the three centuries before the arrival of the Anglo-Normans.

However, the survival of Irish placenames of Norse provenance points to a complex pattern, with a mixed Hiberno-Norse rural population working side-by-side to supply the town of Wexford with essential supplies of food and other commodities. Norse related placenames support the late thirteenth-century documentary evidence for a concentration of Ostmen in the vicinity of Rosslare. Following the arrival of the Anglo-Normans, Mac Murchada's initial grant to Fitz Stephen and Fitz Gerald of Wexford town 'with all its lands' was a strong indication that Forth was under Norse control.[52]

As the importance of the Norse towns became increasingly obvious, the more ambitious Irish kings exploited them as sources of men, ships and taxes.[53] In political terms, the kingdom of Uí Chennselaig, centred on

PRIVATE COLLECTION

Fig. 12 Many of county Wexford's coastal features retain the names given to them by the seafaring Norsemen. These include Cahore, Greenore, Carnsore (*–ore*: headland), Saltee (*–ee*: island). Tuskar Rock off the south-east coast of the county, shown above, contains the Norse element *sker*, a rock, also found in Selskar (seal rock) in Wexford town and Bannow Bay. Wexford got its name from the harbour, called Waesfiord by the Norse.

Ferns, was traditionally remote and insignificant but this was changed by the rising prosperity of the Norse town of Wexford.[54] Diarmait Mac Mael-na-mBó, king of Leinster, gained access to Wexford in 1051[55] and seized Dublin the following year.[56] Control of these two centres of economic and military power remained in the hands of Diarmait's successors for much of the following century and helped them to maintain a dominant position in Leinster until 1171. Following the death in battle of Diarmait Mac Mael-na-mBó in 1072, the power base that he had consolidated in Leinster was fragmented by dynastic conflict and the province remained without dominant leadership until 1132, when his great-grandson, Diarmait Mac Murchada, first asserted himself.[57] His successful bid to establish himself as king of Leinster was facilitated by a power struggle that saw the collapse of the kingdom of Connacht. The importance of the Norse towns was again emphasised in 1137 when Mac Murchada attempted to gain control of Waterford with fleets drawn from Dublin and Wexford.[58] The ambitious Mac Murchada was implicated in the

complex and fractured dynastic alliances that competed for supremacy. Supported by the Norse of Wexford and Dublin and allied with the powerful Muirchertach Mac Lochlainn of Cenél Eógain, Mac Murchada maintained control of Leinster in spite of the opposition of Ruaidrí Ó Conchobair, king of Connacht, and his ally Tigernán Ó Ruairc of Bréifne. In 1166 the Norse of Dublin submitted to Ruaidrí Ó Conchobair[59] and Diarmait's ally Muirchertach Mac Lochlainn was killed in battle. Ó Conchubair marched on Uí Chennselaig and Diarmait, deserted by his own subjects, burned Ferns and submitted to him. Mac Murchada was allowed to retain possession of Uí Chennselaig but before long his enemies (led by Tigernán Ó Ruairc, whose wife, Dervorgilla, Diarmait had abducted fourteen years previously) again marched on Ferns. Perhaps inspired by the origin legend of his dynasty in which Labraid Loingsech was forced into exile and regained his kingdom with the help of allies from Gaul,[60] Mac Murchada, utterly isolated and deserted even by his closest associates, fled overseas in search of foreign aid.[61]

URBAN EXPANSION: THE ANGLO-NORMAN TOWN

The emergence of towns can be attributed to the division of labour between work in the fields and the more economic activities of the market-place, usually associated with the urban dweller. Major periods of expansion were accompanied by an accelerated rate of town building, and the urban explosion which occurred in eleventh-century Europe marked the beginning of the continent's inexorable rise to eminence.[1] Urban origins were associated with pilgrimage sites, the intersection of routeways, river-crossings and navigable estuaries, to which people were drawn by the offer of protection and commercial opportunities. Most towns received a set of privileges defined in a charter of liberties granted to them by the lord on whose land they were situated.[2] The concept of the chartered town or borough had not reached Ireland before the arrival of the Anglo-Normans, but the Norse ports, principally Dublin, Wexford, Waterford, Cork and Limerick, were substantial centres of trade and commerce. The lay settlements which developed around many of the Early Christian monasteries also attracted economic activities normally associated with urban life.[3] The Anglo-Normans were responsible for most of the chartered towns and boroughs founded in Ireland in the twelfth and thirteenth centuries. The recipients of large fiefs established chartered towns as a strategy to lure colonists from Britain.[4] Foundation charters to towns granted plots of land to burgesses within the borough, on which a house could be built and sometimes an outside plot also, for the customary rent of one shilling a year. Other privileges included liberty of movement, trial before equals, freedom from certain taxes and the right to self-administration. In return for these privileges, the town founder received revenue in the form of burgess rent, market tolls and court fines, and the town became a market-place for the produce of his manors. More than 300 chartered boroughs are known to have been established in Ireland by the Anglo-Normans but only about a quarter of that number survive as towns in the modern landscape.[5] The importance of the Norse towns is evident from the fact that three of them – Wexford, Waterford and Dublin – were taken over by the Normans before the end of 1170 and these were among the first towns in Ireland to be granted borough status. Wexford was the first settlement in Ireland to be taken over by the Anglo-Normans and became a capital borough and the administrative centre of a county of the same name.

Fig. 1 Bannow Bay, on the south Wexford coast, was the focus of initial Anglo-Norman landings in Ireland. In May 1169, an advance party of 600, led by Robert Fitz Stephen and Maurice de Prendergast, landed at Bannow Island (right centre of picture; now joined to the mainland by sand-dunes). Diarmait Mac Murchada joined them with 500 men and the combined force marched on Wexford town, which they took from its Hiberno-Norse inhabitants. In May 1170, another small group landed at the promontory of Dún Domhnaill (now Baginbun; left foreground) where they erected a fortification that still survives. After defeating a much larger force of Norsemen from Waterford and Irish from the Déisi, they joined the Norman leader Richard de Clare (Strongbow) who had landed at Passage, and the combined force took the town of Waterford.

Fig. 2   The Bayeux Tapestry records the arrival of the Normans in England in 1066 and the defeat of the English at the Battle of Hastings. Just over a century later, the Normans used similar military expertise to exert control over much of Ireland, after establishing a base in the south-east of the island.

THE ANGLO-NORMANS

Diarmait Mac Murchada's quest for foreign mercenary aid instigated a train of events that resulted in the military conquest of much of Ireland by the Anglo-Normans, and accelerated the introduction of mainstream European influences to Ireland. Diarmait presented his request for assistance to Henry II, king of England and part of France, who granted him permission to hire mercenaries within his kingdom.[6] Mac Murchada directed his recruiting campaign towards the Normans of the Pembroke region in south Wales. For the most part, Diarmait offered money and land in return for military service, but to Richard Fitz Gilbert de Clare (earl of Pembroke, better known as Strongbow) he offered his daughter, Aoife, in marriage and, contrary to Irish custom, succession to the kingdom of Leinster after his death.[7] Among other Cambro-Norman barons recruited by Mac Murchada were the half-brothers Robert Fitz Stephen and Maurice Fitz Gerald, sons of the Welsh princess Nesta, who were promised the Norse town of Wexford with all its lands.[8] He also enlisted help from among the Flemish colony in Pembroke.[9] In 1167 Mac Murchada returned with a small band of Normans and succeeded in re-establishing himself in Uí Chennselaig. Impatient to regain his lost power, he sent messages to Strongbow urging him to come. Eventually, in May 1169, an advance party of Anglo-Normans, 600 strong, landed at Bannow Island on the south Wexford coast, led by Robert Fitz Stephen and Maurice de Prendergast. They were joined by Diarmait with a force of 500 men and the combined army marched on the Viking town of Wexford.[10]

Apart from occasional references in Irish annals, information about initial Anglo-Norman activity in Ireland depends on two almost contemporary sources. Gerald de Barry, a Welsh bishop better known as Giraldus

Cambrensis, visited Ireland in 1185 and subsequently wrote *Expugnatio Hibernica* (The Conquest of Ireland), based on accounts of original participants, including some of his own relatives. *The Song of Dermot and the Earl*, a long poem in French by an unknown author, was compiled using information possibly supplied by Muiris Ó Riagáin, Diarmait's secretary. *Expugnatio Hibernica* gives a detailed description of the capture of Wexford.[11] At first the Hiberno-Norse inhabitants (2,000 strong according to Giraldus and 'confident of their own ability') defiantly came outside the town wall to do battle but, realising the calibre of the attacking force, burnt the suburbs and withdrew inside the wall which was protected on the outside by a deep ditch. The Anglo-Normans attacked the walls but were repulsed. They then set fire to the unprotected ships in the harbour, which may be the origin of the town crest which shows three burning ships with the motto *Per Aquam et Ignem* (by water and fire).

The next morning the attacking force prepared more carefully for the assault but the Norse, unsure of their ability to defend the town and considering that they were impugning royal authority, initiated peace discussions

Fig. 3   The ships in which the Anglo-Normans made the crossing from Pembroke to south Wexford in 1169 were similar to those depicted one hundred years earlier on the Bayeux Tapestry.

The fall of Waesfiord (*Expugnatio Hibernica*)

When Mac Murchada heard of their arrival, he immediately came with about five hundred men. However, he sent his natural son Domnall on ahead of him. He was, although illegitimate, a man of great influence among his people. They renewed their agreements, and oaths were given many times over on both sides to ensure the safety of each party. Then they joined forces and, with a common purpose and complete agreement uniting the two different races, directed both their gaze and their battle line towards the city of Wexford, which is about twelve miles distant from Bannow. When they heard this, the people of the city came out, about two thousand strong, hitherto unvanquished and with great faith in their long-standing good fortune. They decided to meet the enemy not far from their camp and engage in a trial of strength there. But when they saw the lines of troops drawn up in an unfamiliar manner, and the squadron of knights resplendent with breastplates, swords and helmets all gleaming, they adopted new tactics in the face of changed circumstances, burned the entire suburbs, and immediately turned back and withdrew inside the walls. Fitz Stephen and his men eagerly made preparations for the assault. They filled the town ditches with armed men, while the archers watched the ramparts from a distance. With a great rush forward and a mighty shout they all with one accord attacked the walls. But the citizens, very quick to defend themselves, straightaway hurled down heavy pieces of wood and stones and drove them back some little distance, inflicting severe wounds on many. Among these invaders a knight, Robert de Barry, exuberant with youthful hot-headedness and bravely scorning the risk of death, had crept up to the walls in front of everyone else, when he was struck by a stone on his helmeted head. He fell from a height into the bottom of the steep ditch, and in the end just managed to escape by being pulled out by his fellow soldiers. After an interval of sixteen years his molar teeth fell out as a result of the impact of this blow and, even more amazing, new ones grew immediately in their place.

Withdrawing from the walls and rushing eagerly to the shore nearby, they immediately set fire to all the ships they found there. But there was one ship lying at anchor in the harbour, which had come from Britain to trade, which was laden with wheat and wine. The greater part of the crack fighting men had bravely seized this, rowing out to it in boats. But now the anchor rope was deliberately cut by the sailors, and as there was a following north wind, which drove the ship out into the open sea and greatly endangered their safety, it was only with difficulty that they reached land again with the aid of small skiffs and oars. So once again fortune, unvarying only in her inconstancy, had almost deserted Mac Murchada and Fitz Stephen. But on the next day, after the whole army had heard Mass solemnly celebrated, they proceeded to the assault better equipped and with their tactics more carefully thought out, supported by their skill as well as by their military strength, and relying on stratagem no less than on straightforward fighting. When they came up to the walls, the citizens, mistrusting their capacity to defend themselves, and considering they were acting wrongly in resisting their king, set about discussing peace after messengers were sent to them. So peace was restored through the mediation of two bishops who were in the city at that time, and other men of goodwill acting as peacemakers. The citizens surrendered themselves to Diarmait's authority and handed over four chosen hostages for their future loyalty to him. He, for his part, being eager to encourage his followers, decided to reward the principal among them on the occasion of his first success. He therefore immediately assigned the city with all its lands to Fitz Stephen and Maurice according to the obligation incurred in the former agreement. To Hervey of Montmorency he assigned under grants the two cantreds which border on the sea and lie between the two cities of Wexford and Waterford. When all these matters had been settled as they wished, they added the citizens of Wexford to their forces and with an army of about three thousand men turned to attack Osraige.

through the mediation of two bishops who were in the town. They surrendered to Diarmait and gave hostages to guarantee future loyalty. Diarmait immediately granted the town and all its lands, equivalent to the barony of Forth, to Robert Fitz Stephen and Maurice Fitz Gerald. He granted two cantreds on the sea between Wexford and Waterford, the baronies of Bargy and Shelburne, to Strongbow's uncle, Hervey de Montmorency. These were the first land grants made to Anglo-Norman knights in Ireland. The colony subsequently established in the baronies of Forth and Bargy

survived undisturbed for more than four centuries, making the Wexford Pale one of the most anglicised parts of Ireland.

Diarmait added the Norsemen of Wexford to his army and continued his campaign to regain the kingdom of Leinster. His cause was helped by the arrival at Wexford of Maurice Fitz Gerald with one hundred knights and archers in two ships.[12] Leaving Fitz Stephen at Wexford, Mac Murchada marched on Dublin. Possibly fearing a revolt by the Norse of Wexford, Fitz Stephen constructed a fort on a steep rock on the right bank of the Slaney two

PRIVATE COLLECTION

Fig. 4 Pembroke Castle in south Wales was the headquarters of the de Clare earls of Pembroke, known by the soubriquet Strongbow. Richard, the second earl, was the leader of the initial Anglo-Norman activity in Ireland. He claimed succession to the kingdom of Leinster through his marriage to Aoife, Diarmait Mac Murchada's daughter. William Marshal succeeded to the earldom and Leinster through his marriage to Strongbow's daughter, Isabella. The countryside surrounding Pembroke Castle was occupied by Flemish emigrants, many of whom joined the expedition to Ireland.

miles from Wexford at a place called Carrig, indicating that this district was included in the lands granted to him by Mac Murchada.[13] The remains of this first recorded fortification built by the Normans in Ireland, classified as a ringwork castle, is now included in the Irish National Heritage Park at Ferrycarrig.

Following repeated appeals from Mac Murchada, Strongbow obtained 'permission of a kind' from Henry II to come to Ireland. In May 1170 an advance party, led by Raymond le Gros, landed at Dún Domhnaill (now called Baginbun) a headland on the south Wexford coast. They fortified the headland and defeated an army of Norse and Irish from the city of Waterford.[14] Shortly afterwards Raymond joined Strongbow, who had landed at Passage in Waterford Harbour, and the combined forces took the city of Waterford. Diarmait brought his daughter, Aoife, to Waterford where she was married to Strongbow, establishing his right of succession to the kingdom of Leinster.[15] The combined forces then marched on Dublin

which was taken by storm. The three Viking port towns were now in the hands of the Anglo-Normans, effectively giving them control of the seas.

BRITISH LIBRARY

Fig. 5 An Anglo-Norman knight and foot-soldier shown on the seal of Richard de Clare, Earl of Pembroke (Strongbow), leader of the first invaders, who landed at Passage in Waterford Harbour in 1170.

Fig. 6   Following the taking of Wexford, Robert Fitz Stephen fortified a cliff-top site overlooking the Slaney at Ferrycarrig by constructing a bank and ditch across the promontory. This ringwork castle was the first Anglo-Norman fortification to be built in Ireland. Extensive sections of the fortifications survive and have yielded thirteenth-century artefacts. A Crimean War memorial, built in the late 1850s in the form of an Early Christian round tower, is at the centre of the site. The remains of Fitz Stephen's castle is now included in the Irish National Heritage Park.

In May 1171 Mac Murchada died and the situation changed dramatically for the Anglo-Normans.[16] Henry II, alarmed at the prospect of an independent Norman kingdom emerging on the neighbouring island, placed an embargo on all shipping to Ireland and ordered his subjects to return.[17] Strongbow was under military pressure from the Irish and the Norse of Dublin and Fitz Stephen was captured in his fort at Carrig by the Norse of Wexford who then burned the town and imprisoned him on the island of Begerin.[18] Meanwhile Henry, having accepted Strongbow's assurances of loyalty and allowing him to retain Leinster (apart from Dublin), decided to intervene personally and landed at Crook in Waterford Harbour in late 1171.[19] At Waterford, Henry made a formal grant of Leinster to Strongbow, reserving to himself all seaports and fortresses. Before sailing from Wales, Henry had been met by twelve burgesses of Wexford who informed him that they had captured Fitz Stephen and wished to hand him over to Henry for punishment as the first Norman knight to enter Ireland without his permission. Fitz Stephen was brought before the king in

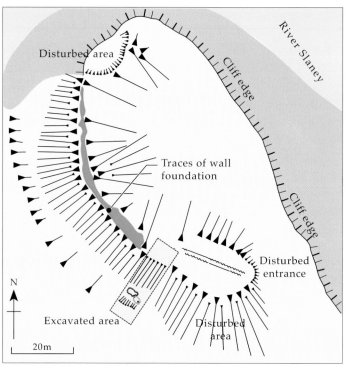

Fig. 7   A plan of the surviving rampart and ditch at Carrig ringwork.

Fitz Stephen's fort at Carrig (*Expugnatio Hibernica*)

Robert Fitz Stephen built a fortress on a steep crag, about two miles from Wexford, called Carrig in the vernacular, and improved by artificial means a place naturally well protected, [described as] a most ill-fortified castle, enclosed by a flimsy wall of branches and sods. The citizens of Wexford and the men of Uí Chennselaig subjected Fitz Stephen to ceaseless attacks. He had been quite unprepared, had not feared an attack of that kind and was surrounded, with only five knights and a few archers. But the Irish realised that they would get nowhere by the use of force, for these men, although few in number, were nevertheless very alert in defending themselves, and in particular a knight, William Not, who in this defence outshone all others in courage. And so they had recourse to their usual weapons of falsehood and lying deceit. They led up to the castle two bishops, of Wexford and Kildare, and others whose habits proclaimed them to be churchmen. They brought along relics also, and then all joined in taking an oath, giving their persons as surety, and asserted under oath that Dublin had been taken [from Strongbow], and that the earl [Strongbow], Maurice and Raymond, together with all the English, were now dead, and that the united armies of Connacht and Leinster were hurrying towards Wexford. They claimed that they had done all this for Fitz Stephen's own good in order that they could convey him safely to Wales with his followers before the arrival of a large force of men hostile to him. In the end, Fitz Stephen believed their assertions and entrusted himself and his men to their pledged word. They immediately killed a number of his men, inflicting severe wounds on some and blows on others, put them in chains and incarcerated them. Almost immediately, rumour, flying with swift wings, made known the true facts of the defeat at Dublin and the approach of the earl. At once the traitors themselves set fire to the whole city [of Wexford] and sailed across to the island of Begerin, which lies at the mouth of the harbour, and which is also called Holy Island, taking with them all their possessions and all the prisoners.

Fig. 8 Henry II visited Ireland in late 1171 to impose his royal authority on his Norman subjects. He granted Leinster to Strongbow but retained all fortresses and seaports for himself. While in Ireland, he bestowed extensive estates on the Knights Templar, including mills in Wexford.

chains at Waterford and, after a spell in prison, was deprived of Wexford and the adjacent lands, which the king then took into his own hands.[20] After wintering in Dublin, Henry traveled to Wexford where he spent seven weeks waiting for favourable weather to make the crossing to Wales.[21] He sailed on 17 April 1172 to face revolt from his sons and ecclesiastical censure for the murder of archbishop Thomas Becket. On his departure he left three knights (William Fitz Audelm, Philip de Hastings and Philip de Braose) in charge of Wexford.[22] Strongbow died in 1176 leaving a baby daughter, Isabella, as heir, and Leinster was taken into the king's wardship.

The arrival of Prince John in 1185 as lord of Ireland signalled a change in emphasis from military domination to colonisation of land. Arriving initially in Ireland as mercenaries, the ambitious Norman knights, welcoming the opportunity to acquire new possessions, quickly seized the initiative and took control of eastern and southern Ireland. The migrations and land-hunger associated with the European population explosion which took place at the end of the twelfth century facilitated the policy of sub-infeudation initiated by the Norman barons, who needed settlers to develop their newly acquired fiefs. Military control was followed by the creation of a hierarchical land-holding system known as feudalism and the introduction of settlers from England and Wales.[23] The subsequent imposition of Anglo-Norman structures on Gaelic Ireland created a complex society and a wide range of settlement features, including the establishment of chartered towns.

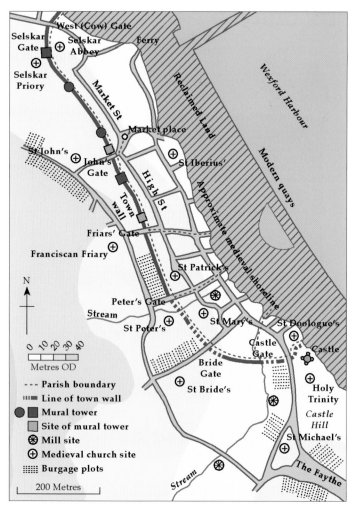

Fig. 9   The new Anglo-Norman lord of Wexford extended the town to the north-west, enclosing the ferry quay and creating the parish of Selskar in the process. Continuous reclamation of land extended the waterfront into the harbour. The narrow burgage strips can be identified in the suburbs outside the town walls. The early thirteenth-century castle was built just outside the town wall, to the south-east of the town, on a natural mound beside the harbour.

associated with Anglo-Norman settlement in county Wexford was the expansion of the Norse port of Wexford and the founding of the new port of Ross. Wexford had the advantage of being an existing settlement with an established infrastructure and trade connections. When Henry II visited Ireland in 1171–72, he took Wexford into his own hands and stayed in the town waiting for favourable weather for his crossing to Wales. On Easter Monday, Henry embarked in Wexford's outer harbour, an early example of the problems caused by the barred haven.[24] His prolonged stay added impetus to the development of the town. In 1173, he granted the town to Strongbow and, for a time, it became the principal town of the lordship of Leinster.[25] In the early thirteenth century, under the Marshal regime, Wexford became the administrative centre of a county of the same name. The takeover of the town by the Anglo-Normans was not

without opposition in the initial stages, when the success of the Anglo-Norman venture still lay in the balance. In 1173, a revolt planned by the Norse of Wexford was prevented only by the arrival from Wales of Raymond le Gros and Meiler Fitz Henry with a large force. Shortly after his arrival, le Gros married Strongbow's sister, Basilia, in the town.[26] A few years later, in 1176, Maurice Fitz Gerald, one of the most prominent of the first arrivals, died, and presumably was buried in Wexford.[27] There is very little information about the transfer of the town from the Hiberno-Norse to the Anglo-Normans. The town was taken over as a 'going concern' and presumably experienced no drastic changes for a considerable period. No immediate alterations to the layout of the existing Hiberno-Norse town were implemented: a limited excavation at Bride Street revealed that property boundaries remained consistent from A. D. 1200.[28]

In 1189, the king gave Strongbow's daughter, Isabella, in marriage to earl William Marshal, the most powerful baron in England, who set about developing the lordship and the town of Wexford.[29] Before Marshal arrived in Ireland in 1200, Wexford had received its first charter from Geoffrey Fitz Robert, the earl's seneschal. Wexford's early charter has not survived but it is referred to in a later charter of 1317, and is mentioned in a charter to New Ross of c. 1285.[30] Burgesses were recorded at Wexford as early as 1172 when Henry II's grant to the Templars included 'Agnile, burgess of Wexford, with all his chattels,' but this could have been a descriptive rather than a legal term, as there is no record of a charter being conferred at that

Fig. 10   An archaeological excavation in 1974, at the corner of Oyster Lane and South Main Street, yielded extensive evidence for medieval occupation, including bronze pins, leather objects, worked antler and nine hundred pot sherds, providing evidence for trade with France and England. A well-preserved post and wattle fence was found at the lowest level which was composed of beach material. No evidence for pre-Norman occupation was discovered. The discovery of numerous oyster shells confirmed the tradition that the lane was the centre of the oyster trade.

Fig. 11 In 1189, William Marshal, the most powerful knight in England, succeeded to the earldom of Pembroke and the lordship of Leinster through his marriage to Strongbow's daughter, Isabella. For almost fifty years, Marshal, who died in 1219, and his five sons who succeeded him in turn, were lords of Wexford. The Marshal dynasty was responsible for developing the early Anglo-Norman town, including the building of the town wall and castle. All of his sons died childless, and in 1247, Leinster was divided among his five daughters. Marshal (foreground), who had been in the Holy Land on crusade, and his son, William II, are buried in Temple Church, London, the principal church of the Knights Templar in England.

could have been a descriptive rather than a legal term, as there is no record of a charter being conferred at that time.[31] Wexford had certainly received a charter by the end of the century, as Marshal's charter to Tintern Abbey in 1200 gave the abbey a burgage in the town.[32]

The town founder received revenue in the form of rent, market tolls, court fines and a variety of other taxes, while the town became a market-place and trading centre for his manors.[33] Trade was strictly regulated with all merchants required to pay prisage, or duty, for permission to sell goods in the town. Breaches in the trading laws were punished by fine in the hundred court. The collection, or farming, of taxes was franchised out to individuals who paid a fixed amount in return. In 1336, for example, John Ruggeleye was farmer of the prisage on wines, beer, fish and flesh in Wexford, paying a rent of £14 a year and in 1338 John Parys was farmer of the ferry.[34]

During the thirteenth and fourteenth centuries, the title Lord of Wexford was held by various families, all of them absentee English peers.[35] Following the death of Marshal's five sons without issue, Leinster was divided among his five daughters. Wexford town and the county palatine[36] passed to his second daughter, Joan; her daughter, of the same name, married the half-brother to Henry III, William de Valence, who then became lord of Wexford town and liberty. Aymer de Valence, who succeeded his father in

1294, granted the town a new charter in 1317, establishing the rights and privileges of the burgesses in legal matters, property, trade and commerce. These included the right to hold burgages in perpetuity for one shilling per annum, common of the lord's woods outside the walls, milling at reasonable rates in the lord's mills, permission to establish merchant guilds and legal protection, including the right to bail from prison in Wexford Castle.[37]

Following the death of Aymer de Valence without issue, the lordship was held by the Hastings family until

WESTMINSTER ABBEY

Fig. 12 At the partition of Leinster in 1247, Wexford town and the county palatine passed to Marshal's grand-daughter, Joan, who married the half-brother to King Henry III, William de Valence, who then became lord of Wexford town and liberty until his death in 1294. William de Valence's tomb and effigy (above) can be seen in Westminster Abbey.

The Cantred of Forth

The cantred of Forth, a seignorial manor attached to the town of Wexford, is represented by the modern barony of Forth with the addition of the parish of Carrig. The southern part of the cantred was known as the manor of Rosslare. To the north, the burgage and other lands associated with the towns of Wexford and Carrig were located along the Slaney estuary. Not all of the land belonging to towns was necessarily held by burgage tenure: the parish of Killiane, for example, was held by a free tenant as part of the borough of Wexford. The large parishes to the south-west of the town were held by hereditary free tenants, principally the Esmonds of Rathaspick, the Rossiters of Rathmacknee and the St Johns in Ballymore. Other free tenants held twenty-three carucates (ploughlands) in various locations, most of them not identified, in lots ranging from one to seven carucates. The military tenures were concentrated in the more fertile south-eastern region. These smallholdings, consisting of six quarter knights' fees and three half fees, resulted in the creation of a complex structure of small parishes, often with detached portions. Not all of the parishes were based on a single manor or landholding unit. For example, there were two small military tenures and a freeholding in both Kilscoran and Tacumshin. The parish of Mayglass, consisting mostly of the episcopal manor of the same name, also included the freeholding of the Waddings of Ballycogley. The principal demesne lands were in Rosslare where eleven carucates were held in the hands of the lord. In 1307 the labours of the Ostmen at Rosslare were worth £9 9s 2d. These were the descendants of the Wexford Vikings who continued to hold land as copyholders with special privileges. Very little information is available on the lower classes of tenant in the cantred. At Ballymore, four carucates were held in gavelkind by tenants-at-will and the English and Irish tenants who held eleven carucates at Ballyregan in the parish of Ballymore and Ballysampson in the parish of Tacumshin must have been in the same category. The almost complete absence of moated sites, usually associated with later waves of settlement, suggests that the comprehensive nature of the initial settlement left no room for further expansion. The location of Forth in the secure south-east led to the establishment of a distinctive society which endured for many centuries.

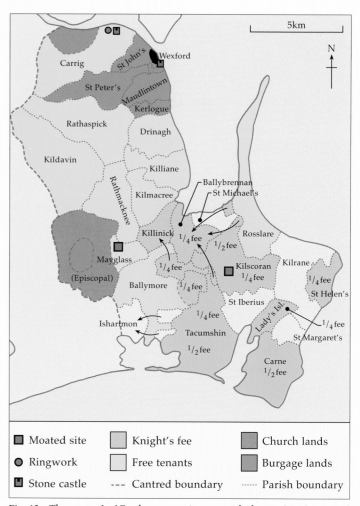

Fig. 13 The cantred of Forth was contiguous with the modern barony of Forth with the addition of the parish of Carrig to the north. The land was mostly held of the lord of Wexford by free and military tenants. The holdings were relatively small, resulting in the development of equally small parishes and townlands. Because of the secure location, Forth, with neighbouring Bargy, were later regarded as the Wexford Pale.

Fig. 14 This fourteenth-century consecration cross (image enhanced digitally) can still be seen, incised on the wall of the ruined medieval parish church of Rosslare at Churchtown in the barony of Forth.

Fig. 15   A 1960s view of the barony of Forth from the south showing Lady's Island lake which is separated from the sea by a barrier of sand and shingle. The distinctive settlement landscape of the barony can be traced to the Hiberno-Norse and Anglo-Normans of medieval Wexford town.

The Ostmen of Forth, 1283

To all seeing and hearing these Letters, Robert of Imer, now Seneschal of Wexford, greeting. Know all you that I, by order of the nobleman, Lord William of Valence, have taken an inquest of the rents, services and customs of foreign Ostmen of the county of Wexford, by the oaths of the subscribed – viz., Henry Wythay, William Marshal, William of Kidwelly, Clement Cod, John the Stewart, Robert of Amera, Robert of Arderne, David, son of Richard, John, son of Philip the Harper, David Cheever, and Adam Hay. Who, being sworn, say that in the time of the Marshals, Lords of Leinster, there were within the county of Wexford, five times twenty foreign Ostmen, very wealthy, possessing many cattle; of whom each in his time was accustomed to yearly render to the bailiffs of Wexford, at two periods in the year, sixpence for his body, that is, at Easter and Michelmas, and twopence on the feast of St Peter ad Vincula [1 August] for each cow belonging to himself; and fourpence at the feast of All Saints, that he should not enter the army; and three oboli in autumn for reaping the corn of his lord at Rosslare for one day in the year; and fourpence for each steer and ox that he possessed, on the feast of St Martin, or to plough for every steer and ox half an acre of land there, at the need of his lord. They say that truly there are not now within the said county but eighty Ostmen, possessing few oxen; and twelve who serve the English, and others, for their sustenance, and possess nothing in goods. And they say that in the time of the Marshals the said Eastmen were accustomed to hold land of whatever lord they wished in the county, paying and rendering the said rents and services to the Lords Marshal. And that our said Lord William of Valence desires to keep them in the same condition, or better, for the health of his soul and of the souls of his ancestors and successors. Nor does he wish that any living people should be borne or sustained of the dead, nor distrained for the dead. The said Eastmen now existing are for ever free from all burdens, rents, and services which the dead were accustomed to sustain while they lived, by command of our aforesaid Lord William Valence. Giving them, by the same mandate of our Lord, licence to hold land of whatever lord they will within the county. Also, that they shall not be severally distrained for any rent to be rendered, or services to be performed, unless they who are living, and according to their ability. In testimony of which I have affixed my seal to these present letters, together with the seal of Thomas Hay, now sheriff, and the seals of the aforesaid jurors.

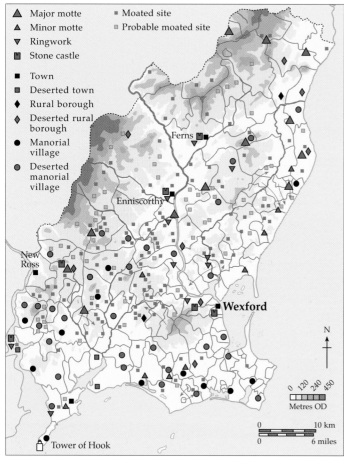

Major motte
Minor motte
Ringwork
Stone castle

Town
Deserted town
Rural borough
Deserted rural borough
Manorial village
Deserted manorial village

Moated site
Probable moated site

Ferns

Enniscorthy

New Ross

Wexford

N

0 120 240 450
Metres OD

0   10 km
0   6 miles

Tower of Hook

Fig. 16 The distribution of Anglo-Norman settlement features in Wexford illustrates the progress and ultimate shape of the colony in the county. Sites are scarce in the north, where the Irish had regained possession by the end of the thirteenth century. Defensive earthworks are located across the centre of the county which was the interface between the Irish north and the English south. Manorial villages are concentrated in Forth and Bargy, which became known as 'the English baronies'. The parochial structure evolved from the landholding system introduced by the Anglo-Normans, as the payment of tithes to the manorial church ensured that manor and parish became synonymous.

1390, when John Hastings, Earl of Pembroke and Lord of Wexford, was slain at the tilt. The title then passed in turn through the female line to Lord Grey and the earls of Talbot and Shrewsbury who held it until Henry VIII, in 1536, under the statute of absentees, removed the power which had given the palatinate lords almost independent status. However, the municipal authority and privileges of Wexford were left intact.

THE BURGESSES
The Anglo-Norman town of Wexford was basically an economic venture and to be successful it was necessary to attract settlers to take up residence as burgesses in the town. The Hiberno-Norse apparently abandoned the town for their rural estates in the barony of Forth, leaving a considerable vacuum to be filled.[38] A 1283 survey of the Ostmen in county Wexford stated that in the time of the

Marshals there were one hundred rich Ostmen in the county, holding lands where they wished but mentioning in particular Rosslare in the barony of Forth. By 1283 their numbers had reduced to eighty and they were in much poorer circumstances. The 'labours of the Ostmen' at Rosslare were again mentioned in 1307.

Although records for Wexford town are very sparse, it is possible to piece together at least an outline picture from the fragmentary evidence. The campaign to attract settlers seems to have been successful initially but the fall in revenue generated by the borough from the mid thirteenth century onwards shows that the early level of achievement was not maintained. In 1246, an income of £42, including £18 burgage rent from the town, suggests that all of the 365 burgage plots in the town at a rent of one shilling each were occupied.[39] By 1298 there were 128 burgages waste in Wexford town[40] and in 1307 the value of the burgages had dropped from £18 to £12, with 127 burgages waste as the tenants had become paupers.[41] By the year 1324 the situation had deteriorated even further with 221 burgages waste and vacant, due in part to the Bruce war.[42] The land granted to burgesses for their one shilling rent was in the form of long narrow strips which gave them a street frontage on which to build and a long garden or back for cultivation.

Archaeological excavations, including the one at Bride Street in Wexford, have shown that property boundaries have remained consistent right back to the twelfth century. In many Anglo-Norman towns burgage strips survive in some form and can frequently be identified on the 1841 Ordnance Survey maps.[43] In the case of Wexford the strips are not so much in evidence within the walls, possibly due to the town's Norse origin and a high density of building. In some cases it is possible to identify the shape of strips where they are reflected in the lines of later building. Outside the town wall, however, the strips can easily be identified in the two medieval suburb areas of the Faythe and John's Street.[44] There is some documentary evidence for these burgages: in 1325 Mary, widow of Aymer de Valence, was assigned sixty-six waste burgages in the north of the town;[45] in 1562 the manor of Kilcloggan (formerly Hospitallers) held twenty-three burgages in John's Street and in 1578 Kilcloggan also held the farm of twenty-four burgages in the Faythe.[46] As well as holding a burgage strip, some of the burgesses held land outside the town. In 1324 certain burgesses held half a carucate (150 statute acres) for a rent of £8, an area perhaps represented by the townland of Burgess at Ferrybank.[47] The town charter also allowed the inhabitants to have common of the lord's woods outside the town's defences.

Fig. 17 The enduring significance attached to the arrival of the Anglo-Normans in Ireland and their first victory at Wexford is highlighted in this 1601 map by John Speed which illustrates the taking of Wexford in 1169 and the arrival of Henry II at Crook in 1171, 'for the conquest of Ireland'.

From these figures, it is possible to calculate an approximate population for Wexford in the mid thirteenth century, presuming that all the burgages were occupied and that there was not multiple ownership of plots. Two methods are employed. The 365 burgesses were heads of households; other people did not enjoyed burgess status and a multiplier of five will give a rough estimate of total population.[48] The other method[49] is based on the theory that medieval boroughs contained 100–120 persons to the hectare. These calculations suggest a population of between 2,000 and 2,400 for the walled town and suburbs. Based on these figures, an estimate of 2,000 for the population of the medieval town seems valid. Gerald de Barry gave the same figure for the Norse town in 1169,[50] indicating that a figure of that magnitude is not unreasonable.

LAND RECLAMATION

Due to pressure on space within the walls, reclamation of land from the harbour was an ongoing process. This would also have been necessary in order to establish a proper waterfront and quay system. At Dublin, for example, the construction of a series of banks between the tenth and thirteenth centuries extended the waterfront by sixty metres.[51] The charter granted to New Ross in 1283 gave specific permission for the extension of burgages by the reclamation of land from the river.[52] At Wexford, the line of the medieval seashore coincided with low-lying parts of the present Main Street. In 1991, pipe-laying operations in the Bullring exposed sea sand several metres below the present road surface. The trench exposed beach material c. 2.5m below the present road surface. An oak timber, about 1.5m long, appeared to be embedded in the sand. Above the sand, a black layer, 20cm in width, containing bones, shells and what appeared to be medieval pottery, was visible. Above that seemed to consist of infill, except for another thin black layer about half-way between the sand and the present surface.[53]

An excavation at South Main Street, between the junctions with Bride Street and Peter Street, provided evidence for extensive medieval land reclamation and consolidation. Revetting consisted mainly of post-and-wattle fences, sometimes reinforced by horizontally laid planks of timber. Reclamation involved the dumping of large deposits of domestic rubbish, with periodic layers of flood material. Over the reclaimed area, a substantial paved street surface was found, with associated pottery dating to the mid thirteenth century. A similar pattern of reclamation was found at North Main Street, from the Bullring to the junction of Monck Street (formerly Ferryboat Lane)[54] and to the north of the town, the natural shore has been exposed at the junction of Slaney Street and Selskar Street.[55] However, just as in more recent times in Wexford, reclamation was not always successful. In 1325, for example, six burgages in the town were of no value because they were submerged by the sea.[56] In 1395 the value of a messuage (a dwelling house with its land) in Wexford was reduced as it had become so much damaged by the subsidence of the soil; it was to be rebuilt and repaired within eight years and rendered 'stiff and staunch'.[57] Eventually one-third of the walled town was constructed on reclaimed land.

Fig. 1   The priory of SS Peter and Paul, better known as Selskar Abbey, was founded early in the thirteenth century by the Canons regular of St Augustine. The curving line of the adjacent street may reflect the circular enclosure of an earlier pre-Norman church. The abbey precinct was divided by the town wall with a connecting gate through a mural tower. Part of the church and tower survive inside the wall. No visible trace survives of the monastic buildings, which were located outside the town wall. The tower was restored as a belfry and sacristy for a church built to the east in 1826.

WEXFORD'S MEDIEVAL CHURCHES

The combination of Celtic, Hiberno-Norse and Anglo-Norman churches, both inside and outside the walls, resulted in a complex medieval parish network in Wexford, consisting of five intramural and five extramural parishes. Unlike the later Anglo-Norman towns which were based on one large parish, the Norse towns had a complex system of small parishes, based on churches located both inside and outside the walls.[1] In Wexford, of the five parishes inside the walls, four of the church dedications – St Doologue's (Olave's), St Mary's, St Patrick's and St Iberius' – were Hiberno-Norse, as the parishes predated the arrival of the Anglo-Normans.

Four churches just outside the gates of the town – Holy Trinity, St Michael's, St Bride's and St Peter's – can also be associated with the Norse town. Of these only the graveyard of St Michael's survives: the others are remembered in the names of streets. Comparisons to other Viking towns are useful indicators of church foundation. Dedications to SS Bridget, Michael, Patrick, Mary, Peter, Olave and Holy Trinity were paralleled in Viking Dublin.[2] Four of these (Holy Trinity, Olave, Mary and Peter) were also found in Viking Waterford.[3]

Inside the wall, considerable ruins of St Patrick's church survive. Like Selskar Abbey, it had a double nave separated by an arcade of four arches

with plank centering. It has a double bellcote on a west gable and a sanctus bellcote over the chancel arch.[4] Only part of the west gable survives at St Mary's, which was a double-nave church similar to St Patrick's and Selskar.[5] It has been described as 'one of Wexford's finest medieval churches', an opinion based on a late eighteenth-century drawing.[6] No visible remains of the medieval church of St Iberius survive but presumably the site is occupied by the present church of the same name, built late in the eighteenth century. The parish church of St Doologue was located near the Castle Gate, south of the Bishopswater stream, but the exact location is not known and has

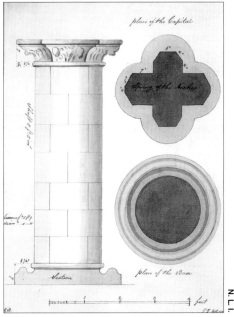

N.L.I.

Fig. 2   St Mary's parish church has been described as one of Wexford's finest medieval churches. This painting of the interior by Gabriel Beranger in 1780 shows the chancel arch and the arcade of 'elegant arches with round columns' on the left, both of which have disappeared. A tomb with the effigy of a woman, also recorded by the artist, is no longer to be seen.

Fig. 3   No visible trace of St John's church survives but a thirteenth-century stone coffin (top photograph), standing upright as a grave marker, indicates the medieval origin of the site. The centre illustration shows the design of the arcade columns, with moulded base and foliate capital, in St Mary's church. The bottom picture shows the surviving remnant of the church in the graveyard at Mary's Lane.

been built over. A bank and fosse uncovered at Barrack Street could be part of the church enclosure.[7] An early nineteenth-century description indicates that the church was close to the water's edge.[8]

THE MILITARY ORDERS

The extramural church of St John, the site of which survives at the junction of John's Street and John's Gate Street, was part of the preceptory of the Knights Hospitallers, brought to Wexford (presumably by Strongbow) who granted them the church of St Michael in the town. Strongbow also made a grant of a free hospital in Wexford to Nicholas Labench and his heirs, before 1176, but nothing more is known about it.[9] A grant of the

Affidavit relating to the boundaries of St Ulogh's Glebe

County Wexford to wit: Thomas Petitt of Ballell in the county aforesaid, farmer aged 82 years and upwards, came this day before me and voluntarily made oath on the Holy Evangelists and said that he resided near the Stone Bridge in the town of Wexford and recollects well the Boundaries of the Church and Church Yard, with the Glebe and Glebe House adjoining, which were formerly situate near said Stone Bridge, and on the site of which several buildings have since been erected, the principal of which is at present occupied as a temporary Barracks, and deponent swears that he has accurately pointed out the boundary of the said Church, Church Yard, Glebe House and Garden, to the best of his recollection and belief, this day to Robert Carty of Rathark Esq., and to Richard Augs. Kidd of the Town of Wexford. And positively swears that there were no buildings to the rear of said Church Yard, but that there was a deep Slob or Slimes in the rear from the boundaries of said Church Yard and Garden to the Harbour of Wexford and that the Dwelling House and Garden now occupied by — was always known and called by the name of the Glebe House and Garden.

Sworn before me this 28th May 1818
Thomas Petitt Thomas Richards

Fig. 5 A Templar knight depicted on a mural in a Templar church in France. Following its foundation in the Holy Land, the Order became powerful, expanding rapidly throughout Europe. In 1172, an extensive grant of estates to the Order by Henry II included mills in Wexford, probably situated on the Bishopswater river and the small stream that originally flowed from Peter's Square to the harbour. They were also granted property in Wexford town, probably by Strongbow. Their preceptory was located on the site of St John's church on the corner of John's Street and John's Gate Street. They were given the income from several churches in the town as well as twenty-three burgage plots in John Street.

churches of SS Patrick, Brigid and Mary Magdalene was confirmed to the Hospitallers by Marshal about 1210.[10]

Their great rivals, the Knights Templars of Kilcloggan, also had a connection with the town as their charter from Henry II granted them mills in Wexford, possibly located on the mill-stream that formerly ran from Peter's Square to the harbour.[11] The Franciscans were the only medieval religious order to be established in Wexford, arriving about the middle of the thirteenth century. Their found-ation, located just outside Friar's Gate (later known as Raby's Gate), is still occupied by the order, providing a direct ecclesiastical link with the medieval town.[12]

SELSKAR ABBEY

The principal Anglo-Norman found-ation was the Canons Regular of St Augustine priory of SS Peter and Paul of Selskar, possibly located on the site of an earlier church, as Irish monastic houses frequently adopted the Augustinian rule in the twelfth century.[13] The foundation has been traditionally attributed to the Roche family, but this cannot be validated. In 1541, following dissolution, an inquisition on the possessions of the priory stated that the name of the founder was not known.[14] It is more likely that the priory was established by the Marshals, as most of the lands held by Selskar were in the barony of Forth, a seignorial manor of the lords of Wexford. The priory held some possessions in the Roche land of Shelmalier East, but these may have been later acquisitions, as, in 1402,

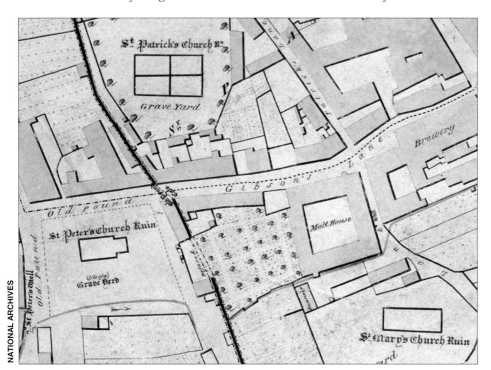

Fig. 4 The O. S. plan of 1840 shows the close proximity of three medieval parish churches, St Patrick's, St Mary's inside the town wall and St Peter's just outside Peter's Gate.

fourteenth century,[18] is well preserved, with battlements, described in 1834 as 'much decayed'.[19] These were restored in the nineteenth century when the tower was re-used as a belfry for a new church.[20] The tower quoins and windows are of dressed Dundry stone. The church is the only part of the complex that survives. Selskar Priory was frequently referred as *juxta* (beside) Wexford, showing that a considerable part of it was outside the town wall, and therefore regarded as outside the town. In 1355, the *Papal Registers* contained a revealing mention of Selskar (and of the perception of Ireland's place in the world!):

> To the bishop of Ferns. Mandate to inform himself touching the destruction by fire of the muniments of the prior and convent of SS Peter and Paul, Selskar by (juxta) Wexford, which is almost at the end of the world in Ireland, and to report thereon, and on the tenor of the said monument under seal to the Pope who will act on the information.[21]

Fig. 6   The tower of Selskar Abbey was a later addition, probably in the fourteenth century when tower building was in vogue. The tower was restored in the early nineteenth century.

Selskar received a grant from the bishop of Ferns of the churches of Ardcavan and Ardcolm, both in Roche territory, followed in 1418 by the church of St Nicholas in Carrig.[15] The priory was certainly founded before 1240 when a synod was convened there by John de St John, bishop of Ferns.[16]

The double-naved church is largely destroyed except for the gables. These contain remnants of west windows and an arcade of four pointed arches separating the aisles. The south wall, now almost completely removed, had four windows with square hood-mouldings.[17] The fortified tower, added possibly in the

Fig. 7   Surviving elements of Selskar Abbey include remains of the twin west gables, the arcade dividing the nave and aisle, and the north wall of the church now incorporated into a boundary wall.

Fig. 8   Inside the town wall, considerable remains of the medieval parish church of St Patrick with surrounding graveyard survive. It had a double nave and chancel, divided by an arcade of arches with plank centering. It has a double bellcote on a west gable and a Sanctus bellcote over the chancel arch. The dedication of the church survives in the adjacent Patrick's Square. Some casualties of the 1798 Rebellion were buried in the graveyard.

Selskar was similarly described in 1463 as 'the monastery of the holy apostles Peter and Paul near (*juxta*) Wexford'.[22] The extramural churches of SS Michael's, Peter's, John's and Magdalene's were also similarly described as near the town.[23] In the 1540s, following dissolution, the precinct of Selskar Abbey contained a church, steeple (presumably the tower), chancel, cemetery, dormitory, a hall, four chambers, kitchen, two stables, lands, granges, barns, orchards, gardens, 'within and without' the town wall.[24]

In 1583, the precinct of the abbey was described as extending:

from the Cowstreet Gate [Westgate] to the cemetery of the parish church of SS Peter and Paul; also an old bake-house and some waste lands and gardens situated between the abbey and the weir[25] leading to the street called Bolane's Land [?Lane; now Trimmer's Lane West], on the south, within the town wall to the Cowstreet gate; also certain tenements and waste lands between the abbey gate and the river Slaney, on the north side, called the Prior's Pill; together with a water-course running near the gate of St John the Baptist, commonly called the Hittelacke [?], with three acres of lands in orchards and gardens; together with the postern [a small side or back door] gate leading from the abbey to the said orchards and gardens,

Fig. 9 St Iberius' church on the Main Street, close to the medieval shoreline, is dedicated to St Ibar of Begerin. It was built in the eighteenth century, presumably on the site of the medieval parish church which had the same dedication. If so, it is the only surviving centre of worship on a medieval site inside the town wall.

NED CULLETON

Fig. 10   As this painting illustrates, the late eighteenth-century ruins of Selskar Abbey were much more intact than at the present time. The south wall of the nave, with four double-light windows and entrance are shown. To the right of the tower, the chancel with east window and gable which were later removed, can be seen. This picture illustrates the dilapidated state of the tower, before restoration of the battlements in the 1820s.

and half an acre of land called Whytt's Park, all held from the Queen, at the annual rent of 5s.[26]

In 1618, an inquisition on the lands of Philip Devereux included a description of the 'ambit, circuit and precinct' of the monastery of Selskar in the town.[27] He held 'two gardens, two acres of land, two orchards, certain gardens, a castle upon the wall of the town, a bake-house, and a gate called the postern gate. He also held a water mill with water-course within the town and Whitt's Park, containing three-and-a-half acres in the parish of Carrig, all parcels of the said monastery'. The precinct of the abbey inside the town wall had been divided by that time as Edward Turner owned

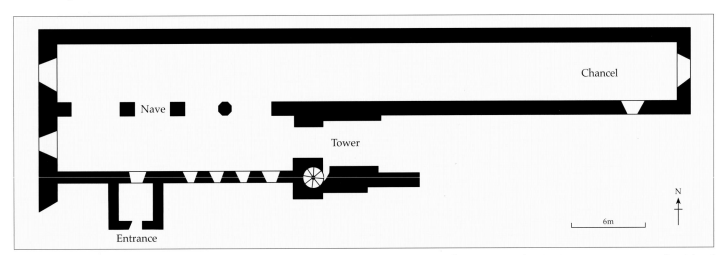

Fig. 11   This 1780 plan of Selskar Abbey shows the complete outline of the structure before the removal of the slender eastern section, to the right of the central tower, to facilitate the building of Selskar church in 1826. The wall of the side aisle, with the entrance, no longer survives. The tower, with spiral stairway, was restored as a sacristy and belfry for the nineteenth-century church. The twin western gables are still standing.

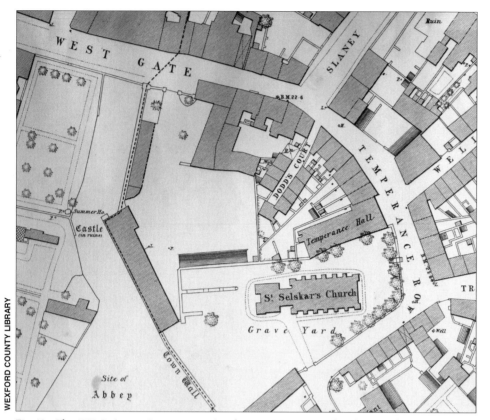

Fig. 12 The 1883 Ordnance Survey town plan shows Selskar Abbey church inside the town wall and also the site of the abbey outside the wall on a vacant space which presumably represents the abbey precinct. A stream which formerly ran across this area was known as the Prior's Pill.

have served an economic function as it allowed the monks to bring goods into the town without having to pay tolls at one of the town gates. As a significant part of the abbey precinct within the wall had been let to lay tenants before dissolution, a considerable part of the conventual buildings, described in the surveys of the 1640s, must have been located outside the walls. Earlier descriptions of the abbey as *juxta* Wexford indicate that, apart from the church, all of the abbey complex was extra-mural.

The depiction of Selskar Abbey on Ordnance Survey maps is not altogether conclusive. The 1841 map has 'abbey in ruins' written across the town wall, possibly indicating that the site was divided by the wall.[28] The large scale map of 1883 shows 'abbey (site of)' outside the wall[29] while the 1903 revision of the six-inch map has 'abbey (in ruins)' inside, and 'abbey (site of)' outside the walls.[30] It is not

ten messuages in 'le Cow Street' in the parish of Selskar, and four enclosures or gardens, of which three were 'outside the gate called the Cowgate and one within'.

Some deductions relating to the extent of the Selskar precinct can be made from these descriptions. Inside the town wall, the abbey possessions were bounded by the curving road now consisting of Temperance Row (formerly Hai Bai) and Westgate Street (formerly Cow Street), extending from the present graveyard gate around to Westgate (Cow Gate).

The precinct included land outside the town wall, which was accessed from the church site by the Abbey Gate and a postern gate. This gate was obviously a weak point in the town's defences and was defended by the construction of the 'castle upon the wall of the town', mentioned in 1618, now erroneously known as the Westgate. The private gate may also

Fig. 13 This late nineteenth-century drawing illustrates the Selskar church tower with restored battlements. Part of the south wall of the nave is still standing. The arcade of arches is more complete than at the present time. The Abbey Gate through the town wall can be seen in the background.

S.P.C.

Fig. 14   This detail from an 1820 painting of Wexford shows the ruins of Selskar Abbey and Gate and also one of the towers on the town wall. A recently-built quay can be seen at bottom left. The picture illustrates the proximity of the abbey to the seashore before extensive land reclamation

clear to what extent the later maps were attempting to clarify the information contained on the original 1841 O. S. sheet. Following dissolution, the abbey church was retained as a Protestant place of worship,[31] thus escaping the fate of other churches in the town which were sold as a source of building stone, some of which was used to repair the damage caused to Wexford Castle by Cromwell's cannon.[32] The same fate may have befallen the domestic buildings of Selskar Abbey outside the town wall as there is no description, either cartographically or pictorially, of their nature. However, the O. S. maps all show a parcel of undeveloped land, stretching from Spawell Road to George's Street, adjacent to the town wall and immediately outside Selskar Gate, which could represent the abbey's holding 'without the wall'.

The expansion of Wexford was greatly influenced by the establishment and locations of church foundations and the extent of that influence can be assessed by examining the distribution of medieval church dedications that survive as modern street names, the majority located in the core area of the Norse town.

R.I.A.

Fig 16   A mid nineteenth-century drawing of a medieval graveslab from Selskar Abbey by G. V. Du Noyer. The depiction of a ship presumably signified that the individual over whom the slab was placed had strong maritime connections. The stone, now very degraded, is secured to the west wall of the tower.

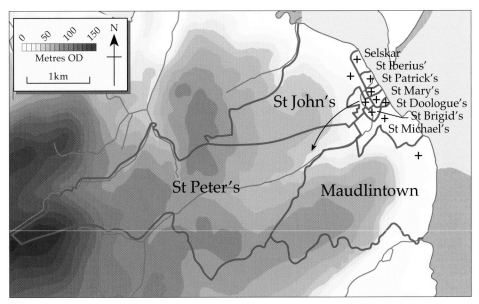

Fig. 15   The medieval parochial structure of Wexford town and liberties was created by the ecclesiastical organisation initiated by the Hiberno-Norse and expanded on by the Anglo-Normans. The complex system of miniscule parishes represent the core area of the Norse town while the larger outlying parishes, with churches close to the town, represent the town's burgage lands.

THE IRISH REVIVAL: THE COLONY UNDER PRESSURE

After a period of relative success, possibly due in part to the blood relationship between the Marshals and the Mac Murchada, the Anglo-Norman colony in the Wexford lordship came under increasing pressure from the Irish from the mid thirteenth century. This was partly due to more efficient opposition from a new generation of Irish leaders and was aided by a complicated partition of Leinster in 1247, with an ensuing long-term damaging effect on the stability of the colony.[1] The partition resulted in the fragmentation of authority and ownership in county Wexford with a consequent slackening in political and financial control. By the end of the century, the Leinster Irish, led by the Mac Murchada, were in general revolt. In 1307 the value of the burgages in Wexford had fallen by almost a half and there were frequent references to districts that were 'waste on account of the Irish wars'.

The requirement to provide ships for foreign wars also placed an economic burden on the town. In 1303 Sir Gilbert de Sutton and Henry Esmond had to provide ships from Wexford for the Scottish expedition[2] and in 1311 the town was ordered to furnish two ships fully armed, with seven weeks' provisions, for the king's service in Scotland against Robert Bruce.[3] The Bruce invasion of Ireland (1315–18), and recurring famines, did much to hasten the decline.[4] Wexford was required, with other ports, to supply men and ships for an expedition against the king of France in 1324 when all ships entering the port were seized for that purpose.[5]

Fig. 1 The Irish chieftains employed professional Scottish mercenaries known as gallowglasses (gall óglaigh: foreign youths), in their conflict with the English administration. This illustration, made in 1521 by the great German artist, Albrecht Dürer (1471–1528), portrays two gallowglasses on the left, accompanied by three Irish warriors, with distinctive Irish hairstyles, on the right.

A COLONY UNDER PRESSURE

The town of Wexford was badly affected by political and economic pressures: a survey of 1324 found that there were 221 deserted burgages in the town and the manor of Carrig, just to the north, was 'destroyed by war'.[6] In 1335 serious discord in Wexford required a prolonged sitting of the court and a special payment of £40 to Robert Poer, the seneschal, for services rendered in quelling conflict between the Irish and English.[7] As a result of the disturbances, the prior of Selskar Abbey claimed that the lands and rents of the abbey had been destroyed by the war of the Irish to such an extent that the monks were considering abandoning the abbey to live with their friends in the countryside.[8] The unrest in the town evidently led to an outflow of people. In 1343 a proclamation was issued to port towns, including Wexford, that all ships were to be arrested and that no

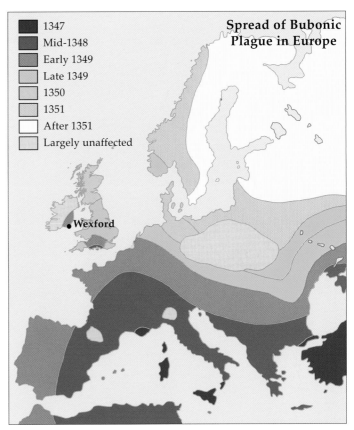

Fig. 3   A cartographic representation of the spread along European sea routes of the devastating plague known as the Black Death.

one, with the exception of merchants, could leave Ireland without the king's warrant.[9] The decline in the colony became more acute after the spread of the Black Death across Europe, reaching Ireland through its ports in 1348. The plague, which lingered on for the rest of the century, principally in the towns, may have reduced the Anglo-Norman population of Ireland by one-third to a half.[10] There is no specific record as to how Wexford fared but, as a principal port, it must have shared the same distressing fate as the other towns.

THE IRISH REVIVAL

The Irish recovery had a dramatic impact on the English colony in county Wexford and by the end of the fourteenth century the north of the county was controlled by the Irish. The Mac Murchada, operating in both cultures, succeeded in regaining the kingship of Leinster and effectively destroyed much of the English colony. An expedition by Richard II did little to remedy the situation and Art MacMurrough Kavanagh – the self-styled king of Leinster – continued to extract a 'black rent' from the settlers. By the year 1400, Wexford had suffered so much 'by the death of burgesses and divers robberies' that the king pardoned all debts owed by the town.[11] By the end of the fourteenth century, the north of the county had been abandoned by

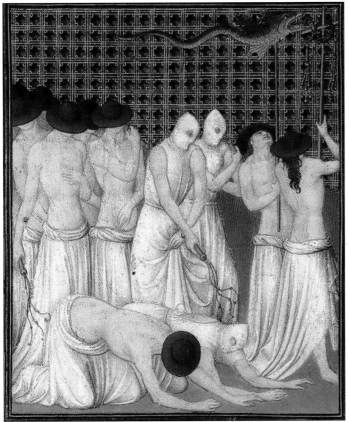

Fig. 2   The disruption caused by the chaotic political situation in fourteenth-century Ireland escalated dramatically with the arrival of the plague known as the Black Death. Appearing in Europe in 1347, the disease spread rapidly along the trade routes and arrived in Drogheda in 1348. The Anglo-Irish, concentrated in the towns, suffered to a greater extent than the more rural Irish population. An estimated mortality rate of 25–35 per cent may have risen to 40 or 50 per cent by the end of the century, due to recurring outbreaks. The horror of the calamity is depicted in this contemporary illustration, executed by the Limbourg brothers, c.1408. Its ravages caused thousands of flagellants to endure doing public penance to expiate sins committed. The bloated dragon is a symbol of the devil, behind the Christian cross. This image is an early technical exercise in foreshortening.

Fig. 4 By the end of the fourteenth century, the threat to the colony in Ireland resulted in two expeditions by Richard II in what were ultimately unsuccessful attempts at forcing the Irish to obey the rule of English law. Jean Creton, a French artist who accompanied the second expedition, portrayed the ships carrying Richard's army sailing into Waterford Harbour, providing a valuable illustration of fourteenth-century shipping.

the settler community and was controlled by the Irish.[12]

In the fifteenth century, English rule became confined to an area around Dublin, protected by an earthen bank and fosse, known as the Pale. In county Wexford the settlers of English extraction were largely restricted to the southern 'English' baronies of Forth, Bargy and Shelburne, insulated behind the natural defences of Forth Mountain and the Corock and Owenduff rivers. Official directives issued in the early fifteenth century acknowledged that the southern baronies of Forth and Bargy were functioning as a second Pale.[13] The settlers were under constant threat from the Irish; in 1416 and again in 1423, the Mac Murchada ravaged Wexford town and suburbs.[14] In 1429, the granting of a £10 subsidy to landowners to build a fortified castle or tower within the Pale initiated the widespread construction of small stone castles, known as tower houses, in both Anglo-Irish and Gaelic lordships.[15] This policy was extended to county Wexford in 1441 when an act was passed for 'building towers upon the waters or river of Taghmon'. The 'waters' were the Corock, with its tributary the Aughnagroagh, which flow into Bannow Bay, and a small river flowing into the Slaney at Polehore.

The rivers were also to be dammed so that by deepening the water a greater obstruction would be created. A further order was issued in 1453 that 'none shall break the

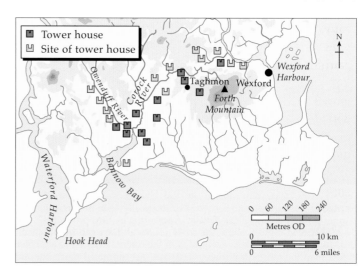

Fig. 5 During the fifteenth and sixteenth centuries, about 170 defended residences, known as tower houses, were built in county Wexford, for security reasons, by the descendants of the Anglo-Norman colonists. Twenty of these were built along the line of the river Corock, and its tributary the Aughnagroagh, to protect the Wexford Pale, consisting mostly of the baronies of Forth and Bargy in the south-east of the county.

Fig. 6   At least six tower houses were built in Wexford town. This detail from an 1820 painting of the town shows the tower of Stafford's castle, built in the fifteenth century. Located between Oyster Lane and Stonebridge on the harbour side of South Main Street, it was later used as the town jail. Urban tower houses were a common feature of late medieval Ireland. The tower over Selskar Gate is the only surviving example in Wexford.

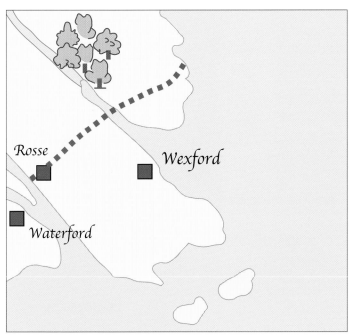

Fig. 7   On a mid sixteenth-century map of Ireland (redrawn by John Andrews), the English Pale around Dublin is defined by a broken line. This detail shows the southern part of county Wexford depicted as an outlying Pale, south of a line from New Ross to Curracloe. Note the representation of forest cover to the north of the Pale boundary.

Stafford's Castle (*Griffith's Chronicles*, 1886)

The Heraldic visitation of the County taken in 1618, gives the pedigree of the Staffords of the Castle in the Town of Wexford, and states that George Stafford, who lived about the year 1480, built the Castle and Hall in Wexford, and his family and posterity resided therein, until the above date. But this is not to be taken as the Castle of the 'King's fortress'. This Castle and hall stood on the sea side, or right of the street into the Town, between the Stone-bridge and Oyster Lane. In the same volume mention is made of Walter Stafford, Esq., of the Bridge and this is the same as the Stonebridge, and this (after dismantling of the Royal Castle by Cromwell, where prisoners had always been confined) was converted into a County Prison, and continued so until the present County Gaol was built near the West Gate, in 1812, when it was converted into a Workhouse, and lately thrown down, and rebuilt as shops and private dwellings by Mr Richard Devereux.

Fig. 8 This tower house was built by the Roches on a clifftop at Ferrycarrig, two miles up-river from Wexford overlooking the Slaney gorge. The castle commanded river traffic to and from Enniscorthy, as well as the ferry, shown here carrying livestock and people across the river narrows.

fortifications of Taghmon in county Wexford nor shall make no ways on the same water from the wood of Bannow to the pill adjoining the river Slaney'.[16] These rivers, with Forth mountain, protected the 'English' baronies of Forth and Bargy and part of Shelmalier West, delineating the distinctive cultural and social landscape of the Wexford Pale.

As many as twenty tower houses were constructed along this important defensive line. The construction of

tower houses was not confined to rural areas as there were at least six built inside the walls of Wexford in the fifteenth century. Hayes's castle was in Hayes's (now Cinema) Lane; Kenny's Hall was located on the harbour side of South Main Street near Kayser's Lane. Part of the lower walls survive in the basement of what is now Penney's store. Stafford's castle, used as a prison in the eighteenth century, stood on the harbour side of South Main Street between Oyster Lane and Stonebridge. Wadding's castle

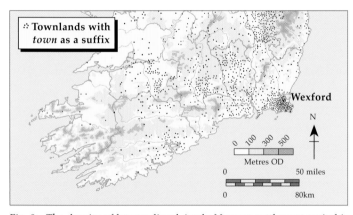

Fig. 9 The density of late medieval Anglo-Norman settlement period is reflected in the distribution of townland names containing the suffix 'town'. The greatest clustering of these townland names in Ireland is found in the heavily settled baronies of Forth and Bargy in south Wexford, many of them containing the names of the original settlers.

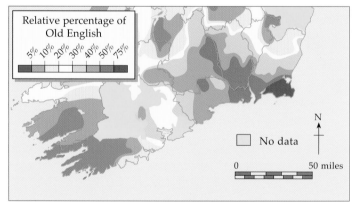

Fig. 10 This map shows the high density of Old English names recorded in the 1660 poll-tax returns. Forth and Bargy in south Wexford had the highest concentration of Anglo-Norman surnames in the country. The map highlights the division of county Wexford between an Irish north and an English south, with a hybrid area in between.

Fig. 11 Killiane Castle, associated with the Hay and Cheevers families, is located close to the shoreline of the southern part of Wexford Harbour. It was built on the liberties of Wexford town, probably in the fifteenth century, and is one of the best preserved tower houses in the county. This eighteenth-century illustration shows the tower with associated bawn (enclosure) to the right. The house to the left of the tower was probably added in the seventeenth century. The building remains substantially in the same condition at the present time.

Fig. 12 Barntown Castle, attributed to the Roches, was built in a commanding position on the slopes of Forth Mountain to control the approaches to Wexford between the mountain and the Slaney.

was located in Peter's Street on the corner of Patrick's Lane. The only surviving tower house in Wexford is the recently restored Selskar Gate tower, built by the monks of Selskar Abbey over a gate in the town wall which divided the abbey precinct.

In spite of the protection afforded by the construction of tower houses and the natural defences of the Wexford Pale, the southern part of county Wexford came under increasing threat from the resurgent Irish. In 1537, when the king resumed the powers and privileges of the Palatinate lords, including the town of Wexford, the sovereign and commons of the town petitioned to enjoy the same privileges as before, claiming that 'the town was surrounded by enemies', and requested a remission of rent in order to repair the town walls which were in very bad repair.[17] The Irish were not always responsible for the chaotic situation in the county as the settlers themselves were sometimes the cause of the mayhem. In 1519, the Roches instigated widespread disorder and in the 1560s the Keatings and the Butlers caused devastation.[18] By the end of the century the county, overrun by the 'rebels', was

'waste and disorderly'. Even Wexford itself was under threat, as in 1598 eighty of the Irish were killed in a skirmish in the town.[19]

DISSOLUTION OF THE MONASTERIES

The situation was further exacerbated by the advent of the Reformation which opened a religious as well as a political divide between the Irish and English. The proclamation of Henry VIII as head of the Irish church in 1536 precipitated profound changes in social and political life.[20] The monastic estates were targeted by the new regime, mainly to gain access to their extensive lands, partly because of a decline in religious life but also because they were regarded as places of refuge for the rebel Irish. The authorities decided to suppress the monasteries and grant their properties to trustworthy men who would protect the land and attract new colonists from England. This process impacted directly on Wexford town where the properties of Selskar Abbey and the Franciscan Friary were confiscated and granted to tenants who were loyal to the crown and the new Protestant religion.

TOWN WALL AND CASTLE

Fig. 1   In this view of Wexford, the line of the town wall is marked by a red line. The sites of the town gates are also shown. This perspective illustrates the narrow, elongated nature of the medieval town. This was even more pronounced before the reclamation of up to one-third of the present area inside the wall. The aerial perspective demonstrates the extent to which the town has spread beyond its medieval core. **A** West (Cow) Gate, **B** Selskar Gate, **C** John's Gate, **D** Friars' Gate, **E** Peter's Gate, **F** Bride Gate, **G** Castle Gate.

THE WALLS OF WEXFORD

Medieval town walls, apart from their obvious defensive function, were symbols of the independence and freedom of medieval towns and acted as lines of economic and social demarcation.[1] The walls played a crucial role in the business life of the town as they defined the different economic zones, within and without the borough, for tax and revenue purposes. They also epitomised the medieval town and the rights and privileges enjoyed by the burgesses. When the Anglo-Normans took Wexford, it already had defences, perhaps even walls of stone.[2] These twelfth-century walls represented an expansion of the town; a seven-metre-wide ditch located twenty metres inside the present town wall could indicate the existence of an earlier

defensive structure.[3] There is no indication so far to show when the Normans strengthened, or replaced with stone walls, the ramparts of the Hiberno-Norse town. The evidence of parochial boundaries, and the architecture of the surviving mural towers, indicates that the Anglo-Norman wall initially followed the line of the Norse defences possibly as far as Cornmarket with a somewhat later extension enclosing the market place, the ferry landing and the conjectured monastic site, creating the parish of Selskar in the process. A description of the town in 1789 stated that the 'old town wall' could be seen running down to the seashore just south of the Bullring.[4] An excavation outside the supposedly later section of wall did not expose the ditch which Giraldus described in his account of

the attack on Wexford in 1169[5] and the mural towers are circular in contrast to the square tower which survives at Cornmarket, suggesting a different period of construction.[6] The apparent absence of mural towers from the southern part of the wall may also be significant. The concentration of Hiberno-Norse extramural churches outside the three southern gates – Castle Gate, Bride Gate and Peter's Gate – is an indication that this part of the town represents the core of Hiberno-Norse Wexford.

Almost all of the northern portion of the wall from Cornmarket to Westgate is still standing, perhaps an indication that it was the last part to be constructed. It is also the most visible because of a lower density of development. Parts of the southern wall failed to survive because it was

Fig. 2   This aerial view shows the outside of the town wall at the north end of the town adjacent to Selskar Abbey. The wall is more visible here as the area outside the wall was not developed for housing. The tower on the wall served as a gate for the abbey, which had possessions on both sides of the wall. The original fabric appears to survive adjacent to the graveyard. The buildings occupying the top third of the picture are on reclaimed land.

built on the marshy ground in the valley of the Bishopswater stream which must have flowed through a culvert in the wall. In 1839, about fifty yards of the town wall, between Peter's Street and Bride Street, to the north of the stream, was knocked by a flood.[7] Urban archaeological exploration has uncovered evidence for thirteenth-century expansion to the north and reclamation of land from the harbour, along the line of the present North Main Street from the Bullring to Monck Street (formerly Ferryboat Lane).[8] An excavation on the east side of the junction of Cornmarket and Abbey Street produced evidence for thirteenth- and fourteenth-century activity, including possible house remains.[9]

No records survive for early murage grants for the building of walls at Wexford but there are

Fig. 3   Selskar Gate from outside the wall. The gate tower was restored in the 1980s. A modern extension (right top) has been added to the town wall. A blocked-up postern gate, with remains of a defensive machicolation above, can be seen to the right of the gateway.

Fig. 4   Access has been opened up along the outside of this section of wall, not all original, between Selskar Abbey and George's Street. The foundations of the early wall are visible in a trench at the fenced-off area. As part of the development, the battlements of the circular mural tower have been restored. The town wall was removed (centre right) to facilitate the extension of George's Street.

The Town Wall
(*Griffith's Chronicles*, 1886)

The town having been much enlarged beyond the walls of the Ostmen, by the influx of new settlers and the increase in commerce created by the settlement of the Normans, a new wall was commenced in the reign of King John, but was not finished until that of Edward III, when Stephen Devereux, Knight, of Ballymagir, completed it, and erected a grand West Gate, near the Abbey of Selskar — an old religious house of the Ostmen. This gate was very near to the large Castle with a gateway under it for a sally-port — and over the new gate Devereux placed his arms, with the following words:-'Nisi Dominus custodit civitatum frustra vigilant qui custodiant eam'. [Unless the Lord protects the city the custodians are helpless]. This gate, with the other gates in the Town, five in number, was taken down in 1759. After the Insurrection of 1798, the gates were erected in a plain manner, and again taken down in 1828.

records for the other Hiberno-Norse towns: Dublin 1215, Cork 1218, Waterford 1224 and Limerick 1237.[10] Presumably, wall-building activity began in Wexford during the first quarter of the thirteenth century. The wall, when completed, was just three-quarters of a mile (1.2km) long. It took a century to build the walls of Kilkenny, which were one-and-a-half miles long,[11] so on that basis, Wexford's town wall may have taken fifty years to complete. An account from 1835 claimed that the walls were completed by Sir Stephen Devereux in 1300, enclosing an area considerably larger than the old Norse town, the wall of which could be traced from the Common Quay to the Courthouse (Common Quay, now covered by extensive reclamation, projected into the harbour close to the present Bullring). Devereux is said to have placed his arms and the inscription 'Except the Lord keep the city, the watchman waketh in vain' over the Westgate. The inscribed stone was still in place in 1759 but,

the gate was demolished in 1794.[12]

The completed wall enclosed an area of forty statute acres (not including later land reclamation from the estuary), compared to the fifty acres of Dublin and Waterford. The Anglo-Norman wall may have

Fig. 5   At Selskar Gate (left) the wall turns to run down the slope towards Westgate (also called Cowgate) which led to the west of the county and the ferry at Carrig, via Spawell Road.

enclosed two elements: the Hiberno-Norse town and the conjectured monastic settlement. This diversity is reflected in the street pattern of the modern town. The surmised Norse town had two streets running parallel to the shoreline (now represented by Main Street and High Street/Patrick's Lane/Mary's Lane), intersected by a number of lanes (including Kayser's Lane) running down the slope to the seashore. The conjectured extension had one street (Market Street, now Abbey Street) connecting the market place (now Cornmarket) to Selskar Abbey and then curving around the abbey precinct to Westgate. Market Street was mentioned in 1280, suggesting that the extension had been completed by that time.[13] A path which ran from the market place along the foreshore to the ferry is now represented by North Main Street (formerly Fore Street) and Monck Street (formerly Ferryboat Lane). The route from the abbey to the ferry survives as Well Lane and Trimmer's Lane.

Historically, there has been a distinction between the 'north' and 'south' ends which persists to the present time. A dispute in 1462 illustrated this distinction very neatly. A parliament held at Wexford in that year heard that for years there had been a division between the commons on the south and those on the north side concerning the revenue in the form of murage tax raised to fortify the town. Each side was responsible for the maintenance of the town wall in its own part of the town. As the south side had the capacity to generate more revenue, there was dissatisfaction with the condition of the walls on the north. The parliament directed that in future the combined revenue should be spent on the entire wall without reference to either side.[14] The area represented by the present

Fig. 6 The precinct of Selskar Abbey was divided by the town wall. This restored gate tower connected the intramural church with the property and buildings outside the wall.

Bullring was presumably held in common by both 'sides'. In 1621 it was referred to as 'the Common Plain', and the adjacent quay was

known as Common Quay, a name still surviving in Common Quay Street.[15]

The town wall, of which two-thirds survives in various stages of

Fig. 7   A section of town wall, viewed from the inside, at the top of Cornmarket adjacent to the site of John's Gate at John's Gate Street (right). Steps to the right of the square mural tower gave access to the wall-walk, traces of which survive, and to the mural tower, through a doorway which is now blocked up. The top of the tower has been restored, probably to coincide with the building of the adjacent Rowe Street church in the 1850s.

preservation, was built near the top of the slope on which the town is situated.[16] References to the collection of murage tolls in 1331 and 1381 for the repair of the town defences indicate that the wall needed on-going maintenance work, so it is probable that part of the original structure may have been replaced.[17] As late as 1537 the mayor reported that the walls were in such bad repair that the town was defenceless and requested a remission in rents for the 'reparation and defence of the town like as Waterford and other towns have'.[18] In places where the structure has been removed, the line of the wall, which is of significant symbolic importance, can be traced. The original fabric survives in places, for example adjacent to Selskar Abbey

where putlog (scaffolding) holes can still be seen. A section of double wall survives at High Street, with the intervening space of three metres packed with earth.[19] Traces of the benched wall-walk can be seen near the mural towers at Abbey Street and Corn-market. Just south-east of the site of Bride Gate, a section of breast work, surviving above the wall-walk, has five musket loops, some of them restored, and indications of battle-ments. Three mural towers survive, a square one at Cornmarket with battlements restored, probably in the 1850s, and two circular towers at Abbey Street, one restored in the 1990s. All towers were entered from the wall-walk at first floor level. A mural tower near St Patrick's church, a square tower near Rowe Street[20] and

another beside John's Gate[21] no longer survive. A reference to a Friar's Tower, 'in or near the town', could indicate the existence of another mural tower near Friar's Gate.[22] A reference in 1561 to 'the gate of the castle of Cow Street' (now Westgate),

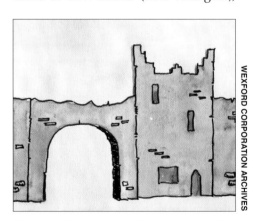

Fig. 8   An illustration from Wexford Corporation records of John's Gate and tower, both of which were removed in the early nineteenth century.

John's Gate

Selskar Gate

West (Cow) Gate

Friar's Gate

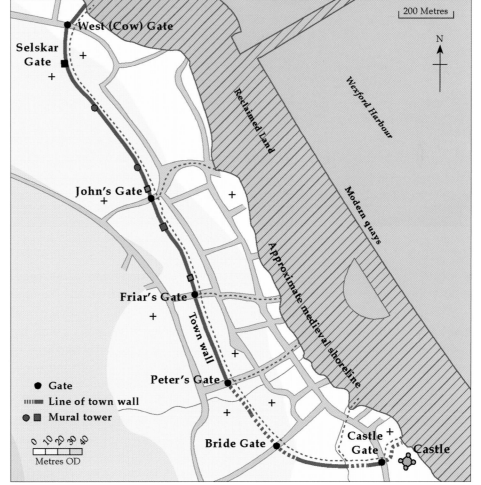

Fig. 9 The sites of seven town gates can be identified in the modern streetscape. The only surviving gate was part of the Selskar Abbey complex and was not part of the street fabric. Five were named after adjacent medieval buildings, the castle and four churches. Westgate provided access to the west of the county. In later centuries, the town wall was breached by George's Street, Rowe Street and King Street.

Peter's Gate

Bride Gate

Castle Gate

Fig. 10 This stretch of town wall viewed from the inside, beside Wexford Arts Centre, has been exposed by the removal of a row of houses at Abbey Street. The section to the left of the tree has been restored. Part of the wall-walk, from which the mural tower was accessed, survives to the left of the tower.

indicates that there was a tower located there also.[23]

The sites of six town gates with associated streets can be identified:[24] Castle Gate, Bride Gate, Peter's Gate, Friar's Gate (later called Raby's Gate)[25], John's Gate and Westgate (also called Cow Gate). The only surviving gate, restored in the 1980s and now called Westgate, was not related to the street complex of the town and was not a public town gate. The excavation at Bride Street in 1988 established the consistency of property boundaries back to the twelfth century and it does not seem possible that a street with all its property boundaries could vanish without a trace. Eighteenth-century Corporation leases refer to a Westgate and a Selskar Gate[26] and the 'fine spa outside of the Westgate' mentioned in 1764 gave Spawell Road, a continuation of Westgate Street, its

name.[27] The surviving gate (now restored) was part of the Selskar Abbey complex, as the abbey had property both inside and outside the town wall. In 1551 the 'tenements of Selskar within and without the walls' included 'two tenements by the great gate of the monastery'.[28] Following the removal of the Westgate, situated only forty metres away, the name survived as a street name and was later transferred to the adjacent Selskar Gate. The site of the original Westgate is clearly named on an 1840 map of the town.[29] The tower over Selskar Gate is actually a small tower house, possibly added in the fourteenth century. The construction of the Westgate has been attributed to Stephen Devereux of Ballymagir. Its location was described as 'very near to a large castle with a gateway under it for a sally-port', a precise description

Fig. 11 The circular mural tower at Abbey Street viewed from outside the town wall.

Fig. 12 From Peter's Gate to Friars' Gate a substantial section of the town wall forms the boundary between the gardens of houses in School Street and High Street. The section shown here is on private property. This is a significant stretch of wall as four different elements can be identified. Part of the parapet survives at **A**, the wall-walk can be seen at **B**, and the wall itself at **C**. The rampart of clay, inside the wall at **D,** probably dates to the mid seventeenth century when houses near the wall were removed and the wall backed with clay as a defence against Cromwell's cannon.

of Selskar Gate (now mistakenly called Westgate). The same source states that the Westgate, with the other town gates, was taken down by the corporation in 1759.[30]

A surviving sketch of John's Gate in 1776 shows a different type of gate with a tower adjacent to, but not over, the gate.[31] In 1684 there was a gun called a 'saker' in this tower. When the town gates were removed by the corporation in the late eighteenth century to facilitate traffic, Selskar Gate survived because it had no associated street and therefore was not being used. Two of the town gates are remembered in street names: Westgate and John's Gate Street.

In a number of towns, including Dublin and Waterford, town defences were constructed along the waterfront. At Wexford, however, there was

Fig. 13 A late eighteenth-century view from outside the wall at Selskar. Selskar Gate was already blocked up at that time. Artistic licence has been used to show the two circular mural towers close together for greater effect. The tower on the end of the wall, to the left, must represent 'the gate of the castle of Cow Street' (Westgate) mentioned in 1561. Inside the wall, the tower of Selskar Abbey is shown before the archway had been blocked up.

Fig. 14   A length of wall at Rope-walk Yard, off King Street, viewed here from the outside, is of vital significance as the wall-walk and parapet survive. Three crenels (openings) survive in the parapet. These have been filled in, with musket loops inserted, presumably in the Cromwellian period. Part of the wall to the left, with musket loops, has been restored. The ground inside the wall at this point has been filled in up to wall-walk level to provide a level surface for car parking.

unrestricted access to the harbour, with narrow lanes leading to numerous jetties along the shore. In 1537, the town was described as 'on one side encompassed'.[32] In 1634, the open nature of the waterfront was noticed by William Brereton who commented that 'there belonged sometimes unto every merchant's house seated on the shore, either a key, or a part interest in a key, or a private way to a key'.[33] A description of the town in 1682 stated that 'Wexford is a walled town on all sides except to the sea-pool or harbour, which washeth the north-east side thereof'.[34] These descriptions imply that there were no waterfront defences at Wexford, at least not of medieval construction. These accounts correspond with the stylised representation of Wexford town on the Down Survey, which depicted the town walled on the land side only, with a series of jetties projecting into the harbour along the waterfront.[35]

Fig. 15   This degraded section of wall, some of it original, runs from King Street to Barrack Street.

Fig. 16   At the top, part of the town wall can be seen incorporated into the structure of a cornstore at Rope-walk Yard off King Street; the middle picture shows the substantial but heavily overgrown wall adjacent to St Patrick's Church. Note the string course for the parapet. The bottom picture records a fragmentary remnant of the town wall at Peter's Square.

Fig. 18   This cross-section of the town wall at Ropewalk Yard shows the parapet, wall-walk, and a diagonal loop through the wall near ground level. The Bishopswater stream flowed under the wall in this vicinity, possibly leading to its collapse due to unstable foundations.

Fig. 17   These pictures feature some details of the town wall. From the top: restored loops at the square mural tower beside John's Gate Street; a loop on the outside of the same tower; a filled-in crenel with musket loop at Bride Street carpark; a loop at Bride Street.

Extensive sections of the town wall survive, in various states of repair, particularly between Peter's Street and Westgate. A continuous stretch of the wall, three to four metres high, exists between Peter's Street and Rowe Street, hidden behind the houses of High Street and School Street. Part of this section, beside St Patrick's Church, consisting of a double wall with the intervening space filled in to form a platform three metres wide, may represent the reinforcement of the wall in preparation for the Crom-wellian siege of 1649. The wall is almost continuous and most visible from Cornmarket to Westgate. The extent and line of the wall where it approached the shoreline at both ends has not been satisfactorily resolved. The line of the wall has been breached by the later streets of King Street,

Fig. 19   The view looking north along the outside of the town wall from George's Street includes a circular mural tower with restored battlements, the tower of Selskar Gate (partly hidden by a tree) and the tower of Selskar Abbey, restored during the 1820s.

Fig 20 A view of the restored circular mural tower from inside the wall at Abbey Street.

Rowe Street and George's Street. Archaeological investigations have uncovered possible remains of the wall at King Street, the foundation trench of the wall at Peter's Street[36]

and the base of the wall at Westgate.[37] The town was divided internally into three wards, with gates on the Main Street, one just south of the Bullring and one at 'Oldgate', just north of Peter's Street.

WEXFORD CASTLE

The principal achievement in urban foundation associated with intense Anglo-Norman settlement in county Wexford was the expansion of the Hiberno-Norse port of Wexford and the founding of the new port of Ross. Henry's prolonged stay in Wexford, which had the advantage of being an existing settlement with an established infrastructure and lively trade connections, added impetus to the growth of the town. Early in the thirteenth century, the palatine of Leinster was divided into the four shires, or counties, of Wexford, Kilkenny, Kildare and Carlow, with

Wexford town as the centre of administration for the county.[38] The premature demise of all five of Marshal's sons, without heir, had a dramatic impact on the lordship: following feudal practice, Leinster was divided equally among his five daughters or their representatives. The liberty of Wexford passed to Marshal's grand-daughter, Joan, who was married to William de Valence, the king's half-brother.[39] Marshal's descendants retained possession of Wexford town and castle for the next three centuries.

The strategic role of Wexford town in the organisation of the Anglo-Norman colony was emphasised by the building of a stone castle. Six early thirteenth-century stone castles existed in the county, located at Wexford, Carrig (a borough on the Slaney three kilometres north-west of Wexford), Ferns, Old Ross, the Island

Fig. 21 Wexford Castle was situated on a natural mound just outside the town wall (the line of the wall is shown in red). Before reclamation, the sea lapped the foot of the mound. The castle was removed in the 1720s and replaced by the military barracks which still occupies the site.

Fig 22   A conjectural drawing of thirteenth-century Wexford Castle, based on historical references. The castle, located just outside the town wall, was located on a natural mound close to the shoreline south of the town. The castle was leveled in the 1720s and replaced by the military barracks.

town, originally lapped by the waters of the harbour before land reclamation. Once considered to be a motte,[46] recent investigation has shown it to be a natural feature composed of glacial deposits.[47] The location of the castle outside the town's defences was not unusual as out of thirty-six towns with castles in medieval Ireland, only four were within the walls; sixteen were on the perimeter and eleven were outside.[48] The location emphasised the independent status of the castle and its occupants and made it less vulnerable to attack from within the town. The charter of 1307 specified that the castle was not part of the borough.[49] An account of 1323 gives a description of the castle and ancillary buildings:[50]

> there is one stone castle in which there are four towers roofed with shingles … but it needs much repair. There is also one hall roofed with shingles and two other houses thatched.

(Greatisland on the Barrow) and Enniscorthy. Five of these were built on seignorial manors. The exception was the castle of Enniscorthy, built by the Prendergasts, holders of the largest fief in the county. All had associated boroughs, with the possible exception of Enniscorthy. Henry II may have ordered the building of a castle in the town before he sailed from Wexford in 1173.[40] A reference to a janitor, or doorkeeper, at Wexford in 1185[41] led to claims that the castle had been built by that early date, but this was unlikely.[42] William Marshal would presumably have initiated a programme of stone-castle building before his death in 1219. His son, also William, was engaged in castle building, as in 1222 and 1225 the service which he owed to the king was cancelled to enable him 'to fortify a castle in Ireland'.[43] Stone castles on demesne land in the county had all been built by 1230: following the death of William Marshal the younger in that year, the castles of Wexford, Ross, Carrig and the Island were taken into the king's hands.[44] The castle of Ferns was not included as it was given in

dower to Marshal's widow, the countess of Pembroke.[45] Wexford Castle was probably built during the first quarter of the thirteenth century by himself or his father, the elder William Marshal. The castle was located on a mound just outside the town wall to the south-east of the

Fig. 23   A stylised depiction of Wexford Castle (re-drawn) from a mid seventeenth-century map indicates that the structure had four towers with conical roofs. The drawing illustrates the castle's location close to the water's edge. The town wall, with Castle Gate, is shown to the right.

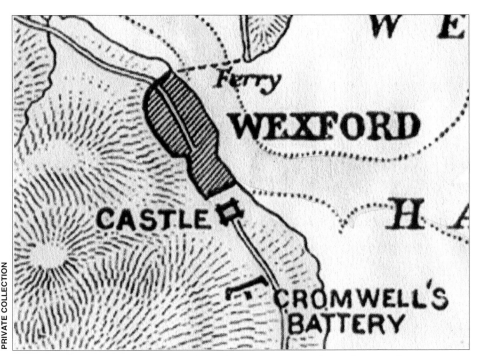

Fig. 24   This nineteenth-century map shows the castle located to the south-east of the town. It also shows the position from which Cromwell's cannon battered the castle in 1649.

The castle was obviously in bad repair in 1323, indicating that it was built early in the previous century. It was presumably one of a group of Leinster castles – including Carlow, Lea, Ferns and possibly Enniscorthy – classed as towered keeps or donjons, which had similar design elements.[51] They consisted of a strong rectangular tower, two or three storeys in height, with a massive circular turret at each corner, a design possibly inspired by Marshal's knowledge of castle construction in France, where the cylindrical keep had its origin.[52] Carlow, where building may have started as early as 1210–15, is considered to be the earliest.[53] However, this theory has been questioned in recent times.[54] Wexford Castle may have been of this type also as it is depicted on a seventeenth-century map as having four towers with conical roofs.[55] The mention in 1323 of 'four towers roofed with shingles' supports this view. Because of its prominence as a landmark, a stylised image of the castle is depicted on Dutch charts of Wexford Harbour.

The profile of the castle is shown as it would appear from the harbour, with only two of the towers visible. The castle is also mentioned as a navigation 'mark' in the written instructions to mariners accompanying one of the maps.[56] Although Wexford Castle was defensive in structure and appearance, its real

significance was to make Wexford town a centre of administration and military control. From their base in the castle, the seneschal, sheriff and other officials of the earl of Pembroke administered his lands and affairs in the county. It was also used as a place of safe-keeping for the earl's belongings which might be needed in the event of a visit to his Irish estates. In 1324, the escheator was mandated to take possession of the late earl's goods and chattels, including a chest containing jewels, which were stored in Wexford Castle.[57] The constable of the castle was responsible for all matters relating to military or police duties. This was especially the case from the late thirteenth century onwards when the castles of Ferns and Enniscorthy, in the north of the county, were under constant threat from the resurgent Irish. In 1323, Wexford Castle was a century old and in need of restoration; the constable was mandated to spend money on the repair of the hall, the kitchen and other rooms. Certain lands were included in the demesne of the castle; thirty acres of arable, one acre of

Fig. 25   This detail, re-drawn from a chart of Wexford Harbour c. 1625 shows an impression of Wexford Castle as it was seen from the harbour. As a prominent landmark, the castle was used for navigational purposes. In profile as seen from the estuary, only two of the four towers were visible.

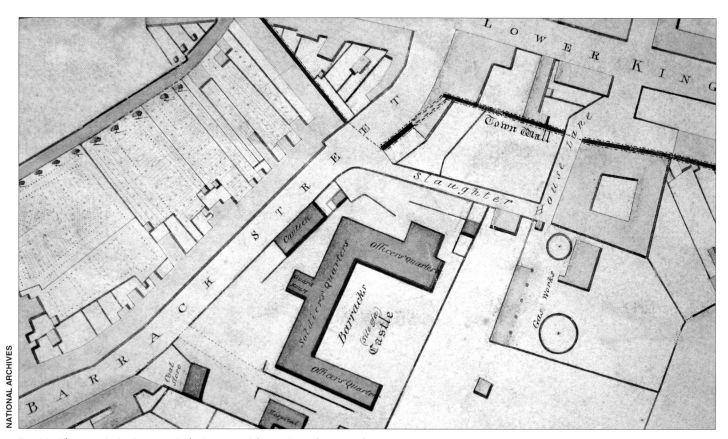

Fig. 26 The 1840 O. S. plan records the location of the castle on the site of the military barracks. It also shows the relationship of the castle with the town wall and the Castle Gate. The foundations of the castle walls were uncovered during mid nineteenth-century construction work.

meadow below the castle and a park with oak trees containing sixty acres used only for the pasturage of cattle, possibly represented by the area known as Townparks.[58] There were also two water-mills near the castle, presumably on the Bishopswater stream in the vicinity of the present-day Mill Road.[59]

Occasional details relating to Wexford Castle's law and order function emerge from the records. For example, in 1310, Muiris Mac Murchada delivered two of the O'Byrnes as captives to Wexford castle and in 1324, hostages of the Mac Murchada, the Ua Brain of the Duffry and the Ó Murchada were delivered to the constable of the castle to guarantee that they would keep the peace.[60] The constable was fined for allowing felons to escape from his custody and in 1356 the town was fined because the pillory was broken.[61]

During the turbulent sixteenth century Wexford Castle, located in the relatively secure south of the county, was a crucial component in the efforts of the authorities to maintain control in the county. This was demonstrated in 1543, when the stone from the recently dissolved Selskar Abbey was used to carry out repairs.[62] As well as serving as a jail, it was also used as a venue for assizes and inquisitions. The effectiveness of the building as a jail was limited; when the Lord Deputy visited Wexford in 1579, he discovered that certain malefactors had escaped. However, he executed those that remained, including one of the principal leaders of the Kavanaghs.[63]

Following the Act of Resumption in 1536, by which the king resumed possession of all the powers of the independent Palatinate lords, the situation in Wexford remained

unchanged, as Henry VIII issued a charter to the town confirming all existing privileges and liberties.[64] In 1609, the charter of James I granted the use of the castle to the mayor and corporation, but it was always referred to as 'the king's castle'. The common land on the high ground to the immediate south was known as Castle Hills, still remembered in the name of Castle Hill Street (officially Kevin Barry Street).[65] The castle continued to be used as the county jail until 1656, when another premises to accommodate prisoners was acquired in the town, possibly because of the dilapidated state of the castle which was continually in need of repair.[66]

The most dramatic period in the history of Wexford Castle occurred during the Civil War of the 1640s, and the subsequent Cromwellian campaign. At the outbreak of hostilities, the Catholic Confederates took control of Wexford and many of the Protestant inhabitants were rounded up and lodged in the castle jail.[67] After the ruthless sacking of Drogheda in 1649, Oliver Cromwell marched south to lay siege to Wexford, the 'Dunkirk of Ireland and a place only famous for being infamous'.[68] The fort on Rosslare point, commanding the entrance to the harbour, was taken, allowing guns to be landed and positioned on Trespan rock to the south of the town, in an area still known as Cromwell's Fort. Cannon fire was concentrated on the castle which had a commanding view of the town, as the attackers believed that 'if the castle was taken, the town would easily follow'.[69] While negotiations were in progress, the attacking army infiltrated the castle and quickly took control of it. The appearance of the enemy soldiers and flag on the castle ramparts generated panic in the town's garrison and they abandoned the walls, many of them fleeing across the river by boat. Apparently without direct orders, the Crom-

wellian soldiers stormed the walls and proceeded to sack the town. Following the Cromwellian campaign, the town was confiscated and granted to English settlers. The castle was not disposed of as it was selected as a strategic garrison in the event of an invasion. Frequent requests were made for the renovation of the structure, no doubt due to the damage caused by Cromwell's cannon. Despite its condition, the castle housed two companies (160 men) which led the mayor to complain of hardship, as the town had to supply them with 'fire and candlelight'.[70] In 1684, the neglected condition of the castle was demonstrated by the fact that the twelve pieces of ordnance were unmounted and equipment in the stores was unserviceable. Only the officers of the two companies stationed there were accommodated in the castle, while the men were quartered in the town. The structure had a narrow escape from destruction in 1690, when the Jacobite leadership ordered that it should be burned. This was prevented by the

Williamite supporters in the town who seized the castle and disarmed the Catholics. Presumably because of its inadequacy for housing a garrison, the castle was purchased by the government in the early eighteenth century and converted into a barracks. The structure was demolished and some of the stones were transported to Killinick where they were used to re-build the church. The troops arrived in 1725, still complaining that the town would not pay 'fire and candle', and by 1728 there were three companies of foot quartered in the barracks.[71]

Not all of the medieval fabric of the castle was removed. In 1847, excavations under the barracks floor exposed the foundations of a western tower and wall seventeen feet in thickness, extending southwards.[72] The possibility that the remains of the castle survive, hopefully to be recovered in the future, makes this a site of tantalisingly rich archaeological potential which could add greatly to our knowledge of five centuries of Wexford's history. This site must be monitored carefully.

TRADE AND TRIBULATION: WEXFORD BEFORE CROMWELL

Wexford's growth was greatly influenced by two factors: its geographical situation as part of the Irish Sea trading network, and the relative security of its location within the Wexford Pale. The town was also an important fishing centre and excavations at Bride Street showed that a variety of fish was caught.[1] Despite the problematical harbour, Wexford's advantageous location in relation to British and continental ports enabled the town to grow as a significant trading centre. The shallow estuary and the difficult channel did not present a great problem to the shallow-draught ships of the Norse founders of the town, and the difficult navigation of the harbour may have been regarded as a form of security.

Wexford's strategic situation in relation to Britain and the continent became even more crucial when the opening up of the New World placed Ireland centre-stage in the Atlantic world. Unlike England, Ireland did not adopt the new Protestantism during the sixteenth-century Reformation, creating another source of religious and political friction between the two islands. Ireland was viewed as a natural ally of Catholic France and Spain, England's continental opponents, and the political and military control of Ireland became an urgent priority. The advent of the Spanish Armada in 1588 led to the construction of coastal defences in county Wexford at Duncannon and probably at Rosslare Point. Tudor England's control of Gaelic Ireland was finally achieved by the defeat of a combined Spanish and Irish force at the Battle of Kinsale in 1601 and the subsequent Flight of the Earls. During the seventeenth century, the situation escalated into political as well as religious conflict, culminating in the Confederate and Cromwellian wars of the 1640s. Wexford's cataclysmic involvement in these events ushered in a dramatic new phase in the town's evolution.

PADDY DONOVAN

Fig. 1   Wexford's connection with its harbour and the sea is typified by the locally built Wexford cot, a traditional flat-bottomed craft that is designed to cope with the sandbars and mudflats of the estuary. The versatile cot is made in different sizes, depending on intended use, and it can be powered by sails as well as oars. The ones shown above are kept in the cot safe at Maudlintown. A mussel dredger can be seen in the background.

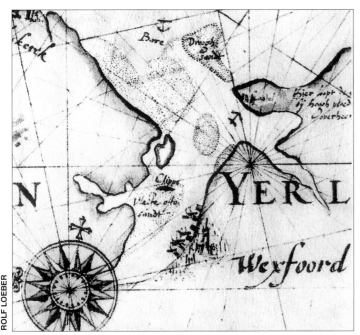

ROLF LOEBER

Fig. 2 The production of early seventeenth-century Dutch charts of Wexford Harbour, like the one shown here, is an indication of the town's significance as a port in a European context. The harbour, with its bar, channels and sandbanks, is recorded in impressive detail as well as the location of secure anchorages. The town is shown with ships berthed at its projecting jetties. A castle on Rosslare Point indicates that it was fortified before the 1640s. Interestingly, Glascarrick is included as a settlement of significance on the east coast.

SHIPPING AND TRADE

During the visit of Henry II to Wexford in 1172, £40 was spent on herrings to feed his retinue[2] and for centuries the herring fishery was vital to the town. Fishing was not confined to the seas near at hand as Wexford fishermen were killed in an affray on the Isle of Man in 1217.[3] Specific references to Wexford's maritime activities are meagre, but it is possible to construct at least an outline impression of the scope and nature of the town's trading pattern. The first record of trade related to the Anglo-Norman attack in 1169, when Giraldus recorded that a ship had just arrived from Britain with a cargo of corn and wine.[4] The need to import corn is significant as it indicates that Ireland's self sufficiency in grain would only be achieved with the introduction of Anglo-Norman manorial agriculture, although corn continued to be imported in times of scarcity.

During the thirteenth century, New Ross, because of its superior location and harbour, emerged as the principal port of the lordship of Leinster, and Wexford was reduced to secondary status. This was reflected in the returns for the great custom on wool and hides, introduced in 1275. From 1275 to 1279, the returns from Wexford averaged £6 10s compared to £690 from New Ross. By 1345, the figure for New Ross had dropped to £109 and Wexford had risen slightly to £11.[5] The

merchants of Wexford exported principally fish, cloth, mantles, wool and hides while importing mainly wine and salt. Corn was both imported and exported, depending on supply and demand. In 1293, William Chatnell paid customs duty of £8 14s on forty-one hogsheads of wine landed at Wexford from St Emelian in France[6] and in 1390 the ship *Nicholas* from Wexford was in the cloth-importing trade from Bristol. Although most of Wexford's small ships traded across the Irish Sea, some ventured further afield. In 1303, two Wexford ships were importing wine from Bordeaux, and in 1383 two Wexford ships loaded salt in Le Collet, also in France.[7]

Wexford was Ireland's leading fishing port in the fifteenth and early sixteenth centuries. Many small vessels of local and English ownership were based in the port and the trade in fish led to very close contacts with Bristol.[8] Fish, particularly herring, was Wexford's most lucrative export in the sixteenth century.[9] For example in 1566, Patrick Furlong of Wexford unloaded herrings at Chester; the *George* of Wexford discharged eighteen barrels of white herring and 10,000 red herring; the *John* of Wexford brought thirty barrels of white herring and 10,000 red herring and Bristol imported 'two burdens of codfish' from Wexford in 1591.[10] Salmon was also a significant item of export. In 1388, Henry Lane and John White had permission to export eight casks of salmon from Wexford and Waterford to England.[11] The oyster beds in Wexford Harbour were renowned and their economic contribution to the town is remembered in the name of Oyster Lane, where taverns specialising in oysters advertised their wares by piling oyster shells outside the door. Numerous oyster shells were recovered from the archaeological excavation in Oyster Lane in 1976.

PRIVATE COLLECTION

Fig. 3 For centuries, the Slaney gabbard was used as a bulk carrier to transport goods on the river and in the harbour. Up to fifty-five feet long with a fourteen foot beam, it could carry a cargo of thirty tons.

PRIVATE COLLECTION

Fig. 4   The city of Chester, on the river Dee near the Welsh border, made a trade agreement with Wexford in 1539 which lasted for almost a century. As both ports had difficult harbours and small ships, an agreement of this nature was mutually beneficial.

During the sixteenth century, Wexford's trading activities intensified in spite of the 'barred haven'. Although the town was adversely affected by the Irish revival, an improved trading situation may have been due to its location within the Wexford Pale, in contrast to New Ross which was more exposed to attack from the Mac Murchada and their allies. Wexford also suffered from competition with Waterford as there were disputes between the two ports over payment of custom dues. This was resolved to Wexford's disadvantage: in 1562, the free citizens of Waterford were acquitted of all customs payment in Wexford.[12] Paradoxically, the nature of the harbour added to the town's trading activities, as the merchants were forced to maintain their own fleet of small ships due to the inability of bigger foreign craft to gain access.[13] These small ships, some of only six tons' burden, may have been a sea-going version of the Wexford cot, one of the longest existing and most seaworthy of the traditional craft of north-west Europe.[14] The thirty-six Wexford ships trading with the Somerset port of Bridgewater in 1560 were presumably cots, as they were best suited to navigating its difficult harbour. Recent research in Bristol University has highlighted Wexford's trading connections with the Bristol Channel ports and with Bridgewater in particular.[15] Wexford's small boats took the largest part in the early sixteenth-century import of Welsh coal to Ireland, first recorded in 1504. In 1587, of

twenty-four ships carrying coal from Milford, fifteen were from Wexford, bringing wood and fish on the outward voyage.[16] Perhaps due to its increased status as a port, Wexford entered into a trade agreement with Chester in 1539, an early example of a 'twinning' arrangement. This agreement persisted until at least 1628, when it was the cause of a dispute between the two ports.[17]

In the sixteenth century, the magnificent woodlands of Ireland were exploited for their commercial potential and Wexford was well placed to export the timber from the

Trade agreement between Chester and Wexford, 1539

Be it known unto your worships, both mayor, council and commons of Chester in England that we, sovereign council and commons of the town of Wexford in Ireland, do certify unto you that we be content that your citizens be free of paying of custom with us for ever, upon condition that our burgesses may be so free with you in like manner, certifying us of the same, and also to make restitution of such as you took of late of some of our burgesses. In witness and testimony of the premises we the said sovereign council and commons, to these presents have set to our town seal of office the 20th day of May in the 30th year of the reign of our sovereign lord King Henry VIII.

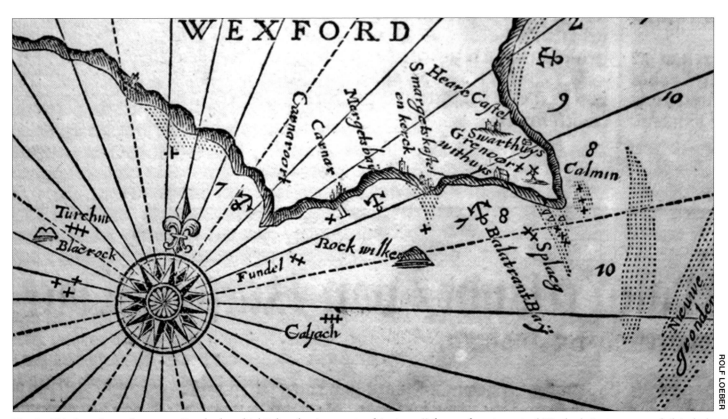

ROLF LOEBER

Fig. 5   This late sixteenth-century Dutch chart highlights the dangers to shipping off the south-east coast of Wexford. Features recorded include Tuskar, Splaugh and Blackrock. Castles, houses and windmills are shown because they were useful aids for navigating the dangerous waters.

forests of the Duffry and Shillelagh in the north-west of the county, becoming a booming timber town in the process. A small amount of timber was being exported in the late fifteenth century[18] but the process was greatly accelerated following the dissolution of the monasteries in the 1530s and the early seventeenth-century plantation of north county Wexford, as new landlords sought to maximise the income from their newly-acquired estates.[19] The timber was floated down the Slaney to Wexford and exported mainly to the Welsh ports. From the middle of the century, the wood was made into beams, boards, rafters, laths, oars, ship planks, pipe staves and poles before export. The skill of Wexford wood-workers was well known, as in 1548 the Lord Deputy requested the mayor to send four workmen, 'skilled makers of laths', to repair the roof of Dublin Castle.[20] In 1568 Wexford, with other ports, was ordered by the Lord Deputy not to export boards to Scotland for building galleys as the ships were being used to disturb the peace in Ireland. The following accounts describe a typical cargo: in 1586 the *Saviour* of Wexford, burden six tons (probably a cot), master and merchant Richard Morrow, unloaded 100 boards (£1) and 1,000 laths (5s) at Milford. The following year the Cornish ports of St Ives, Fowey, Penzance and Padstow received from Wexford and Youghal 512 boards (£5 10s), forty-eight great beams (£5), forty-seven small beams (£2 10s), and

seventy-eight oar ends (£3 5s).[21] A report in 1583 suggested that, as timber could be abundantly supplied in Ireland, ships should be built for the navy at Cork, Youghal, Wexford and Belfast but there is no evidence to show that this advice was implemented.[22]

In 1586, Sir Henry Wallop, an army officer, acquired the castle and friary lands of Enniscorthy and in the

Fig. 6   An archaeological excavation at Oyster Lane in 1976 uncovered evidence for medieval occupation. The discovery of numerous oyster shells supported the belief that the lane was the centre of Wexford's oyster industry. The archaeologist, Pat Wallace (standing, on right), of Wood Quay fame, is now the Director of the National Museum of Ireland. The late John Scanlon (standing, on left), a stalwart of the Wexford Historical Society, was a pioneering radio expert and photographer.

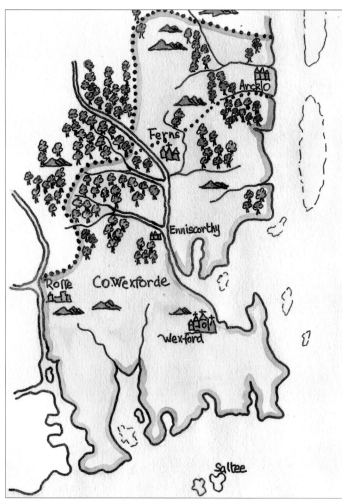

insatiable demands for timber of the ironworks established along the Slaney in the seventeenth century. The port of Wexford benefited from the trade associated with this enterprise.[26] In 1626 the importation of Norwegian timber was recorded at Wexford for the first time and this trend was set to continue indefinitely.[27]

Perhaps because of decreased prosperity, many Irish ships were sold to Spain in the late 1580s, presumably to take part in the Spanish Armada that sailed against England in 1589. The small capacity of Wexford ships would hardly have been adequate for the Armada. Wexford, of necessity, had to retain its fleet of low tonnage craft as bigger foreign vessels were unable to navigate the barred haven. Wexford and Waterford were the only ports that maintained the numbers of their ships successfully and in 1598 they had more ships than all the other Irish ports combined. A contemporary account recorded that 'there belongeth more ships to the cities of Waterford and Wexford than to all Ireland besides'.[28] Wexford's exports of timber, barrel staves, hides, tallow, woolfells and herring were valued at £4,000, twice that of the once dominant New Ross.[29]

However, by the end of the sixteenth century, a combination of political and commercial influences led to a marked decline in commercial activity in the ports of the south and east of Ireland. This happened principally during the Elizabethan period when the efforts of English

Fig. 7 The forests of north and west county Wexford were recorded by sixteenth- and seventeenth-century cartographers both as landscape features and for their commercial value. This image is based on a map produced by Baptista Boazio in 1599. Following the setting up of a lumber industry in Enniscorthy in the late sixteenth century, the north Wexford forests were rapidly depleted by indiscriminate felling.

following year he was given a lease on the lands of Selskar Abbey.[23] He established a lucrative lumber industry in Enniscorthy to exploit the extensive forests in the north of the county. He reported that 'in the woods, not far from my home in Enniscorthy, there is as good and as great a store of plank and of timber needful for shipping to be had as in any place I do know either in England or Ireland'.[24] By 1598 he had a contract with Wexford to supply pipestaves and hogshead staves for export. Because of the unsettled state of the county, he had to maintain a garrison at Enniscorthy. The Slaney was the safest and most efficient means of communication and transport between the two towns and to protect this vital link the authorities in Wexford built a strong barge, propelled by twelve oars, and defended by two cannon and thirty muskets.[25] The supply of timber in Ireland was not limitless, however, and the forests were rapidly depleted by indiscriminate felling. The demise of the forests was hastened by the

HORE'S *HISTORY*

Fig. 8 In 1586, Sir Henry Wallop, an army officer, was granted Enniscorthy Castle and the lands of the Friary. Shortly afterwards he acquired the lands of Selskar Abbey. He set up a lumber business in Enniscorthy to exploit the great forests in the north of the county. The timber was floated down the Slaney to Wexford for export.

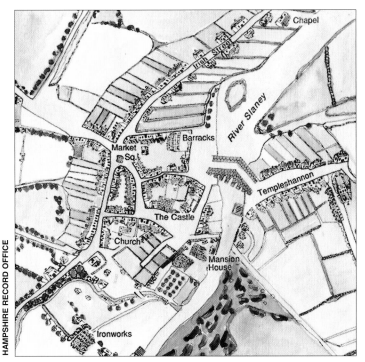

Fig. 9   Located at the head of the tidal waters of the Slaney, Enniscorthy's early origins were focused on St Senan's Early Christian foundation at Templeshannon. The settlement expanded in the medieval period following the construction of the Prendergast castle on the west bank of the river in the thirteenth century and the foundation of a Franciscan Friary. The growth of the town as an industrial centre engaged in the lumber business is recorded in this early eighteenth-century map.

trading interests to retain the profits of all branches of commerce in English hands, linked with a natural political dislike of the native Irish intercourse with France and Spain, proved effective. By the close of the sixteenth century, the economic situation was worsening further because of a decline in the Irish fishing industry, due in part to the disappearance of fish shoals but also because of the growing importance of the Newfoundland fishery from which fish had been landed in Ireland as early as 1537.[30] The deteriorating political and economic circumstances would eventually bring about drastic changes in mid seventeenth-century Wexford.

REFORMATION AND COUNTER-REFORMATION

Shortly after the proclamation of Henry VIII as head of the Irish church, at a parliament in Dublin in 1536, the dissolution of the monasteries led to the confiscation of the property of Selskar Abbey and the Franciscan Friary.[31] In the case of Selskar, the dissolution may not have caused much resentment as by that time the Augustinian Priory had lost much of its significance as a religious house.[32] The Franciscans, on the other hand, were very active and were particularly prominent as opponents of the reformed religion.[33] The king granted the confiscated properties to trustworthy men who would protect the land and attract

new colonists from England. This process impacted directly on Wexford town where the properties of Selskar Abbey and the Franciscan Friary were granted to lay tenants who were loyal to the crown and the new Protestant religion.

The conservative townspeople, although loyal to the crown, defied the authorities, as did the rest of Ireland, and generally chose a religion that was not that of the civil authority. The resolution by the people of Wexford, and Ireland, to opt for a religion which was anathema to that of the civil authorities, while wishing at the same time to give full allegiance to that authority, was without parallel in the rest of Europe and resulted inevitably in civil and religious discord.[34]

This situation evolved because the native Irish and the Old English were prepared to defy anti-Catholic legislation and the government had difficulty in enforcing it. From a political perspective, the natural alliance between Ireland and England's Catholic enemies, principally France and Spain, made it imperative for the Elizabethan English to assert military and political control. This was made even more urgent, from an English perspective, by Ireland's new strategic significance in the Atlantic world, following the opening up of the Americas. By the end of the sixteenth century, the arrival of Spanish-educated Irish priests had a political

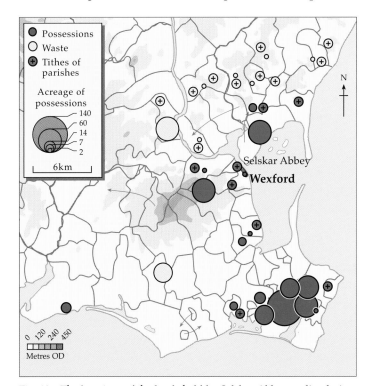

Fig. 10   The locations of the lands held by Selskar Abbey at dissolution. The abbey held scattered parcels of land in the south-east of the county, principally in the barony of Forth. Some of the lands west of the Slaney were described as 'waste', because of raids by the Irish.

Possessions of Selskar Abbey, 1540
The manor of Ballyreilly (Kilrane parish, Forth)

Townland	Parish	Barony	Acreage	Value
Kisha	St Iberius	Forth	55	27s 6d
Grange	St Iberius	Forth	60	30s
Rathmore	St Iberius	Forth	40	20s
Churchtown	Tacumshin	Forth	40	20s
Allenstown	St Iberius	Forth	140	70s
Graheeroge	Ballymore	Forth	14	7s
Blackhall	Bannow	Bargy	11	5s. 6d
Carrig	Carrig	Shelmalier		2s 8d
Newbay	St Peter's	Forth	60/1 castle	6s 8d
	Ishartmon	Forth	7	3s 6d
St Margaret's	St Margaret's	Forth	2	1s
Kilmacree	Kilmacree	Forth	7	3s 6d
Killiane Little	Killiane	Forth	2 tenements & gardens	1s
Ballyla	Ardcolm	Shelmalier East	60	13s 4d
Ardcavan	Ardcavan	Shelmalier East	7	1s
Killurin (waste)	Killurin	Shelmalier West	60	20s
Tikillin (waste)	Tikillin	Shelmalier East	2	8d
Ballinaslaney (waste)	Ballinaslaney	Shelmalier East	2	1s
Baldwinstown (waste)	Kilcowan	Bargy	40	20s
Killisk (waste)	Killisk	Ballagheen South	2	1s
Kilmallock (waste)	Kilmallock	Ballagheen South	2	1s
	St Nicholas (waste)	Ballagheen South	2	1s
	Killila (waste)	Ballagheen South	2	1s
13 tenements in Wexford town:	58s 8d			

Tithes of parishes

Carrig	£14	St Helen's	£6 13s 4d	Killiane	£13 6s 8d
Kilmacree	£13 6s 8d	Ishartmon	£14	St Margaret's	£5 6s 8d
?Ballemen	13s 4d	Killurin (waste)	£3	Ballinaslaney (waste)	
Tikillen (waste)	£1 6s 8d	Rathale (waste)	10s	Kilmallock (waste)	13s 4d
Killisk (waste)	13s 4d	St Nicholas (waste)	13s 4d	Ballyvaldon (waste)	6s 8d
Ardcolm	£8	Ardcavan	£6 13s 4d	Killila (waste)	13s 4d
Skreen (waste)	6s 8d	Rectory of Selskar & St Tullocks:	£26 13s 4d	St Peter's juxta Wexford	£2 13s 4d

Total value of all rents of the priory of Selskar (except the waste lands): £129 0s 10d

dimension, as the authorities regarded them as harbingers of Spanish support for the rebellion known as 'the Nine Years' War', which erupted in Ulster in 1595, led by Hugh O'Neill and Hugh O'Donnell. In 1601, England's worst fears were realised when 4,000 Spanish, led by Don Juan del Aquila, landed at Kinsale in county Cork. The Spanish were surrounded by an English army and when O'Neill marched south to join them he was comprehensively defeated; the Spanish surrendered and returned home. The battle of Kinsale completed the Tudor conquest and is regarded as marking the end of Gaelic Ireland.[35]

When the Counter-Reformation got under way following the Council of Trent in 1563, Wexford port was well placed to ship students to the newly established Irish colleges on the continent. Wexford students flocked to seminaries in Louvain, Lisbon, Salamanca and Douai, among others, and, after ordination, were carried back in

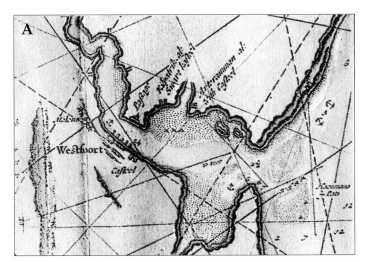

Fig. 11 (A) Detailed instructions for the navigation of the harbour are given in this early seventeenth-century Dutch chart. Landscape features, natural and man-made, are used as navigational aids. These include Forth Mountain, Trespan Rock, Wexford Castle and Artramon Castle. Five windmills are shown on what is now known as Windmill Hill. A series of five projecting jetties are shown along Wexford's waterfront. (B) A detail (re-drawn) from a 1612 Dutch map of the Wexford coast showing six projecting quays at Wexford with ships berthed beside them.

Wexford ships. The rejection of the official religion resulted in the ultimate sacrifice for some. In 1579, a religiously-motivated revolt by Viscount Baltinglass alarmed the government and his attempt to escape through the port of Wexford with his accomplice, a county Wexford Jesuit named Robert Rochford, led to the execution of Matthew Lambert, a miller, who was accused of hiding the fugitives, and the five sailors who attempted to give them passage abroad. All the names of the three Wexford town sailors are known: Robert Meyler, Edward Cheevers and Patrick Kavanagh.[36] In 1590, Christopher Roche, a Wexford student from the Irish seminary in Louvain, was arrested in Bristol and died in prison in London.[37]

By 1580, priests returning from continental seminaries were beginning to have an impact and by the end of the century the majority of people were attending Mass. This was particularly true of county Wexford as out of one hundred Irish seminarians in Salamanca in the years 1592–1617, ten were from the county. In 1595, the Lord Deputy reported that at Wexford 'divers Jesuits and Seminaries are lately landed'.[38] These continental educated priests – particularly Daniel O'Druhan, who returned from Salamanca in 1591 and was made vicar apostolic of the diocese of Ferns in 1607 – revitalised the Catholic church. One of the most famous of the Counter-Reformation priests was a Wexford man, William (Candidus) Furlong, who became a Cistercian in Spain. He returned to his native town in 1609 and acquired a reputation for healing and holiness that brought many to the Catholic church. He died in 1616 and was buried in St Patrick's churchyard. By the early seventeenth century, mass was being said daily in Wexford and in 1620 the friars rented a house in High Street and built a thatched chapel in Archer's Lane, between High

Street and Main Street.[39] In 1622, the Friary was rebuilt and reoccupied by a legal stratagem as it was located outside the town wall.[40] In 1624, Daniel O'Druhan's successor, John Roche, a native of New Ross, was appointed bishop of

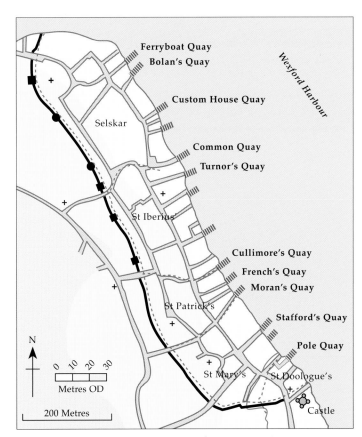

Fig. 12 Since its foundation, Wexford had a series of quays projecting into deep water, accessed by a system of approach lanes. As the spaces in between were reclaimed, the quays were extended further and the lanes got longer. Most of these quays and lanes were owned privately, leading to rivalry and fragmentation in the commercial life of the town. As some quays were known by the names of their owners, names changed when the quay and the approach lane changed hands.

Fig. 13   During the Penal Laws, many young men sailed from Wexford to study for the priesthood in one of the Irish Colleges on the continent, before returning to minister in Ireland. The Irish College in Louvain, Belgium, run by the Franciscans, was a popular destination.

Fig. 14   As part of Counter-Reformation strategy and in response to restrictions imposed by the Penal Laws, Irish Colleges mushroomed in the Catholic countries of Europe to train seminarians for the priesthood.

Ferns. He had been ordained in Douai in the Spanish Netherlands and had extensive experience at the highest level on the continent, including the Vatican. He took up residence in Wexford town and played a leading part in reorganising the church in the diocese and the town. Although the Catholic Church operated with a tacit degree of official toleration, it was functioning illegally, and discretion was essential. Roche frequently used the alias 'J. R. Turner', indicating that he stayed with the Turner family, who were wealthy Catholic merchants in the town. By the time he died in 1636, there were thirty priests in the diocese, as well as the friars in Wexford town.[41] In 1633, the official view of the state of religion in Wexford, and in Ireland in general, was set out by Justice Hugh Cressy in a letter to the Lord Deputy:

> This county, which doth contain the most ancient English planters, and were lately the most forward professors of the reformed Christian religion in the kingdom, by the pernicious confluence of priests, who have raised among them a Romish hierarchy of bishops, commissaries, vicar-general and parochial priests of their own, to the great derogation of His Majesty's

Fig. 15   The coat-of-arms of three burning ships with the motto *Per aquam et ignem* (by water and fire) granted to Wexford in the early seventeenth century, may have been inspired by the burning of a ship in the harbour when the town was taken by the Anglo-Normans in 1169.

royal power, and to the establishing of a foreign state and jurisdiction in all things ecclesiastical, are now in a sort become principally Romish and popish; and so, as themselves confess do even groan under the burden, I mean the secular and common people...[42]

The justice admonished the jury to abide by the law, 'but all in vain, for they are all recusants, not one Protestant among them'.

Another visitor to Wexford, Sir William Brereton, also commented on the state of religion in the town in 1634:

most of the women are bare-necked and clean-skinned and wear a crucifix in a black necklace hanging between their breasts. It seems they are not ashamed of their religion nor desire to conceal themselves; and indeed in this town there are many papists.

Even the town officials were not reluctant to show their allegiance to the Catholic religion. The mayor and sheriff left the judges at the door of the church to attend mass, 'which is here tolerated and publicly resorted unto in two or three houses in this town, wherein are very few Protestants', while the judges went to the Protestant church, where there was a 'slender congregation'.[43]

By the 1630s, the Protestant clergy were unable to compete with new Catholic priests arriving from colleges in Europe and the Catholic Church succeeded in becoming

fully organised in Wexford town. However, this success was achieved at a price. The collection of recusancy fines was no longer implemented on a large scale but the government had other means of imposing financial penalties. These were felt particularly in Wexford, from which there were many complaints of increasing poverty at this period.[44]

The town was very dependent on fishing, particularly herring, which were so abundant in 1612 that a six pence per barrel toll was demanded by the customs officials of the town from the many boats attracted from Devon and Cornwall.[45] The plight of Wexford was exacerbated by the disappearance of the lucrative herring shoals from the south-east coast. A contemporary commentator lamented that 'the fish begins to wander from our shores'.[46] In 1629, there was great distress in the town, with three hundred tenements deserted. The hardship was partly caused by the 'cessing' (an obligation to supply provisions) of soldiers on the inhabitants. Trade was made more difficult by the lack of buoys and markers in the harbour and danger from pirates.[47] The economic slump which followed the disappearance of the herring was highlighted in an account from 1635:

[Wexford] is seated upon a brave spacious harbour, capacious of many thousand sail, but it is much prejudiced and damnified by a most vile barred haven, which notwithstanding, is better than formerly. Two narrow banks of sand run along on both sides of the channell, or passage.

Fig. 16   The significance of the fishing industry to Wexford for many centuries is demonstrated by the use of a fish motif on the mayoral seal.

DENIS O'CONNOR ARCHIVE

Fig. 17   Nicholas French was consecrated bishop of Ferns in 1645 and lived in this house in Peter's Street (Gibson's Lane). The house was close to three churches: SS Mary's, Patrick's and Peter's.

Trade much decayeth in this town, and it is very poor, by reason of the herring-fishery here failing. They report here an incredible multitude of herrings ordinarily taken in one night, in this vast and large harbour, by five or six men in one boat of ten tuns burden; sometimes to the value of £20, sometimes £40, sometimes more. This was affirmed to me by one that ordinarily fished here, and took this proportion. Now of later times the herrings having forsaken the coast, this town is much impoverished and decayed, their quays go to ruin, and are in no good repair. There belonged sometimes unto every great merchant's house seated on the shore, either a quay, or part interest in a quay, or a private way to the quay. Their haven was then furnished with 5,000 sail of ships, and small vessels for fishing, and now naked.

The turbulent political and social events of the seventeenth century in Ireland had profound consequences

for Wexford. James I granted a newly revised charter to Wexford in 1609, in response to a request from the town. This may have been intended to encourage loyalty to the Protestant religion, but in reality this was not achieved.[48] The charter was mostly a rehearsal of earlier versions but it did give the town authority to set up a Guild of Merchants to regulate business. An undertaking by the Guild of Butchers, in 1621, to hold bull-baiting twice a year on the 'common plain of Wexford', last recorded in 1770, is recalled by the name of the square known as the Bullring at the centre of the town.[49] The renewal of the charter led to the granting of a coat-of-arms to the town in 1618, consisting of a ship in flames, with the motto *per aquam et ignem* (by water and fire).[50]

Hopes for a relaxation of anti-Catholic legislation on the accession of James I in 1603 had not been realised and political tensions in Ireland intensified.[51] Mass continued to be celebrated although some efforts were made officially to prevent the open expression of the Catholic religion. In 1603, the Lord Deputy reported that 'Wexford has with some insolence set up the public exercise of the Mass' and that he had 'written to those commanding them on their allegiance to desist'.[52] The government could exercise some control over those who held public office; in 1613, for instance, Richard Wadding, 'a known malicious papist', was deprived of the mayoralty for refusing to take the Oath of Supremacy. In 1612, the property of the Hospital of Lepers of Maudlintown, to the south of the town, was targeted by the crown. For some reason, perhaps because of the valuable service it provided, the hospital had escaped confiscation at the dissolution of the monasteries. It was claimed that the Prior, with the brothers and sisters, had converted the possessions to their own use and it was taken into the king's hands. The property consisted of the townlands of Maudlintown, Pembrokestown, Rochestown and Mulgannon.[53]

Although religious oppression continued to be of paramount concern, a greater focus on the confiscation of land held by Catholics caused widespread apprehension. Dramatic change was epitomised by the widespread transfer of land from Catholic to Protestant ownership.[54] The Catholics were mostly of old stock, either Gaelic or Anglo-Irish. To distinguish themselves from the native Irish and the newly arrived Protestant English, and in order to show their loyalty to the crown, the Anglo-Irish increasingly called themselves Old English, although by that time they had assimilated much of Gaelic culture. Following the accession of Charles I in 1625, the political situation in England deteriorated rapidly and the king offered concessions, known as 'graces,' to Irish Catholics in return for £40,000. The resentment generated by the failure to implement the promised reforms further alienated the Catholic community.[55]

THE REBELLION OF 1641

Against a background of political, economic and religious friction, the Irish and the Old English, forced into an uneasy confederation, began to contemplate armed rebellion. The situation was exacerbated by the eruption of Civil War in England between king and parliament in August 1642, with the Scots entering the war on the side of parliament. In Ireland, the rising erupted in Ulster in 1641, the insurgents claiming not to be rebels but supporters of the king. Atrocities were committed by both sides, but

Fig. 18 This late sixteenth-century map shows that a fort existed on Rosslare point before the construction of a fortification there in 1641. The Confederate fort may have been a restoration of an existing structure.

Confederate Defences at Wexford (Depositions TCD)

Thei have trenched their walls round about the Towne eight foote deepe and 24 foote broade. Likewise thei have thrown down eight foote within the Towne, houses and pales from end to end. Thei have pitched great timber from the Ferrie Banke southwards 'till they reach against Pole Kaye, and thence westwarde into the side of the Channell, and after thei took a good shipp of one Mr Nugions, of Dublin, and did her sink in the syde of the Channell within the tymbers, with her sterne to the Towne, and her mysone-maste standing for the tyinge of the sea-board end of her chaines to stopps. The other end is to be brought to a great Capson by their Forte upon Pole Key. The mastes of Captaine Bartle his shipp, thei are chained with Iron betweene each two of them, being nine in number, and 60 Fathomes longe, and the cables of his shipp thei have turned to that use. Thei found four peces of ordinance in Mr Nugions shipp, of 6 foote long or thereabouts. The field-brass-piece which was found in the Castell of Fernes, nine foote long, of King Henry the Eighth, these five are sent on their Forthe. In the course of a short time after, they erected a Fort on the south point of the land, or the Rosslare side, which still retains the name, and another, [long since disappeared] on the north side, called Fort St Margaret, now Raven Point.

---

those inflicted on Protestant settlers, particularly in Ulster, were deliberately exaggerated to create a massacre myth for propaganda purposes. In 1642, a meeting of the Confederate Catholics at Kilkenny established an executive supreme council, as well as a legislative general assembly. In the autumn of 1641, a great hosting of the principal gentry and burgesses of Wexford was held on the hill of Carrig to consider the state of affairs in the town and country. A decision was taken to declare for the

Catholic confederacy, and Wexford town mustered 800 men to support the rebellion.[56] Confederate activists in the town were also involved in recruiting support in the county: for example, John Wadding, an alderman of Wexford, swore in fifty men for the Confederate army at Baldwinstown.[57] Witness statements taken after the rebellion indicate that the townspeople were fully committed to the Confederate cause and describe the preparations made for the protection of the town.[58] In anticipation of a siege, extensive work was carried out on

Fig. 19 The mid seventeenth-century Down Survey map shows two forts at the entrance to Wexford Harbour, on the point of Rosslare to the south and on the Raven to the north.

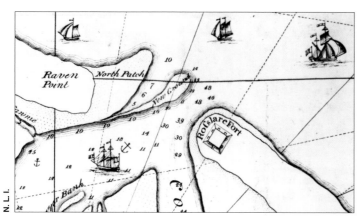

Fig. 20 Rosslare Fort is shown as a square enclosure in this detail from the 1764 Scalé and Richards map which illustrates the fort's commanding position in relation to the entrance of Wexford Harbour.

the town defences and captains were appointed for the parishes: Martin White for St Mary's and St Doologue's; Patrick Ffrench for St Patrick's; Nicholas Hay for St Iberius' and Nicholas Cheevers (the mayor) for Selskar. Richard Stafford was made governor of the castle. A trench, eight feet wide and twenty-four feet deep, was dug on the outside along the length of the town wall. On the inside, houses and fences within eight feet of the wall were levelled to make access easier. The harbour was fortified by a timber boom stretching from Ferrybank towards Pole (now Paul) Quay. A moveable chain, stretching from a ship sunk at the end of the boom to the 'fort on Pole Quay', allowed access to the port. A fort was erected at the mouth of the harbour on Rosslare Point, and armed with nine cannon guns. An earlier fortification was presumably restored for the purpose, as a fort, possibly built at the time of the Spanish Armada, is shown in this location on a late sixteenth-century map.[59] A fortification of some kind, known as Fort Margaret, was erected on the Raven Point, the northern arm of the harbour entrance.[60] However, it is not clear if it was ever completed as it apparently took no part in subsequent events.

The establishment of a Catholic administration allowed the public practice of religion and mass was again celebrated in the old churches of Wexford. In February 1642, the oath of confederation was administered to all the male inhabitants. Catholic supremacy almost inevitably led to aggressive sectarian behaviour. According to witness statements after the rebellion, leading Protestants in the town were imprisoned and mistreated in Wexford Castle. Out of eighty Protestants attempting to escape by sea, only one allegedly survived when their frigate foundered outside Wexford Harbour, 'either by accident or design'. Another deposition stated that the rebels made a declaration that 'they would not suffer English man, woman or child, or

anything that was English to remain alive, and burned all the bibles they could meet with, saying 'What will you do now, your bibles are burnt'. The traditional empathy with Catholic Spain was expressed by displaying the Spanish colours and the slogan 'God bless the king of Spain, for but for him we should all be slain'.[61]

A new bishop of Ferns, Nicholas French, was consecrated in the town in 1645 and lived in Peter's Street.[62] The highlight of the decade for the Catholics was the visit to the town of the papal nuncio, Archbishop Rinuccini, at Easter 1647. Rinuccini sailed down the Slaney from Enniscorthy and was met by a fleet of boats and given a tumultuous welcome. Cannon thundered from the town walls and from ships in the harbour as bands played to greet him. In the presence of a military guard of honour, he was given an official reception by the corporation. A liturgical reception was held in St Peter's church and after celebrating Easter Mass he remained in the town for several days. His diary described his welcome in Wexford as the greatest manifestation of loyalty to the Holy See that he had received in Ireland.[63] However, Rinuccini was also a divisive influence, as his opposition to a peace initiative in 1646 split the Confederacy into opposing factions. Wexford, where the nuncio's proclamation against a declaration of peace was nailed to the door of St Mary's church, initially supported Rinuccini. But when Rinuccini excommunicated those who supported the move for peace, the mayor and burgesses protested.[64]

Because of its advantageous location, Wexford was used as a port by the Confederates from the beginning of the rebellion. To ensure a supply of shipping, an eminent ship-builder, Anthony Van Kaat, was brought by the Confederate authorities from Flanders, with skilled workmen, to construct ships from the timber that was

---

Wexford in 1644 (*Griffith's Chronicles*)

M. Boullay le Gouz, a French gentleman, whose travels in Ireland, in 1644, have been published by Mr Crofton Croker, thus notices the castle: The Town is very populous, owing to its great commerce. The fortress is a small square, regularly enough fortified, and washed by the sea. At the foot of this Castle are many ruins of old Churches, amongst others that of the Holy Trinity, towards which the women have great reverence, and come there in solemn procession. The oldest march first, and the others follow, then take three turns round the ruins, make a reverence to the remains, kneel and recommence this ceremony many times. The people of Wachesford came chiefly from France.

Fig. 21 (A) Confederate flag. (B) Seal of the Catholic Confederation of Kilkenny, combining the symbols of harp and crown.

readily available on both sides of the Slaney.[65] In early 1642, a frigate laden with ammunition for the insurgents, sent by General Eoghan Roe O'Neill, arrived at Wexford from Dunkirk. It was followed shortly afterwards by Colonel Thomas Preston, who returned from Flanders to command the Confederate army in Leinster. The charter of a ship from Dunkirk to secure Wexford Harbour is an indication of the significance of the supplies and reinforcements being landed at the port. In September 1642, the Lord Justices complained about the activities of the Wexford ships:

> The rebels had gotten a ship of Dunkirk of good strength at the harbour of Wexford to annoy us and to secure the arrival of their expected supplies from foreign parts. Since which time we hear that seven or eight ships more, some of them carrying twenty-four pieces of ordnance, are come thither in aid of the rebels, that they have brought in and landed at Wexford a very large proportion of arms and munition, great ordnance and field pieces, and from France and Flanders some principal commanders of this nation that have served in foreign parts.[66]

Although the English parliamentarian navy controlled Irish waters, Wexford was the Confederate naval headquarters and the chief focus for the importation of arms from Antwerp and other continental ports.[67] The town became the Confederates' principal conduit with continental ports and a source of much-needed supplies and financial support, as this report from 1643 highlighted:

> Wexford is the port into which all their [the rebels] ammunition and assistance from foreign ports comes, and there is doubtless much at this time, and from thence they transport all the native commodities, which being of little value amongst them, yields them great benefit being transported.[68]

It was as a centre of privateering that Wexford caused most problems for the authorities. The Confederate command, based in Kilkenny, instructed their agents in Flanders to find able honest men who would sail to Ireland and protect the coast. In return they would be allowed to enrich themselves by the prizes taken. During the next year, at least twenty letters of marque were issued to captains of foreign frigates allowing them to hinder at sea all enemies of the 'Catholic cause' in Ireland and all opponents of Charles I, king of England, thereby involving Irish privateers in the Thirty Years' War which had been raging in Europe since 1618. Wexford, as the nearest harbour in Ireland to Britain and the continent and in an ideal position to control strategic shipping lanes, was an obvious haven for the privateers. The difficult approach, which was curiously similar to Dunkirk, provided its own protection and the town was also defended by forts at the entrance to the harbour, on

Fig. 22 The highlight of the 1640s for the Catholics of Wexford was the visit to the town of the papal nuncio, Archbishop Rinuccini at Easter 1647. After celebrating Mass in St Peter's he remained in the town for several days. This illustration shows the title page of a book published by Rinucinni several years later after his return to Rome.

Fig. 23 The Confederates employed Anthony Van Kaat, a skilled shipbuilder from Flanders, to construct ships in Wexford. His shipyard was situated at Kaat's (Cat's) Strand Lane just outside Westgate. Before land reclamation, this lane, shown above, ended at the seashore.

the Raven and Rosslare points. A worried government report of 1642 described Wexford as:

> a place plentiful in ships and seamen, and where the rebels have set up Spanish colours on their walls in defiance of the king and kingdom of England, and have gotten in from foreign parts great store of arms and ammunition and where they profess openly that they will make another Dunkirk and infest us in all parts of the coasts of the kingdom, and so intercept the passage between Chester and Dublin as to hinder all intercourse between that place and this.[69]

By the mid 1640s a cosmopolitan privateering community composed of Irish, Flemish, French and even

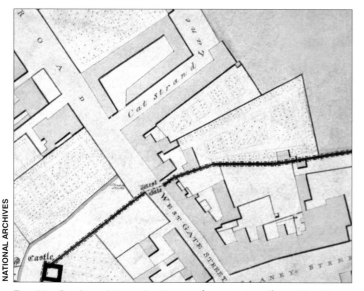

NATIONAL ARCHIVES

Fig. 24 Cat Strand Lane, leading to the site of Anthony Van Kaat's shipyard, is recorded on the 1840 O. S. town plan. The reclamation of land from the harbour is shown at centre right.

English had established themselves at Wexford, with as many as seventy-four individuals involved in the privateering business. The chief naval officer was William O'Doran, of Wexford extraction but born in Flanders. Frigate owners included the Marquis of Antrim, who had two ships at Wexford, and the papal nuncio Rinuccini, who had four.

The privateering fleet consisted of Dunkirk frigates, small fast vessels laden with cannon and men, regarded as the most sophisticated warships in early modern Europe. By the mid 1640s, there were twenty-one frigates and

Fig. 25 During the Confederate War of the 1640s, forty Wexford-based Dunkirk frigates, crewed by a privateering community made up of Irish, French, Flemish and even English, cruised the seas looking for enemy shipping. Up to 1,900 prizes were taken, bringing short-term prosperity to Wexford but ultimately leading to bloody retribution.

almost 200 cargo ships in Wexford and within a few years this figure had doubled. Packs of Wexford-based frigates cruised the seas between the Bay of Biscay and the Baltic and wreaked havoc on enemy shipping. English vessels were the most common prizes, followed by Scottish and Dutch ships. Irish ships supplying enemy ports were also taken, with occasional victims from Germany, Spain, France and Turkey. A contemporary observer estimated that Irish privateers took 1,900 prizes, not counting ships that were sunk in naval battles. These prizes, and their varied cargoes, brought prosperity to Wexford town and county. A contemporary pamphlet reported that 'the inhabitants of Wexford had enriched themselves by robbing and pillaging at sea all English merchants they could light on since the war began, and made a trade of that piracy'.

However, the prosperity was confined to those directly benefiting from privateering as reports referred to land: by the 1660s they owned twenty per cent, largely in Connacht. As for Wexford, the wealth generated by the privateers was to prove the town's undoing. A contemporary parliamentarian's account commented that 'God showed that he had a further controversy against such a place, and people, who enriched themselves with spoil of the innocent ... and therefore God so ordered it, as to make them vomit up again their stolen riches'.[72]

CROMWELL

In August 1649, Oliver Cromwell, leader of the victorious parliamentarian army, landed at Dublin with a highly trained, well equipped army of 12,000 men, determined to avenge supposed massacres of Protestants and to impose government authority by implementing a policy of 'conquest, confiscation and colonisation'. The brutal killing of more than 2,000 people after the taking of Drogheda was a deliberate tactic intended to strike terror in other Confederate towns which might be considering resistance.[73] Viewed from a wider perspective, the atrocities associated with Cromwell in Ireland can be likened to the excesses connected with the taking of fortified towns in Germany during the Thirty Years War,

TOMÁS HAYES

Fig. 26 The clay rampart, built inside the town wall as a defence against Cromwell's cannon, survives in the vicinity of St Patrick's church (to the left). In the 1970s, the rampart was landscaped and planted with shrubs. Unfortunately, the plants were allowed to grow unchecked and the top of the wall is now completely overgrown.

hardship in the town. In 1648, the mayor, Michael Bolan, claimed that there was 'extreme poverty and general want' and that he 'found it a hard task to get bread in the mouths of the common people'. By 1649, food was so scarce and expensive in the town that the inhabitants would have starved but for the prizes taken by the frigates.[70] Despite internal friction, the uprising continued for seven years as the bitter civil war in England did not permit the government of Charles I to intervene decisively. By the end of the decade, the Confederacy had split into opposing factions and the country was reduced to a state of destitution by war. Nevertheless, the Confederate Catholic regime that controlled much of Ireland from 1642 until 1649 has been described as 'one of the most successful revolts in early modern history'.[71]

The ultimate failure of the rebellion proved to be devastating, as it led to Cromwell's campaign of retribution and the destruction of the Catholic land-owning elite. Before the war, Catholics owned sixty per cent of Irish

BRITISH LIBRARY

Fig. 27 Oliver Cromwell as governor of Ireland. In Wexford, his name is synonymous with bloodshed and religious fanaticism.

Fig. 28   The rocky outcrops **(A)** overlooking the town to the south-east provided Cromwell's gunners with a strategic location from which to bombard the castle **(B)**. Part of this area is still known as Cromwell's Fort. After the fall of the castle, the town was quickly taken.

as armies in both cases, imbued with religious zeal, were convinced that they were doing God's work.[74] After the ruthless sacking of Drogheda, Cromwell marched south to lay siege to Wexford, the 'Dunkirk of Ireland and a place only famous for being infamous'.[75] Colonel David Sinnott had been appointed governor of the town to prepare it for a siege, but the townspeople, alarmed at the appearance of Cromwell's fleet of twenty ships at the mouth of the harbour and terrified at the prospect of the massacre at Drogheda being repeated, were inclined to surrender.[76] Cromwell's army made camp to the north-west of the town, in the vicinity of Spawell Road. The fort on Rosslare point, commanding the entrance to the harbour, was inexplicably abandoned by its garrison at the approach of a squadron of the attacking army, and the fort and two

frigates fell to the Cromwellians.[77] This allowed the English fleet to enter unopposed into the harbour to unload provisions, guns and ammunition. The landing probably took place to the south of the town, as the guns were positioned in that area for the subsequent attack. Following the capture of Rosslare Fort, Cromwell initiated negotiations for surrender, but these were interrupted by the arrival of 500 reinforcements who crossed over from Ferrybank, bringing to 4,000 the number of defenders in the town. The Confederate leadership, concerned that the port of Wexford should not be taken, attempted to send in further relief but this was refused.

Cromwell moved his forces to the south of the town and his siege guns, brought ashore from the fleet, were erected on the Trespan Rock, in an area still known as Cromwell's Fort. As a second wall had been built inside the town wall and the intervening space of four metres packed with clay (partly surviving between High Street and School Street) as a reinforcement against artillery – 'ramparted with earth, very thick' – cannon fire was concentrated on the castle which was just outside the wall with a commanding view of the town. The attackers believed that 'if the castle was taken, the town would easily follow'.[78] When the castle was breached, the Governor, James Stafford, with three others, were sent out to discuss terms. While these negotiations were in progress, the attacking army gained entry to the castle and quickly took control of it. Stafford was somehow implicated in this as Cromwell later observed that 'he yielded up the castle to us'.[79] In the early eighteenth

Fig. 29   The Bullring in the centre of the town, referred to as the market-place in 1662, has been traditionally associated with the massacre of townspeople following the taking of the town by Cromwellian soldiers.

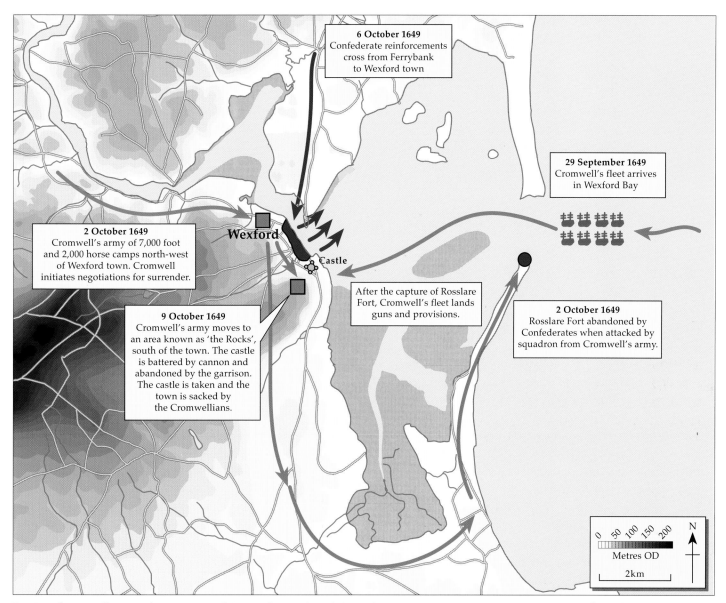

Fig. 30 This map illustrates the movement of Cromwellian and Confederate forces in and around Wexford in October 1649. The capture of Rosslare Fort facilitated Cromwell's success. The sacking by Cromwell was the lowest point in the town's history and brought the medieval phase to an end.

century, descendants of the townspeople killed by Cromwell's army claimed that Stafford was paid £500 to betray the castle.[80] The appearance of the enemy on the castle ramparts terrified the town's garrison and they abandoned the walls, many of them fleeing across the river by boat. Apparently without direct orders, the Cromwellian soldiers stormed the walls and sacked the town. The townspeople huddled together at the market place, where, in Cromwell's own words, his soldiers 'put all to the sword that came in their way … not many less than 2,000'. The Bullring was referred to as the market-place in 1662, so the tradition linking it with the massacre

Fig. 31 According to tradition, Cromwell occupied a large house on the Main Street, known as Kenny's Hall, during his stay in Wexford. Its location (A) is shown on the 1840 OS town plan. The building is currently occupied by Penney's department store.

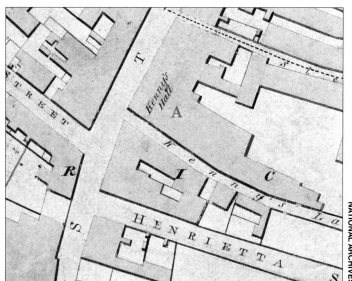

is well founded.[81] Some attempted to escape by boat but several hundred were lost when two boats overturned because of overloading. Among the dead were priests, including six Franciscans who were killed in front of the altar in their church. Regret was expressed by Cromwell himself, and some of his supporters, for the destruction of the town, as it would have made excellent winter accommodation for the army, but it was seen as a 'just judgement' by God on the inhabitants for the way they had treated 'divers poor Protestants'.[82]

During the siege, the townspeople had removed some of their goods across the harbour to Ferrybank, but the occupying soldiers still got a 'rich booty'. A large array of abandoned material was confiscated for the parliamentary authorities. Great quantities of iron, hides, tallow, salt, pipe and barrel staves reflected the trade in the port, much of it based on the timber industry; 100 cannon were also seized, as well as a large number of ships and boats, including one almost completed frigate in the shipyard (presumably the one operated by Anthony Van Kaat just

---

Cromwell's account of the taking of Wexford to the speaker of the English parliament, October 1649

Upon Thursday 11th instant (our batteries being finished the night before) we began to play betimes in the morning, and having spent near 100 shot, the Governor's stomach came down, and he sent to me to give leave for four persons entrusted by him, to come unto me and offer terms of surrender, which I condescending to, two field officers, with an alderman of the town and the captain of the castle, brought out the propositions enclosed, which for their abominableness, manifesting also the impudency of the men, I thought fit to present to your view, together with my answer, which indeed had no effect; for whilst I was preparing of it, studying to preserve the town from plunder that it might be of more use to you and your army, the captain, who was one of the commissioners being fairly treated, yielded up the castle to us; upon the top of which our men no sooner appeared, but the enemy quitted the walls of the town, which our men perceiving, ran violently upon the town with their ladders and stormed it. And when they came into the market place, the enemy making a stiff resistance, our forces broke them, and then put all to the sword that came in their way. Two boatfuls of the enemy attempting to escape, being overpressed with numbers, sunk, whereby were drowned near 300 of them: I believe in all there were lost of the enemy not many less than 2,000 and I believe not 20 of yours were killed from first to last of the siege. And indeed, it hath not been without cause been deeply set upon our hearts, that we intending better to this place, than so great a ruin, hoping the town might be of more use to you and your army: yet God would not have it so, but by an unexpected providence, in his righteous justice, brought just judgement on them, causing them to become a prey to the soldiers, who in their piracies had made preys of so many families, and made with their bloods to answer the cruelties which they had exercised upon the lives of divers poor Protestants, two of which I have lately been acquainted with. About seven or eight score poor Protestants were put by them into an old vessel, which as some say bulged by them, the vessel sunk, and they were all presently drowned in the harbour. The other was thus, they put divers poor Protestants into a chapel, which since they have used for a Mass house, and in which one or more of their priests were now killed, where they were famished to death.

The soldiers got a very good booty in this place, and had they not had opportunity to carry their goods over the river whilst we besieged it, it would have been much more. I could have wished for their own good they had been more moderate. Some things which were not easily portable, we hope we shall make use of to your behoof [advantage]. There are great quantities of iron, hides, tallow, salt, pipe and barrel staves, which are under commissioners hands to be secured. We believe there are near 100 cannon in the fort [the castle] and elsewhere in and about the town. Here is likewise some very good shipping; here are three vessels, one of them of 34 guns, which in a week's time would fit to sea; there is another of about 20 guns, very near ready likewise; and one other frigate of 20 guns upon the stocks, made for sailing, which is built up to the uppermost deck, for her handsomeness sake I have appointed the workmen to finish her, here being materials to do it, if you or the Council of State shall approve thereof. The frigate also taken by the fort is a most excellent vessel for sailing, besides divers other ships and vessels in the harbour.

This town is now in your power, that the former inhabitants I believe scarce one in twenty can challenge any propriety in their houses, most of them are run away, and many of them killed in this service; and it were to be wished that an honest people would come and plant here, where are very good houses, and other accommodations fitted to their hands, and may by your favour be made of encouragement to them; as also a seat of good trade, both inward and outward, and of marvellous great advantage in the point of herring and other fishing. The town is pleasantly seated, and strong, having a rampart of earth within the wall fifteen foot thick.

Fig. 32   A nineteenth-century illustration of the massacre in the market place, of the townspeople of Wexford by Cromwellian soldiers. The market cross is inaccurately represented in the form of a Celtic cross. The atrocity is rendered more horrific by portraying all of the victims as women and children.

outside Westgate), as well as other ships and boats in the harbour. Many of the defenders of the town were conscripted into Cromwell's army.[83] Very few of the former inhabitants remained to claim their houses as most of them had been killed or dispersed. Another observer commented that 'we have near eighty ships and one hundred boats to fish in, of which there is a fine trade. God hath spoiled the spoiler, abundance of plunder and rich. It is a fine spot for some godly congregation, where house and land wait for inhabitants and occupiers. I wish they would come'. According to tradition, Cromwell stayed in a large house known as

Kenny's Hall on the Main Street, the cellar of which survived until recent times.[84]

The sacking by Cromwell was the lowest point in Wexford's often turbulent history and brought the town's medieval phase to a bloody end. The 'most English of towns', once considered to be part of the Pale, was in ruins, its population scattered, and its ecclesiastical, social and business infrastructure decimated. Wexford's future depended on an influx of new families, combined with the survivors of the *ancien régime*, who would rebuild the town and guide it through religious and political crises into the modern era.

CROMWELLIAN CONFISCATION AND COLONISATION

The events of the 1640s, 'the war that finished Ireland', had far-reaching consequences for Wexford and the rest of the country. In 1610, most of the land was owned by 2,000 Catholic gentry; in 1641, 59 per cent of the land of Ireland was owned by Catholics; by 1660, this had collapsed to 22 per cent and by 1703 only 14 per cent of the land remained in Catholic hands. Ireland still had a majority Catholic population, but the land and political institutions were now controlled by a Protestant minority. This generated an Anglican ascendancy which would control Ireland for more than two centuries, resulting in the implementation of far-reaching societal changes.[1] Although Wexford had prospered during the Confederate war, there was immense disruption to the economic life of the town from 1650 onwards, following the expulsion of Catholic inhabitants and merchants. The loss of Catholic merchants impeded economic recovery, as the demise of these old Catholic families led to a reduction in shipping and, more crucially, in overseas trading contacts.[2] Before Cromwell, an Old English mercantile elite dominated all the major towns, including Wexford, although the majority of inhabitants consisted of native Irish. The confiscations which followed the Cromwellian campaign introduced a colonial frontier in which the majority Irish population was dominated by a privileged English elite.

N. L. I.

Fig. 1   This mid seventeenth-century map of Wexford is the first known cartographic representation of the town. Although schematic in execution, the map conveys considerable information about the town's topography. The town wall is depicted with battlements, mural towers and gates. The castle, shown outside the wall to the south, has four towers with conical roofs. The Franciscan church is shown outside the wall to the west. The waterfront has seven jetties projecting into the harbour. The streets of the town are designated by three rows of substantial houses; two small cabins beside the wall may reflect the type of thatched house that was knocked in preparation for the Cromwellian siege.

Fig. 2 Wexford town is located at the extremity of a ridge sloping from the high ground known as Forth Mountain (235m), 5km to the south-west. The town and harbour can be seen in the top right section of the picture. A concentration of Irish townland names on this high ground suggests that the poor quality land remained in the hands of the Irish, subsequent to the arrival of Anglo-Norman settlers.

Subsequent to the Cromwellian campaign, the authorities embarked on a ruthless campaign against the many Confederate soldiers (known as 'tories') who continued to attack government targets from the hills and woods. An order was made in Wexford in 1655 for the apprehension of tories, with rewards offered for noted 'outlaws'.[3] Areas of the country not controlled by the government, including part of county Wexford, were declared 'outlawed'; inhabitants could be executed or transported simply for living in a place where attacks were launched on Commonwealth forces.[4] The residents of a zone along the coast between Dublin and Wexford were excluded from protection unless they came in and surrendered to the authorities.

The governor of Wexford was ordered to report how this zone should be established around Wexford, who would be permitted to live within it, and who should be excluded. A claim in 1722 to commonage rights on Forth Mountain by the people of the town and neighbourhood, could have dated to this period.[5] Reclamation of waste land on the mountain began in the 1650s.[6] As part of the campaign, garrison commanders were ordered to destroy houses that might shelter rebels within two miles of towns. This edict was implemented in Wexford; in 1658, fishermen who returned to the town were imprisoned because they disobeyed the two miles edict. They were freed on condition that they would not continue to live in

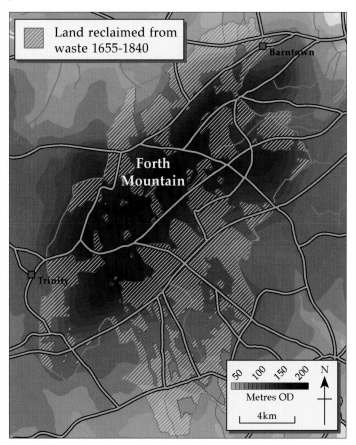

Fig. 3 The reclamation of land which began in the 1650s on Forth Mountain (shown as commonage on the Down Survey) suggests that people who had been expelled from Wexford by the Cromwellian regime were forced to occupy the marginal upland environment.

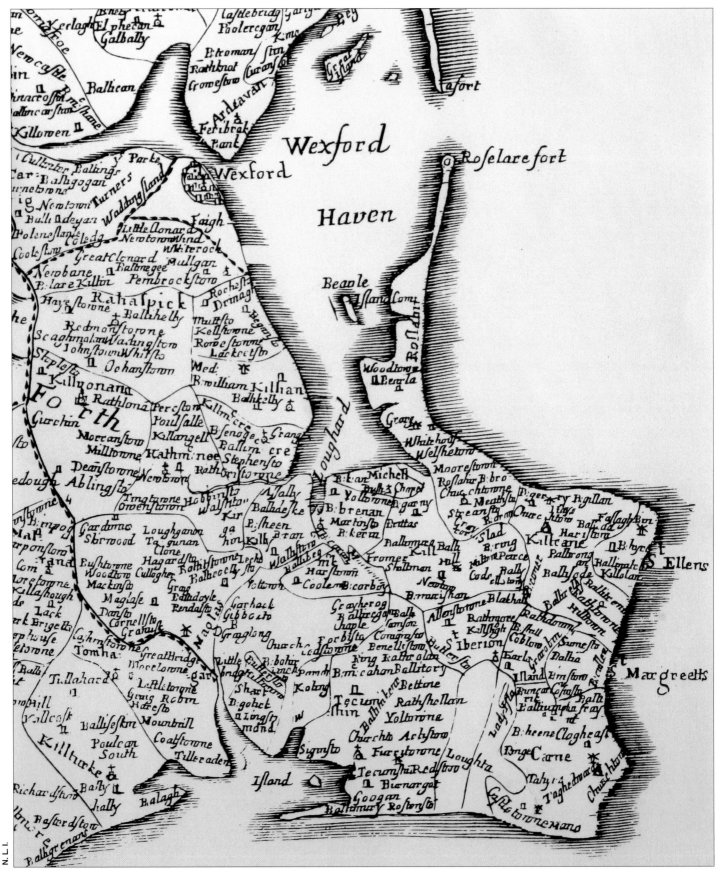

Fig. 4   Following the Cromwellian campaign in Ireland, the estates of Catholic landowners who had been active in the Confederate war were confiscated. Surveyors compiled the *Down Survey*, which mapped estates that were to be appropriated. Wexford town and liberties and all of the barony of Forth were seized and granted to new English, Protestant owners. The *Down Survey* is a rich source for landscape and placename studies.

Fig. 5   As part of a campaign to impose law and order, a new jail was established in Stafford's Castle on South Main Street, between Oyster Lane and Stonebridge. The castle continued in use as a jail until 1812. This image of the castle is from a view of the town painted in 1820.

freed on condition that they would not continue to live in the town.[7] These restrictions presumably contributed to the expansion of the fishing community in the southern suburb of the Faythe. The scorched earth policy implemented by the government produced famine conditions, which, combined with an outbreak of Bubonic plague, led to a demographic disaster, resulting in the deaths of 20–25 per cent of the population. In 1650, an outbreak of plague in Wexford town caused many deaths; conditions were so bad that the garrison was moved outside the town to Drinagh and other locations.[8] Combined with the war casualties of the 1640s and transportation, this resulted in a likely population loss, at a national level, of at least 33 per cent, between 1641 and 1654 (from *c.* 2 million to *c.* 1.3 million).[9]

The aftermath of the Confederate uprising revolutionised subsequent political and social development. The Cromwellians, who had helped Parliament to defeat the Confederates, either as investors (known as 'adventurers') or soldiers, were to be paid in land. In 1652, the Act of Settlement decreed that all landowners who had fought as Confederates were to lose their estates and receive lands in Connacht in exchange. Two surveys were carried out to facilitate the confiscation of land: the *Civil Survey* (1654–56)[10] established land ownership and value in 1640, while the *Down Survey* of 1654 mapped the lands that were to be forfeited.[11] The many changes in land ownership during the second half of the seventeenth century were later recorded in the *Books of Survey and Distribution*.

Nearly half of Ireland was confiscated by the English parliament and transferred from Catholic to Protestant ownership; Catholic owners were to vacate their estates and migrate across the Shannon. The possibility of removing all Catholics to the west was considered, but in practice only some landowners were transplanted, as the new owners petitioned that labourers and tradesmen should be allowed to remain to work on the land. Many soldiers and adventurers who received grants of land made a quick profit by selling them on; others married Irish women and some of their children were raised as Catholics.

Wexford, with other port towns, was reserved by parliament for the army, adventurers and creditors. Wexford Castle and Rosslare Fort were retained for the defence of the kingdom. Initially, it was determined that the town should be cleared of all previous inhabitants,

S.P.C.

Fig. 6   The suburb of the Faythe, the Irishtown of Wexford, located to the south-east of the town on level ground between 'the rocks' and the seashore, may have expanded as a fishing hamlet in the post-Cromwellian period when fishermen were expelled from the walled town. This detail from an 1820 painting depicts the long straggling nature of the suburb with fishing craft off-shore. The recently-built Rocklands House is shown at centre left.

but, as law and order was restored, many of them filtered back to provide a badly needed workforce. Others, whose services were indispensable, even succeeded in occupying their former houses, but as tenants-at-will, not as owners. In 1654, a petition from Wexford to the Commissioners for Irish Affairs asked for guidance concerning the numbers of Irish Papists that would be permitted to live in the town, including Catholic Irish women who had married Protestants, and Catholic men who had turned Protestant. The response stipulated that no Irish Papist could remain in the town, without authorisation, after May 1655.[12] The issue of mixed marriages was persistent and contentious. In 1652, the wife of Francis Harvey, merchant, was dispensed and permitted to live in the town with her husband until the following year while Anthony

Harrison's wife was allowed to remain in the town during the fishing season, but then was to be transplanted. William Morton, secretary to the Revenue Commissioners, made himself 'incapable of continuing his employment' when he married a Papist, and was dismissed from his post.[13]

In 1652, efforts made by the recently arrived settlers to improve living conditions in the town included the appointment of a physician and schoolmaster. Initially, ruinous houses in the town were let at a reasonable rent for seven years to tenants who would repair them. In 1657, the 'people of Wexford' who had received 'rebel lands and house', in 'satisfaction of debts', because they had spent more than £10,000 on building and repairing houses and quays, and 'gaining ground out of the sea', successfully

N.L.I.

Fig. 7   Thatched houses in the suburb of John's Street at the turn of the twentieth century. Note the gas-light bracket on the left-hand wall.

N.L.I.

Fig. 8   A row of thatched houses c. 1900 at Slippery Green (now Thomas Street) with Bride Street church in the distance.

Fig 9   The long south-eastern suburb of the Faythe from the 1840 O. S. town plan. The two shipyards are shown at top right. The recently-constructed Trinity Street, William Street and New (Parnell) Street had not been fully developed. Maritime activity is emphasised by the presence of four rope-walks.

PRIVATE COLLECTION

Fig. 10 Some of the transplanted Irish were forced to work in the demanding conditions of the Caribbean sugar plantations.

petitioned for long leases of thirty-one years. Land reclamation was ongoing as part of the redevelopment of the town. There were frequent references at this period to 'lands gained from the sea' or 'ground took from the strand'. In 1662, after the Restoration, the king granted to Wexford Corporation 'all the strands from the present high-water mark as far as shall hereafter be gained out of the sea within the liberties and franchises of the said Corporation'.[14]

The new regime in Wexford moved quickly to implement sanctions against Catholics and to impose law and order. In early 1650, the Poor Clare nuns were driven out of their convent and banished from the town; they were subsequently awarded £20 per annum. The discontinuity imposed by the Reformation and re-settlement was epitomised by the abandonment of the older parish centres where the churches, still with thriving graveyards, mouldered into ivy-covered ruins.[15] The exception in Wexford was the church of St Iberius' which was taken over for use as the Protestant place of worship. The churches of SS Peter, Michael, John and the Holy Trinity, outside the walls, were demolished, with the stones of the last three being used to repair the castle. The Franciscan friary, 'with an elaborate sumptuous chappell and a spacious walled precinct', became a ruin.[16] In 1652, Wexford was one of the ports which provided ships for the transportation of 3,000 men to foreign parts and in the following year the town authorities were instructed to transplant all 'Popish priests without exception'.[17] Four

Wexford Franciscans were captured in 1654 and hanged in the neighbourhood of the friary.[18] In 1656, a jail was established, initially in Bride Lane (now Mary's Lane) but after a short period in Stafford's Castle, on the corner of Oyster Lane and South Main Street, which continued in use as a jail until 1812.[19] Priests, in particular, were targeted, because of their role in dissuading Catholics from attending Protestant services. In 1658, it was proposed to send three 'Popish priests' who were in Wexford jail to 'the American Islands' and to institute a search for 'Mass books and other Popish trash'. In the same year the Justices of the Peace were instructed to apprehend the 'many Popish Priests and seminaries' who were still in the county. Some of these priests were taken into custody; in 1659, for example, 'Popish priests', Francis Stafford, Thomas Hore and Thomas Hanton, petitioned not to be sent to the Atlantic islands of Aran and Inishbofin because of their age and other infirmities.[20]

A concerted effort was made to remove 'undesirables' from the town. In 1654, all 'rogues, beggars, idlers and wanderers', unless they could give a good account of themselves and show that they were leading a productive life, were handed over to Captain Morgan and others, for shipment to the West Indies. Irish children and Irish in

Fig. 11 Monck Street, in the north end of the town, was constructed in the post-Cromwellian era and named after George Monck, Duke of Albemarle, who acquired extensive properties in Wexford.

CENSUS OF 1659 – Wexford town and liberties

	Tituladoes	English	Irish	Names
Wexford				
East Ward	143	70	73	Thomas Lowe Esq, mayor of Wexford Town, John Cotterell, Paul Wakefield, Robert Phillips, Constantine Neale, William Reynolds, Christopher Dobson and Anthony Cauldron, gents.
West Ward	161	64	97	Hugh Hobbs, Michael Lewling, Thomas Pilkington, John Roberts and Richard Neale, gents.
South Ward	259	115	144	Ambrose Andrews, Valentine Chyttwood, George Linnington, Charles Huddle and William Barker, gents.
North Ward	118	52	66	James Roe, John Walton, Francis Harvey, Robert Wilkinson, Isaac Freborne and William Cleburne, gents.
The Suburbs				
Faigh	92	12	80	
Bride Street	15	2	13	
St John Street	74	16	58	
Weststreet	34	9	25	
Maudlintown	6	0	6	

Principal Irish names and their number
Murphy – 14; Codd – 13; Synott – 11; Welsh – 7; Doyle – 6; White – 6; Connors – 5; Devereux – 5; Furlong – 5; Redmond – 5

Town and Liberties of Wexford: English – 340; Irish – 562; **Total – 902**

Fig. 12   The 1659 'census' of Ireland (an abstract of the poll-tax returns) provides a partial list of adults over fifteen years of age. Single adult females and most single adult males who were not servants or gainfully employed were excluded. The names of English property holders were recorded, but only the numbers of Irish. These figures reveal that 62% of title holders were Irish. This figure dropped to 56% inside the wall but rose to 82% in the suburbs. The south ward of the town had the highest population while the north had less than half that amount, reflecting the historic north/south division. In the suburbs, where 25% of the occupants lived, 82% were Irish, with the highest numbers in the Faythe, followed by John's Street. Many of the surnames recorded did not continue in the town but some became part of the profile of Wexford names. These included Phillips, Reynolds, Dobson, Hobbs, Pilkington, Roberts, Barker, Roe and Harvey. The principal Irish names recorded (mostly of Anglo-Norman origin) are typical examples of the surnames found in the town and county. A multiplier of 2.5 gives an estimated overall population of 2,255, not much greater than the estimated population of 2,000 at the end of the twelfth century. This 'census' is the earliest detailed demographic depiction of Wexford town.

hospitals were included. Two years later, demands were still being made for the removal of 'loose and idle persons of the Irish nation' who were a cause of 'idleness and profaneness' among the inhabitants. The Governor, Colonel Sadler, was ordered to arrange the 'speedy removal of the Irish' but this was never fully achieved.[21] In

M. GIBBONS

Fig. 13   'Cromwell's Fort', built in the 1650s on the island of Inishbofin off the coast of county Galway in the west of Ireland, was used as a concentration camp for Catholic priests, including some from Wexford.

an effort to curb lawlessness in the town, the Commissioners ordered that no one, English or Irish, should be given a license to sell intoxicating drink indoors. This directive was intended to abolish inns and alehouses which were regarded as meeting places for disaffected persons. Almost inevitably, this order was not effective. By 1660 there were nine taverns in the town, seven of the proprietors having English surnames.[22]

There is evidence for transplantation of Wexford people who had lost their lands, although some succeeded in having their convictions rescinded. There were so many petitions lodged in Wexford against transplantation that a committee was set up to deal with them. Punitive action was taken against some who failed to transplant; for example, in 1655, Dudley Kavanagh was shipped to Barbados for not transplanting but Edward Furlong and James Keating of Wexford were excused because of old age. For some ship owners, the transporting business proved to be lucrative. In 1655, John Devereux of Wexford was given permission to transport all Irish natives to

Fig. 14 George's Street, first mentioned in 1666, was developed in the north end of the town, possibly along the line of an existing laneway. It was a popular location for eighteenth-century Georgian town houses. In the early nineteenth century, the street was extended beyond the town wall.

nineteen women as well as children.[23] The issue of transplantation lingered on for some time. In 1659 an inquiry was held to determine the part played in the rebellion by Richard Devereux, Redmond Baron, John Murphy and Edmond Doyle, who were held in Wexford jail for not transplanting.[24]

In spite of the official policy of preventing Catholics from living in the town, they still made up more than half the population by the end of the decade; out of a population of 2,255 in 1659, 1,400 were Catholics.[25] Many of them occupied the suburb areas of John's Street and the Faythe, to the west and south of the walled town.[26] The Catholic population was further increased after the Restoration of the monarchy in 1660 when some of the former inhabitants returned, hopeful of recovering their property and status. Fifty-six Wexford sea captains and masters, describing themselves as the 'ancient natives', who had been in the royal service since 1651, petitioned the king on behalf of those 'who escaped the sword of the usurper and the heirs of those who sacrificed their lives in his majesty's service'. There is no indication that their request for the return of their former property and possessions in the town received any attention. When expectations were dashed in the vast majority of cases, many of those who returned to the town chose to rent their former dwellings and to work under the new proprietors. The tension caused by this situation may have been responsible for the formation of a militia troop in Wexford Castle, following the appointment of Colonel Solomon Richards as governor in 1658. The banning of unlawful assembly in 1665 and the stationing of two companies (120 men) in the castle in 1666 are indicators of a growing sense of confrontation in the town.[27]

America who were prisoners for not transplanting, and Captain John Norris was given leave to ship men, women, vagrants, idlers and beggars to the plantations of America from Wexford, Ross and Kilkenny. In the same year, the marshal of the Four Courts in Dublin delivered all Popish priests and other malefactors in his custody to Robert Coleman, captain of a Wexford frigate, to be shipped to Barbados; the list included four priests, sixteen men and

---

Description of Wexford c. 1680 (Hore)

This Barony of Forth contains within its limits Wexford, a very ancient corporate town, the description of whose pleasant and profitable situation, beauty, strength, pious monuments, and structure, may be delineated by more dextrous pen and more amply acquainted and better informed judgement. A slender elegy of the eminently deserving things does but detract from their real and due estimate. The town is governed by a mayor and bailiffs. There are two burgesses sent from thence to all parliaments in Ireland. It is in the diocese of Ferns. To render an exact account of the numerous commodities that town is constantly supplied with all, the frequentation of merchants and strangers from almost all parts of Europe, the sending from thence to all parts of the known world, the exquisite knowledge of the natives in the art of navigation, very many of them familiarly having traversed the ocean to the most remote regions and coasts discovered by Americus Megellanus Vespusius [sic], and Drake, capable to navigate and in a martial manner to command the greatest ship, and best provided with offensive and defensive arms, from the Gallion to the Galliot, whose valiant resolution, activity and strength of body, in many late engagements at sea, is remarkably known to all admirals in Europe. Their inviolate fidelity and loyal affection to their dread and dear sovereign Charles II, King of England, and their zealous and incessant services for his majesty and inseparable attendance on him during his exile, would require a grand volume: not to mention the abundance of all sorts of corn, flesh, butter, tallow, hides, wool, timber, incredible quantity of fish and its variety, the market is supplied with all.

TRADE AND COMMERCE

Economic development was a priority for the new owners and measures to improve trade and fishing were immediately initiated. Serious restrictions were in place regarding the landing of merchandise and in 1651, a decree was issued that all ships carrying goods, both for import and export, had to use either Common Quay or French's Quay. This move was obviously aimed at maximising the collection of taxes. The customs officers requested that 'a convenient house' should be set aside for their use. A decision was also taken to improve the navigation of the harbour by the provision of buoys and beacons and to investigate the possibility of building a public quay. The Corporation was also given permission to provide a ferry boat, 'for the common use', to land goods and passengers on the Ferrybank side of the harbour. An unusual regulation was introduced at all Irish ports, including Wexford, banning the export of Irish wolf hounds, due to the increase in the killing of cattle by a growing wolf population.[28]

The return of the herring shoals helped to boost the economic life of the town as a huge catch was recorded for 1654. The significance of the fishing business to the town's welfare was reflected in a survey of 1662 which mentioned twelve 'red herring houses' and five 'fish yards' and in the same year the mayor and Corporation were given permission to make by-laws for the regulation of herring fishing and the fishing trade in general. The owners of quays benefitted greatly from increased catches of fish as each boat owner had to contribute half a maze (half a barrel) of herrings per annum in landing rights. The quays could be more than one hundred yards long so they were capable of accommodating many boats.[29] A 1674 report observed that 'almost every house hath a quay or wharf to the water side'.[30]

The lucrative timber trade was also regulated and four officials were appointed to oversee the felling and sale of trees in 1652. A 'convenient place' was selected in the town for use as a public timberyard. After more than a century of logging, trees must have been getting scarcer and in 1656 a directive was issued prohibiting the exportation of timber, and for the preservation of wood in and about Wexford. At the same time, an order was made that timber belonging to the state and private individuals should not be mixed in the wood yard at Wexford. Presumably because of the growing scarcity of trees in county Wexford, the governor, Colonel Sadler, applied for £45 payment for bringing a great quantity of timber from Dundrum in county Dublin, and storing it in the town. The customs figures indicate that the port made a dramatic recovery during the second half of the seventeenth century. From a low of £510 in 1632, Wexford had become the leading port in the south-east by 1693 with customs returns of £6,851, compared to £6,651 for Waterford and £1,196 for Ross.[31] An account of the town from c.1680 emphasised the international nature of Wexford's trade and remarked on the seafaring tradition and navigational skills of the port's mariners.[32]

The change in ownership was epitomised by the change in the surname profile in the town. The old, predominantly Anglo-Norman names were replaced by English names such as Croxton, Hornibrooke, Wilbore, Marre, Grogan, Hobbs, Leynam, Wesley, Evans, Hix, Mansfield, Wallis, Fortune, Taylor and Sadler. The names of some of the new proprietors are remembered in street names in the town. Principal among these was George Monck, Duke of Albemarle, after whom Monck Street was named. Monck, governor of the town in 1662, had received a grant of the ferry of Wexford in 1658. After restoration, he acquired further lands with extensive privileges, including permission to build a quay at Ferrybank on the far side of the harbour. Other Cromwellian settlers gave their names to Raby's Gate (formerly Friar's Gate), Batt Street, Archer's Lane, Ivory's Lane, Hayes's Lane and Grogan's Road.[33] Surviving records give some indication

KEVIN WHELAN

Fig. 15   The new administration banned the export of wolfhounds from Irish ports, including Wexford. This was due to the threat to livestock from a menacing wolf population, possibly because of the extremely disturbed state of the country during the previous decade.

Fig. 16 During the era when the Penal Laws against Catholics were in force, the traditional pilgrimage site of Our Lady's Island, in the barony of Forth, attracted pilgrims in great numbers. In August and September, vast crowds of people continue to be drawn to the Island to take part in the ceremonies and to walk the pilgrim route around the circuit of the Island.

of the state of Wexford in the 1650s and 1660s. In 1662, the principal public buildings were granted by the crown to the Corporation; these included the townhall, with the rooms at the west end and cellars underneath, a clockhouse, the tholsel and the council chamber. The locations of these buildings cannot be established but the townhall was probably on the sea side of the present South Main Street, where, because of the steep slope, all the houses were built over cellars.[34] A survey of the town was carried out in 1662 under the Act of Settlement, but it may not have included all properties. It listed seventy houses, thirteen of them thatched and four 'caged' (timber-framed), as well as twenty-five ruined houses. Industrial establishments included twelve red herring houses, five fish yards, twelve tan pits, three malt-houses, a ruined water-mill, a forge, a brewhouse and a hospital. Street names mentioned in the survey were, for the most part, synonymous with parish church dedications. The name of (St) George's Street was first recorded in 1666, an indication that it was of post-Cromwellian origin.[35]

The tension generated by the ever increasing number of Catholics in the town inevitably led to a growing unease and the introduction of further anti-Catholic measures by the Protestant minority. An account written by the governor, Solomon Richards, in 1682, noted that 'the greatest number of the inhabitants are Irish, but the magistracy are all English or Protestants'.[36] In 1674, an order was issued that all convents, seminaries, friaries,

nunneries and Popish schools in the town and county were to be dissolved. Four years later, a proclamation by Sir Nicholas Loftus, the governor of the town, ordered all Catholics to surrender their arms within twenty days; no Papist was to 'ride with, carry, buy, use or keep' any kind of weapon without a licence. A further proclamation was issued forbidding any Catholic to keep a market outside the walls of Wexford or to reside in the town unless he had lived there for most of the past year, to attend a fair carrying arms or to meet by day or night in great or unusual numbers; all Popish clergy were ordered to transplant, and were to be apprehended if found in the town or county.[37]

LUKE WADDING

In spite of anti-Catholic legislation, the Catholic community in Ireland had made some progress at an organisational level by the early 1670s. In Wexford, the Protestant church was well established within the town, as its Vestry Books from about 1662 indicate, but it made little attempt to evangelise the Catholic population.[38] Politically, the town was controlled by the Protestant

Fig. 17 Mary's Lane gets its name from the medieval church of St Mary's, which is located behind the black door in the centre of the picture. In penal times, the upper floor of the house with dormer windows was used as a mass-house and, for generations, was known as 'the oratory'.

CONFISCATION · AND · COLONISATION

Description of Wexford in 1682 by Solomon Richards

The town of Wexford stands in the end, or rather the beginning of the barony of Forth. Tradition agreeing with Mr Camden, saith it was first called 'Menapia,' then 'Weisford.' It is now called Wexford, in Irish Loch Garman. It's a walled town on all sides, except to the sea-pool, or harbour, which washes the north-east side thereof. It's of the form of a half oval, divided the long way. It has gates for entrance – extends itself in length from north-west to south-east about five furlongs. It was in good order, and very populous since the last rebellion, but much depopulated in its taking by Oliver Cromwell. Since that, brought by the English into a flourishing condition, but now about two-thirds of it lies in its ruins, through the decay of the herring fishery, which was so great that about the year 1654, there were made and entered in the custom house of Wexford above eighty-thousand barrels of herrings, and it was even thought above forty-thousand more were made that were not entered. Which trade is so decayed, that about the year 1678, there was not above two hundred barrells made in the whole town – nor is there above two hundred barrels made this year, 1682. The greatest number of the inhabitants are Irish – but the magistracy are all English, or Protestant. Its greatest honour is that it was the first town in Ireland that submitted to the English government – for when Robert FitzStephen first landed at Baginbun, he presently marched to Wexford, and it surrendered to him, and the Lordship thereof, together with a large district of land adjacent, was given to him by Dermot MacMurrough, the then Irish King of Leinster … It was formerly divided into eight parishes, viz. – St Iberius, St Selskar's, St Patrick's, St Mary's, St Toolock's, St John's, St Peter's, and St Michael's – a monastery also, but now ruinated, and under one minister. The monastery of St Selskar was once famous, but now lies in its ruins, and without the walls; the abbey – ruined alsoe, but still possessed by priests and friars. The government of this town of Wexford is by a mayor, two bailiffs, and twenty-four burgesses. It sends two burgesses to parliament. It has a well frequented market on Saturdays. At the south-east end of the town stands the castle, just without the walls. It is a great old antique building, said to be raised by King John at the time of his being in Ireland. Doubtless it is of great antiquity. Cromwell battered it, and had it rendered on his own terms. It usually was a garrison, but now not so. The town and castle are washed on the north-east side by the mouth of the River Slaney, dilated into a pool of about six leagues in circumference, two necks of land from north and south pointing at each other over the harbour's mouth, without [outside] which lies the bar, at least a league at sea.

WEXFORD COUNTY LIBRARY

Fig. 18 Ballycogley Castle was the ancestral home of the Waddings, who came to Ireland during the Anglo-Norman settlement. They lost their lands in the Cromwellian confiscation. Luke Wadding went to Paris and returned as a priest to Wexford in 1668.

minority with the Corporation periodically issuing statutes forbidding Catholics to live within the town walls. Although anti-Catholic directives were not strictly enforced, they deprived Catholics of civil rights, forcing them to practice in a clandestine manner. For pragmatic reasons, Catholic merchants had been allowed to return to the town as trade had slumped badly in their absence. It was against this background that Luke Wadding was appointed to the town in 1672. A member of the well known Anglo-Norman family of Ballycogley Castle, Wadding left Wexford after the sacking by Cromwell to attend university in Paris where he was eventually ordained a priest.[39] Following an academic career on the continent, he was appointed Vicar-General of Ferns diocese in 1668 by Bishop Nicholas French, who was living in exile since the Cromwellian period. After a short stay in New Ross, Wadding moved to Wexford where he set about establishing parochial structures. He refused to be consecrated as coadjutor 'because of the present state of the people, the extreme poverty here, the uncertainty of the times and a hundred other reasons'.[40] Rather surprisingly, given the political climate, he succeeded in starting parochial registers which survive to the present time; the surnames recorded show that the Catholics in the

Fig. 19 Continuity of tradition in the baronies of Forth and Bargy is epitomised by the funeral custom of placing a wooden cross in a thorn bush near the cemetery. The sacred tree has obvious mythological connotations but the practice may be a reference to the crown of thorns. Once widespread, this custom is now confined to the parish of Kilmore.

parish church for the Catholics of the town, estimated at 2,000 in 1700, a status it was to hold until the middle of the nineteenth century.[45] A claim, in 1690, by Rev. Alexander Allen, the rector of St Iberius', that the Catholic community had 'several chapels fit for the free exercise of their religion, both within and without the walls of the town, and whereunto several Protestant inhabitants had given liberal donations', may not have accurately represented the true situation.[46]

Solomon Richards, writing in 1682, said that the town had been 'much depopulated' when it was taken by Cromwell but that the English had brought it to a 'flourishing condition' since that time. Two-thirds of the town was then in ruins because of the collapse of the unpredictable herring fishery.[47] Against this background, the accession of the Catholic James II to the throne in 1685 gave hope to his co-religionists in Wexford, as in Ireland as a whole. His charter to the town in 1687 was mostly a confirmation of earlier charters, aimed at preserving the rights of the burgesses.[48] There was a general increase in lawlessness and disorder with some anti-Protestant activity.

After the arrival of James in Ireland in 1689, Protestant fears increased, particularly after a bill introduced in the Dublin 'patriot parliament' of 1689 – designed to repeal the acts of settlement and establish religious toleration – threatened the very basis of Protestant power.[49] In Wexford, the Catholic majority took control, helped by the fact that the mayor, Edward Wiseman, and the governor of the castle, Colonel Butler, were Catholics. The mayor took possession of St Iberius', the Protestant church in the town, and allowed 'the rabble' to vandalise

town were predominantly of Old English origin. Even more unexpectedly, he was given permission to build a public chapel inside the walls of the town, believed to be located between High Street and the town wall, opposite the Theatre Royal.[41] Details of the building, which took twelve years to complete, were recorded meticulously in his notebook.

In 1678, an abortive 'popish plot' in England and an upsurge of anti-Catholic activity had repercussions in Ireland. These included the execution of Oliver Plunkett, the bishop of Armagh, the expulsion of bishops and priests and the closure of mass houses.[42] In Wexford, Wadding was arrested but released with the help of Protestant friends. Following the death of Nicholas French, Wadding was consecrated bishop of Ferns in 1683 but died four years later and was buried in the Friary church. He is perhaps best remembered for his carols, some of which are still sung in Kilmore church during the Christmas period.[43] Wadding's chapel did not survive after his death as in 1697 a thatched mass house in Back Street, in the possession of Patrick Murphy, was forfeited to the crown.[44] The Franciscan friary then became the

---

Bishop Wadding's Notebook

In my chapel booke I find the charge I have beene from the year 1674 til this year 1686 in removing the great heap of dunge, in building the house, ceilinge, thatchinge, washinge, making the altar, rayles, pulpit, confessional, seats, bankes, the wall nere the rampart and the wall nere the street, doors, glasinge, paveinge, floringe and all things else from time to time as in my chapel booke of six sheetts of large paper: £53 14s 9d.

The names of friends who did contribute to this worke are in chapel booke folio 1: £8 12s 7d.

All pictures, ornaments of altar and chapel given by myselfe and others are in my chapel book folio 3 which with moderation may be valued: £40 0s 0d.

Total cost: £102 7s 4d.

Fig. 20 Wadding's notebook gives details of the building of the chapel at High Street for a total cost of just over one hundred pounds.

HILARY MURPHY

Fig. 21 Members of the Kilmore singers who perform the traditional carols, some composed by Luke Wadding, during the Christmas period. From left: Paddy Busher, Robbie Whelan, Jack Devereux, Liam Sheil, Johnny Devereux.

For Christmass Day

This Christmas day you pray me sing
My Caroll, to our new born King,
A God made man, the Virgin's Son,
The word made flesh, can this be don;
Of me I pray noe more require
Than this great mysterie to admire.

Whom Heaven of Heavens cannot containe,
As scripture doth declare most plaine,
In a pore stable is born this day
Layd in manger wrapt in hay
Of me I pray no more require
Than this great mysterie to admire.

Excerpt from a Christmas carol
composed by Luke Wadding

the church furniture and artefacts. After the defeat of James II at the Boyne, Butler left to join the king on his flight to France, leaving instructions that the castle should be set on fire. However, the Protestants, led by Captain Thomas Knox who, with others, escaped from Wexford jail, declared for King William and held the castle and town against the 'Irish rebels' until the arrival of reinforcements.[50] The political position of the Catholics was now more exposed than ever. After another lost war and viewed with harsh suspicion by the authorities because of their Jacobite sympathies, they were exposed to the full rigour of the Penal Laws.

WEXFORD BOROUGH COUNCIL

Fig. 1   The power of the Corporation (now the Borough Council) is symbolised by the fur-trimmed gowns worn by the members and the maces carried by the town sergeant. The first mention of gowns being granted to citizens of Wexford occurred in 1171 when a group from the town sailed to Pembroke to meet Henry II before his departure for Ireland. They offered to release the imprisoned Robert Fitz Stephen and the king presented them with robes.

Early references to burgesses suggest that Wexford was given a charter shortly after the town was taken over by the Anglo-Normans. In 1171, a deputation of twelve burgesses from Wexford, led by Murchadh Mac Murchada, sailed to Pembroke to meet Henry II before he embarked for Ireland. The king presented expensive robes to the Wexford burgesses to mark the occasion.[1] Burgesses were again recorded at Wexford in 1172 when Henry II's grant to the Templars included 'Agnile, burgess of Wexford, with all his chattels'.[2] These early references to burgesses may have been descriptive rather than legal, as there is no record of a charter at that time. Before Strongbow's successor,

William Marshal, arrived in Ireland in 1200, Wexford had received its first charter from Geoffrey Fitz Robert, Marshal's seneschal. This charter established the administrative structure by which the medieval town was

Privileges granted to the burgesses of Wexford

Burgages held forever at a yearly rent of 1s
Preferential legal treatment
Trial by a jury of equals
Bail before trial
Non-burgesses could only trade in the town with official permission
The right to establish guilds (associations) to organise trade and commerce
Freedom from tolls throughout the kingdom
No permission required to arrange marriages
The right to dispose of property
Use of the lord's mills at a reduced rate
Commonage in the lord's woods outside the town wall

WESTMINSTER ABBEY

Fig. 2 William Marshal's great grandson, the French–English nobleman Aymer de Valence (1275–1324), earl of Pembroke, succeeded as lord of Wexford in 1296. He granted the town its first surviving charter in 1317. His magnificent tomb and effigy can be seen in Westminster Abbey.

governed, but it has not survived. It is referred to in a later charter granted in 1317, and it is also mentioned in a charter to New Ross of *c.*1285.[3] Wexford had certainly received a charter by the end of the century, as Tintern Abbey's charter, granted by Marshal about 1200, gave the abbey a burgage in the town.[4] Wexford's first surviving charter dates from 1317, and was granted by Aymer de Valence, Earl of Pembroke, who succeeded to the Lordship of Wexford through his father's marriage to a Marshal heiress.[5]

These provisions formed the basis for further charters issued over the following five centuries. In 1411, Henry IV granted a new charter, adding to the privileges of the previous one. A charter from Edward IV added some further provisions. These included a direction that all forestallers (anyone buying goods outside the town gates) should be arrested and, if convicted, should be jailed and fined. The sovereign was to set the cost of bread and beer and anyone found guilty of price-fixing would be imprisoned or pilloried. No foreigner was allowed to buy skins inside the town and burgesses were exempted from expeditions against the king's enemies.[6]

Following the Act of Resumption in 1536, by which the king resumed possession of all the powers of the independent Palatinate lords, the situation in Wexford remained unchanged, as Henry VIII issued a charter to the town confirming all its privileges and liberties. In 1590, a ratification by Elizabeth I of previous charters contained extra directives including permission to use the punishment of the ducking-stool and stocks. An order that the residents should be armed and drilled was a response to the disturbed nature of the county at that time.[7] In a charter granted by James I in 1609, the sovereign is referred to as the mayor, and Maudlintown and Killiane are described as being part of the liberties of the town. Corporation lands were held in openfields up to that time, as permission was granted to the mayor to divide the commons of the town into enclosures surrounded by ditches and hedges, in an early reference to seventeenth-century land enclosure. In 1687, James II granted Wexford a charter but this was annulled after he was deposed by William of Orange.[8] Throughout the centuries, Aymer de Valence's charter of 1317 remained the basic blueprint by which the administration of Wexford was regulated. Subsequent versions made minor adjustments in response to political and economic expediency.

Following the passing of the Irish Municipal Corporation Bill in 1841, Wexford was deprived of its Corporation, because it had less than 12,000 inhabitants within the borough. Strenuous efforts by local politicians obtained a new Charter of Incorporation for the town, but with greatly reduced powers. Almost all of the land formerly held by the Corporation had been alienated into private ownership.[9] The town boundary delineated at that time still defines the jurisdiction of the Corporation, now referred to as the Borough Council.

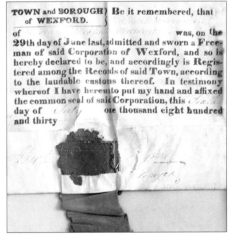

WEXFORD BOROUGH COUNCIL

Fig. 3 A freeman's certificate from the 1830s. Conferred initially only on residents of the borough, landlords from around the county, who had residences in Wexford, were making freemen of men from their estates to strengthen their political support in the town in the eighteenth and nineteenth centuries.

EIGHTEENTH-CENTURY WEXFORD: RECOVERY AND REPRESSION

The upheaval in land ownership, demographic patterns and religious structures during the seventeenth century generated intense social and cultural trauma as the native elite was swept aside. Society was dominated by a new, Protestant and British landed class which would monopolise the economic, political and social pinnacle of Ireland for two centuries. From the end of the seventeenth century, restructuring the landscape revolved around initiatives prompted by the new estate owners. These included a phase of house, demesne and village building, agricultural and infrastructural development, the exploitation of natural resources, and settlement reorganisation. The Catholic community, at a low ebb after two failed rebellions, was viewed with suspicion by the authorities as potential supporters of the Jacobite cause. After the turbulence and suffering of the seventeenth century, the quieter eighteenth century was a period of gradual recovery for Wexford, as the resilient old inhabitants adapted to their drastically changed circumstances.

As conditions in the town improved, the new Protestant owners refurbished old streets in the town by building new houses. They were joined in this venture by the landed class from around the county who regarded a base in the town as a social, economic and political asset. This impetus led to investment in Wexford's infrastructure during the last decades of the century. However, the town's progress was built on volatile social and political foundations. Forged over two centuries of discrimination and inequality, the frustration and anger of Irish Catholics led to an ever increasing level of political activity and was given sharper definition by the new enlightened doctrine of equality and justice which sparked the American and French revolutions. By the end of the century, this doctrine had won support across class and religious boundaries. Wexford county and town were centre-stage in the ensuing catastrophic confrontation with the hard-line administration.

In the early years of the eighteenth century, a Penal Code was enacted, directed at the Catholic religion but also designed to deprive Catholics in perpetuity of political and economic power which might lead to the recovery of their confiscated estates.[1] Although Catholics were prohibited from the professions and public life, no concerted effort was made to exclude them from the provisions trade and it was in this area that urban Catholic wealth grew, particularly in port towns like Wexford.

Fig. 1   A late eighteenth-century perspective of Ferrycarrig from up-river by Gabriel Beranger, shortly before the construction of the bridge. The road approaching the ferry can be seen to the right of the castle. The illustration of the traditional ring-netting method used for fishing salmon is of particular interest. One end of the net having been anchored on the shore, the other end was pulled out in a semi-circle by the boat on the left and then hauled back to shore by the men on the right, trapping any fish that had been caught in the loop.

Fig. 2 Nicholas Sweetman, of Newbawn, appointed bishop of Ferns in 1745, ushered in the start of a new era for the Catholic church in the diocese. He built a fine house in Back Street (High Street) which still survives. His rosary beads (inset), a memento of Salamanca where he studied, is preserved by the Sweetman family.

Fig. 3 This substantial house built by Bishop Sweetman in Back (High) Street has been divided into two modern dwelling houses.

Fig. 4 The holy water font inside the main door of the Franciscan Friary has a dedication to Fr Peter Colfer, a member of the community in 1771.

THE PENAL LAWS

The implementation of the Penal Laws climaxed in the first two decades of the eighteenth century but by 1730 had relaxed somewhat, even though the 1697 Act of Banishment – directed against the clergy – was still in force. Somewhat paradoxically during the same period, essential Catholic ecclesiastical structures and religious practice were established along Tridentine lines, and by 1730 there was a rudimentary parochial system in county Wexford.[2] In 1731, a report on the state of 'Popery' in the county recorded thirty mass-houses, ten recently built, and ten temporary altars.[3] The heaviest concentration of temporary altars was in the barony of Forth south of Wexford town, a strong indication that the construction of mass-houses was forbidden by the predominantly Cromwellian landlords of small estates in this region.

The appointment of Nicholas Sweetman of Newbawn as bishop of Ferns in 1745 ushered in a new era for the Catholic church in the diocese. A man of great leadership ability and a staunch Stuart supporter, he orchestrated diocesan affairs for almost half a century.[4] Initially obliged to live unobtrusively in lodgings in Back (High Street), he later built a house there which is still occupied. The revived state of the Church at mid century in Wexford, where the friary served as the parish church, is an indication of progress made under his stewardship.[5] There were six priests in the town: three Franciscans, the bishop and his two assistants. There were six masses on Sundays, one with sung vespers, and three on week-days. Sharing the friary as a parish church led to constant friction between the bishop and the friars, an irritant that persisted during his episcopate. Unlike his predecessors, who were interred in the friary, the bishop was buried in the Sweetman plot in Clongeen graveyard after his death in 1786.

URBAN EXPANSION

There is very little evidence for expansion in the town during the early years of the century. A bill for the improvement of Wexford Harbour, submitted to

Books contain some information relating to income from the port.[7] For example, every oyster boat had to contribute a proportion of its catch to the Corporation; ships were fined 40s for throwing ballast into the harbour and the Corporation leased out Common Quay to a private individual. Anne Street postdates the coronation of Queen Anne in 1702. It leads from the Main Street to the Quays, possibly constructed along the route of an existing lane. It was never a residential street but a centre of business, as it still is at the present time. The only major event was the demolition of the medieval castle in the 1720s, and the construction of a military barracks on the site. In 1731, the

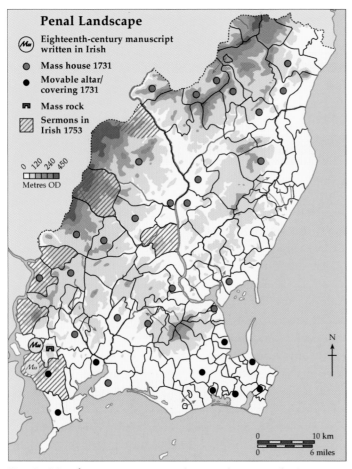

Fig. 5 Mass-houses, temporary altars and mass-rocks in county Wexford in 1771. The concentration of moveable altars in the barony of Forth indicate that the landlords in this area were active supporters of the Penal Code. The medieval parish layout shown here (now referred to as civil parishes) was abandoned after the Reformation, and the Catholic and Protestant churches organised dual parochial systems which bore little relationship to the obsolete medieval divisions.

stones from the castle were used to build the church at Killinick.[8] A visitor's account in 1748 describes the town as having 'some handsome buildings' with the walls 'so broad that a coach might drive upon them', and gates still in use. He described a mineral well or spa, covered by a small structure, outside the Westgate, which attracted

Fig. 6 In the 1720s, Wexford's medieval castle was knocked and was replaced by a military barracks. The barracks (at top) with surrounding wall is shown in this detail from an 1820 painting of the town.

many visitors to the town, but not as many as formerly.[9] Some of these wells survive in what is now Spawell Road. The spa was popular in the late seventeenth century and early eighteenth centuries; visitors included satirical writer Jonathan Swift and his friend 'Stella'.[10] In spite of economic progress, the underlying volatility in the town was highlighted by an incident that occurred in 1757. Because of a fear of impending famine, with ensuing high prices, a protest against the exportation of corn and foodstuffs led to 'riots and disturbances'. A 'very audacious and insolent mob' of several hundred committed outrages by 'stripping ships of their sails [presumably to stop them from leaving port] and breaking open granaries and houses'. Rather surprisingly, there were no soldiers stationed in the barracks and the town officials requested that the army should be sent in to 'quell the mob and protect lives and property'. The threat of famine was real, as the corn merchants agreed to put one barrel of corn, from every

Fig. 7 A detail from the 1820 picture showing a troop of cavalry from Wexford barracks escorting a coach across Wexford's new bridge.

Fig. 8 This detail from the 1820 painting illustrates the spread of villas at the north end of the town. The harbour at the bottom of the gardens was reclaimed in the late nineteenth century and is now occupied by houses, a road and a railway. A coach and four is shown on Spawell Road. The location of Kaat's shipyard can be seen at left centre. The precise depiction of a Slaney gabbard (with the single sail) is of particular interest.

merchants agreed to put one barrel of corn, from every twenty exported, in a storehouse, to be sold in small quantities to 'the poor of the town', and that no meal, potatoes, wheat, eggs or fowl would be shipped out.[11]

The regeneration of Wexford during the later part of the century led to an upsurge of house building by increasingly successful business families. A further dimension was the decision of some ascendancy families in the county to build or acquire town houses, principally for social or political reasons. These houses were concentrated on the modern Main Street, Selskar Street, Monck Street and George's Street. At that time, business

Fig. 9 The reputation of the spa waters in Wexford was widely acclaimed. Visitors included satirical writer Jonathan Swift and his enigmatic friend 'Stella', both referring to the spa in correspondence.

Fig.10 In the late seventeenth and early eighteenth centuries, mineral wells or spas outside the Westgate attracted many visitors to the town. The remains of these wells survive in what is now Spawell Road.

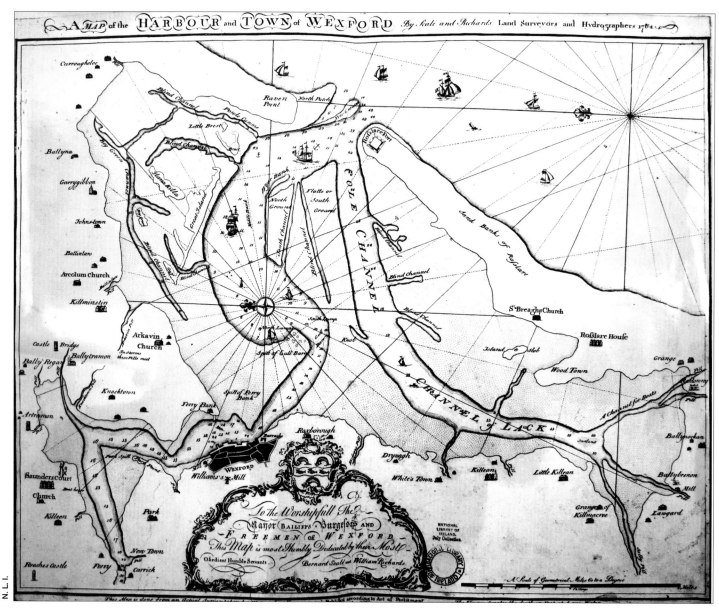

Fig. 11   In an obvious effort to encourage the use of the port by shipping, the mayor and freemen commissioned Scalé and Richards, 'land surveyors and hydrographers', to produce this chart of the harbour in 1764. The chart is extremely detailed, showing channels, depth in feet, islands and sandbanks. It includes many landscape features which were used as navigation aids, including castles, churches, houses and windmills. An outline of the town shows a windmill on Windmill Hill, the recently-built barracks and the uneven nature of the waterfront. The chart, possibly the first which focused exclusively on the harbour, highlighted the daunting challenge presented by the hazardous approach to the port, particularly on a first visit.

premises were clustered in Cornmarket and Back Street. High-profile county families included the Marquis of Ely of Loftus Hall (Church Lane); the Colcloughs of Tintern Abbey and the Harveys of Bargy Castle (George's Street); the de Rinzeys of Clobemon House (Westgate House) and the Tottenhams of Tottenham Green (Bullring).[12]

Although Catholics were prominent in business, political life in the town was monopolised by the Protestant minority.[13] The acquisition of a dwelling in the town ensured that members of county ascendancy families became freemen, with the potential for political advancement. The admission of freemen was historically based on 'continued habitation' but this was

subsequently widened by qualifications of birth, apprenticeship and marriage. The process was further diluted in 1662 by an 'Act for encouraging Protestant strangers and others to inhabit and plant in the kingdom of Ireland', which made it easy for Protestants to become freemen of towns in which they resided. As only freemen had voting rights, they were pivotal to the political control of the town, particularly in the second half of the eighteenth century when members of the county ascendancy began to use the town as a power base. It became customary for the mayor and burgesses to nominate friends and relations, not necessarily living in the town, as freemen. The political implications of this

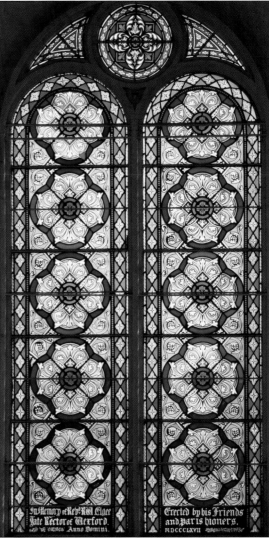

Figs 12–13 St Iberius' church, dedicated to the Early Christian St Ibar of Begerin, was built in the 1760s on the site of the medieval parish church of the same name. The belfry was added in the nineteenth century. The decorative stained-glass east window in St Iberius' church was installed in 1867, in memory of Rev. R. Elgee, rector of Wexford. St Iberius' is the only church with medieval connections within the walled town.

were demonstrated by the mayoral election of 1776: of the 323 freemen who voted, 200 were from the county, 22 from outside the county and a minority of 101 from the town itself. The election was won by the conservative Loftus faction which subsequently dominated politics in the town until Catholic Emancipation in 1829, at the expense of the liberal Grogan/Colclough/Harvey grouping. As it became almost impossible to become a freeman except with the patronage of the dominant Loftus and Neville grouping, they retained control of the town through the strategic appointment of freemen without any regard to their place of residence. This devious system was typified by 'Lord Ely's Fethard freemen', a group of small farmers and fishermen from the Loftus estate who were created freemen of Wexford solely to vote as directed by their landlord.[14] Not surprisingly, the exclusion of the Catholic community

from the political process resulted in the emergence, at a national level, of pressure groups, some (such as the rural based Whiteboys) operating as secret societies. Other associations, most notably the Catholic Committee, frequently supported by displaced Catholic gentry, were dedicated to achieving civil rights through exclusively political means.[15] In 1830, a select committee enquiry into complaints about illegal electoral practices in Wexford revealed the extent of the corruption and determined that only residents and apprentices in the town should be admitted as freemen, but by that time the Corporation was no longer dominated by a Protestant minority.[16]

A description of Wexford written by Amyas Griffiths in 1764 portrays a town that was still medieval in some respects but also recognisable to the modern reader.[17] The town is defined very much in the context of the wall, with the Main Street running from the Barrack Gate in the south to the

Amyas Griffiths' description of Wexford in 1764

Before Cromwell's time [Wexford town] was well enclosed, part of the walls are yet standing, with four gates, one at each quarter of the town. The Main Street from the Westgate to the Barrack Gate is about three-quarters of a mile in length. Outside of the Westgate is a fine spa, reckoned by skilful physicians to be an infallible cure for many disorders, among others the scurvy, gout and decay. It creates an appetite and certainly dispels melancholy, etc. Beyond the South [Barrack] Gate stands the barrack, a large, low building forming a little square. I have heard that it can contain four companies completely. From this barrack runs a very broad street upwards of a mile in length named the Fierth, commonly styled Faith. The cabins which compose this suburb or outlet are very snug and commodious, and the dwellers are a set of the most industrious people on the earth. Their employments are mostly weaving nets or spinning hemp.

In the midst or heart of the Main Street is the Bullring, where the courthouse, with an excellent clock, etc., stands. About fifty yards from the courthouse, southwards, is the new church, which (when finished) in miniature will come nigh in beautiful structure, workmanship, materials, etc., to any in Dublin. Between the church and the barracks, a little above the Jews Bridge, lies the gaol. It is but ordinary, yet built exceeding

strong, with a courtyard, etc. In John Street, north-west of the town, is the chapel; it is one of the prettiest I have ever seen, with a friary, garden, etc., belonging to it. The chapel yard is esteemed the best walk about the town. We have a prodigious number of other streets, lanes and quays, as the Flesh Market, Cornmarket, Back Street, Shambles, Kaiser's Lane, Ferryboat Quay, Meadow's Quay, Bennett's Quay, the Common Quay, Gibson's Lane, the Custom House Quay, which is the chief or principal of all the other quays, half of which I have not mentioned. The Custom House quay is small, but vastly pretty, with seats all round, a good warm watch house, and an excellent custom house, with convenient stores, etc.

I procured the number of houses in the town and suburbs from a collector of the hearth money who told me that there were exactly to a house, 1300, and in the confines of the walls 650 slated houses. For ale and oysters Wexford is noted as having the best on earth. The chief exports are corn, which annually exceeds upwards of 2,000,000 [possibly exaggerated] barrels, herrings, beer, beef, hides, tallow, butter, etc., and they trade to all parts of the globe, but in particular to Liverpool, Barbados, Dublin, Norway and Bordeux. Wexford imports brandy, rums, sugars, wines, dyestuffs, porter, fruit of all foreign kinds, salt, timber and hops. Wexford is as celebrated for its fine women as its beer and oysters.

Westgate in the north. Griffiths mentions only some of 'a prodigious number' of streets, lanes and quays, including names (Bullring, Cornmarket, Kayser's Lane, Common Quay) that are still in use. He refers to some public buildings: the courthouse in the Bullring; the gaol at Jews' Bridge (Stonebridge); the friary church ('the prettiest I have ever seen'), and St Iberius' church which was then in construction. Half of the 1,300 houses were outside the walls, showing that the town had extended well beyond its medieval boundary. He particularly noticed the suburb of the Faythe, where 'the very broad street' was lined with 'very snug and commodious cabins' and the inhabitants, 'the most industrious people on earth' who were mostly employed 'weaving nets and spinning hemp'. His detailed account of the spa well indicates that it was an important feature, social as well as medical, in the life of the town at that time. His final comment that 'Wexford is as celebrated for its fine women as for its beer and oysters' possibly gives an insight into his personal memories of the town!

His comments on shipping and trade depict a bustling, cosmopolitan port, exporting mostly fish and agricultural produce and importing luxury goods. The description of Wexford ships trading with 'all parts of the world' echoes the account of 1680 which mentioned 'the exquisite

knowledge of the natives in the art of navigation', many of them having crossed the ocean 'to the most remote regions and coasts', emphasising the role played by the sea in the

Fig. 14 The seal of the Corporation set up in 1788 to improve the harbour. It later became the Ballast Office of the Port of Wexford.

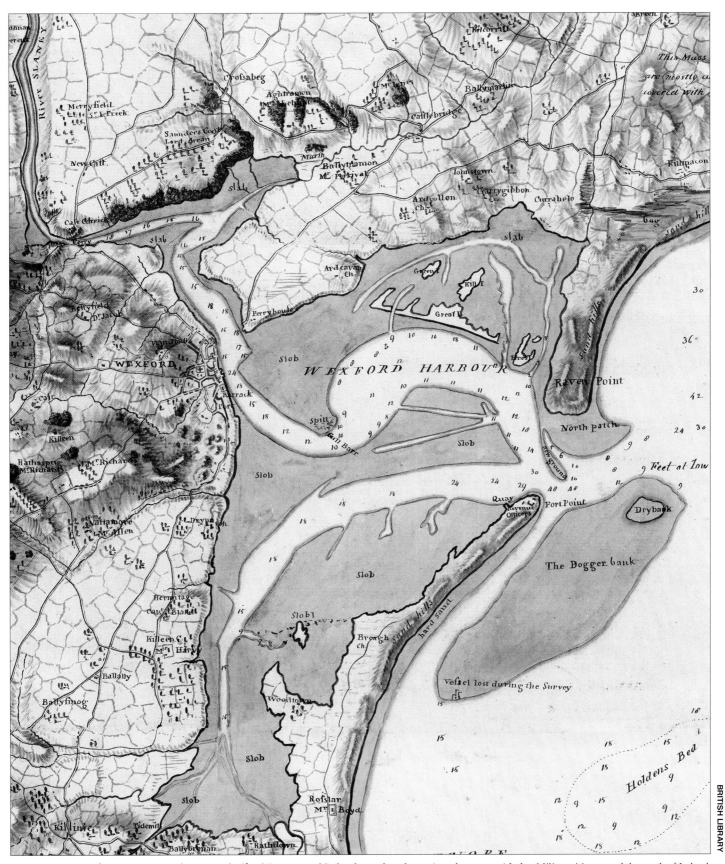

Fig. 15   In 1776, Charles Vallancey (1725–1812), Chief Engineer of Ireland, produced a series of maps entitled a *Military itinerary of the south of Ireland*, identifying strategic military locations, including this very fine map of Wexford Harbour and hinterland. The bar, channels, depths and islands are shown. The map actually shows the site of a vessel wrecked during the survey. On land, locations of big houses and demesnes are included, possibly as sources of supplies for the military. A bog and sandhills at Curracloe could mark the existence of a previous entrance to the harbour.

N. L. I.

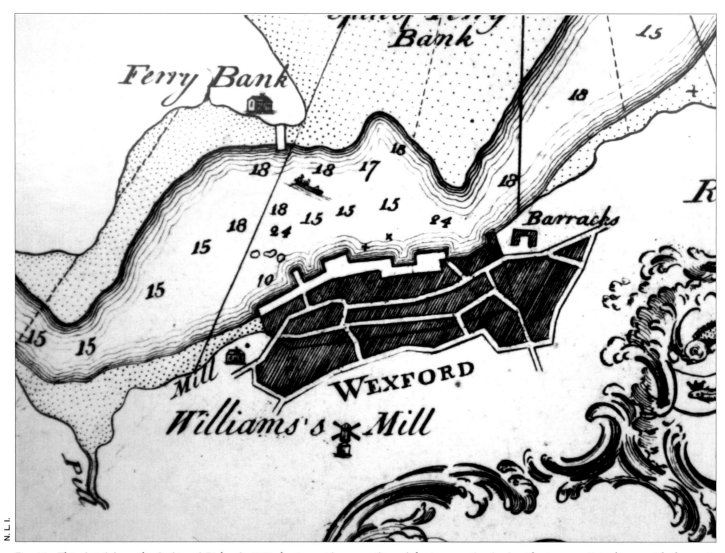

Fig. 16   This detail from the Scalé and Richards 1764 chart provides an outline of the town and suburbs. The town wall is shown with the roads leading from the town gates. The road leading to the ferry quay is also included, with the ferryboat crossing to a pier and inn on the Ferrybank side. A water-mill is placed just outside Westgate, also Williams's mill, presumably at Windmill Hill. The waterfront has projecting jetties with the deepest water shown at what is now Crescent Quay. The position of rocks in the harbour, presenting a hazard to shipping, are also recorded.

life of the town. Wexford's maritime tradition was epitomised by John Barry, who sailed for Philadelphia as a young man. During the American War of Independence, he became known as 'the father of the American navy'.[18]

In the last quarter of the century, initiatives to improve infrastructure indicate that the town was experiencing expansion and economic growth. In 1772 a Quay Corporation, the original Harbour Authority, was set up with full responsibilities for shipping, quays and harbour with all passages leading to them. In the same year a Bridge Corporation was set up, consisting of a group of subscribers who would contribute to the building of a bridge across the Slaney, a project that was completed more than twenty years later. An application to the government in 1781 for the removal of John's Gate indicates an increased volume of traffic from the hinterland. Ten years later, the tower beside the gate was

leased by the corporation (and presumably demolished) for the purpose of widening the street.[19] The other town gates were also presumably removed at this time. The

WEXFORD COUNTY LIBRARY

Fig. 17   A townhouse known as Castle House or Taylor's Castle, built in the eighteenth century at Castle Hill, to the south-east of the town.

N. L. I.

Fig. 18   In 1764, the suburb of the Faythe was described as a 'very broad street lined with very snug and commodious cabins' where the inhabitants, 'the most industrious people on earth', were mostly employed 'weaving nets and spinning hemp'. The maritime connection was further indicated by four rope walks and a lane known as Fishers' Row. This late nineteenth-century photograph shows the broad street with some of the original thatched houses.

removal of the gates may also have been related to the growth of the town beyond the walls. In 1788, it contained 1,412 houses, with 9,178 occupants, an increase of 112 houses on the number recorded for 1764. An expanding town placed more demands on the administration and concerns were raised about the lack of price regulation, especially on essential items such as coal, meat and bread. Efforts were also made to improve the environment by keeping the streets 'free from dung, rubbish, filth and other obstructions, and preventing swine from going at large therein'.[20] Directives in 1793 give the Corporation power to 'remove all encroachments, or nuisances whatsoever, as well as doors, stairs, or cellars projecting into the streets or lanes, or of shop windows or windows shutters, frames, pent-houses, sheds, or standings, in or upon such streets or lanes, as also of sinks or uncovered sewers from kitchens or from malt-houses, breweries or distilleries, in such manner as the corporation shall think fit or expedient'.[21] These regulations portray a crowded town, teeming with people involved in domestic and industrial activity of all kinds which, because of the

WEXFORD COUNTY LIBRARY

Fig. 19   A company dominated by the liberal wing in the town was formed in 1794 to construct a bridge across the Slaney. The contract was given to Lemuel Cox, from Boston, who completed the work in 1795.

John Barry 'father of the American navy'

John Barry, born about 1745, was a member of a barony of Forth sea-faring family. The place of his birth is a matter of conjecture but it is known that his parents were buried in the church at Rosslare. The family must have been reasonably well off as the young Barry received a good education, possibly in Wexford town. As a young man of fourteen, he sailed for Philadelphia in the United States where he may have had family connections. He went to sea as a cabin boy but rapidly rose through the ranks to command his first ship in his early twenties. An expert navigator, he quickly acquired a reputation as a skillful and successful mariner and was given a series of high-profile commands. On the outbreak of the revolutionary war, Barry was assigned the task of outfitting the navy ships that put to sea from Philadelphia. He was also given a captain's commission in the Continental Navy and command of the brig *Lexington*. Barry had a highly successful naval career during the war, commanding a number of ships. He wrote a signal book in 1780 to improve communications at sea. In 1783, in the final naval battle of the American Revolution, commanding the *Alliance* in the Gulf of Mexico, he defeated an English ship named the *Sybil*.

After the War of Independence, Barry returned to maritime trading until 1797, when the navy was revived on a permanent basis and he was appointed senior captain in the Federal Navy by his friend, President Washington. Commanding the forty-four gun frigate the *United States*, Barry served as squadron commander of the fleet for the next seven years, holding the courtesy title of Commodore. He died at a relatively young age in 1803 and was given a full military burial in Philadelphia. Because of his outstanding contribution over seventeen years, he became known as 'the father of the American navy'. Four U. S. navy ships have been named in his honour. Statues of Barry stand in front of Independence Hall in Philadelphia (erected in 1908) and in Franklin Square, Washington (erected in 1914).

In 1956, a bronze statue of John Barry, presented to the town of Wexford by the American navy, was erected on the Crescent Quay in Wexford town. It was viewed by President John F. Kennedy during his emotional visit to Ireland in 1963 where he was greeted by large crowds in his ancestral county of Wexford. The Barry connection is marked annually by a wreath laying ceremony. Much remains to be discovered about the Wexford background of the Barry family. Wexford County Library has recently acquired a cache of Barry records from Philadelphia.

Fig. 20 The Market House and Assembly Rooms was constructed at Cornmarket in 1775. The ground floor originally had arched openings, giving direct access from the street to the market area; the first floor had a large ballroom and supper room to facilitate the social life of the many ascendancy families who had houses in the town. It was used for a period during the twentieth century as the Town Hall and is now the vibrant Wexford Arts Centre.

confined space, spilled out into the narrow streets and lanes with obvious implications for health and sanitation. Efforts to improve the situation were not immediately effective, as several years later it was observed that 'the health of the inhabitants would be much improved by removing nuisances in the town'. Some development was taking place; in 1793, Allen Street, a new, wider street constructed by Robert Allen between Patrick's Square and the Main Street, was paved by the corporation.[22]

By 1788, Wexford, with forty-four ships, was the sixth busiest port in Ireland.[23] The presence of 200 herring boats added to the congestion in the harbour.[24] The county had become one of Ireland's principal grain producing regions and numerous small ships were employed in carrying malt to the Dublin breweries and distilleries, from the 210 malt-houses in the town.[25] Because of the dangerous entrance to the harbour, many ships had been damaged or wrecked, with obvious detrimental consequences for the commercial

Fig. 21   By the end of the eighteenth century, Wexford town was among the top malt-producing centres in the country. Much of the malt was brought by ship from malt-houses in the town to Dublin breweries.

JOHN HAYES

Fig. 22 A new Tholsel was constructed in 1794, on the narrow site of the old courthouse at the southern junction of the Bullring and the Main Street. The upper storey contained offices for the mayor and town clerk as well as the court of conscience. The ground floor, which had archways opening on to the Bullring, accommodated the fish market. This photograph shows the building in the late nineteenth century.

life of the port and a number of bills were introduced to improve facilities. A body with its own seal, called the Corporation for Improving the Town and Harbour of Wexford, was appointed to enhance the harbour by deepening the channel and building quays along the waterfront from Ferryboat Quay in the north to Paul Quay in the south. The group then became the Ballast Office of the Port of Wexford, with full powers to regulate shipping, to improve the harbour and to build quays, wharves and docks.[26] This initiative began the process which led to the creation of the unified modern waterfront.

A significant economic and social initiative led to the construction of the market house (now the Arts Centre) in Cornmarket in 1775. The ground floor originally had arched openings, giving direct access from the street to the market area. The first floor had a large ballroom and supper room to facilitate the social life of the many ascendancy families who had houses in the town. The most dramatic project began in 1794, when a Company of Shareholders was set up to build wooden bridges across the Slaney at Wexford and up-river at Ferrycarrig. The constitution of this company was political as it was controlled by the liberal grouping in the town, perhaps an indication that they were more forward thinking and progressive than their conservative opponents. Some of the members were later involved on the rebel side in the 1798 Rebellion. Evidence for a growing prosperous Catholic merchant class in the town is provided by the company membership, where they were heavily represented; the sole requirement was a substantial subscription.[27] This company was more dynamic and successful than its predecessor in the 1770s; a subscription

R.I.A.

Fig. 23   This drawing of c. 1850 by George Victor Du Noyer shows the timber bridge at Ferrycarrig, completed in 1795. An access road has been quarried through the rock to the left of the fifteenth-century Roche castle, built to command the river and the ferry crossing.

Shareholders in Wexford Bridge, 1794

Cornelius Grogan	£1,000	Loftus Richards	£200	John Colclough	£100
Miss Hatchell	£1,000	Matthew Keugh	£200	James Harvey	£100
Right Hon. Marquis of Ely	£500	Christopher Taylor	£200	William Hatton	£100
Beauchamp Bagenal Harvey	£500	Arthur Leared	£200	Matthew Hughes	£100
Thomas Grogan Knox	£500	Mrs Eliza Hatton	£200	Richard Waddy M.D.	£100
Arthur Meadows	£500	Robert Sparrow	£200	John Couzens	£100
William Kearney	£500	Nicholas Dixon	£200	Henry Gird	£100
Richard Neville	£500	John Grogan	£100	Richard Gainfort	£100
John Cardiff	£500	Ebenezer Jacob	£100	William Hughes	£100
Charles Stanley Monck	£500	Patrick Prendergast	£100	Miss Bridget Corish	£100
Robert Carty	£500	Rev. William Eastwood	£100	Miss Margaret Corish	£100
Mrs Mary Hobbs	£500	John Johnstone	£100	Andrew Rock	£100
Anthony Lee	£500	Ambrose Hughes	£100	Mrs Dorothy Archer	£100
Miss Mar[y]anne Carty	£500	Patrick Keating	£100	Mrs Fisher	£100
James E. Devereux	£400	Miss Mary Corish	£100	Thomas Richards	£100
John Lightburne	£300	Nathaniel Hughes	£100	John Redmond	£100
Narcissus Huson	£200	John Cullimore	£100	Nicholas Sinnott	£100
Miller Clifford	£200	Thomas Jones	£100	William Boxwell	£100
John Connick	£200	William Archer	£100	John Hay	£100
Robert Mayler	£200	William Devereux	£100	George Lacy	£100
Christopher Richards	£200	John Pettit	£100	**Total**	**£15,000**

The 'First Rebellion'

WEXFORD COUNTY LIBRARY

In 1793, following a protest over the payment of tithes, two men were lodged in Wexford gaol. A large number of protestors converged on the town to demand their release. They were confronted at Windmill Hill by fifty soldiers, led by Major Charles Valottin. Valottin and John Moore, the leader of the protestors, came forward to negotiate but when Valottin observed one of his officers being held by the protestors, he plunged his sword into Moore. Moore struck Valottin with a scythe and both men fell to the ground, mortally wounded. The military immediately opened fire and many protestors were killed. Others, while fleeing, were killed by a military patrol at Bettyville. Five more were captured hiding in a hayloft and hanged on Windmill Hill. The shock of the incident reverberated through town and county and helped to generate the momentum that culminated in the Rebellion of 1798. The Corporation erected an obelisk to Valottin at Windmill Hill and he was also commemorated by a church memorial.

Fig. 24   The memorial in St Iberius' Church reads: *Sacred to the memory of Charles Vallotton Esq., a major in the army and a captain in the 56th regiment of infantry. Who, in the suburbs on the eleventh day of July, 1793, when zealously co-operating with the civil power in support of the mild and beneficent laws of his country, received a mortal wound from a savage hand. Thus untimely fell this accomplished gentleman, not less admired and beloved for every social quality than he was eminently distinguished on every occasion by the enterprise and gallantry of a soldier. Reader lament with every good man the irreparable loss and strive to emulate his many virtues. The Corporation of Wexford, with becoming gratitude, erected this monument to perpetuate their high respect for his inestimable character.*

Fig. 25 Very little commercial development took place in Wexford during the eighteenth century. The Corporation was dominated by estate owners who had residences in the town but whose economic interests lay elsewhere. Their principal contribution was the construction of town houses, principally along the Main Street and in George's Street. As Catholic businessmen gained more influence towards the end of the century, the pace of development began to quicken with the building of the Assembly Rooms, the construction of the bridge and an initiative made to improve the quays.

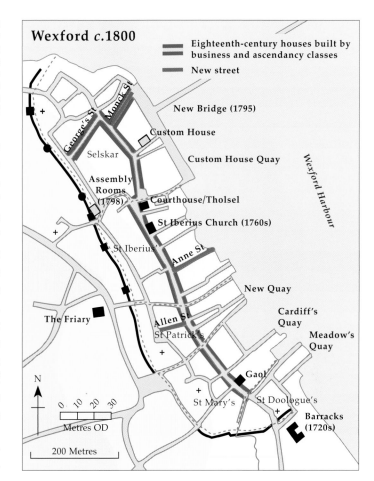

list was opened to raise £12,000 for the Wexford bridge and £7,000 for Ferrycarrig. A committee of nine, with Cornelius Grogan as chairman, supervised the project. The contract was awarded to Lemuel Cox, an engineer from Boston, who completed the Wexford bridge in 1795; the Ferrycarrig structure was completed shortly afterwards. The other significant development in the town was the construction of a new Tholsel in 1794 on the site of the old courthouse at the southern junction of the Bullring and the Main Street. The upper storey contained offices for the mayor and town clerk as well as the court of conscience. The ground floor, which had archways opening on to the Bullring, accommodated the fish market.[28] The Marquis of Ely's contribution consisted of the erection of a fountain in Cornmarket in 1795.[29] It was later moved to the Bullring where it remained until the late nineteenth century.

Wexford had been relatively isolated from civil disorder and violent confrontations during the eighteenth century

---

At a General Quarter Sessions, held at Wexford, the 12th day of January, 1791

Whereas divers nuisances have been permitted to remain on, or near to, the highways, in the neighbourhood of Wexford, to the very great annoyance of passengers, and in particular to the inhabitants of said town. Now, in order more efficiently to have nuisances removed, and to prevent the like offences in future, we, the undernamed magistrates, presiding at said quarter sessions, do give public notice, that we will immediately put into strict force the several statutes against nuisances, and will punish, to the utmost rigour of the law, all persons offending against the said statutes, and do pledge ourselves to support all persons legally acting against them; and that no person may in future plead ignorance, the following abstract of statutes, particularly relating to nuisances, is hereby annexed.

After forty-eight hours notice to occupiers of land or houses to remove dunghills, dirt, rubbish, or any other nuisances opposite the same, or to make sewers for water to pass, on complaint of neglect, shall, for every such offence, forfeit 20s.

Every person who shall lay any turf, dung, dirt, rubbish, or the scouring of any ditches or drains, or other filth, or any stones or timber, upon any part of any road, or within twenty-one feet of the centre of the road, or dig any pit, or make any ditch, or build any wall that may encroach on any road, or leave any car or cart in the night-time, from sunset to sunrise, on any part of any road, or in the streets of any city or town, or winnow any corn on any road or street, or skin or leave the carcass of any dead horse, mule, or ass, within one hundred yards of the centre of any road, or scrape the gravel off any road, shall, upon conviction by oath of one credible witness, or on the view of any magistrate, forfeit 10s. And any turf, dung, dirt, straw, rubbish, corn-filth, or scouring of ditches or drains, or stones which shall be found laid upon any part of any road, any person may take and carry away the same, and apply it to his own use, without being sued or prosecuted for so doing.

The inhabitants of the town and vicinity of Wexford may be assured that all legal complaints, for the removal of the abovementioned nuisances, will be pointedly attended to in Wexford by the Mayor, and on all presented roads, by the subscribing Magistrates.

Isaac Cornock, B[ostock] R[adford] Jacob, Mayor, Matthew Keugh, Ebenezer Jacob, Richard Newton King, Henry Hatton, John Grogan, Cornelius Grogan

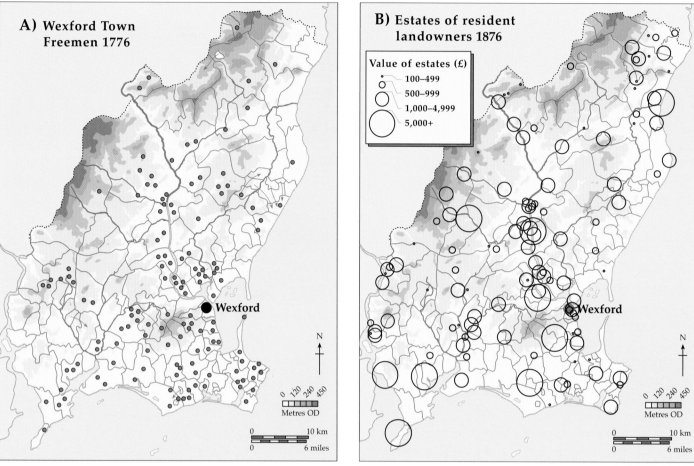

Fig. 26   A) Originally based on residency in Wexford, by the late eighteenth century the office of freeman was being exploited for political reasons. Powerful landlords from around the county made freemen of their tenants as a means of gaining a political power-base for themselves in the town. B) There was a noticeable concentration of estates on the beautiful stretch of the Slaney flowing between Enniscorthy and Wexford town. Gentry family from these estates sustained the social life of Wexford town in the eighteenth century. Town houses were financed by a spike in rents in the second half of the century. This surge lasted until 1815 and generated considerable income for the ascendancy class.

until, in the growing instability of the 1790s, the tragic episode already described took place in 1793 at Windmill Hill, just outside the town. The incident became known as

'the first Rebellion' and initiated a sequence of events that culminated in the Rebellion of 1798.[30] This rebellion became the defining event in the history of county Wexford.

Corn complex at Peter's Street (Gibson's Lane)

THE 1798 REBELLION: A WEXFORD TOWN PERSPECTIVE

The Catholic elite, dispossessed in the 1650s, continued as an 'underground' gentry, either as tenants on the lands which they had previously owned, or in exile on the continent.[1] After the war of William and James, they were viewed with suspicion as Stuart sympathisers in league with England's Catholic enemies on the continent. However, not all of the dispossessed Catholic gentry class left for Europe. Many remained as tenants and middlemen and the political leadership which they provided during the Jacobite phase was frequently carried through to the United Irishmen. When the dismantling of the Penal Laws began in 1778, the Jacobite claims to land ownership were abandoned by the upper ranks of Catholic society,

backed by the Catholic Church because of fears of the 'French disease' which had decimated the Church in France. The universal ideas of liberty, equality and justice ignited revolutions in America and France and were the inspiration behind the establishment of the United Irishmen in Belfast in 1791, with the principal aim of overthrowing a political system based on sectarian privilege and replacing it with a secular democracy. These events, combined with the frustration and bitterness generated in the Catholic community during two centuries of social, economic and religious exclusion, generated intense upheaval during the crucial last decade of the eighteenth century. The merging of the United Irishmen with the more

militant Defenders in 1795 was greeted with alarm and led to the foundation of the Orange Order to protect loyalist interests. A campaign of military terror initiated by the authorities caused a state of turmoil. At the end of May 1798, the country, and in particular county Wexford, rose in bloody rebellion. Although not directly involved in the initial stages of the rebellion, Wexford town quickly became embroiled in the shock waves of this climactic event.

The Rebellion of 1798 has been described as 'the most ferocious civil war in Ireland and one of the most bitter in modern European history'.[2] It seemed anomalous that the Rebellion was most intense in Wexford, a region regarded as quiet and prosperous, but

Fig. 1   In 1998, during the bicentenary commemorations of the Rebellion of 1798, memorials were erected to honour individuals who were involved, and to mark the locations of significant events. This impressive bronze sculpture depicting a group of pikemen is one of the most evocative. It is situated at Barntown, beside the New Ross road, 10km west of Wexford, with the site of the battle of the Three Rocks on Forth Mountain in the background.

Fig. 2   The United Irish banner used the motif of the 'new strung' harp and the cap of freedom.

the reasons can be found in the volatile political and social mix in the county. In south Wicklow and north Wexford, where the most successful Protestant settlement outside of Ulster was located, there was rising tension as competition for property and status between Catholic and Protestant middlemen generated antagonism. The division of the Protestant gentry in Wexford into the hard-line Loftus and more liberal Colclough factions intensified political instability. The United Irish organisation spread into the north of the county and began to recruit. Some members of the more radical Protestant group had links with the north of Wexford, which may explain their interest in and subsequent involvement with the United Irishmen: the Grogans of Johnstown Castle held land in the north and both the Harveys of Bargy Castle and the Colcloughs of Tintern Abbey had links with the family of Miles Byrne of Monaseed, one of the early United Irish leaders in the county. The United Irish organisation in county Wexford remained intact until the eve of the insurrection when Anthony Perry, a leading Protestant United Irishman in the

Gorey area, was arrested and forced under torture to reveal details of the command structure in the county, leading to the arrest of three of the southern leaders, Edward FitzGerald, Bagenal Harvey and John Henry Colclough.[3] Their arrests probably contributed to a delay in mobilisation in the south of the county. Although arms continued to be surrendered – with the encouragement of Bishop Caulfield, the Catholic bishop of Ferns – reports of atrocities by the military in Wicklow and Carlow led to a rapid escalation and on 26 May the rebellion erupted and swept quickly across north Wexford.[4]

News of the Rising was brought to Wexford by Edward Turner of Newfort, near Screen, whose house had been raided for arms, and by loyalist refugees seeking protection. The military in the town was slow to react, partly because a troop of cavalry had gone to Ballyteige to arrest John Henry Colclough. Eventually, a detachment of 120 men of the North Cork Militia, augmented by a small troop of the Shelmalier cavalry, marched north from the town to investigate. Confident that a disciplined force could rout a much larger mob, they

confronted a 2,000 strong rebel force at Oulart Hill. Competently led by Edward Roche and Fr John Murphy, the rebels were completely victorious and only a handful of North Cork survivors arrived back in Wexford.[5] This comprehensive defeat at Oulart Hill, with the loss of so many troops from the Wexford garrison, had serious implications for the defence of the town against rebel attack. News of the defeat sowed panic, leading to talk of evacuation by some loyalists. On 28 May, the confident rebels followed up their victory at Oulart by advancing on Enniscorthy which they took after a stubborn battle with the garrison. This resulted in even more refugees flooding into Wexford, bringing alarming news of rebel successes. It now seemed likely that an attack was imminent. Jonas Watson, a retired officer who had served in the American war, set about organising the defence of the town which had a garrison of 400 North Cork Militia. The town walls were patrolled, thatched cabins near the walls were demolished as a fire risk and the town gates were guarded by artillery pieces. A request for reinforcements from Duncannon Fort resulted in the arrival of 200 troops

Fig. 3   This sketch of the Battle of Ballyellis shows the intimate ferocity of the struggle in 1798.

under Colonel Maxwell, augmented by yeomen from Taghmon. The United Irishmen in the town remained quiet, biding their time until the arrival of the main rebel army. By this time the town was crammed with loyalist refugees. When some sought to escape by ship, the captains, who were United Irishmen, refused to sail. The mood of the loyalists darkened when a group returned with the bodies of the dead from Oulart Hill. In desperation, the military leadership sent Edward FitzGerald and John Colclough to Enniscorthy to plead with the rebels to

Mountain overlooking Wexford, preventing the garrison from retreating to Duncannon or New Ross. The sight of so many rebel camp-fires on the high ground above them caused consternation among the loyalist population. Spirits in the camp must have been high as, at this stage, the United Irish were in a strong position in the county and were not yet aware that the Rising had failed tragically in other counties. In the late evening, a column of 200 troops from Duncannon Fort, led by Colonel Fawcett, advanced slowly up the western slopes of Forth

Fig. 5 Bagenal Harvey was one of the United Irish leaders who was arrested at the start of the Rebellion. He was later freed from Wexford jail and led the rebel army at the battle of Ross.

Furlong. The short action resulted in a total victory for the rebel group and, crucially, included the capture of vital arms and artillery. On hearing of the episode, Fawcett with his panicky troops retreated quickly to Duncannon, depriving Wexford of reinforcements.

The town now faced a further threat from a group of rebels who gathered at Ferrybank on the far side of the harbour where they set fire to

Fig. 4 A late eighteenth-century painting of Bargy Castle, home of Bagenal Harvey. The castle incorporates the fifteenth-century house and hall, built by the Rossiter family, whose principal seat was at Rathmacknee Castle in the barony of Forth. The castle is still occupied as a private dwelling.

disperse. This approach was greeted with contempt by the rebel leadership who detained FitzGerald as a hostage and sent Colclough back with a message demanding the surrender of the town. Colclough was then dispatched to Forth and Bargy to persuade the United Irish forces there not to rise but he went to stay in his home in Ballyteige Castle.

On 29 May, the rebel army of more than 10,000 marched south and camped at the Three Rocks on Forth

Mountain and, unaware that the rebels were already in position a short distance ahead, decided to camp for the night at Taghmon. A second detachment of 100 troops, following behind with the artillery, missed Fawcett's camp in the dark and continued on towards Wexford. The rebel leadership, alerted of their approach, decided that they would be attacked by the Bantry battalion of 1,000 men, led by Thomas Cloney, John Kelly, Robert Carthy and Michael

Fig. 6 Ballyteige castle, near Kilmore, the home of United Irishman, John Henry Colclough. After the Rebellion, Colclough was captured, with Harvey, on the Saltee Islands and both were executed on Wexford Bridge.

the toll-house on the bridge. Although the fire was extinguished by soldiers from the garrison, it made it difficult for loyalists to escape from the town over the damaged bridge. At this point, a troop of 200 men, brought out to look for the over-due reinforcements from Duncannon, was attacked and defeated by the rebels at Belmont, a short distance to the north-west of the town; the American War veteran, Jonas Watson, was one of the fatalities.[6] After this incident the garrison of the town was in disarray. Bagenal Harvey, still in jail, was prevailed upon to write to the rebels asking them to spare the town. When the message had been sent, Maxwell, with the garrison of 1,000 men, abandoned the town, hoping to retreat to Duncannon Fort through the south Wexford countryside. This left only a unit of the Wexford yeoman infantry

under the command of the mayor, Ebenezer Jacob, a liberal Protestant, to protect the town. In response to Harvey's letter, the United Irish leadership sent a message demanding surrender, unaware that the garrison had already marched out to the south, and moved their force to Windmill Hill, just above the town. At this point, rebels on the Ferrybank side of the harbour took the initiative by repairing the bridge and entering the town unopposed. The remaining yeomen abandoned their guns and tore off their uniforms. Bagenal Harvey, released from jail, paraded through the streets accompanied by United Irishmen from the town who had previously not broken cover. Wexford town was organised into two separate corps drawn from the Faythe and John's Street, each with its own distinctive identity. The long broad

street of the Faythe, to the south of the town, was home to the seafaring community; John's Street, parallel to the town wall on the west, was occupied by craftsmen and traders. The John's Street corps was captained by the exuberant Dick Monaghan, better known as Dick 'Monk'.[7]

Monk, an ex-shoeblack, corn factor and United Irishman, was the popularly appointed mayor of John's Street, an extramural proto-industrial suburb. As Handcock expresses it: 'Dick Monk was called the Mayor of John's Street, a suburb of people of a low class like himself, amongst whom he used to administer gratuitous justice and was as absolute in his adjudication as the mayor of the town and probably equally just'.[8] When the rebellion broke, Monk flamboyantly headed the 300-strong John's Street corps. The Faythe, another suburb

Fig. 7   On 29 May, the United Irish army set up camp at the Three Rocks on Forth Mountain, south-west of Wexford town. That evening, a detachment of one hundred troops, part of a larger force marching from Duncannon Fort to reinforce the garrison in Wexford, approached the mountain, unaware of the presence of the rebel army. A section of the rebel army attacked and routed the government force in what became known as the battle of the Three Rocks. An obelisk commemorating the victory was erected in 1938. This view that the rebels would have had of the town is now obscured by forestry.

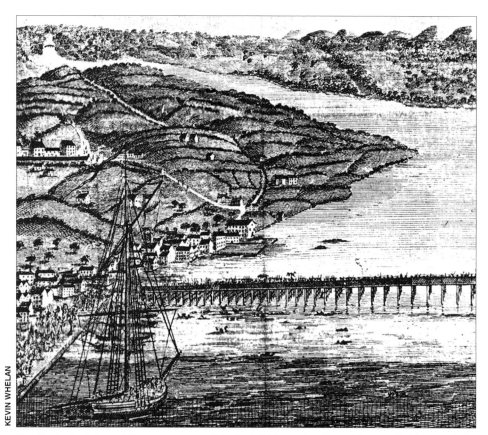

KEVIN WHELAN

Fig. 8 A depiction of the massacre on Wexford Bridge taken from Musgrave's history of the Rebellion. The ship in the foreground presumably represents the prison ship. The illustration also contains evidence for the late eighteenth-century development of the town, including a length of straight quayfront below the bridge and land reclamation associated with new houses at left centre. Villas are shown along the road to Ferrycarrig, which can be seen in the distance.

from the monolithically Protestant Corporation. These included Edward Frayne (the £300 a year tanner), John Herron (grocer and chandler), John Murphy (hardware shop owner), Patrick Prendergast (maltster and merchant), John Scallan (sloop owner), Edward Sutton (merchant) and John Howlin (ex-American privateer and sloop owner). Their very real achievement in maintaining order in the town over the three weeks has been obscured by an event that illustrated what happened when their control was terminated – the Wexford Bridge massacre.

The town was remarkably well disciplined for the duration of what was referred to as the Wexford Republic. The committee of public safety, the passwords, the printed proclamations, the rationing system, the district committees, the rebel navy – all these were substantial achievements in the turbulent hurly-burly of a fully fledged rebellion.[9] More than any other episode in the 1798 rebellion,

with a strong sense of maritime identity, also had its own corps, as did the more mercantile district of Selskar. These represented enduring social divisions within the town. A fascinating climax to this decade of politicisation was 'the embryo republic' (Musgrave) in Wexford town, controlled by a small directory composed of that distinctive United Irishman merger of radical Protestant reformers and Catholic activists who had provided the leadership in the town in the 1790s – Matthew Keugh, Bagenal Harvey, William Hatton and Nicholas Grey, Edward Hay, Robert Meyler, Robert Carthy and William Kearney. The second tier of control consisted essentially of the Catholic merchants of the town, especially those radicalised in the 1790s and part of the generation schooled in the 'Rights of Man', and conscious of their exclusion

KEVIN WHELAN

Fig. 9 Just before Wexford was taken by government forces, the United Irish leaders, Bagenal Harvey and John Henry Colclough, fled the town and took refuge in a cave on the Saltee Islands, off the south coast of the county. They were arrested by the military following the betrayal of their hiding place. Both men were brought to Wexford where they were court-martialled and executed.

they mark a close parallel to the experience of the French Revolution – and a tantalisingly brief glimpse of the potential had there been a successful United Irish coup in Ireland.

When the main rebel army marched into the town, the citizens offered them hospitality and hung appeasing green flags and boughs from their windows. There was no general violence or looting, but when the rebel leaders realised that Maxwell had tricked them, they launched a search for yeomen and prominent loyalists. By evening, 100 prisoners had been taken (some found on ships in the harbour) and lodged in the jail. Two loyalist prisoners were piked to death by the rebels: John Boyd, who was found on one of the ships, and George Sparrow, who was killed in the Bullring. The town remained peaceful with Ebenezer Jacob acting as liaison between the loyalist population and the rebels.

The main rebel army continued to occupy the camp on Windmill Hill and on 31 May were joined by Cornelius Grogan of Johnstown Castle at the head of 2,000 men from Forth and Bargy, bringing the strength of the army to 20,000 men. The return of Edward FitzGerald and John Henry Colclough (who had been captured but released by the fleeing government forces) meant that there was almost a full complement of the United Irish leadership present and a council meeting was held in the town to decide on strategy. At this stage, the leadership realised that the rising had failed elsewhere and that they would have to break out of the county to have any hope of success. The army was split into two divisions; the northern division, under Edward Roche of Garrylough, would attack Gorey and Newtownbarry (Bunclody), and the southern, led by Harvey (who was appointed as commander-in-chief)

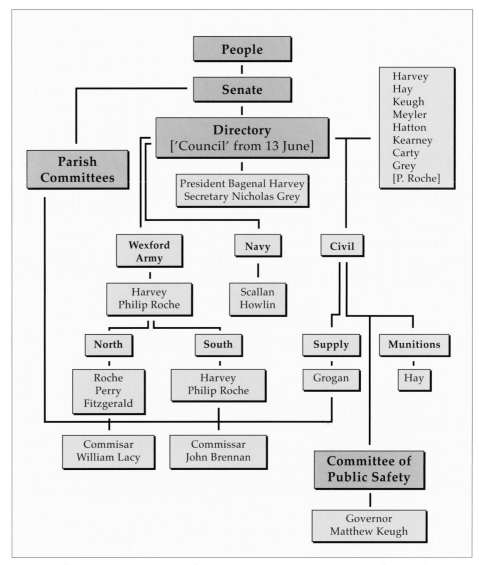

Fig. 10 Schematic representation of the revolutionary administration established by the United Irishmen based in Wexford town.

would march against New Ross. A governing committee was set up for Wexford town consisting of Matthew Keugh, William Kearney, Ebenezer Jacob and Cornelius Grogan.

Most remarkably, a 'Republic of Wexford', with a novel administration system, was also established to run the county, with an eight-man directory of four Catholics and four Protestants. This short-lived organisation, based in Wexford town, functioned well, observing discipline and order in difficult circumstances. There was no damage to property and reprisals were remarkably restrained. It also ran the army, the nucleus of a navy, a food distribution system and a print shop.[10] On 31 May, the northern division of 10,000 men left Windmill Hill to attack Gorey and Newtownbarry. The two Wexford town corps went with them as part of the division led by Fr John Murphy.[11] Harvey adopted a more relaxed approach, delaying his departure to host a dinner for his officers in his George's Street residence before leading his division out late in the evening for the planned assault on New Ross. However, the capture of Wexford, the county town and port, proved to be the pinnacle of the United Irish success; even as the two armies

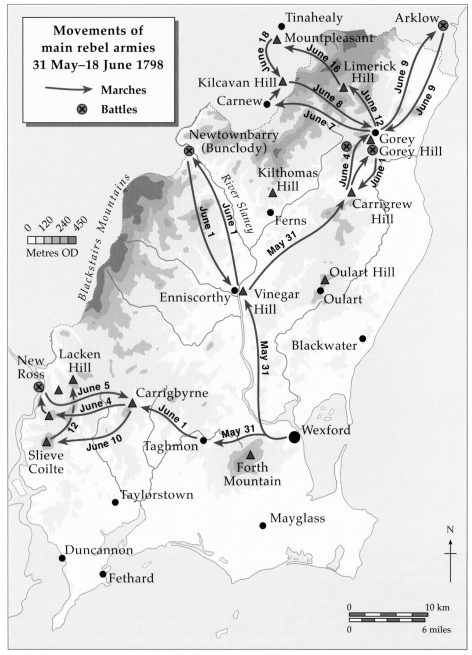

Fig. 11   The movements of the rebel armies in county Wexford and the location of the principal battles during the first half of June, 1798. Although Wexford town was of great strategic significance it escaped destruction, as it was abandoned in turn, without a fight, by the garrison and the rebels.

marched towards their destinations, a government counter-offensive led by General Lake was moving into place.

The insurgents who were left in control in Wexford town, under the command of Matthew Keugh and his committee, concentrated on consolidating their position. Because of concern about a naval attack, four fishing boats were fitted out as a rudimentary navy, and ordered to patrol the harbour mouth, presumably crewed by fishermen and sailors from the town who had an intimate knowledge of the bar and sand-banks in the estuary. The guns from Rosslare Fort were also deployed to defend the harbour entrance. The four 'navy' boats had immediate success as they captured several grain ships which helped to supplement supplies in the town. The food reserve was further augmented by Cornelius Grogan who initiated a system for bringing grain and livestock into the town from the south of the county. Blacksmiths were organised by Edward Hay to set up a pike making factory in the Bullring; small groups were dispatched into the countryside to cut the long poles which were required to make suitable handles. The presence of volatile elements in the town made the maintenance of law and order and the safety of prisoners a priority. Keugh's efficient leadership and the establishment of volunteer companies of townsmen prevented mob action and anti-loyalist activity. Sporadic killing of prisoners continued to take place on Vinegar Hill.

The second day of June was a turning point in the Rebellion. Lake launched a counter-attack on the rebel forces with reinforcements moving into position on the west and north of the county. The rebel leadership began to vacillate, an indecisiveness that had not been apparent in earlier engagements, possibly due to the news that the Rising had failed elsewhere. Matthew Keugh was aware of this following the capture of Lord Kingsborough, hated commander of the North Cork Militia, by the boats patrolling Wexford Harbour, as he traveled by ship from Arklow to Wexford. The ship was carrying newspapers which contained details of the collapse of the Rising in Dublin. The rebel army in the north of the county experienced setbacks at Gorey and Bunclody, followed by a victory at Tubberneering and the taking of Gorey. After a fiercely contested battle on 5 June, the southern division failed to take New Ross and this was followed four days later by a decisive defeat at Arklow. Military atrocities during the battle of Ross were followed by a massacre of loyalists at Scullabogue near Carrigbyrne. In an

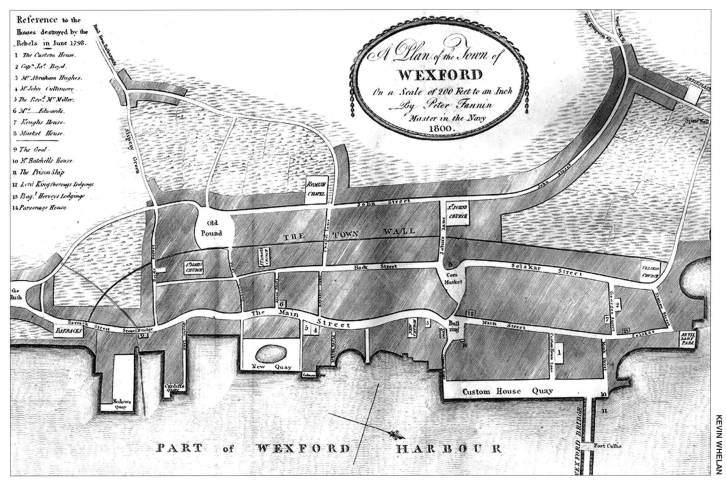

Fig. 12   This plan of Wexford drawn in 1800, by Peter Fannin, a master in the navy, records the places in the town that had connections with the 1798 Rebellion. It provides useful information on the growth of the town, particularly the waterfront which still had a series of projecting jetties, apart from the section near the bridge where the straight length of Custom House Quay had been constructed as far as the Bullring.

attempt to retrieve what was now a desperate situation, a new command structure was established. Edward Roche became commander-in-chief, Fr Philip Roche took over the southern division and Anthony Perry the north. Harvey was recalled to Wexford town to become president of the administrative council with Keugh remaining as governor of the town. Roche was to be based in Wexford town so that he could communicate with both divisions. Following his appointment, he issued a proclamation which was a classic example of republican language and sentiment.

Following the defeat at Ross, the leaders in Wexford town managed to maintain law and order but there were continuous threats to the safety of the loyalist prisoners. On 7 June, a party

of rebels stormed the jail and took out twenty-five prisoners with the intention of shooting them. The prisoners were saved by the intercession of Fr John Corrin, the parish priest, who succeeded in persuading the rebels to let them live. However, some of the prisoners were sent to Vinegar Hill where they were later executed. On 10 June, a battalion of men who had been stationed in Wexford town since the beginning of the Rising were sent to Vinegar Hill, perhaps in an effort to put an end to atrocities there. The removal of this disciplined force from the town weakened the position of the moderates and allowed the more militant supporters of Thomas Dixon to pursue their more extremist agenda. The rebel leadership in the town

became increasingly anxious, knowing little of what was going on elsewhere in the county. Checkpoints were manned in and around the town to monitor movement and lookouts were also stationed on the coast in case of a naval attack on the town. As the position of the government forces in the county grew stronger, the United Irish leadership in Wexford town held a crisis meeting to discuss their situation. They were also concerned about the extremists who had to be constantly restrained from acts of violence, resulting in tensions between the different rebel groups in the town.

At this point the government forces sent an offer of a negotiated settlement. The United Irish leaders agreed in principle, knowing that the loyalist prisoners, especially the high-profile

Kingsborough, gave them some bargaining power. A delegation was sent to discuss terms with Lake. Thomas Dixon succeeded in being appointed to the delegation and effectively sabotaged the initiative. Following this incident, the authority of moderate leaders in the town weakened even further with Dixon's group in control of the streets. However, the return of the moderate Wexford battalion from Vinegar Hill restored Keugh's wavering authority. On 19 June, reports of a new offensive by the government forces caused consternation in the town, exacerbated by reports of British naval ships outside Wexford Harbour. In the confusion, Dixon arrived back from Shelmalier East with a company of pikemen and installed them in the barracks. Fr Philip Roche left his southern division camped on Forth Mountain and attended an emergency council of war in Wexford. It was decided to gather a new army of 5,000 men, including the Wexford town units, and to confront the government forces approaching from the west, led by General John Moore. Roche, assisted by Colclough and Cloney, led the new force out towards New Ross and engaged Moore's army in a well fought but ultimately inconclusive battle at Goff's Bridge near Foulksmills.

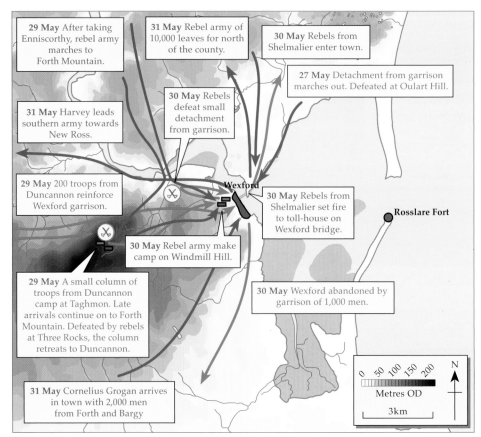

29 May After taking Enniscorthy, rebel army marches to Forth Mountain.

31 May Rebel army of 10,000 leaves for north of the county.

30 May Rebels from Shelmalier enter town.

27 May Detachment from garrison marches out. Defeated at Oulart Hill.

30 May Rebels defeat small detachment from garrison.

31 May Harvey leads southern army towards New Ross.

29 May 200 troops from Duncannon reinforce Wexford garrison.

Wexford

30 May Rebels from Shelmalier set fire to toll-house on Wexford bridge.

Rosslare Fort

30 May Rebel army make camp on Windmill Hill.

29 May A small column of troops from Duncannon camp at Taghmon. Late arrivals continue on to Forth Mountain. Defeated by rebels at Three Rocks, the column retreats to Duncannon.

30 May Wexford abandoned by garrison of 1,000 men.

0 50 100 150 200
Metres OD

3km

N

31 May Cornelius Grogan arrives in town with 2,000 men from Forth and Bargy

Fig. 13   This map of rebel and government forces movements in and around Wexford during the 1798 Rebellion illustrates the scale of activity that was focused on the town. It also highlights the importance that both sides attached to Wexford port, which had the potential to provide access for foreign intervention.

When the leaders arrived back in Wexford, they discovered that a shocking atrocity had been inflicted on the loyalists prisoners. With the United Irish leadership and most of the fighting force involved in the clash with Moore, Dixon and his battalion of Shelmalier East pikemen remained behind and could not be restrained by Keugh and other civilian leaders who were still in the town. Dixon decided to put the loyalist prisoners on trial. A panel of seven judges tried the prisoners who were dragged from the

---

Proclamation issued under Edward Roche's name, 7 June 1798

Countrymen and Fellow Soldiers!

Your patriotic exertions in the cause of your country have hitherto exceeded your most sanguine expectations, and in a short time must ultimately be crowned with success – Liberty has raised her drooping head; thousands flock daily to her standard; the voice of her children every where prevails – let us then, in the moment of triumph, return thanks to the Almighty Ruler of the universe, that a total stop has been put to those sanguinary measures, which of late were but too often resorted to by the creatures of government to keep the people in slavery. At this dreadful period, all Europe must admire, and posterity will read with astonishment, the heroic acts achieved by people, strangers to military tactics, and having few professional commanders. But what power can resist men fighting for liberty! In the moment of triumph, my countrymen, let not your victories be tarnished with any wanton act of cruelty; neither let a difference in religious sentiments cause a difference amongst the people. To promote an union of brotherhood and affection amongst our countrymen of all religious persuasions, has been our principal object; we have sworn in the most solemn manner, have associated for this laudable purpose, and no power on earth shall shake our resolution. To my Protestant soldiers I feel much indebted, for their gallant behaviour in the field, where they exhibited signal proofs of bravery in the cause.

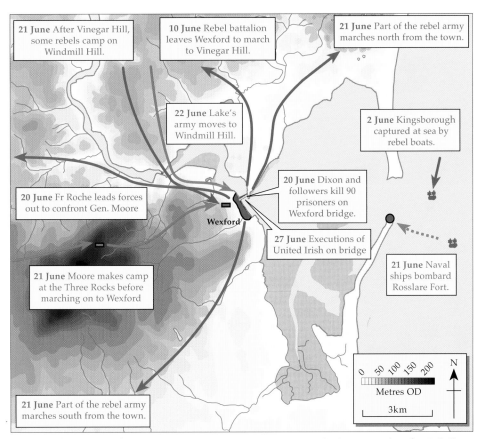

21 June After Vinegar Hill, some rebels camp on Windmill Hill.

10 June Rebel battalion leaves Wexford to march to Vinegar Hill.

21 June Part of the rebel army marches north from the town.

22 June Lake's army moves to Windmill Hill.

2 June Kingsborough captured at sea by rebel boats.

20 June Fr Roche leads forces out to confront Gen. Moore

20 June Dixon and followers kill 90 prisoners on Wexford bridge.

Wexford

27 June Executions of United Irish on bridge

21 June Naval ships bombard Rosslare Fort.

21 June Moore makes camp at the Three Rocks before marching on to Wexford

21 June Part of the rebel army marches south from the town.

0 50 100 150 200
Metres OD
3km
N

Fig. 14 The second phase of military movements around Wexford town. After the Rebellion, Wexford's significance was acknowledged by the construction of a road, still known as 'the new line', across the width of the county, providing direct access from Duncannon Fort to the town in the event of further emergencies. A Martello Tower, constructed in the early nineteenth century on Rosslare Point to defend the harbour entrance, fell victim to erosion before the end of the century.

jail, the market house and the prison ship, invariably condemning them to death. They were then marched to the bridge where they were piked to death and the bodies thrown into the harbour. By evening, ninety loyalists had been murdered and the macabre killing spree only stopped when Edward Roche arrived from the north of the town with a newly recruited force of pikemen. The moderates among the United Irishmen must have been shocked at this atrocity, apart from the fact that it deprived them of their only bargaining power in a surrender situation. They must also have realised that, because of it, none of them could expect mercy following victory by government forces. On the morning of 21 June, the United Irish in Wexford town could hear the distant sound of artillery as the government

forces began the final assault on the rebel camp on Vinegar Hill. Keugh convened a meeting of the leaders, including Philip Roche and Thomas Cloney, in his house in George's Street, and agreed to ask Lord Kingsborough to accept the surrender of the town. Ebenezer Jacob was reinstalled as mayor. Kingsborough received the surrender and the United Irish officers handed their swords to him. Delegates were dispatched to bring news of the surrender to Generals Moore and Needham, and principally to the commander-in-chief, General Lake. As they rode out, the ominous sound of cannon fire from naval ships attacking Rosslare Fort could be heard.

The messengers informed Moore at Taghmon of the surrender of Wexford and he proceeded to move his forces to the Three Rocks overlooking the town.

The delegates heading towards Enniscorthy met parties of the rebel army streaming towards Wexford after the defeat at Vinegar Hill, some of them outraged to hear that the town had been surrendered. The rebels entered the town in search of food and Edward Roche's battalion made camp on Windmill Hill. The town was now in a state of confusion with the exhausted rebel army in no state for another confrontation. Harvey and Colclough fled, planning to go into hiding on the Saltee Islands.

When Moore's army arrived at the Three Rocks, the rebel outposts at Windmill Hill sounded the alarm. Edward Roche held a meeting of his officers and it was decided that the northern division of several thousand men would retreat across the bridge and into the open countryside. The two priests, John Murphy and Philip Roche, also led several thousand of their men out of the town, but to the south, taking the same route into the baronies of Forth and Bargy that the town garrison had traveled three weeks previously. The two groups succeeded in breaking out through the Wicklow Mountains and the Scullogue

Fig. 15 A miniature of Edward Roche of Garrylough. A lock of his hair is twined inside the frame. Roche proved to be one of the most capable United Irish leaders in Wexford.

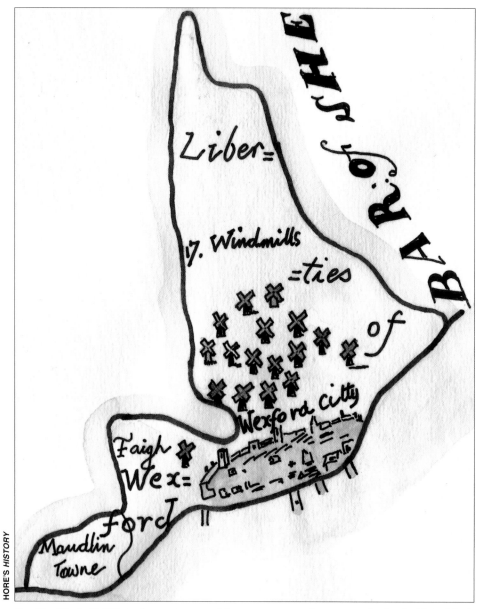

Fig. 16 Windmill Hill, to the north-west of the town, was used as a campsite by the United Irish army and the government forces. This 1770s map of Wexford recorded seventeen windmills on the high ground above the town, showing that the placename was highly apt. The presence of so many windmills indicated the extent to which Wexford was involved in the corn industry.

On hearing this, Kingsborough wrote to Lake telling him that the town had been surrendered to him and Lake decided to spare the town, allowing Wexford to escape massacre and destruction for the second time. Lake and Moore made camp on Windmill Hill and their soldiers launched a campaign of terror as they searched for rebels. Lake offered an amnesty to rebels who handed in weapons but few were willing to take the chance. Fr Philip Roche and the wounded John Kelly were arrested and thrown in jail. Two of the captured insurgents were court-martialed and hanged on the bridge, the first of many executions. Harvey and Colclough, whose escape to the Saltee Islands had been reported to the authorities, were captured and imprisoned. Within three days of entering the town, Lake was in complete control with most of the south Wexford United Irish leadership in prison. On 25 June, Matthew Keugh, Philip Roche and seven others were led out for execution by hanging on Wexford bridge. Other leaders who went to their deaths on the bridge included Bagenal Harvey, Cornelius Grogan, Patrick Prendergast, John Henry Colclough and John Kelly. The corpses of the Protestant rebel leaders, Harvey, Grogan and Keugh, were subjected to particularly brutal treatment. In a macabre twist of fate, Grogan, Harvey, Colclough and Keugh had been part of the committee responsible for the construction, only four years earlier, of the bridge that now became their gallows.[13]

Although Wexford town was not centre-stage at the outbreak of the '98 Rebellion, it inevitably became the focus of attention by both sides in the conflict because of its strategic significance. It had a substantial loyalist population but was the natural headquarters of the liberal cadre of United Irish leaders, some of

Gap, but were eventually defeated after heroic resistance. Not all of the rebels fled from the town; many, including some of the southern leaders, remained behind, presumably hoping for mercy from the government. Meanwhile, Moore, not wishing to enter the town before Lake, advanced a small detachment into the town to secure the prisoners. As they rode in unopposed through John's Gate, Thomas Dixon escaped across the bridge with his wife and

followers.[12] After the prisoners were freed, Moore sent in two detachments of troops to guard the town for the night. Loyalist bands combed the town for rebels and many were caught and hauled off to prison. Keugh, the former governor, was imprisoned in his own house in George's Street.

On the morning of 22 June, Lake, not knowing that the town had already fallen, rejected the offer of the surrender and the emissaries rode back to inform the United Irish leadership.

Fig. 17   Wexford's first bridge, shown here in a detail from an 1820 engraving, played a macabre role in the town's involvement in the events of '98. The first group of rebels who entered the town crossed the bridge from Ferrybank. Ninety loyalists were murdered on the bridge by an extremist rebel element, led by Thomas Dixon. After the re-taking of the town by government forces, United Irish leaders were executed on the bridge, including Harvey, Grogan, Colclough and Keugh, all members of the committee that had been responsible for its construction only four years earlier.

whom had houses there. Taken by the rebels and government forces in turn, Wexford was the only town in the county to escape destruction and massacre. Following the appointment of Edward Roche as commander-in-chief, the town became the command headquarters where decisions relating to strategy were taken. In the dying throes of the Rebellion, before the arrival of the government forces, the two rebel army divisions left from Wexford town in their successful attempt to break out of the county. Most of the leaders who remained behind were executed on the bridge. The liberal wing of Wexford politics was decimated, leaving the hard-line conservative faction in firm control. Perhaps unfairly, Wexford is remembered most for the sectarian killings that were perpetrated on the bridge which were more than matched by the campaign of terror carried out by the army following the surrender of the town.

The 1798 Rebellion and its aftermath threw Ireland into turmoil and evoked memories and fears of the bloody rebellion of 1641. The decade that began with the founding of the United Irishmen, with aspirations for an Irish 'fellowship of freedom', was to close with increased sectarian bitterness. Politically, the crisis was manipulated to engineer a legislative union between Ireland and England, achieved by the Act of Union in 1801.

Fig. 18   A propagandistic representation of the murder of loyalists on Wexford bridge by George Cruikshank, Charles Dickens' celebrated illustrator. Intended for an English audience, Cruikshank's illustrations attributed stereotypical qualities to the Irish to make them appear as racially inferior.

Fig. 19   This aerial perspective illustrates the strategic nature of Forth Mountain (left foreground) in relation to Wexford (top right). From their camp on the mountain the rebels had a commanding view of the town. The military road built after the Rebellion can be seen in the right half of the picture.

The Croppy Boy

It was early, early all in the Spring,
The small birds whistled and sweet did sing,
Changing their notes from tree to tree,
And the song they sang was 'old Ireland free'.

It was early, early all in the night,
When the yeomen cavalry gave me a fright,
To my misfortune and sad downfall,
I was taken prisoner by Lord Cornwall.

Lord Cornwall he said unto me
That I should tell on one, two or three;
But I'd rather die on the gallows tree
Than be an informer on my family.

It was in his guard house where I was laid,
And in his parlour that I was tried,

My sentence passed and my spirits low,
When to Geneva I was forced to go.

As I was going up Wexford street,
My own first cousin I chanced to meet,
My own first cousin did me deny,
And the name he gave me was 'the Croppy Boy'.

As I was going up Wexford hill,
Oh who could blame me to cry my fill,
I looked behind and I looked before,
But my own dear mother I ne'er saw more.

It was in Duncannon this young man died,
And in Duncannon his body lies,
All you good people that do pass by,
Pray the Lord have mercy on the Croppy Boy.

KEVIN WHELAN

Fig. 20   This illustration of the Croppy Boy by Jack B. Yeats is taken from a ballad sheet published as a Broadside by the Cuala Press in 1935.

In the aftermath of the Rebellion, a military road (still known as 'the new line') connected Wexford town with Duncannon Fort. In the town, this involved the building of a new road along the marshy valley of the Bishopswater stream, giving the military direct access to their quarters in Barrack Street. This section of road played a central role in Wexford's industrial and economic growth for more than a century.

1798 seared itself into the conciousness of Wexford. The songs, folklore and popular memory were a vehicle for transmitting a powerful sense that the rebellion had defined the distinctive character of the county. This perception was dramatically deepened by the centenary and bicentenary commemorations, in which Wexford town featured prominently. The Pikeman in the Bullring became an iconic image.

URBAN GROWTH: TRADE AND INDUSTRY

During the nineteenth century, political, economic and infrastructural advances ushered Wexford into the modern era. Catholic Emancipation added dramatically to the architectural profile of the town as well as significant social change brought about by greatly enhanced educational opportunities. Expansion in shipping and trade was adversely effected by the advent of the steamship, eventually leading to the construction of a new port at Rosslare Harbour. The town's diminishing stature as a port was balanced by the arrival of the railway late in the century. Although Wexford escaped the worst excesses, the town's modernisation was obscenely bisected by the Great Famine of mid century.

Because of the effective control maintained by the United Irish leadership and a fortunate escape from a direct assault, Wexford town suffered relatively little damage to property during the 1798 rebellion. Despite the trauma of the event and the emigration of some Protestants,[1] the townspeople quickly made efforts to resume normal living and commercial activity. These efforts proved to be successful, as Wexford achieved growth in population and commercial prosperity in the early decades of the century, with the other port towns.[2]

Following the Act of Union in 1800, the hard-line conservative grouping lost ground to the liberals. In the aftermath of the rebellion, initiatives were taken to improve conditions in the town. With security considerations high on the agenda, repairs were carried out to the town wall and gates in 1804, but the gates had been removed to facilitate traffic by 1835.[3] In the early years of the nineteenth century, as part of the precautions against an expected French invasion, Rosslare Fort was selected for the construction of a signal tower. A Martello tower, similar to the one at Baginbun, was constructed in or near the fort, but was demolished by coastal erosion before mid century.[4]

In 1801, the Grand Jury established a diocesan school in Spawell Road, in an effort to encourage Protestants to remain in the town. The school continued in use until 1872.[5] The construction of two major public buildings in the town early in the century can be attributed to post-rebellion concerns about law and order. A new courthouse, commissioned by the Grand Jury in 1802, was completed on the quays opposite the bridge in 1808. Four years later a new jail (on the site of the present County Hall) was built at Spawell Road.[6]

The town's cultural life was enhanced by the building of the Theatre Royal in High Street in 1832.[7] In the middle of the twentieth century, it would become the home of what is now the world-renowned Wexford Festival Opera.

S.P.C.

Fig. 1 This *c.* 1820 panoramic view of Wexford from Ferrybank conveys a good impression of the early nineteenth-century town. A cavalry troop is shown crossing the recently constructed toll-bridge, which is attracting considerable traffic from the Castlebridge direction. The newly-built courthouse can be seen at the town end of the bridge. Villas are shown on the outskirts of the town and to the south the fishing suburb of the Faythe occupies the low ground between the high ground of 'the Rocks' and the seashore. The newly constructed quay is crowded with sailing ships and the traffic in the harbour includes fishing boats and cargo-carrying Slaney gabbards. A close examination shows the dockyard and the military barracks.

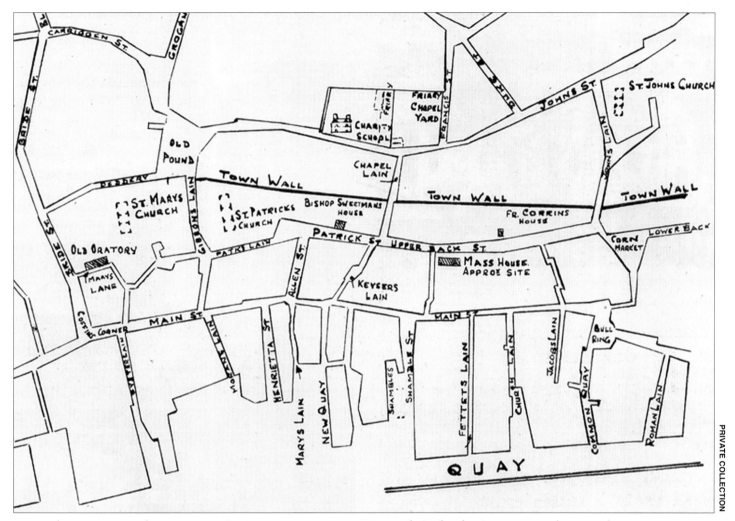

Fig. 2 This early nineteenth-century map of unknown origin concentrated on Catholic church infrastructure in the town. The newly-built quay is shown stretching from the bridge to Anne Street. The map provides a useful record of the names of many of the old laneways leading to the quays.

URBAN GROWTH

Early in the century, new streets were added to the town's infrastructure: Rowe Street, built by the Rowes of Ballycross (near Bridgetown) and Charlotte Street, presumably named after Charlotte, Princess of Wales, who died in 1817; in the south of the town, Trinity Street and New Street (later Parnell Street) were constructed on reclaimed land. In the aftermath of 1798, the new road constructed by the military from Duncannon Fort to Wexford necessitated the construction of a road (now Distillery Road and King Street Upper[8]) along the marshy valley of the Bishopswater stream, giving direct access to the military barracks in Barrack Street.

In the early decades of the nineteenth century, a small but wealthy coterie of Catholic families rose to supremacy in the business and commercial life of the town, paving the way for political power following Catholic Emancipation in 1829.[9] In 1833, they had gained sufficient control of the Corporation to elect William Whitty, a grain merchant from the Faythe, as the first post-Cromwellian Catholic

mayor of Wexford.[10] Two of these families, the Devereuxs and Redmonds, dominated all aspects of life in Wexford for the rest of the century.

By the early nineteenth century, a growing trend towards bigger ships made improvements to the

Fig. 3 In 1807, the political tension in the county was epitomised by a duel at Ardcandrisk (on the right bank of the Slaney, just above Ferrycarrig) in which liberal (and alleged to have United Irish connections) John Colclough, of Tintern Abbey, was killed by William Alcock, a supporter of the conservative group. Colclough was waked in the family's George's Street residence and his funeral to Tintern was reputed to have been the biggest ever seen in Wexford.

S.P.C.

Fig. 4   The new courthouse, completed on a site opposite the bridge in 1808, is shown in this detail taken from the 1820 view of the town.

approaches and to the quay system a priority. In 1806, a special gabbard was commissioned to carry out continuous dredging in the harbour.[11] The need for modernisation was recognised as important for the whole county: in 1807, the Grand Jury allocated £236 to build a stone quay, forty-five feet in length, south of the bridge.[12] The existing system of numerous small jetties projecting into the harbour, owned by various competing private individuals, was an added complication. The Harbour Corporation addressed this fragmentation by taking control of the approach lanes. During the early decades of the century, an embankment was built parallel to the shore line, allowing the enclosed area to be filled in and reclaimed from the harbour.[13] A long quay front was created in the deep water along the outside of the embankment, stretching from the bridge to the southern end of the town. This new quay was straight, except for a crescent section near the centre, curving inwards around

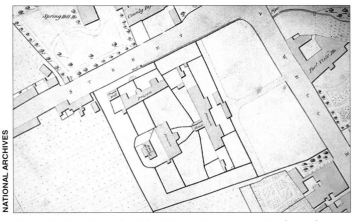

NATIONAL ARCHIVES

Fig. 5   In the aftermath of the '98 Rebellion, a new jail, shown here on the O. S. town plan of 1840, was built on the corner of Spawell Road and Hill Street. The county infirmary can be seen at the top of the picture.

the location where deepest water was shown on contemporary maps. This may have been necessary because of the difficulty in building an embankment in deep water or it may have been done deliberately to provide extra berthage in the most suitable area. The upgrading of the quay system was offset by a failure to carry out any improvements to the harbour, which presented a permanent obstacle to shipping as the trend towards bigger vessels continued. In an effort to ensure the safety of vessels entering and leaving the shallow harbour, pilots were taken on board from a station set up at Rosslare Fort.[14]

Enniscorthy acted as an important collection point for agricultural produce which was sent by lighters down the Slaney to Wexford for export. Imports of coal, timber and other commodities were carried on the return journey.

Fig. 6   The jail was taken over by the County Council in the early twentieth century and became the County Hall in 1931. Only the women's prison, shown above, survives of the prison complex.

Two new quays were built in Enniscorthy and an initiative to increase trade by improving the Slaney navigation was discussed in 1832. The proposal included the building of a canal from Pouldarrig to Brownswood at a cost of £33,000, but the plan was never implemented. At that time the annual traffic on the river between the two towns was 36,000 tons, despite navigational impediments.[15] In early nineteenth-century Ireland, a number of new mini-ports were developed in tillage areas, in the sheltered waters of the harbours of larger ports based on new infrastructure of road, quay, granaries, mills, malt-houses and dwelling houses. Examples included Ballincurra (Cork), Blennerville (Tralee), Westport (Mayo) and Castlebridge, situated on the eastern shore of Wexford's inner harbour, beside the marshy estuary of the Sow and Castlebridge rivers. Castlebridge's potential was recognised in the late eighteenth century as in 1792, when the adjacent land was

Fig. 7 Castlebridge, to the east of the inner harbour, was developed as a corn centre in the early nineteenth century as a strategy to avoid paying tolls on Wexford bridge and to the Corporation. The canal constructed from the corn centre to the harbour still survives.

Fig. 8 A detail from the 1820 view of the town showing the traffic on the road to the bridge from Castlebridge. Boats in the harbour include a fishing smack and a cot. The Slaney gabbard at top right may have been on its way from Castlebridge with a cargo of corn.

described as 'most conveniently adapted to erect thereon stores, malt-stores, breweries or distilleries, being bounded by a navigable river, capable of admitting lighters of 30 tons burthen'.[16]

The construction of a toll-bridge at Wexford in 1795 meant that farmers from 'over the water' bringing corn to the town were compelled to pay for the privilege of accessing the port. This provided the incentive for the establishment of an alternative market and in 1805, to avoid the tolls on the bridge, a centre for corn-drying, milling and malting was built by the Dixon family at Castlebridge. A canal was constructed to connect the complex to the harbour and produce was transported by large cots, known as gabbards, directly to the ships at Wexford quays.[17] This forestalling process had a significant economic impact on Wexford as in 1814 the mayor and Corporation lost a legal claim that the town was entitled to tolls on corn purchased in the interior of the county and brought by lighter to Wexford quays for delivery to malt-houses in the town.[18] The threat to the corn trade in Wexford town was significant: in 1832, an advertisement for the sale of a new corn store and kiln at Castlebridge described it as 'being situated in one of the best corn markets in Ireland and within a few feet of the canal, from which the corn can be shipped with the greatest facility and convenience'. In 1837, Castlebridge was described as being remarkable for its extensive trade in corn. It was claimed that nearly all of the produce south of Arklow and east of the Slaney was brought to the extensive stores, mills and malt-houses in Castlebridge to avoid the tolls on Wexford bridge. At that time, the complex was owned by

Patrick Breen, whose predecessor had cut a canal to the Slaney in 1810. The stores had a capacity of 40,000 barrels and 65,000 barrels were exported annually. The corn was sent by boats of twenty tons' burden to Wexford quays, whence it was shipped without any extra charge.[19] The bridge was made toll-free in 1852 but the corn business at Castlebridge, which passed to the Nunn family, survived until 1973.[20]

The building of the quayfront at Wexford resulted in the creation of a new service street (the modern quay), parallel to the Main Street, and the provision of a

Fig. 9 A gabbard at Castlebridge (from a photograph). These shallow-draught boats were capable of carrying up to twenty tons' burden.

Fig. 10   The Crescent Quay represents the deep pool around which the original Viking town was founded. After the building of the quays on reclaimed ground in the early nineteenth century, the flow of water was changed and the Crescent silted up. A railway bridge was built across the Crescent in the late nineteenth century. In the present century, a marina was constructed outside the Crescent as part of a waterfront development.

considerable acreage of reclaimed land for development, although not for immediate use. The infill needed to consolidate for a considerable time before building could take place. As the reclaimed land was only slightly above sea-level, the potential for flooding was a problem, as it still is. Many plots remained vacant in the 1840s, particularly around the Crescent Quay where it may have been necessary to put in a deeper infill because of the depth of water. Ownership posed a greater obstacle to long-term usage as the reclaimed land was added to the narrow medieval burgage plots along the east side of the

Fig. 11   On the 1840 Ordnance Survey Town Plan, much of the reclaimed land bordering the Crescent Quay remained undeveloped.

Fig. 12   Charts of the harbour invariably show the deepest water along the quays in the vicinity of the Crescent. This detail from Vallancey's 1770s map records twenty-four feet in that area. It also records a windmill at Windmill Hill above the town to the north-west.

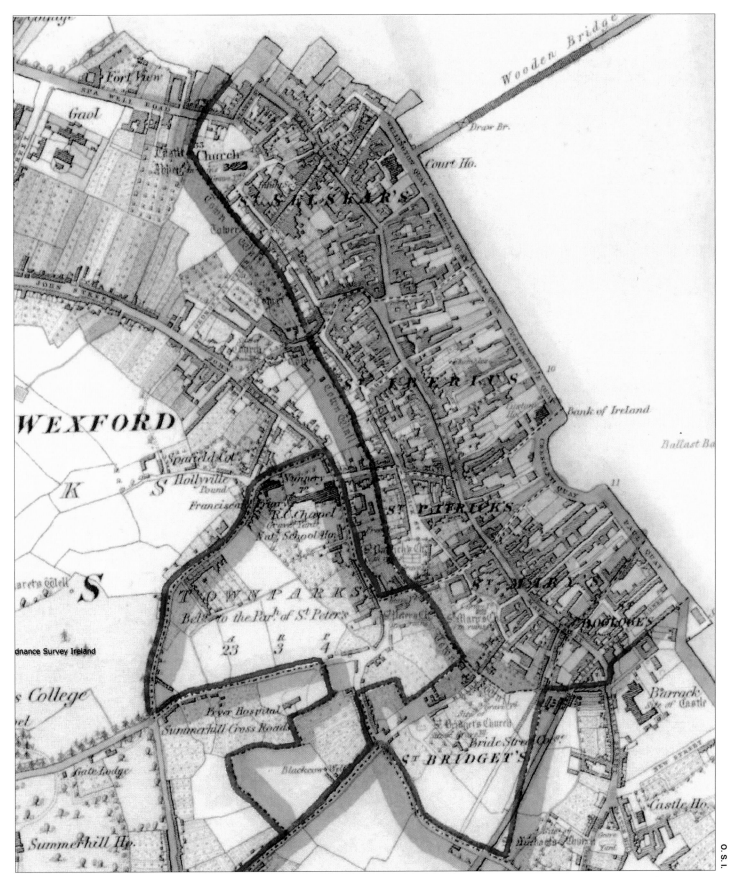

Fig. 13 The 1842 Ordnance Survey six inch coloured maps, with the town plans of 1840, provided the first accurate, detailed cartographic depiction of Wexford town. Apart from the extramural suburbs of the Faythe and John's Street, the town had expanded little beyond the area defined by the town wall. Parish boundaries are shown in green, townlands in red. The colouring on plots in the town is believed to be decorative.

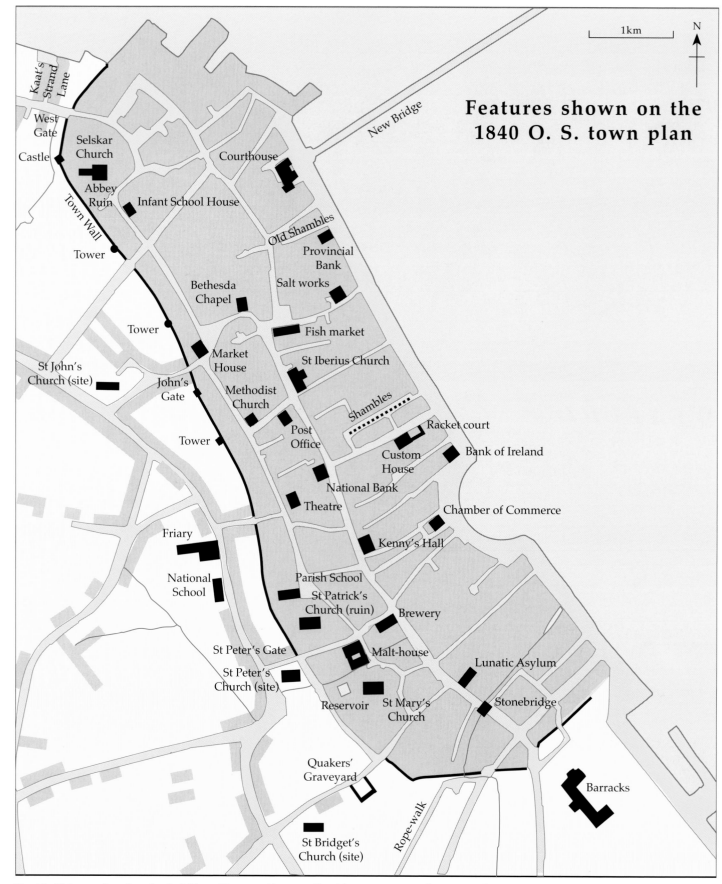

1km

N

Features shown on the 1840 O. S. town plan

Kaat's Strand Lane

West Gate

Castle

Selskar Church

Abbey Ruin

Town Wall

Infant School House

Courthouse

New Bridge

Tower

Old Shambles

Provincial Bank

Bethesda Chapel

Salt works

Tower

Fish market

St John's Church (site)

Market House

St Iberius Church

John's Gate

Methodist Church

Shambles

Tower

Post Office

Racket court

Custom House

Bank of Ireland

National Bank

Chamber of Commerce

Theatre

Friary

Kenny's Hall

National School

Parish School

St Patrick's Church (ruin)

Brewery

St Peter's Gate

Malt-house

Lunatic Asylum

St Peter's Church (site)

Reservoir

St Mary's Church

Stonebridge

Rope-walk

Barracks

Quakers' Graveyard

St Bridget's Church (site)

Fig. 14   This map, based on the O. S. Town Plan, provides a profile of the town in 1840. The town with its medieval layout of streets and lanes, was still very much defined by the town wall. Some indications of modernisation are provided by a Chamber of Commerce, banks and a theatre.

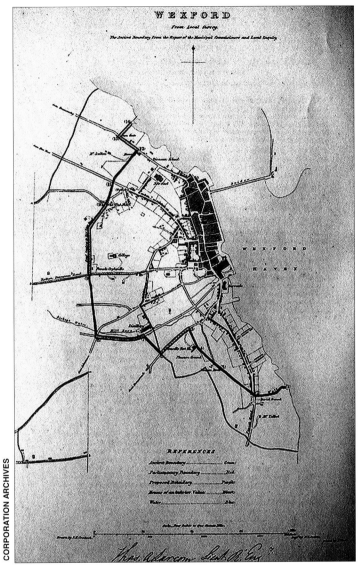

Fig. 15 When Wexford was re-incorporated in 1846, the urban boundary was extended to include a large area outside the town walls.

Fishers' Row, by an embankment built by John E. Redmond. It was planned to construct a new road to Maudlintown (the modern William Street/Trinity Street). New roads had also been constructed from Wexford to Duncannon Fort, New Ross and Enniscorthy, and a new road to Ferrycarrig bridge was planned. Two attempts at introducing regulations for 'cleaning, lighting and paving' the narrow streets had been rejected by public meetings but gas lighting had recently been installed on the quays. Water was supplied to the 1,820 houses in the town by pipes laid down by the Corporation for improving the quays, by wells and by the public conduit in the Cornmarket. A 'small and neat theatre' had been built in Back Street in 1832 and a 'house of industry and lunatic asylum' was established in the old jail in South Main Street in 1816.

The O. S. maps provided the first accurate cartographic representation of the town. The 1840 town plan, in particular, printed at a scale of 1:1056, is extremely informative, providing details on streets and lanes, public buildings, historic features and land-use.[22] On the landward side, the town had not significantly expanded beyond the medieval walled core, plus the two traditional suburbs of the Faythe and John's Street. On the seaward

Fig. 16 This Corporation boundary marker at Windmill Hill is the only survivor of the expansion of Wexford borough in the 1840s.

Main Street, resulting in long narrow properties with multiple owners between the Main Street and the quay, clearly identifiable on the 1840 O. S. town plan. The awkward shape of these plots, combined with difficult access, led to haphazard, piecemeal development, which has survived down to modern times. Along the quays, an industrial and commercial strip of warehouses, timber-yards, coal-yards and grain-stores were built to take advantage of the import and export trade. Two significant buildings constructed on the new Crescent Quay were both commercial – the Bank of Ireland and the Chamber of Commerce – an indication of growing economic activity in the town.

A comprehensive description of the town was compiled by Samuel Lewis in 1837, containing details of new buildings, trade and commerce and social activity.[21] The quays had been extended to the south-east as far as

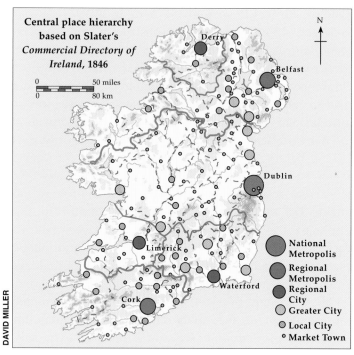

Fig. 17 In 1846, Wexford was included with eight other towns among the fourth-ranked urban centres in Ireland. In the south-east region, it came second, with Kilkenny and Clonmel, after Waterford.

side, land reclamation had reached the line of the present quays, apart from the recent extension. The on-going process of land reclamation from the harbour to the north and south of the town is illustrated. The Ordnance Survey recorded Wexford's medieval pattern of streets and lanes, dominated by the town wall and medieval church sites, with the addition of some new streets. An identical layout is clearly identifiable in the nucleus of the modern town, demonstrating the town's medieval genesis and a millennium of continuity.

Wexford's status was reduced by the Irish Municipal Corporation Bill of 1841 which deprived towns with fewer than 12,000 inhabitants of their corporations. Wexford's mayor and officials appealed against the downgrading and succeeded in obtaining a new charter for the town in 1846. However, under the Municipal Act, Wexford was stripped of much of the power formerly exercised by the Corporation.[23] A survey carried out at the time to establish the Corporation's right to the lands of the town and its liberties found that the old administration had allowed the leasing system to fall into complete disarray and that the Corporation property had become almost exclusively confined to the parish of St John's, starving the town of much needed revenue from rents.[24] On the eve of the Great Famine, lack of revenue may have contributed to an opinionated description of Wexford in 1845, accompanied by an equally prejudiced opinion of other major Irish towns:[25]

The town as a whole is an ill-paved, filthy, repulsive place, most of its thoroughfares orientally narrow, and multitudes of its houses squalid, disgusting and pestiferous. No large or second rate town of Ireland seemed so malodorous and generally disagreeable as Wexford, excepting Galway, the Irish town of Athlone and the English town of Limerick.

This view might be compared to a milder comment from the notoriously ugly John Philpot Curran who remarked in 1798 that 'he never beheld a more indifferent looking town in his life', to which his local friend replied 'why then it is like yourself – it is much better than it looks!'

THE GREAT FAMINE

Between 1700 and 1845, the population of Ireland expanded dramatically from three million to eight-and-a-half million, due in part to the increased use of the potato as an easily produced nutritious food. The success of the versatile potato, when it was efficiently grown using lazy-bed cultivation, meant that foodstuffs which had formerly formed part of the staple diet (particularly butter and oats), were sold to provide cash for rent and other necessities, creating a precarious over-dependence on a single crop, particularly among the labouring and cottier classes. By the 1830s one-third of the population (three million people) relied utterly on the potato for over ninety per cent of their calorie intake. Following the end of the Napoleonic Wars in 1815, the demand for agricultural produce plummeted and the economy went into a sharp depression. This further deepened dependence on the potato. When blight appeared in 1845, the effect was immediate and devastating.[26]

Fig. 18 Wexford Union Workhouse was constructed in 1838, to the north-west of the town, on a site overlooking the Farnogue valley. At the height of the Famine, it catered for over 1,000 destitute people per annum. It served as Wexford General Hospital until 1993.

Although not the only famine experienced in Ireland during the eighteenth and nineteenth centuries, the trauma of the horrific Great Famine of 1845–51 led to permanent changes in all aspects of Irish life.[27] When blight struck the potato crop in 1845, the inability to provide an alternative food supply led to a major humanitarian disaster. The impact on the population was staggering. As well as the million people who died from hunger and related diseases, another million fled the country. Because of political ideology, the official response saw the Famine as an opportunity to replace the 'backward' potato with grain, regarded as a more 'civilised' crop. It was also seen as a chance to modernise estates by ridding them of a 'surplus' pauper tenantry. Official relief was limited to public relief works, which gave employment nationally to 700,000 men at their height. The Famine inflicted devastating and permanent changes on Irish society. In the decade after 1841, the population collapsed from eight million to six-and-a-half million, a loss of twenty per cent. Sustained emigration continued and by 1901 the population had dropped to four and a half million, almost half the pre-Famine level.

The Famine impacted most severely on the densely populated regions along the western seaboard. Wexford town and county escaped the worst horrors of the catastrophe but it did impact on the labouring and cottier classes, and the county suffered from the resulting prolonged agricultural depression.[28] Under the Poor Law Act of 1838, Wexford Union Workhouse was constructed in 1842, on a site to the north of the town overlooking the valley of the Farnogue stream, with capacity for 600 inmates. By 1845, 290 destitute people had been admitted, having been first obliged to surrender their small-holdings. Following the failure of the potato in 1845, the Workhouse was authorised to substitute vegetable soup, oatmeal, rice and bread.[29] In Wexford, it was suggested that the town's nineteen malt-houses should cease operations so that the corn could be conserved for those in need.[30] Relief schemes were initiated in 1846, as numbers in Wexford Workhouse continued to rise. Wexford Harbour Commissioners proposed employment for 200 men by deepening the channel from the quay to the harbour mouth and building a new bridge at Kaat's Strand.[31] The bridge was eventually constructed in 1856, but not as a famine relief scheme. Conditions deteriorated even further following the abolition of price control by a new Whig government at Westminster. In 1846, Wexford merchant, Richard Devereux, volunteered to import 100 tons of Indian meal at cost and in the following year he temporarily closed Bishopswater distillery so that the grain could be used to feed those in need. In 1848, he was instrumental in establishing the St Vincent de Paul Society in the town to help those in dire straits. The need for the Society was highlighted by a report in 1847:[32]

> The numbers of unfortunate creatures begging relief are surprising and many a disheveled form, the emaciated face, the tottering step which tells a tale of poverty, misery and hunger indescribable by words, with cheeks like scorched leather, eyes shrunken and a voice sounding as if from a tomb, beseech you, in accents almost inaudible from weakness, for relief for God's sake.

The increasing numbers in Wexford Workhouse served as a barometer for deepening distress in the south-east of the county.[33] Designed to cater for 600 inmates, it contained over 1,000 people by 1848, with 270 of those from the Wexford town electoral division. In 1847, 3,289 people

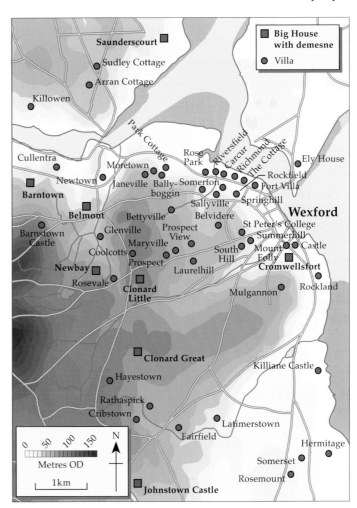

Fig. 19 Big Houses and villas were built in the vicinity of Wexford by members of the landed gentry from the county and successful businessmen from the town. The dwellings were mostly located to the west and north-west, on the high ground overlooking the harbour.

were given relief in the Wexford Union, rising to 4,425 in the following year. In the same year, the death of a whole family from starvation, near Wexford town, caused consternation as it was believed that Wexford had escaped the worst consequences of the Famine.[34] As conditions improved, evictions and famine-related diseases swelled numbers in Wexford workhouse, showing that the town and surrounding area continued to suffer in the aftermath of the Famine. There was also a prolonged agricultural depression which impacted on the entire farming community. The county was depopulated by emigration, with many embarking at Wexford for Liverpool where they took ship for America.

SHIPPING AND TRADE

During the eighteenth century, Wexford's success as a port was based on a fleet of small ships suited to the difficult nature of the harbour. The town's seafarers were mostly engaged in the coastal trade or fishing for oysters and herring, with up to sixty cots fishing out of Wexford Harbour.[35] In 1804, Wexford experienced a repercussion from the Act of Union, when a petition to Westminster to form a company in the town to fish the Nymph Bank off the south coast met with failure, because of objections from English fishing ports.[36] Fishing failed to expand significantly during the nineteenth century, partly due to

lack of proper facilities but also because of the unpredictable nature of the herring shoals. Because of its insecure nature, those directly involved in the fishing industry found it difficult to rise above a subsistence level. The fishing suburb of the Faythe was described in 1834 as 'a very long, poor suburb, chiefly inhabited by fishermen'.[37] Shipping, on the other hand, entered a boom period, particularly from 1850 to 1880, partly because of the construction of a shipyard in the town. This was located on reclaimed land beside an extension to the south-east of the quays built by John Edward Redmond, whose family would play a vital part in the town until the early twentieth century.[38] In 1836, Redmond launched the *Town of Wexford,* the only steamship built in the town, to provide a ferry service to Liverpool. The paddle ship operated successfully for sixteen years until she was wrecked near Holyhead in 1852.[39] In 1837, 110 registered vessels, crewed by 600 seamen, were engaged in the coastal and cross-channel trade, carrying mostly agricultural produce. The ships were supported by the malt industry; in 1831, thirty-eight malt-houses produced 80,000 tons of malt, most of which was shipped to Dublin.[40] As well as the seamen who sailed in local ships, Wexford sailors found employment in other ports, including in ships of the British Navy, many of whom never returned. Typical of these was Edward Percival,

Fig. 20   A detail from an 1820 panoramic view of Wexford depicts a port crowded with sailing ships. It may be somewhat misleading as the vessels would not have been under full sail while anchored or tied up at the quayside. The ships are concentrated along the new quay close to the bridge.

Fig. 21   A mid nineteenth-century view of Wexford dockyard at Trinity Street looking east. The yard was constructed by the Redmonds on reclaimed land early in the century. The painting shows a bustling scene with ships being repaired in the dockyard and work being carried out on fishing boats in the foreground. To the left, other ships are waiting to be dealt with. Logs required for making planks are scattered about. The dockyard was incorporated into the Star Iron Works late in the nineteenth century. At present, the waterside site is vacant, awaiting development.

master's mate on the Royal Navy frigate, *Havannah*, who was killed in action in the Adriatic Sea in 1813. The captain and officers had a monument erected to his memory in St Iberius' church.

By mid century, a fleet of merchant shipping had been built up in Wexford, trading to the Baltic, the Mediterranean, Canada, the Americas and Africa.[41] For over fifty years, the two Devereux brothers, John Thomas and Richard, were the principal shipowners in Wexford with almost sixty schooners, brigs and barques between them. They traded principally with Galatz on the Danube, carrying coal on the outward voyage and returning with wheat and yellow corn and were also involved in the Mediterranean fruit trade.[42] In 1837, their first schooner, the *Slaney*, was built in their own shipyard, followed by others in quick succession; most of their other vessels were Canadian built.[43] The bigger ships were off-loaded into barges, or 'lighters', outside the harbour, to at least partially overcome the problem of the bar, and towed into the quays by a steam tug purchased by Richard Devereux.[44] By mid century, it was possible to improve the navigation of the harbour as a steam dredger had been acquired to deepen the channel.[45] The Devereux brothers were by no means the only shipowners in the town; the Allen family, for example, had many ships following the

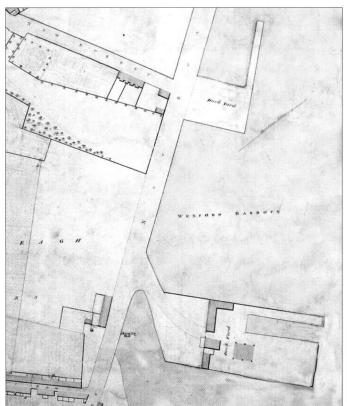

Fig. 22   Early nineteenth-century land reclamation to the south of the town led to the creation of Trinity Street, New (Parnell) Street and the two dockyards shown above on the 1840 O. S. town plan.

'The Fishermen of Wexford' by John Boyle O'Reilly

There is an old tradition sacred held in Wexford town,
That says: 'upon St Martin's Eve no net shall be let down;
No fishermen of Wexford shall, upon that holy day,
Set sail or cast a line within the scope of Wexford Bay'.
The tongue that framed the order, or the time, no one can tell;
And no one ever questioned, but the people kept it well.
And never in man's memory was fisher known to leave
The little town of Wexford on the good St Martin's Eve.

Alas! Alas for Wexford! Upon that holy day
Came a wondrous shoal of herring to the waters of the bay.
The fishers and their families stood out upon the beach,
And all day watched with wistful eyes the wealth they might
*   not reach.*
Such shoal was never seen before, and keen regrets went
*   around,*
Alas! Alas for Wexford! Hark! What is that grating sound?
The boat's keel on the shingle! Mothers, wives, ye well may
*   grieve,*
The fishermen of Wexford mean to sail on Martin's Eve.

'Oh, Holy Virgin! be their guard', the weeping women cried;
The old men, sad and silent, watched the boats cleave through
*   the tide,*
As past the farthest headland, past the lighthouse, in a line,
The fishing fleet went seaward through the phosphor-lighted
*   brine.*
Oh! Pray ye wives and mothers; all your prayers they sorely need
To save them from the wrath they've roused by their rebellious
*   greed.*

Oh! white-haired men and little babes, and weeping
*   sweethearts pray*
To God to spare the fishermen to-night in Wexford Bay.

The boats have reached good offing, and, as the nets are
*   thrown,*
The hearts ashore are chilled to hear the soughing sea-wind's
*   moan.*
Like a human heart that loved, and hoped for some return,
To find at last but hatred, so the sea-wind seemed to moan.
But ah! the Wexford fishermen, their nets did scarcely sink
One inch below the foam, when lo! The daring boatmen
*   shrink*
With sudden awe and whitened lips and glaring eyes, agape,
For breast-high, threatening, from the sea uprose a human
*   shape.*

Defying the dread warning, every face was sternly set,
And wildly did they ply the oar, and wildly haul the net.
But two boats' crews obeyed the sign, God-fearing men were
*   they*
They cut their lines and left their nets, and homeward sped
*   away;*
But darkly rising sternward did God's wrath in tempest
*   sweep,*
And they, of all the fishermen, that night escaped the deep.
Oh, wives and mothers, sweethearts, sires! Well might ye
*   mourn next day;*
For seventy fishers' corpses strewed the shores of Wexford
*   Bay.*

Mediterranean and Black Sea trade. They were engaged in the cotton trade from the southern United States, carrying emigrants on the outward voyage, and the *Menapia* traded trinkets for palm oil on the west coast of Africa. However, as the century progressed, the steamship eclipsed the sailing ship, especially for deep-sea trading. The Allen family ships were sold off in the 1870s, followed by the Devereux fleet in the 1880s, bringing to an end the golden era of sail in Wexford port.[46] The steamships did bring some benefits to the town: in the 1860s the 'superior steamer', *Troubadour,* sailed weekly to Liverpool and the *Fire fly* to Bristol, carrying passengers and agricultural produce; there was also a steamship service between Wexford and Dublin.[47]

In the 1880s, there was still considerable activity in the port with fifty-three vessels engaged in the coasting trade, one screw steamer, two tug-boats and a variety of fishing boats.[48] The Staffords of Cromwell's Fort, who began to buy schooners in the 1890s, were the last sail owners in Wexford. They were engaged mostly in the coastal trade as the malt trade between Wexford and Dublin continued to give steady employment to sailing vessels when other routes were taken over by steam. Two of the Stafford schooners were sunk by German submarines during the First World War. After the war, the Staffords bought small steamships and formed the Wexford Steamship Company. The last Wexford-built sailing ship afloat was the schooner *Antelope,* built by Wexford Dock Yard in 1886.[49]

Shipwrecks

Because of Wexford's extensive involvement in maritime activity, ships and sailors were inevitably lost at sea. The treacherous nature of the south-east coast and the approaches to the harbour meant that many disasters happened close to home. The fate of ships that disappeared in foreign parts frequently remained a mystery. The dangers of the harbour and bar exposed the herring cots to particular danger, as much of their fishing took place in winter. Two ballads recall disasters that befell the herring fleet: 'The fishermen of Wexford' recalls a storm in 1762 in which seventy fishermen lost their lives, and 'The Faythe fishing craft' commemorated a lesser

Fig. 23 This monument in St Iberius' church was erected by the shipmates of Edward Percival, an officer on the Royal Navy frigate, *Havannah*, who was killed in action in the Adriatic Sea in 1813.

disaster in 1833.[50] In the same year the sloop *Hawk* of Wexford, was wrecked on the bar. The risk associated with living in Rosslare Fort was highlighted in 1835: twelve people drowned when the market boat returning from Wexford to the fort overturned.[51] The vicissitudes of life at sea were illustrated by a particularly dramatic wreck and rescue that occurred in 1837. An emigrant ship named the *Glasgow* struck the Barrels Rock, off Carnsore, and began to sink. The Wexford schooner, *Alicia*, homeward bound, arrived on the scene. The captain, Martin Walsh, in spite of

Fig. 24 Because of numerous wrecks off the treacherous south-east coast, a lighthouse was completed on Tuskar Rock in 1815. During the construction, a severe storm resulted in the loss of ten men's lives.

high seas, managed to rescue 82 of the 111 people on board before the ship went down. Walsh brought the survivors to Wexford where they were cared for by the townspeople. A collection was made to return them to their homes, mostly in the west of Ireland. Subsequently, Walsh and his crew were honoured in every port they sailed to, particularly in Glasgow, the home port of the wrecked ship. Sadly, a few years later, the *Alicia* and her crew disappeared in a storm on the return trip from the Black Sea with a cargo of corn. However, not all hazards at sea were weather related; in 1851, the schooner *Sibyle* of Wexford, owned by John Barrington, was boarded and robbed by pirates on the Bospherous near Istanbul.[52]

The frequency of wrecks off the Wexford coast forced the authorities to take action. In 1815 a lighthouse was completed on Tuskar Rock, but at a cost of ten lives, lost in a storm during construction.[53] A lifeboat station, which earned a worldwide reputation over the next century, was established at Wexford in 1838, alternating between the town and Rosslare Fort until 1927, when it was transferred to Rosslare Harbour.[54]

Fig. 25 Early nineteenth-century boats off the suburb of the Faythe, the part of Wexford mostly associated with maritime affairs.

INDUSTRY

Industrial activity in Wexford was traditionally based on the processing of fish and agricultural produce. Corn mills were located at Mill Road on the Bishopswater stream and at Peter's Street (also known as Gibson's Lane) on a small stream (now underground) that originated in Summerhill and flowed to the harbour through Peter's Square. In 1840, a brewery was located beside these corn-stores at the corner of Peter's Street and Main Street.[55] Other breweries were located in Maudlintown and Spawell Road where a water-powered flour mill was later located on the site of the brewery.[56] Corn was also ground at Windmill Hill above the town, where sixteen windmills were shown on a 1770s map with another one in the field behind the Christian Brothers Primary School. There were also a number of small tanneries around the town,

Fig. 26 This view of Wexford can be dated fairly accurately to the 1860s. The spires of the twin churches, completed in 1858, are shown prominently on the skyline, and the original bridge, replaced in 1858 by a new structure up-river at Carcur, continued in use for a short period, mostly for foot traffic. Apart from the Quay and the Catholic churches, the town is not shown in any detail. The main focus is on the quays and harbour where a variety of boats and ships are shown. Among them are two paddle-steamers, illustrating the move from sail to steam, which led to a decline in the port of Wexford.

particularly in the John's Street area where no fewer than six were recorded.[57]

The emergence of the malting business in the eighteenth century was Wexford town's first major industrial enterprise. The malting process took place in tall, narrow malt-houses, three or four storeys high, sometimes built around a central courtyard. Malting consisted of the preparation of barley or other grain for brewing and distilling, by steeping, germinating and drying. In 1806, an inquiry into the malt industry found that thirty-three licensed malt-houses in Wexford paid £31,077 in excise duty.[58] As many as 210 malt-houses were recorded in Wexford at the end of the eighteenth century, but this had been reduced to thirty-eight by 1831, perhaps in fewer but bigger buildings; the 80,000 barrels of malt produced were primarily shipped to Dublin.[59] By 1845, the number of malt-houses had halved but in the period 1846–66 the quantity of malt on which excise was paid increased by sixty per cent, suggesting greater production in fewer premises.[60]

The Redmonds were involved in banking and property ventures rather than industry and greatly influenced the development of the town.[61] In the 1830s, John Edward Redmond reclaimed an extensive area from the harbour stretching to the south-east from Paul Quay, leading to the creation of Trinity Street, part of William Street and New Street (later Parnell Street). As part of the project, he constructed a wharf for steamships and a dockyard where ships were built for the rest of the century.[62] The dockyard was Wexford's first major industry; in 1843, when it was owned by Robert Sparrow, sixty ships' carpenters were employed.[63] Service industries were set up to supply sails,

Fig. 27 A number of Wexford's malt-houses have been successfully converted into apartment blocks. The example shown here is situated at the town end of the Faythe, known as 'The Swan' because of the fountain.

JOHN HAYES

Fig. 28   The Folly Mill Iron Works (better known as Pierce's) was established on the site of the Folly Corn Mill in 1839, beside a new road built by the military in the post-1798 period. Power was initially supplied by the Bishopswater river. The founder, James Pierce, was a highly-skilled inventor and craftsman and the industry, specialising in farm machinery, prospered for over a century. The site is now occupied by a Tesco supermarket.

ropes and other necessities; in 1840 there were five rope-walks in the town, four in the Faythe and one at King Street.[64] A German visitor to Wexford in 1842 commented on the 'new, broad and handsome quay' and observed that a great many vessels were built in the town where 'American and Baltic timber and Irish oak are everywhere to be seen'. He also admired a machine, which was not in use anywhere in Germany, called 'Parkin's patent slip', which raised or lowered ships, as required, in the well-equipped dockyard.[65]

The land opened up by the road, constructed subsequent to '98 as part of the 'new line' to Duncannon Fort, was occupied by Wexford's two major nineteenth-century industries. In a logical extension of the malting industry, the Devereux family and a Mr Harvey set up the Bishopswater distillery in 1827. Water for the distilling process was obtained from the nearby Bishop's Well, believed to be of superior quality. Power was provided by harnessing the Bishopswater stream to drive a water-wheel, later augmented by steam power. Covering several acres, the distillery had the most modern equipment and included a granary, a malting department and a bonded warehouse, cut out of solid rock. Later in the century, another warehouse was erected on Crescent Quay to supply the export trade, mostly to Bristol and Liverpool. Overseas business was managed by a London agent. The distillery was regarded as a 'model industrial concern' and gave employment to 'a great number of hands'.[66] Although renowned for the quality of its whiskey, due to the temperance movement and an increase in excise duty, production of whiskey fell by 35 per cent in the period

1846–66,[67] but the business continued throughout the nineteenth century.

The Folly Mill Iron Works (better known as Pierce's), the other industry to occupy a premises along the new road, was founded in 1847 by James Pierce from Kilmore.[68] The success of a small foundry set up by Pierce in Allen Street in 1839, where he specialised in making fire fans, enabled him to move to the large twenty-acre site (previously occupied by the Folly Corn Mill and Maltings), which had the added attraction of water power

PETER MILLER

Fig. 29   Fire fans, initially produced by Pierce's, were successfully manufactured by all three iron foundries in Wexford. The examples shown here are on display in the Irish Agricultural Museum at Johnstown Castle. The Doyle model has a distinctive swan's neck design. Mowing machine seats with the names of the foundries are shown over the fans.

Fig. 30   In the early twentieth century, the Doyle family of Selskar Iron Works built Auburn Terrace, beside the factory at Redmond Square. The houses were occupied by members of the family until the 1950s.

provided by the Bishopswater stream. Power was later provided by steam and oil. Pierce was a highly skilled inventor and craftsman and created technically demanding products such as the railings for the twin churches in 1858, and elaborate cast-iron conservatories for Edermine House and Castlebridge House. He also secured the contract to build a new bridge at Carcur in 1856. However, his main products were agricultural implements and machinery, particularly mowing machines and ploughs. Pierce was succeeded by his son Philip, and the factory was controlled by the family until 1964. By 1900 they were the biggest employer in the county, with a workforce of 400. The foundry produced bicycles for the first two decades of the twentieth century, as well as an expanded range of farm machines. As the use of tractors became more prevalent, Pierce's failed to modernise with inevitable consequences. As the demand for their 'horse era' products declined, the viability of the foundry diminished and, in 1964, the sale of the company marked the end of an era in Wexford. At the height of production, Pierce's had offices at Rue de Flandre in Paris and in Rio de Janeiro. These are remembered in housing schemes built by the Pierces for their workers at Avenue de Flandre (overlooking the factory), and at Casa Rio and Alvina Brook, as the names suggest, built along the Bishopswater stream.

Later in the century, two other iron foundries specialising in agricultural machinery were established in the town, one at the north end, and one at the south, strategically located close to the quays and the north and south railway stations. Matthew Doyle, originally from the north of the county but who had worked in Pierce's for many years, set up the Selskar Iron Works on reclaimed land opposite the north station in 1880.[69] Their wide range of high-quality agricultural machinery was very successful and the industry flourished, employing sixty men. The

family encountered financial difficulties after the War of Independence and the foundry eventually closed down. The site is now occupied by the Dunne's Stores complex.

The Keane family, who had founded the Star Iron Works in Cappoquin in the early 1880s, combined in 1897 with the Hearn family of New Ross to establish the Wexford Engineering Company (also known as the Star Iron Works), sited on reclaimed land to the south of the town off Trinity Street, formerly occupied by Wexford Dockyard.[70] The factory was built to the highest specifications and involved the reclamation of further land from the harbour and the construction of a shipping wharf

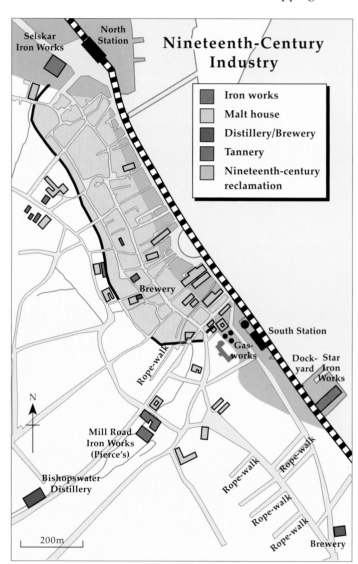

Fig. 31   There is an obvious connection between nineteenth-century land reclamation and industrial development. The dockyard was located on reclaimed land to the south-east of the town. Later in the century the site was extended to accommodate the Star Iron Works. The biggest concentration of malt-houses was located on reclaimed land between Oyster Lane and King Street, around the mouth of the Bishopswater river. The opening up of the marshy valley of the same river led to the establishment of the Bishopswater Distillery and Pierce's Iron Works. The seafaring suburb of the Faythe had four rope-making industries while the 'industrial' suburb of John's Street had malt-houses and tanneries.

Fig. 32   This prize-winning sample of Drinagh cement is preserved with a plaque stating that 'limestone cooked with mud from Wexford Harbour made world's hardest cement to withstand 2,500 lbs PSI in 1908'.

and railway siding. Ambitious early plans included the setting up of a base in Romania, serviced by Wexford shipping. By 1908 the Star was up for sale due to financial difficulties and was eventually purchased by the Hearn family. The plant continued to produce high-quality agricultural machinery, in spite of competition from Pierce's and the advent of the tractor, until its sale as a going concern in 1964.

The limestone deposits to the south-east of the town supported considerable industrial activity for over a century. In the 1830s, 20,000 tons of limestone were shipped annually from quarries near the shore of the harbour at Drinagh.[71] Limestone quarrying continued during the century and in 1871, a cement works with the most up-to-date equipment was established at Drinagh, ideally sited to use the proposed Wexford–Rosslare railway as transport.[72] The product, manufactured by the most up-to-date machinery, was of the highest quality and took first prize at international industrial exhibitions at Cork and Dublin. By 1888, expansion saw the installation of a 250 hp steam engine and the construction of a 110 feet high brick chimney. At the height of production the enterprise employed 150 men. In 1918, the concern was sold to the London Portland Cement Syndicate and was closed within a year. Strenuous efforts by Alderman Richard Corish to have the Drinagh cement factory re-opened were briefly successful but it closed down permanently in 1923. The tall brick chimney, to the east of the Rosslare road, still marks the site of the factory.

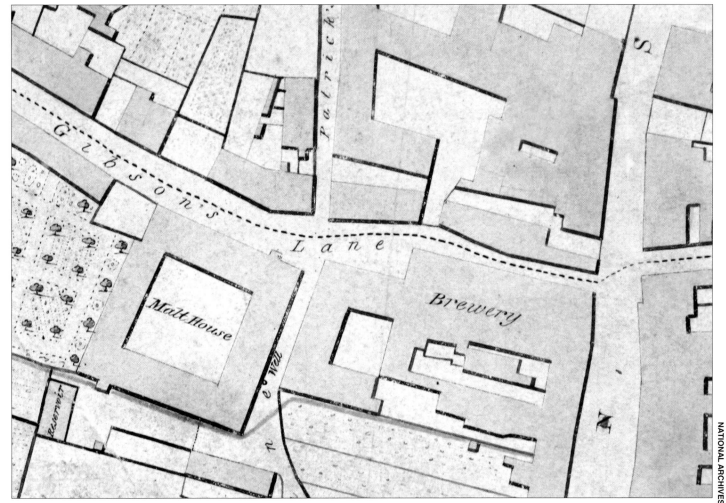

Fig. 33   Peter's Street (also known as Gibson's Lane) has been a centre of the milling industry since medieval times. Power was provided by a small stream, shown on the 1840 O. S. town plan, which is now culverted. At that time, the corn business included a malt-store and brewery.

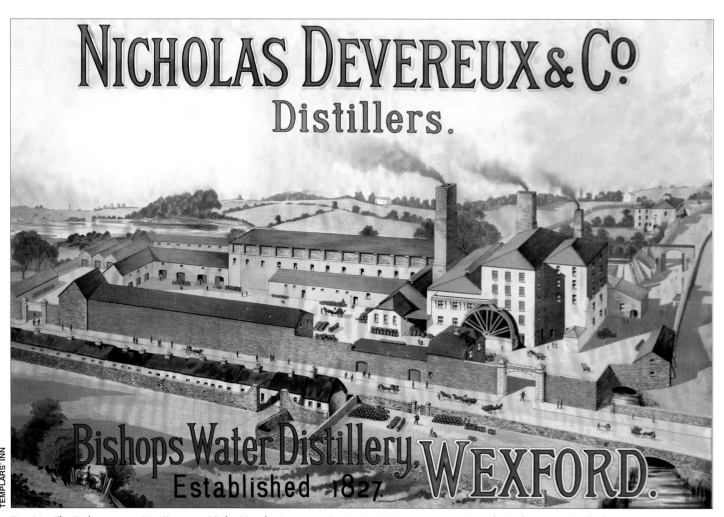

Fig. 34   The Bishopswater Distillery, established by the Devereux family in 1827, got its name from the Bishop's Well, which provided a supply of superior water. The advertisement shown above illustrates the extent of the industry later in the century. Many features are shown, including the mill-wheel and mill-race. Distillery House, accessed through an archway, can be seen at centre right. The row of thatched cabins along Distillery Road may have been occupied by the workers. Nothing survives of the complex except the arched entrance. The map of the site shown below is taken from the town boundary map of 1846. The small sample bottles of the product in 1887 are in private ownership.

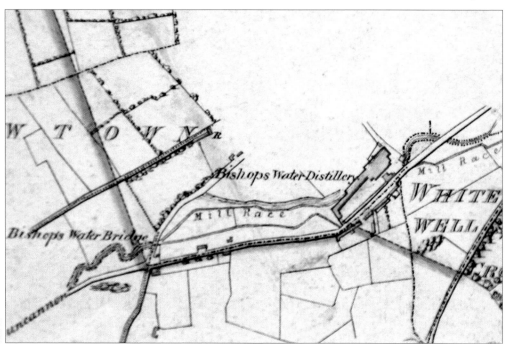

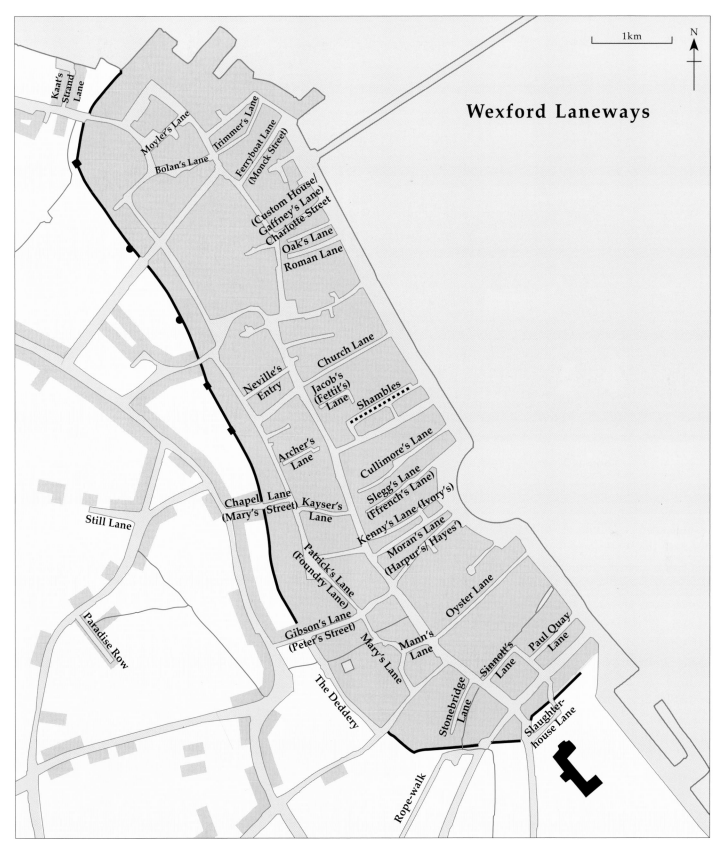

Fig. 35 Wexford's laneways are an integral part of the town's history and fabric and are worth preserving. Some have lost their character due to the removal of the original boundary line. Most of the lanes led from the Main Street to the waterfront and originated in the early days of the town, typified by the Viking Kayser's Lane. The lanes led to jetties and were extended as the waterfront was pushed further into the harbour by land reclamation. Many of the lanes and jetties were in private hands and names changed with ownership. Some were residential, containing rows of thatched cabins. The value of the lanes as routeways was diminished by the opening up of a new street along the waterfront in the early nineteenth century and many became derelict. In recent times, some of the lanes are again being utilised because of infill building between the Main Street and the waterfront.

Thomas Moore (1779–1852)

Thomas Moore, son of a Catholic merchant from Kerry and Anastasia Codd of Wexford town, was born at Aungier Street, Dublin. A student in Trinity College at the time of the 1798 Rebellion, he associated with known United Irishmen, including Robert Emmet, and had 'a deep and ardent interest' in United Irish politics. Because of his involvement, he was questioned by the authorities in early 1798. He later wrote a biography of Lord Edward FitzGerald. His United Irish experience intensified his sense of identity as an Irish Catholic and found expression in his songs and satires. Immensely successful as a writer in his lifetime, Moore was ranked with Scott and Byron; his oriental narrative poem, *Lalla Rookh*, was widely translated. He is best remembered for his songs, known as 'Moore's Melodies', which were wildly popular on both sides of the Atlantic. He was called 'the national poet of all oppressed peoples' and impacted on the national poetry of Europe. His Wexford connection is marked by a plaque on the house in Cornmarket (the centre house above) where his mother, Anastasia Codd, was born. In his diary, he described a visit to Wexford in 1835, during which he called to the Presentation Convent where he played on the organ and sang some of his lyrics.

Fig. 36   This aerial view shows the reclaimed lands of the south slob, divided by the wide drainage channel. In the foreground, the Wexford to Rosslare railway skirts the edge of the slob. A failed reclamation embankment extends to Rosslare point in the middle distance.

LAND RECLAMATION

The reclamation of land from the shallow waters of Wexford Harbour, continuous since medieval times, was an integral part of nineteenth-century urban growth. Reclamation work was carried out by John Edward Redmond to the south of the town in the 1830s and members of the family continued to be involved in similar projects later in the century. As early as 1813, efforts were made to reclaim the mudflats (known as 'slobs') in the shallow northern and southern parts of Wexford Harbour but these attempts ended in failure. An 1838 plan to reclaim 20,000 acres was opposed by the town's merchants and ship owners. They claimed that by making the channel deeper, Wexford's large fleet of small vessels would become redundant and they would no longer have a monopoly on business in the town.[73] In 1840, an Act of Parliament provided government aid for reclaiming waste land in Ireland. This prompted the formation of a Scottish syndicate with the aim of reclaiming extensive lands along the coast of county Wexford, including the North and South Slobs of Wexford Harbour.[74] The proposal involved extensive changes to all of the harbour, including the entrance and the channel. Not surprisingly, this initiative met with major resentment from local

Fig. 37   This watercolour by Wexford artist Mai McElroy depicts the pumping station on the north slob. As the slob was below sea-level, the station was needed to pump excess water into the harbour.

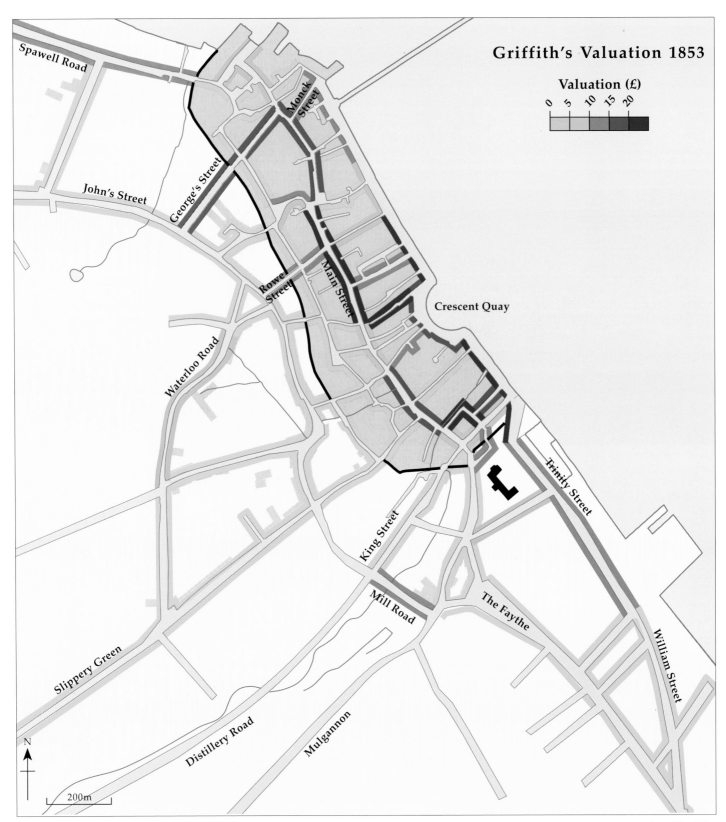

Griffith's Valuation 1853

Valuation (£)

0   5   10   15   20

Fig. 38   By mapping the average rateable valuations of streets, recorded in *Griffith's Valuation*, it is possible to create an economic and social profile of the town in 1853. The most valuable commercial area was concentrated on the reclaimed land between the Crescent Quay and King Street where there was a high density of malt-stores. The highest valued residential properties were located in George's Street and parts of the Main Street. The relatively late developed residential areas of Spawell Road, Monck Street and Rowe Street were of average value. The properties in the oldest streets, lanes and suburbs were of the lowest rateable value, indicating that the houses and businesses were sub-standard and occupied by the poorest social stratum. The communities in these areas probably retained the most enduring and traditional lifestyle whereas new developments presented high-value economic opportunities. During the twentieth century, the high-valued commercial areas decayed and fell in value but in the buoyant economy of recent years urban renewal has led to the regeneration of some derelict areas and an increase in their commercial worth.

landowners, merchants and politicians, who considered it a threat to their own interests. It was alleged that the proposed reclamation would make the already problematic navigation of the harbour even more difficult and would cause serious flooding in the town. After prolonged and intensive opposition, the project was eventually abandoned.

However, despite strenuous objections, the venture was taken up by an Irish group headed by John Edward Redmond. Work started on the embankment of the North Slob in 1847 and was completed two years later, giving badly needed employment during the Great Famine. Canals were constructed to drain the 2,400 reclaimed acres, allowing excess water to be removed by a pumping station. The soil proved to be fertile and was ready for cultivation within a few years. In 1854, work started on the embankment for the South Slob and was successfully completed. Unlike the North Slob, the soil failed to solidify, leading to the bankruptcy of the company in 1870. Ironically, the soil subsequently hardened and became financially viable for the new owners. By lessening the flow of water in the harbour, the reclamation of the slobs contributed to the silting-up of the channel and the growth of the bar at the entrance to the harbour.[75] The reclaimed slobs proved attractive to wildfowl and waders and in 1974 the Wexford Wildfowl Reserve was opened on 270 acres of the North Slob, which was increased to 470 acres in 1990.[76] The Redmonds continued their involvement in reclamation and by the 1870s they had reclaimed an area to the north of the town. This achievement was marked by

Fig. 39 During the 1860s, the Redmond family continued their involvement with reclamation by recovering the area now known as Redmond Square from the harbour. The achievement was marked by the erection of an obelisk known as the Redmond Monument.

IRENE ELGEE

Fig. 40 In this pre-reclamation drawing from *c.* 1860, the area that became Redmond Square is under water. The shoreline is marked by a stone sea-wall near the junction of North Main Street and Slaney Street. The substantial houses along Westgate Street are shown on the right.

Fig. 41   An early twentieth-century photograph of a steam train crossing the Crescent bridge. Following the arrival of the railway, the spectacle of trains travelling along the waterfront must have been a source of wonder and entertainment. Both sailing and steamships are berthed at the quay.

the erection of an obelisk, honouring various members of the Redmond family, located in the centre of the newly recovered land which was given the name Redmond Place (now Redmond Square). In 1874, Wexford's first railway station was situated on this stretch of reclaimed land and an embankment built to carry the railway along the edge of the harbour enclosed a further stretch of slob for eventual recovery.[77]

THE ARRIVAL OF THE RAILWAY

The construction of a rail link between Wexford and Dublin was of major infrastructural, social and economic significance.[78] The idea was first mooted by the renowned English railway engineer, Isambard Kingdom Brunel, during a visit to Dublin in 1844, when he proposed that a new rail line to a port in Milford Haven in Pembrokeshire should be connected by steamer to a port in south-east Ireland, which would be linked to Dublin by rail. Irish railway entrepreneurs were reluctant to become involved so the Great Western Railway (of England) formed the Waterford, Wexford, Wicklow and Dublin Railway to construct a line from St Stephen's Green in Dublin to

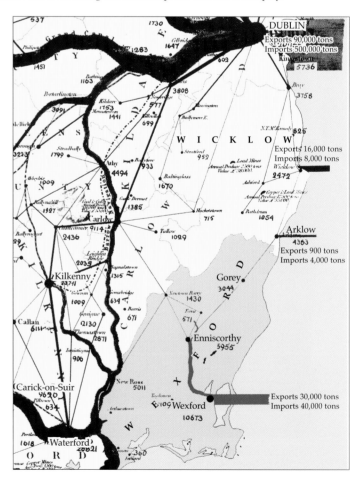

Fig. 42   This map prepared for the Railway Commissioners in 1837, depicting relative quantities of traffic, portrays Wexford as a minor port with a limited hinterland. The economic implications possibly contributed to a delay of over thirty years before the railway reached the town.

Fig. 43   The large-scale 1883 O. S. town plan contains detailed information on late nineteenth-century Wexford. Apart from the arrival of the railway, the town portrayed in these maps remained relatively unchanged until the mid twentieth century.

Waterford, with a branch line to 'a pier in the sea or on the shore of Greenore Bay, near the town and port of Wexford', on a route just to the west of Wexford town. Other competing proposals were put forward, but the scheme was shelved with the onset of the Great Famine in 1845. The project was revived in the 1860s by the Dublin, Wicklow and Wexford Railway which opened a rail line to Enniscorthy in 1863. In the following year, the Waterford & Wexford Railway Company was formed to construct a rail line across south Wexford to connect with the Dublin line at Carrig, north of Wexford, with a branch line west of the town to Greenore, where a pier was to be constructed. Five years later, the same company applied for permission to the Wexford Harbour Commissioners to run a tramway along the quays to connect the two railways, instead of building a rail line to the west of the town. The permission was granted but the Company was required to construct a quay and wharf on wooden piling along the length of the waterfront to take a second line of rails.

In 1871, the Dublin Wicklow & Wexford Railway Company opened a temporary station at Carcur, beside the new bridge, and three years later the line was extended to a new terminus opposite the old courthouse (just north of the present bridge). By 1872 the Wexford–Dublin line was open for service. The difficulties experienced by the two railway companies and the town authorities in attempting to reach

Fig. 44   Wexford's North Station was completed in 1891. Temporary stations had previously been in operation at Carcur and on the quay opposite the courthouse. The South Station was opened at Trinity Street in 1885.

THE QUAY, WEXFORD.

Fig. 45   The advantages of having a railway on the quay is illustrated in this early photograph which shows a railway wagon either loading from, or unloading to, a paddle-steamer. In comparison to other pictures, very few ships are berthed along the quay, a sign of things to come. Unloaded cargo includes the timber in the foreground. Some of the buildings along the quay, such as the red-brick structure to the left, are still in use.

agreement on a rail line along the quays delayed the work of continuing the line to Rosslare for a considerable time. Various schemes, including the filling in of the Crescent, were proposed and rejected. Eventually, in 1880, work started, including the construction of a bridge over the Crescent, and the Rosslare line opened two years later. In 1885, a new station, known as Wexford South, was opened near Trinity Street, for the convenience of residents in that part of the town; the present North Station was opened in 1891. By 1889, a great number of Wexford people were renting seaside premises for the summer season in Rosslare, facilitated by the railway, a custom that continued for much of the following century.

Conclusion

Wexford town experienced dramatic change during the course of the nineteenth century. The introduction of major manufacturing projects ushered in a late industrial revolution. In spite of the difficult harbour, the middle of the century saw a boom in shipping but when sailing ships were superseded by bigger steamships, Wexford experienced a catastrophic decline with much of its maritime activity transferring to the new port of Rosslare.[79] The most dramatic innovation during the century was the connection of the town to the railway system, which had far-reaching social and economic implications. Wexford's leading businessmen, the Devereuxs and Redmonds, dominated politics in the town during the century.[80] The Redmonds emerged as the principal political family in the south-east, several of them serving as MPs for different constituencies. John Redmond succeeded Parnell as leader of the Irish Party in Westminster where he was responsible for bringing a Home Rule Bill before parliament in 1914. The Bill was postponed because of the political situation in Ireland and the outbreak of war in Europe. After his death in 1918, he was buried in the family vault in St John's cemetery in Wexford.[81]

Friary tower from Mary's Street

ECCLESIASTICAL EXPANSION

Fig. 1   During the nineteenth century, Wexford's skyline was punctuated dramatically by the addition of Catholic churches. Apart from their religious significance, the church spires provided an emphatic social and political statement following the liberating effect of Catholic Emancipation in 1829.

The economic and infrastructural growth experienced by Wexford in the nineteenth century was paralleled by spectacular ecclesiastical expansion. By the end of the eighteenth century, prosperous and educated Catholic merchants were playing an influential part in public life, including church affairs. The success of the Devereux and Redmond families, by far the richest in the town, accelerated the growth of Catholic practise and the building of infrastructure.[1] As the application of the Penal Laws relaxed, the need for Catholic education in the town was quickly addressed. The Franciscans opened a classical school in Gibson's Lane (Peter's Street) before 1800, followed by a diocesan Catholic seminary at Bunker's Hill (Michael Street) in 1811.[2] This establishment was replaced by the foundation of St Peter's College in 1819, on lands belonging to the Redmond family at Summerhill, for the purpose of educating clerical students at home, instead of sending them to the continent.[3] The education of Protestant children was catered for by an infant school in Abbey Street, a primary school at Patrick's Square and a diocesan secondary school at Spawell Road,[4] also attended by the children of some wealthy Catholic families.[5] These were not the only schools; the Wexford Poor School, founded in 1809, catered for 300 boys and the Lancastrian Schools were established in the town with the support of Richard Devereux.[6] The demand for education can be gauged from the recording of twenty-eight schools in the town in the 1820s, many of them in private houses, catering for small numbers of pupils.[7]

Before Catholic Emancipation in 1829, the provision of church accommodation was confined to improving the Friary church where a north transept was added in 1812 due to a growing congregation. Further work, including the erection of side galleries around the walls, was carried out in 1827.[8] A lay committee set up at the time to upgrade the church grounds was composed of the town's wealthiest Catholics.[9] In 1833, a spacious library was built in the Friary to house a collection of books and documents acquired from the Franciscan College in Louvain.[10] The only significant undertaking in the town was the construction of Selskar Church by the Protestant community in 1826, in the grounds of Selskar Abbey, as a 'chapel of ease' for St Iberius'. This was controversial as it involved demolishing part of the medieval abbey. All households in the town, irrespective of religion, were obliged to contribute towards the cost. Furthermore, the spiky neo-Gothic design by architect John Semple, incorporating the medieval tower as the sacristy and belfry, was unpopular.[11]

Fig. 2   In 1826, Selskar Church, designed by John Semple, was controversially built in the grounds of Selskar Abbey. The abbey tower was restored and used as a sacristy and belfry.

Fig. 4   In 1800, a Protestant diocesan secondary school was built at Spawell Road.

In the more liberal post-Catholic Emancipation era, there was a surge in church building projects, not all for the Catholic community. A Methodist church was constructed in Rowe Street in 1835, a Friends' Meeting House in Patrick's Square in 1842 and a Presbyterian church in Anne Street in 1844. The first post-Emancipation Catholic church to be built in the town was the chapel of St Peter's College, constructed in the 1830s. John Hyacinth Talbot, of Castle Talbot, who helped to finance the work, acquired the services of the flamboyant architect, Augustus Welby Pugin, to design the chapel,

Fig. 5   The Presbyterian church built in Anne Street in 1844 has recently been sensitively restored by the church authorities.

through his English relation, John Talbot, earl of Shrewsbury, who was Pugin's patron. This was the architect's first introduction to county Wexford where he subsequently designed a further eight churches.[12]

The introduction of religious orders, almost all of them involved in education, had profound long-term implications for the future of Wexford and its inhabitants. The Presentation Order arrived in the town in 1818 and established a convent and school at Francis Street, beside the Friary.[13] They were followed by the Mercy sisters in 1840, who took over an orphanage built by the Redmond and Talbot families. Richard Devereux was a major benefactor, building a convent and school for the Order at Summerhill.[14] Richard Devereux also sponsored the establishment of the Christian Brothers in the town, funding schools in 1849 and 1853 at the Faythe and George's Street. In 1873, he built a monastery and adjacent school for the Brothers at Joseph Street; the St John of God Sisters were given the house and school in the Faythe.[15] During the second half of the century, a further

Fig. 3   The Friends' (Quakers') Meeting House built in Patrick's Square in 1842 is now used as a bandroom. In the 1850s, the Quaker graveyard was incorporated into the site for the Church of the Assumption at Bride Street.

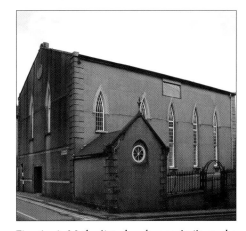

Fig. 6   A Methodist church was built at the junction of Back (Mallon) Street in 1835. It is no longer used for its original purpose.

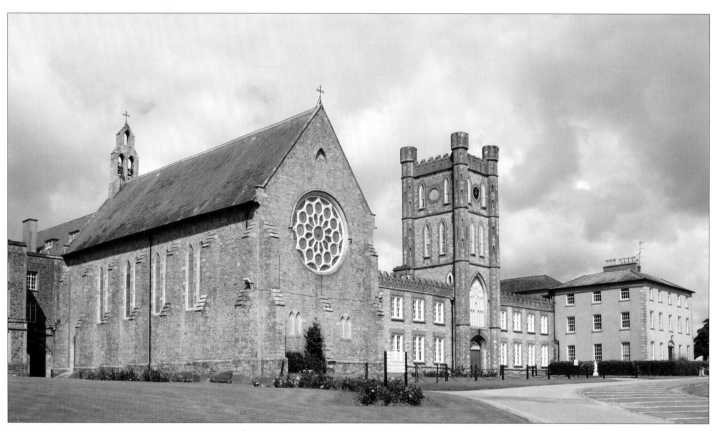

Fig. 7 St Peter's College was founded at Summerhill in 1819, as a diocesan Catholic seminary, in a house (on the right) and on lands donated by the Redmond family. During the 1830s, an extension with tower, and a church designed by renowned architect A. W. Pugin, was constructed.

three orders of nuns were established in the town, two of them involved in education. In 1866, the Loreto sisters arrived in the town, staying in a house in George's Street until Richmond House on Spawell Road, the centre of the present complex, was purchased for the Order. The Perpetual Adoration Order was established in Wexford in 1875, moving from a temporary residence at Rockfield House at Spawell Road to a new convent beside Bride Street church in 1887. In 1871, the St John of God sisters arrived, occupying temporary accommodation at Sallyville until 1881, when their convent at Newtown Road was completed.[16]

As the infrastructure and confidence of the Catholic Church grew, supported by a wealthy middle class and a swelling number of priests, devotional activity also increased and was given added impetus by the traumatic psychological impact of the Great Famine. The religious fervour was typified by the enthusiastic response to Fr Mathew's visit to the town in 1840 as part of his revivalist Temperance crusade, and to the founding of the Catholic Young Men's Society. It was also evident in an extremely high

BRIAN DOYLE

Fig. 8 Until the 1930s, St Peter's College church retained the original Pugin rood screen, separating the nave from the chancel.

Fig. 9 Original Pugin design elements in St Peter's College church include the highly ornate altar and stained glass window.

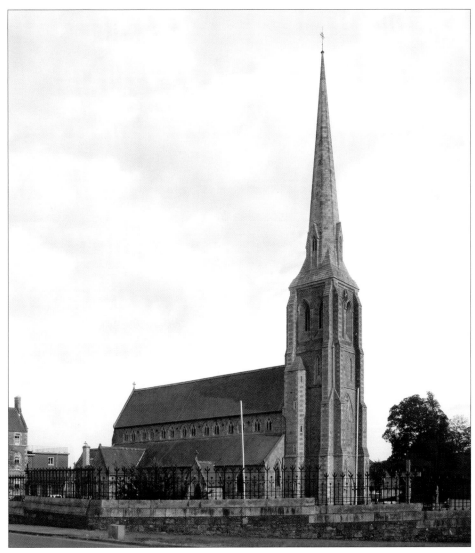

Fig. 10   One of the twin churches, the church of the Assumption, generally referred to as Bride Street church, was completed in 1858, close to the site of the medieval church of St Brigid.

Fig. 11   The interior of Bride Street church. The original design was changed by the removal of the altar when the sanctuary was modernised in the post-Vatican II period.

Fig. 12   A light from a window by stained-glass artist, Harry Clarke, in Bride Street church.

Fig. 14 This statue of Rev. James Roche was erected in the grounds of Rowe Street church to acknowledge his leading role in the building of the churches at Bride Street and Rowe Street.

Fig. 15 The Perpetual Adoration Order still occupies a convent built for them in the grounds of Bride Street church in 1887.

Fig. 13 The church of the Immaculate Conception (popularly known as Rowe Street church) was built beside an extension of Rowe Street from the town wall to John's Street. The twin churches were designed in the style of Pugin, by Wexford architect Richard Pierce (who had worked with Pugin), and was built by Thomas Willis. The ornamental railings were manufactured by Pierce's Foundry.

attendance at mass and other devotional practices.[17] Against this positive background an initiative to provide much needed new church accommodation in the town was assured of widespread support. In 1850, a public meeting decided to build not one, but two new churches in the town. Rev. James Roche was appointed Parish Priest shortly afterwards and became the driving force behind the building project.[18]

The bishop stipulated that both churches should be identical in plan to avoid 'jealousy and unpleasant comparisons amongst the towns-people', reflecting the historical antagonism between the north and south of the town.[19] The church for the south end of the town (dedicated to the Assumption) was to be sited outside the town wall at Bride Street, on a mostly vacant plot which contained the site of the medieval

Fig. 16 Richard Devereux, wealthy business-man and shipowner, was a major benefactor and philanthropist in nineteenth-century Wexford, contributing to the building of schools, convents and churches.

Fig. 17   During the 1850s, a four-storey Romanesque bell-tower was added to the north gable of the Friary. This architectural embellishment is a fine example of sympathetic development.

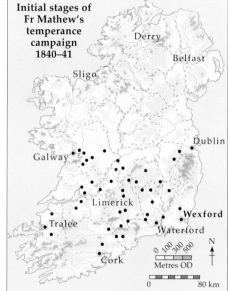

Fig. 19 Fr Mathew received an enthusiastic welcome in Wexford when he visited the town during his temperance campaign of 1840–41.

church of St Brigid, and a Quaker graveyard.[20] The church for the north end (dedicated to the Immaculate Conception) was also located outside the town wall, on a site at the junction created by John's Street and an extended Rowe Street. This choice of site involved the demolition of some houses along John's Street and part of the town wall, including a mural tower.[21] These much-loved churches became popularly known by the names of their adjacent streets, Rowe Street and Bride Street.

The wealthy business sector of the town made a significant contribution to the cost of the churches, but most of

WEXFORD COUNTY LIBRARY

Fig. 18   The Mercy Order arrived in the town in 1840 to take charge of an orphanage built at Summerhill by the Redmond and Talbot families. Richard Devereux erected a convent for the nuns. The complex was sold in the 1980s and the site is now occupied by a housing estate.

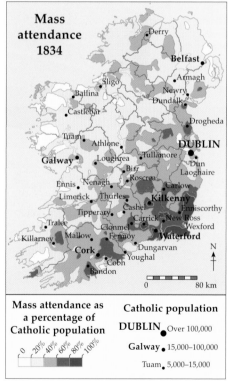

Fig 20 The extraordinary levels of Mass attendance (80–100%) in county Wexford in 1834, the highest in the country, explains the huge support for church-based initiatives in the town during the nineteenth century.

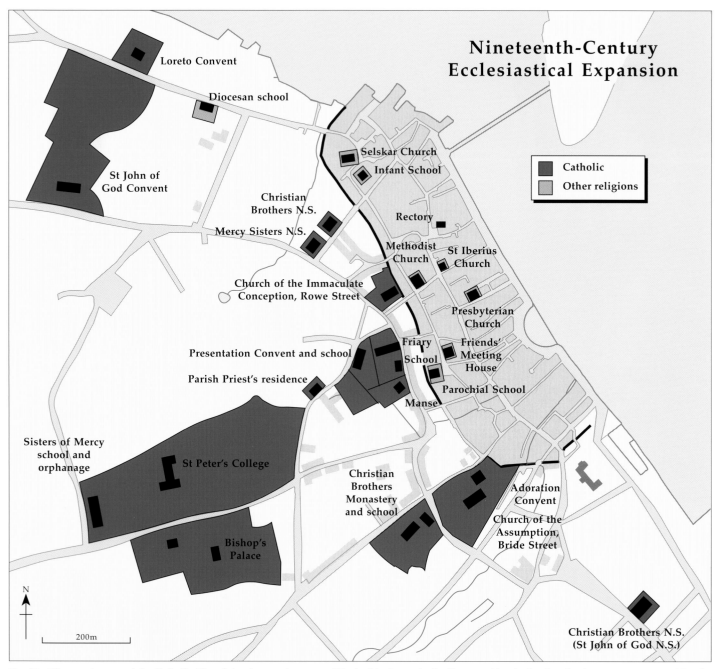

Nineteenth-Century Ecclesiastical Expansion

Loreto Convent

Diocesan school

St John of God Convent

Selskar Church

Infant School

Christian Brothers N.S.

Mercy Sisters N.S.

Rectory

Methodist Church

St Iberius Church

Church of the Immaculate Conception, Rowe Street

Presbyterian Church

Presentation Convent and school

Friary School

Friends' Meeting House

Parish Priest's residence

Parochial School

Manse

Sisters of Mercy school and orphanage

St Peter's College

Christian Brothers Monastery and school

Adoration Convent

Church of the Assumption, Bride Street

Bishop's Palace

Catholic

Other religions

N

200m

Christian Brothers N.S. (St John of God N.S.)

Fig. 21   The renaissance of the Catholic Church in nineteenth-century Wexford is dramatically illustrated by the land and infrastructure acquired by the Church during that period, all located outside the core area of the town. Some land has been sold but much remains in the possession of the Church.

the £54,000 was raised by elaborate collection methods from the entire community.[22] Wexford architect, Richard Pierce – who had acted as clerk of works for Pugin's church-building projects in county Wexford, Killarney and Maynooth – was selected to design the churches. Pierce, who also built churches in his own right, was deeply influenced by Pugin's Gothic Revival philosophy.

Pierce's builder, Thomas Willis, completed the main structure of the churches by 1858. The decorative work, executed by Thomas Hardman and Thomas Earley, both of whom had been involved in Pugin's Irish projects, was not completed until 1881. Built of a conglomerate red sandstone, quarried at Park to the north of the town, Wexford's twin churches were Pierce's finest work, the soaring spires

punctuating Wexford's skyline in an eloquent expression of resurgent Irish Catholicism.[23] During the same period, a four-storey Romanesque bell-tower was added to the north transept of the Friary as part of major renovations, completing the visual transformation of the Wexford skyline.[24]

The dramatic advances made in the industrial, economic and infra-structural life of Wexford during the

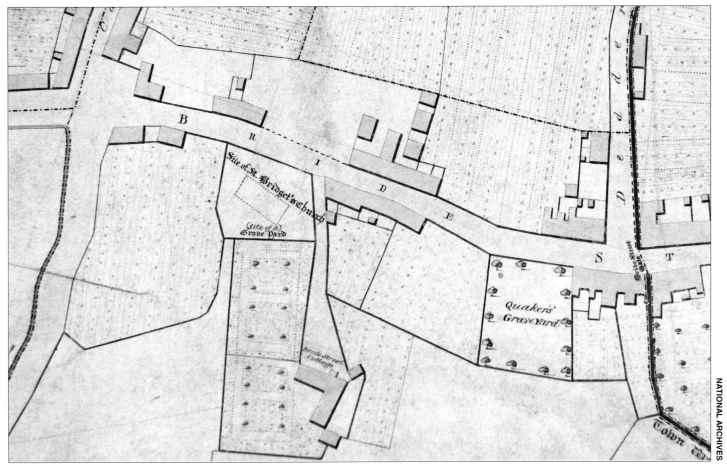

Fig. 22   Bride Street church was built on a plot of ground south of Bride Street, just outside Bride Gate. The location contained the Quaker graveyard and the site of St Brigid's medieval church. Roche's Road was subsequently constructed to connect the church with Peter's Square and School Street.

nineteenth century were accompanied by parallel growth in religious institutions and personnel. This was made possible partly by the dedication and ambition of an educated clergy but also, and in large part, by the support of powerful business interests in the town. The introduction of highly visible churches and religious institutions fundamentally changed the character of the town, creating a profile that has survived until recent times. Ultimately, the greatest impetus for social change came from the vastly improved educational opportunities made available by the religious orders.

THE MODERN TOWN

By the end of the nineteenth century, Wexford's industrial and shipping boom was in decline. The transfer of shipping to the new port of Rosslare was balanced partially by the presence of the railway, but, as bigger steamships began to dominate maritime trade, Wexford's role as a port dwindled inexorably as the century progressed. The Harbour Board struggled to cope with the difficult nature of the bar at the harbour entrance, where ships and fishing boats frequently grounded. In January 1903, a storm enlarged the bar to such an extent that no ships could enter the estuary. In April, however, twenty-eight vessels and thirty-nine fishing-boats entered the port and a Liverpool sucking dredger, the *Tulip*, had been engaged to dredge the bar at a cost of £100 per week.[1] In spite of endemic problems with the bar, the Staffords, an enterprising Wexford family, continued to trade with sailing ships, owning eleven schooners up to 1919. The topography of the harbour was altered dramatically in the mid 1920s by the erosion of the Rosslare sandspit.[2] The peninsula had been subject to erosion for some time and was eventually breached by a storm in 1924. So extensive was the breach that the Fort Village and lifeboat station at the extremity of the point had to be abandoned. The Fort and two kilometres of sandspit were eventually completely submerged, creating a much wider entrance, but still too shallow to be advantageous to shipping.

O. S. I.

Fig. 1   An early twenty-first century aerial perspective of Wexford, showing the expansion of the town to the west, sandwiched between the New Ross and Duncannon roads. The extension to the waterfront, including a new marina, has been completed. Wexford Golf Club is at bottom centre.

THE NEW CENTURY

The twentieth century was heralded by the Boer War, which began in South Africa in 1899, the first of many wars that blighted the century. The distant war impacted directly on Wexford as the Wexford Militia was among the Irish regiments sent to the front. The nationalist disposition of the early twentieth-century town is reflected in newspaper reports of the activities of the Gaelic Athletic Association, the Gaelic League and frequent reports on 'the land question'. In the first decade of the century, sporting headlines were made by the great Wexford boxer, Jem Roche, who fought, but lost, against the world heavyweight champion, Tommy Burns, in Dublin. Castlebridge's victory against Limerick in the 1910 All-Ireland hurling final provided another sporting highlight. Entertainment was provided by variety concerts in the Theatre Royal, magic lantern shows and balls in the Town Hall. The Corporation, engaged in ongoing disagreement with the Gas Board, decided to demolish the Tholsel in the Bullring and to open a new street known as John's Road.[3]

In 1911, an industrial dispute impacted severely on the economic life of the town.[4] Following the establishment of the Irish Transport and General Workers Union in Wexford, a strike by the dockers brought them an increase in wages. Presumably encouraged by the dockers' success, workers in Pierce's foundry began to join and were immediately dismissed. When the I. T. & G. W. U. retaliated by 'blacking' an essential consignment of coke, Pierce responded by closing the ironworks, resulting in hardship for the families of 400 workers. The Star and Selskar Iron Works closed also, in a united effort at resisting unionisation. Negotiations between the two sides proved unsuccessful and, as the situation deteriorated, 150 R. I. C. men were brought in to maintain law and order. Their arrival led to clashes in the streets which resulted in the death of one man. After four months, circumstances were made even more desperate by the introduction of 'blackleg' labour by the employers. Eventually, intervention by the local clergy resulted in a resolution of the crises.

WORLD WAR I

The political mood of the town was dictated by John and Willie Redmond, members of the prominent Wexford Catholic family. John was M. P. for Waterford and Willie for East Clare. In 1890, John became leader of the Home Rule party following the death of Parnell.[5] Redmond succeeded in bringing a Home Rule Bill before the house at Westminster, only to see it postponed by the outbreak of World War I. The Redmonds, underestimating the

Fig. 2 The widespread centenary commemorations of the 1798 Rebellion had a political and religious dimension. An attempt to use the occasion as an opportunity to unite the Irish Parliamentary Party was not successful as Redmondite Wexford decided to hold separate events. By claiming that the Rebellion was 'for faith and fatherland', the writings of Wexford Franciscan, Fr Patrick Kavanagh, gave a distinctively Catholic character to the commemorations. The 350-strong Wexford Borough Centenary Committee held many ceremonies during the year, including an assembly at Three Rocks on Forth Mountain. A decision was taken to erect a '98 monument in the Bullring as a permanent '98 memorial. The commission was given to Irish sculptor and nationalist, Oliver Sheppard, whose design of a pikeman in heroic pose was accepted. The larger than life sculpture took some time to complete and was eventually unveiled in 1905. The town was decorated with evergreens, flags and banners for the spectacular event, to which 15,000 travelled by train from all over the south-east of Ireland. The monument was highly acclaimed and 'The Pikeman' is now part of Wexford's heritage. Sheppard also sculpted the Fr Murphy monument in Enniscorthy (1908), the Willie Redmond bust (1930; now in Redmond Park) and the Death of Cúchulainn (unveiled in 1935 in the G. P. O. as the 1916 Rising memorial).

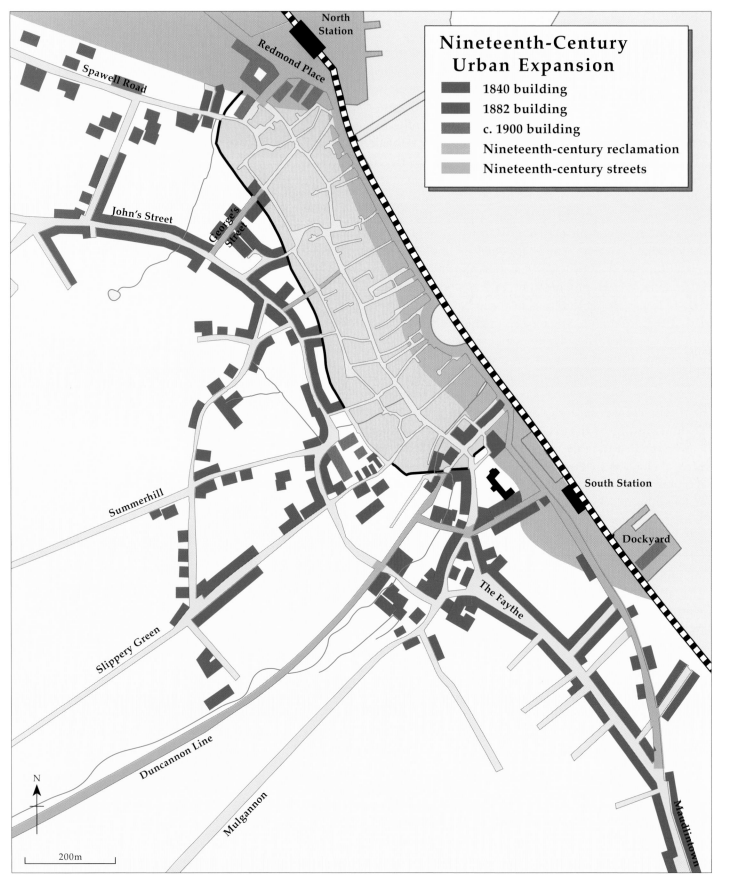

Nineteenth-Century
Urban Expansion

■ 1840 building
■ 1882 building
■ c. 1900 building
□ Nineteenth-century reclamation
□ Nineteenth-century streets

North
Station

Redmond Place

Spawell Road

John's Street

George's
Street

Summerhill

Slippery Green

Duncannon Line

Mulgannon

The Faythe

South Station

Dockyard

Maudlintown

N

200m

Fig. 3 At the beginning of the twentieth century, the town's housing stock was substantially the same as in 1840. The principal additions were concentrated in the south of the town which had been opened up by land reclamation and the construction of the Duncannon Line.

Fig. 4 As bigger steamships became common place, the endemic difficulties with access to Wexford Harbour, and the arrival of the railway, led to the development of a new harbour at Rosslare. This inevitably resulted in the eventual abandonment of Wexford port.

threat of Unionist opposition, supported recruitment for the British army as they believed that it would forge a common Irish identity and lead to Home Rule.[6] Numerous young men from Wexford town and county volunteered for active service. The families of those who died in the trenches were awarded a bronze plaque which became known as a 'dead man's penny'.[7] Willie Redmond, true to his convictions, became an officer in the British army and died at the Battle of Messines Ridge, near Yprès in Flanders. His brother, John, died in 1918

Fig. 5 John Redmond, a member of a prominent Wexford family, dominated Irish politics for thirty years. His hopes for achieving Home Rule by constitutional means were dashed by the outbreak of World War I. He died in 1918 and was buried in St John's graveyard in the family mausoleum. Long neglected, it is currently being restored, an indication of the revival of Redmond's reputation.

and was buried in the family mausoleum in St John's graveyard in Wexford town.

Wexford was the location for two activities directly related to the war, one of them – the manufacture of shell cases for the British army in Pierce's foundry – being of considerable economic value to the town. In the final days of the war, because of its tactical location, Wexford was selected as the base for a squadron of U. S. navy sea-planes which patrolled the sea lanes off the south-east coast in search of German submarines. (Two schooners owned by Stafford's of Wexford had been sunk by submarines during the conflict.[8]) With 426 personnel, the unit also had a battery of heavy guns at Rosslare, a marine detection centre at Kilrane and an air-ship base at Johnstown Castle. The planes completed ninety-eight patrols before the end of the war and destroyed several submarines. The Americans departed soon after the war ended.[9]

Fig. 6 In the last days of World War I, a base for a squadron of U. S. navy sea-planes was set up in Wexford Harbour. Extensive accommodation was constructed at Ferrybank where the American slipway still survives .

THE 1916 RISING

The Easter Rising of 1916 was denounced by John Redmond, but he also deplored the executions of the leaders following the failure of the Rebellion.[10] The Redmondite Wexford Corporation passed a motion opposing the Rising but four years later it was rescinded, a clear indication of the shift in political sympathies.[11] In county Wexford, activity associated with the 1916 Rising was focused mainly on Enniscorthy, which was taken over by Republican forces.[12] However, during the subsequent War of Independence, there was considerable action by Republican forces in the county. In Wexford town, the Doyles of Selskar Iron Works, whose ancestors had been active in 1798, made guns, bullets and grenade casings for the Republican forces. The foundry was raided on several occasions but nothing was found. The Doyles received a final warning and moved their weapon-making operation out of town.[13] The contentious treaty of 1921 was carried by

Fig. 7   The families of soldiers killed in World War I were presented with bronze medallions inscribed with the name of the lost relative. These became known as 'dead men's pennies'.

a narrow majority in the Dáil but opposed by the anti-Treaty group, led by De Valera.[14] Following the establishment of the Irish Free State and the setting up of a provisional government, a bloody civil war broke out between the opposing factions. There was considerable activity in county Wexford by anti-Treaty forces, particularly aimed at the disruption of train services. Wexford town was strongly pro-Treaty and when Michael

Fig. 8   This early twentieth-century advertisement for Pierce bicycles used attractive girls (presumably from the town) in what was the latest fashion, to encourage sales. For some unknown reason, all of the girls are carrying horse-whips.

Collins addressed a public meeting in St Peter's Square in 1922, special trains carrying supporters to the town were intercepted by anti-Treaty activists.[15] During his stay, Collins visited the Mill Road Iron Works and was presented with a Pierce bicycle. The saddest episode of the Civil War in county Wexford coincided with the cessation of operations by the anti-Treaty side. In February 1923, a number of Republicans were captured in a house at Horetown, Foulksmills and lodged in Wexford jail. Three of them, John Creane, Patrick Hogan and James Parle, were executed at the jail a month later. Initially buried in Kilkenny, they were later re-interred in the Republican plot at Crosstown. A few weeks after the executions, thirty-nine Republican prisoners escaped from Wexford jail.

Fig. 9   The profile of buildings shown in this early twentieth-century photograph of South Main Street is still recognisable. The low building with a dormer window to the right, on the corner of Oyster Lane, was removed in recent times. Cobble-stone shores bordered the unsurfaced street. The use of slates as damp-proofing on walls was a feature of buildings in Wexford and is still in evidence in the town.

SHIPPING

In spite of endemic problems with access to the port, the Staffords established the Wexford Steamship Company in 1930 and acquired three modern motorships, the *Edenvale, Kerlogue* and *Menapia*.[16] During World War II, Staffords' ships were involved in carrying much needed supplies to Ireland, mostly from neutral Lisbon. The *Edenvale* was attacked by German aircraft on four occasions and in 1943 the *Kerlogue* was attacked by RAF aircraft (presumably by mistake), resulting in injury to the captain and three crew members. The motor vessel *Begerin*, owned by Wilsons of Wexford, was bombed and sunk by a German plane while bringing coal from south Wales. The eight-man crew took to the lifeboats and survived.[17] In December 1943, the *Kerlogue*, under Captain Donohue of Dungarvan, carried out an epic rescue in the stormy Bay of Biscay of 170 German survivors from ships recently sunk by the British navy. The Wexford ship spent ten

TONY RECK

Fig. 10   The small, Stafford-owned *Kerlogue*, shown here off the Hook Lighthouse, was involved in the dramatic rescue of 170 German sailors in the Bay of Biscay in 1943. She was one of the last Wexford-owned ships to continue to use the port until the 1960s.

hours rescuing the sailors from the sea. Disregarding Allied orders to land at Fishguard, the captain took his overcrowded ship to neutral Cork where the German sailors were interned until the end of the war.[18] The greatest war-time tragedy with Wexford connections was the sinking of the Great Western Railway mailboat, the *St Patrick,* in June 1941. The ship was bombed by German aircraft eighteen miles from Fishguard and went down with the loss of thirty lives.[19] A memorial to the thirteen Wexford seamen who lost their lives during the war was erected at the Crescent Quay in 1956. The *Edenvale, Kerlogue* and *Menapia,* until they were sold in the 1950s and '60s, were the last Wexford-owned ships. With them ended a maritime tradition that stretched back to the foundation of the town.

URBAN EXPANSION

Local government was reformed in 1898, by replacing Grand Juries and Boards of Guardians with County Councils. The first meeting of Wexford County Council took place in Wexford Courthouse the following year. The Council acquired the former jail in 1905 but it was used as a convent and barracks until 1931, when it became the Council's headquarters. (Only the women's prison survives as the complex has been much modified in the course of several renovations.[20]) Wexford Corporation also acquired new accommodation in 1949, when it moved from the Town Hall (now Wexford Arts Centre) to the Municipal Buildings at Wygram. Formerly the Tate School, the red-brick structure was funded in the 1850s by a bequest from William Tate.[21] Wexford town experienced limited expansion in the first three decades of the century with the provision of new Corporation housing confined to small schemes at Hill Street, Distillery Road and St Ibar's Villas. However, during the 1930s, the rate of house building away from the core urban area increased dramatically.[22] The principal schemes were at Wolfe Tone Villas (94 houses), Maudlintown (154 houses) and Whiterock View (62 houses). After a lull during the war years, the expansion of the town to the west continued during the 1950s and '60s with major Corporation housing developments at St Aidan's Crescent (58 houses), Bishopswater (128 houses), Corish Park (132 houses) and Kennedy Park (126 houses).

Fig. 11 The former jail was taken over by the newly formed County Council in 1905 but was not used as the County Hall until 1931. The complex has been subsequently modified and, of the original buildings, only the women's prison, the perimeter wall and the entrance (shown above) survive.

RECOVERY

During the 1950s, there were indications that the town was emerging from the doldrums of the previous fifty years. Wexford Opera Festival was inaugurated in 1951, and from modest beginnings developed into a world-renowned event. The 'Festival', as it is popularly known, continues to be of immense economic and promotional value to the town. Significantly, it was this cultural initiative that gave Wexford an international profile and helped to generate the impetus that facilitated the town's renaissance during the second half of the century. Another event of the decade with international significance was the erection of the John Barry memorial on the Crescent Quay in 1956. In the late 1950s, the town reverberated to the sound of pile-drivers as a new bridge was built, on the site of the original structure, from the north quay to Ferrybank. The 1795 bridge heralded the town's eighteenth-century expansion and similarly its modern successor can be seen as a symbol of the town's recent prosperity. The cultural life of the town received a significant boost in the 1970s when the Corporation, with the support of the Arts Council, made the old Town Hall in Cornmarket available as Wexford Arts Centre, still a vibrant component of Wexford's creative life.

Fig. 12 The Tate School, at Windmill Hill, was occupied by the Corporation in 1949 and became the Municipal Buildings.

Fig. 13   The construction of a new bridge, on the site of the late eighteenth-century structure, symbolised the revival of Wexford's fortunes during the second half of the twentieth century. In the 1990s, in a skillful engineering operation, the original concrete superstructure was replaced in metal.

However, in the short term, the town's economic life was experiencing decline rather than growth. As difficulties with the bar led to continuous problems in the harbour, the number of ships coming into Wexford declined steadily and by the mid 1960s the port was closed.[23] The town's traditional industries were also struggling to survive, particularly Pierce's Foundry and the Star Iron Works. In the early 1960s, they were bought by the Smith Group which set up a car assembly plant in the Star premises and operated a limited business in Pierce's.[24] Both enterprises were sold in the 1990s: the site of Pierce's is now occupied by a branch of the Tesco supermarket chain and a major development, to be known as Trinity Wharf, is proposed for the waterside location of the Star. By the 1970s, determined efforts to attract new industry to the town were meeting with some success,

Fig. 14   In the early 1950s, a major scheme of 132 Corporation houses built west of the town was named Corish Park, in honour of Richard Corish who was mayor for twenty-five consecutive years. Now a settled community in the middle of other housing estates, Corish Park was surrounded by open countryside when it was first built.

Fig. 15   In the 1970s, because of a growth in residental properties to the west of the town, a new Catholic parish of Clonard was created, with its own church and community centre. The initial church was inadequate for expanding numbers and was rebuilt in the 1990s. The Clonard area is now one of the principal centres of population in greater Wexford.

Fig. 16   Following the closure of the port, in the 1970s a successful mussel industry was established in Wexford Harbour. Mussels are sown and harvested by a fleet of purpose built mussel dredgers which add vibrancy, colour and character to the waterfront.

partly due to the establishment of the Whitemill Industrial Estate to the west of the town. The absence of commercial shipping allowed the potential of Wexford's shallow harbour to be exploited as a centre of aquaculture. By transplanting seed mussel to the mudflats, the Lett family set up an innovative mussel industry with a processing plant at Batt Street. Dredging was carried out initially by individual fishermen in Wexford cots, but, as the industry

Wexford
Town

Habitats

	Infralittoral gravel and sand		Moderately exposed infralittoral rock
	Infralittoral muddy sand		Infralittoral mud
	Infralittoral mixed sediment		3km

N

Fig. 17   By the deposition of silt and sediment, complex currents of river and sea have formed a varied series of habitats, resulting in a rich and varied ecological environment in Wexford Harbour, making it very suitable for mussel aquaculture.

Fig. 18   Among the many items brought up by the mussels dredgers, the broken clay pipes, some centuries old, form a link with the hundreds of Wexford fishermen who fished the harbour over the years.

Fig. 19 In the 1980s, the Irish National Heritage Park was developed at Ferrycarrig in a marshy area beside the newly constructed ring road. The park contains recreations of domestic and ceremonial buildings from Ireland's early history, reconstructed according to the the best available archaeological advice. The Early Christian church site is shown here.

ringroad was constructed to the west of the town to relieve traffic congestion. Connecting the Dublin road at Ferrycarrig with the Rosslare road at Drinagh and linked to the town by four connecting roads, this was a major infrastructural initiative and was essential to the future growth of the town. Industry benefited by the setting up of the Kerlogue Industrial Estate and the Wexford Business Park, adjacent to the ringroad to the south of the town convenient to Rosslare ferryport. In the 1980s, the Irish National Heritage Park, highlighting a series of replicated archaeological monuments, was developed as a successful tourist attraction on marshy ground beside the ring road at Ferrycarrig. The implementation of the government-sponsored Urban Renewal Scheme in the late 1980s led to the regeneration of the north end of the town. In conjunction with a housing development at Westgate, the Selskar Abbey gate tower and a circular mural tower were restored. The run-down Redmond Square area was completely refurbished as a shopping area, bringing vitality back to what had become a neglected part of the town.

matured, the large purpose-built mussel dredgers, now such an attractive presence in the harbour, were acquired.

In the 1980s, as traffic through the town increased, especially from Rosslare along the quays to the bridge, a

Fig. 20 This aerial view shows the extension to the waterfront constructed in the late 1990s in conjunction with a main drainage scheme. Considerable infill building can be seen between the Main Street (marked at centre left by St Iberius' church) and the quay. The large white building at centre right is the new White's Hotel. The fleet of mussel dredgers is berthed alongside the new quay front.

Fig. 21   Wexford's intimate Main Street, meandering along the length of the medieval town, contains an attractive array of retail outlets and is Wexford's principal shopping area. Mostly pedestrianised, the vibrant atmosphere and character of the street attracts social as well as commercial activity.

In some respects, changing patterns in the use of the Main Street symbolise the transformation of the town during the second half of the twentieth century. Located in the heart of the medieval town, the winding, congested thoroughfare has been transformed from having two-way

Fig. 22   The controversial design of the projecting portico of the new White's Hotel in Abbey Street sits uneasily with the adjacent town wall on the opposite side of the street, and the medieval tower of Selskar Abbey.

traffic and double parking in the 1960s to a vibrant shopping precinct with an attractive range of shop fronts. This change has been facilitated by the introduction of pedestrianisation in the town, most recently in North Main Street. The profile of retail units has been transformed in response to modern consumer demands. Most traditional shops have been replaced by an eclectic range of outlets, offering an amazing array of products, ranging from discount shops to exclusive clothes and consumer goods. Because of its appeal to the public, the Main Street is also the centre of financial services and food outlets. As in all medieval towns, traffic is an endemic problem and it is essential that imaginative traffic management continues to be given priority to ensure the continued success of the town centre. In spite of struggling with traffic, Wexford, with a few exceptions, has not resorted to the large-scale relocation of retail outlets to the periphery of the town. The colourful character and atmosphere of the Main Street, created by centuries of usage, make it a vibrant town centre to which people are instinctively attracted for social as well as

Fig. 23   The waterfront in the south of the town at Paul Quay and Trinity Street. The extended quay and walkway is in the foreground. The building at left centre, built in the early 1990s on the site of the former gasyard, was the first high-rise apartment block to be constructed in the town.

business reasons. In order to capitalise on this unique economic asset, the integrity of the town should be safeguarded by retaining the commercial vitality of the Main Street, rather than moving retail outlets to soulless shopping malls.

As business began to prosper, attention turned to the many derelict sites, particularly in the old laneways between the Main Street and the Quays. During the past twenty-five years, many of these have been built on to allow expansion of existing businesses or to facilitate the establishment of new ventures. Some town-centre housing initiatives were also included. These have included the conversion of malt-houses into apartments as well as the construction of new infill apartment blocks. As activity in the town increased, it became evident that services would have to be upgraded and in the late 1990s work started on a main drainage scheme and effluent treatment plant. To facilitate this, the quay was imaginatively extended, creating a significant waterfront amenity for the people of the town. As an ancillary aspect of the main drainage scheme, the archaeological record of the town's medieval origins was significantly enhanced.

During the past thirty years, residential housing has progressed at an unprecedented pace. Corporation housing schemes have been concen-trated to the west of

the town in Townparks and Coolcotts. In the 1970s, the shift of population to this area led to the creation of the parish of Clonard and the building of a new parish church.[25] As the demand for housing grew, property developers produced numerous housing schemes, again mostly to the west and south-west of the town but with smaller infills wherever land became available. The decentralisation of the Environment Protection Agency and the Department of Agriculture, Food and Forestry to Johnstown Castle accelerated demand for houses and services. The late twentieth- and early twenty-first century saw a big rise in residential units. One of the biggest projects, known as Clonard Village, is currently underway to the west near the ring road. Private houses at the upper end of the market tend to be located on minor roads outside the town, most of them with views of the harbour and river. These dwellings are located principally at Coolballow, Coolcotts Lane, Clonard Road, Whiterock Hill, Park and at Newtown on the main road to New Ross. In-fill in the town core has included high-rise apartment blocks and multi-storey carparks. A feature of the town's regeneration has been the provision of five new hotels in the town and environs, one of them, White's Hotel, on the site of its eighteenth-century predecessor, bringing the number of hotels to six.

Fig. 24   This view looking from over Bride Street church towards Forth Mountain illustrates the expansion of residential estates to the west. Whitemill Industrial Estate is visible at centre left. The green spaces of the GAA park and St Peter's College can be seen in the foreground.

INDUSTRY

Industrial activity in the town is mostly concentrated in estates at Whitemill, Kerlogue and Drinagh but substantial enterprises are also located on independent sites, some on the Ferrybank side of the harbour. Smaller businesses are catered for by the excellent Kerlogue Enterprise Centre. Transport is facilitated by easy access to the ring road and the proximity of freight services at Rosslare Harbour. The eclectic group of industrial concerns based in Wexford leaves the town with an unemployment level of five per cent, just above the national average. In recent years, the contribution of immigrant workers, particularly in the construction and hospitality areas, has been considerable. The principal indigenous business concerns include Celtic Linen, Kent Engineering, the Pettit Group, Cleary & Doyle Development Group, Senator Windows, Griffin Hotels and Wexford Cheese Factory. The main foreign enterprises include the Financial Services Groups PFPC and Equifax, ABS Pumps, Theo Benning and Waters Technology. Industrial growth has been hampered by the lack of a sophisticated broadband system, in spite of the installation of a fibre-optic system in the early years of

the century. According to the 2006 census, seventeen per cent have broadband access, compared to twenty per cent at national level.[26] The lack of a third-level education institute is also a major drawback as students from the five excellent secondary schools in the town must leave to acquire further education, and perhaps to work, in other urban centres. Twenty-one per cent of the population of the county have a third-level education:

Fig. 25   Kerlogue Industrial Estate and the Drinagh Business Park to the south of the town, at the junction of the ring road and the Rosslare road.

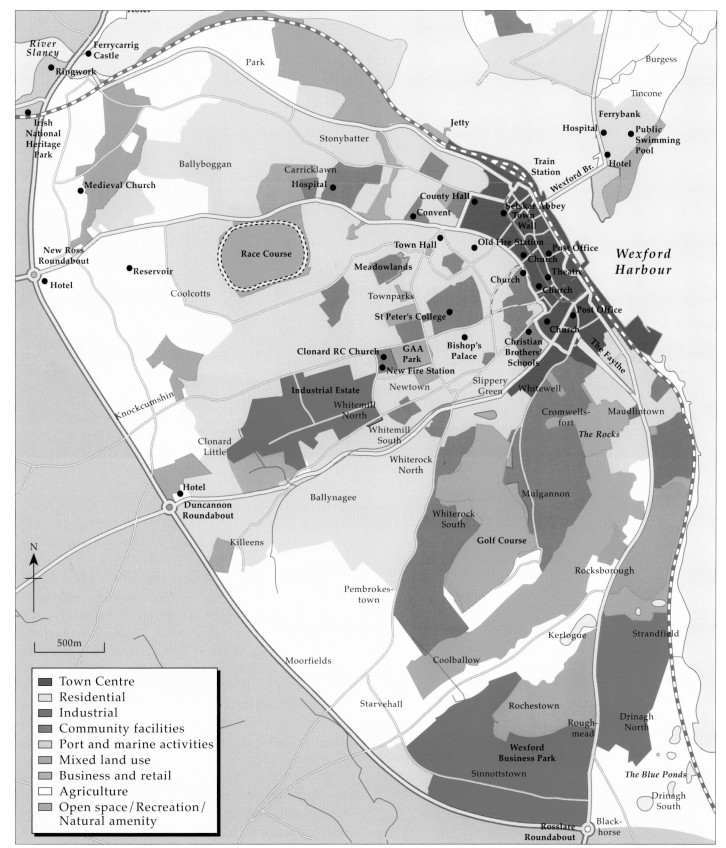

Fig. 26   This map uses data from the Development Plan of Wexford town and environs, 2002, which takes the ring road and the waters of the harbour as the edge of the urban area. Land use within that space has been divided into nine categories or zones, some actual, others proposed, designed to cater for all aspects of life in the town, including residential, economic, recreational, environmental and leisure. A priority should be to concentrate future growth within the ring road, preventing wasteful and unsightly sprawl in the surrounding countryside. In 2008, the urban boundary was expanded to encompass the area within the ring road, which gives a sharp boundary to the modern town. This expansion doubled the urban population.

Fig. 27   Clonard Village project under development adjacent to the Duncannon Line to the west of the town, just inside the ring road. As well as residential units, the complex incorporates shopping units and other services including a large retail park.

eleven per cent of these have a degree or higher, compared with nineteen per cent at national level. The lack of a locally-educated workforce inhibits potential investors in the town, particularly in IT and knowledge-based industries.

Fig. 28   The economic boom of the late twentieth and early twenty-first century has been epitomised by the construction of ultra-modern car showrooms on the periphery of the town .

SPORT AND LEISURE

Wexford has a well-established sport and leisure infrastructure on land and sea. Water-based activities are focused on Wexford Boat and Tennis Club at Carcur and there is also a thriving Wexford Sub-Aqua Club. Annual regattas organised by cot-sailing enthusiasts at Maudlintown have lapsed in recent years but deserve to be revived as the vernacular cot is so synonymous with Wexford Harbour. With up to five teams, the traditionally strong G. A. A. town clubs received a boost through the establishment of the Park Complex on the Ferrycarrig Road in the 1980s and the up-grading of Wexford Park at Clonard in the 1990s. Wexford Wanderers Rugby Club, also located at Park, has an active and dedicated membership. Soccer in the town has received a boost by the high quality Michael Wallace Wexford Youths' soccer complex at Crossabeg near Ferrycarrig. Golf was formerly associated with Rosslare Golf Club, established following the arrival of the railway in the late nineteenth century.[27] The founding of Wexford Golf Club in 1961, on the high ground of Mulgannon to the south of the town, was also a significant social and infrastructural initiative. Further expansion in the 1980s and '90s resulted in the creation of an eighteen-

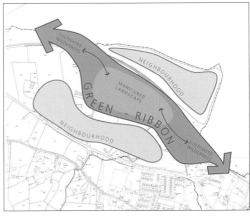

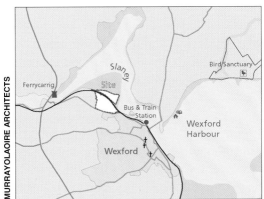

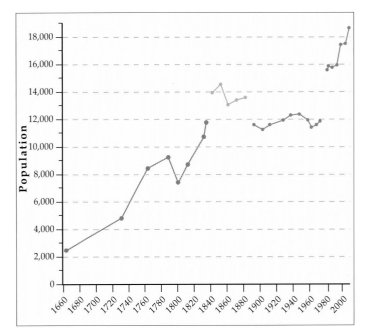

Fig. 29 These plans for a proposed waterside development at Carcur and Park on the Ferrycarrig road, including residental, sport and leisure as well as areas of ecological interest, signal expansion along the estuary to the north-west of the town.

hole course. A major initiative led to the opening of a championship layout and a new clubhouse in 2007.

FUTURE TRENDS: EXPANSION AND CONSERVATION

The development of Wexford is constrained by the need to respect the town's heritage and layout and the requirement for archaeological investigation, particularly in the medieval core area. An informed and sensitive plan is essential not only for the residents but also for the tourism industry, which contributes significantly to the town's economy. This type of approach is clearly articulated in the Development Plan for the town and environs, published jointly by Wexford County Council and Wexford Borough Council in 2002.[28] The Plan recognises the bypass as a significant edge-feature, connected to the town by radial routes which provide a basic structure for the town's expansion. Future models for the town's growth are postulated, including linear expansion to the north and south, serviced by the railway. The Plan aspires to control and direct activity in a sustainable manner, towards an eventual ideal model for the town's growing population. If achieved, this scenario should maximise the benefits of living in a medium-sized town by facilitating social contact, movement and a comprehensive range of services. The town centre is seen

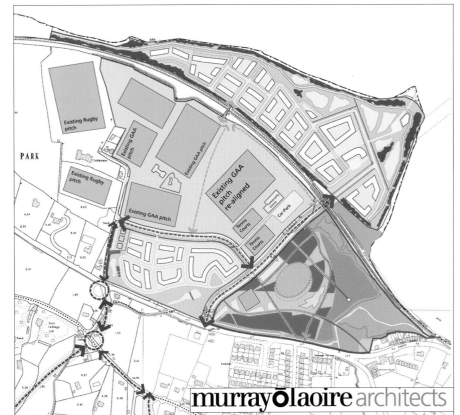

Fig. 30 This diagram offers an estimate of population in Wexford town and environs since the mid seventeenth century. It is not possible to produce a continuous graph of population as the census boundary was changed in the 1880s and again in the 1970s. The brown line until 1840 represents estimated population of the town and suburbs. The dip before 1800 corresponds to the aftermath of the 1798 Rebellion. The population of the town actually rose during the Famine as people gravitated to the town seeking assistance. A dip in the 1860s was presumably due to emigration. The population of the town and greater urban area has been rising steadily since the 1980s.

as having a clear structure that is attractive to pedestrians in both scale and use but the need for a co-ordinated parking plan is stressed. The under-utilisation of space in the town centre and the potential for in-fill is highlighted, particularly between the Main Street and the waterfront.

The significance of high-quality landscape features in the vicinity of the town is emphasised, with special reference to Ferrycarrig, the Slaney estuary and the Trespan Rock escarpment, and it is proposed that their value should be integrated into development. The National Heritage Areas of the Slaney Estuary, Carrig River and Wexford Harbour also get special mention. The plan demonstrates a sound understanding of the town's medieval origins and proposes a clear strategy for protecting and displaying surviving heritage features. It underlines the need to preserve the medieval street layout and the recognition of the town wall and gates as an effective boundary of the medieval town centre. The conservation of the wall, with an adjoining pathway giving access along the circuit, is advocated. The option of opening up medieval graveyards as parks or gardens of remembrance is also encouraged. Other heritage related proposals include the protection of zones of archaeological potential and the listing of arch-itecturally significant buildings.

The objectives and proposals contained in the Development Plan illustrate that, at planning level, there is an informed vision regarding the need to respect the town's heritage and environment. Since the publication of the Plan, considerable expansion has taken place in the town and environs, including some in-fill building in the town centre. However, apart from development-related archaeological investigations, little has been done to conserve the town's medieval legacy. It is essential for the future of the town and its citizens that what is in essence an inclusive, imaginative Development Plan is not diluted by over-pragmatic economic and political considerations.

It is also imperative that the compact character and dense fabric of the town can be protected by rigorously preventing sprawl outside the line of the ring road. As environmental sustainability becomes an ever more important issue, dependence on the car will inevitably be curtailed. In Wexford's future, its inherited historical character as a high-density town can be an asset rather than a weakness. Liveability will also be an increasingly important factor and Wexford town can continue to score highly on that front, if its vibrant cultural life, varied habitats and intimate scale can be protected and enhanced. As the poet Patrick Kavanagh said, 'On the stem of memory, imagination blossoms'.

Quayfront, early morning

THE PERSONALITY OF WEXFORD

The charm and character that distinguishes Wexford has been created over the past millennium by a complex combination of environmental, cultural and economic influences. The location on the Slaney estuary determined the town's foundation and the occupations of the people. The current residents are descended from disparate groups who were attracted to the town from overseas for various reasons. The gene pool of the inhabitants is derived from four principal ethnic reservoirs: the native Irish, the Viking and Hiberno-Norse founders, their racially diverse Anglo-Norman successors, and the Cromwellian English. The town's personality has been shaped by the traumatic events associated with the advent of the different groups. The societal mix was greatly influenced by the town's strategically viable location close to busy sea routes. The arrival of numerous foreign ships and the global horizons of seasoned local mariners introduced a cosmopolitan and outward-looking element, with an inevitable broadening of attitudes and ideas. The Wexford accent is inherited from the rich mix of languages and dialects heard in the town over the centuries. This legacy is deeply embedded in the town's heritage: the distinctive Wexford greeting 'Howya hon?' may well be an echo of the Viking word *hon*, meaning a fine young fellow. The town's complex genetic tapestry is woven from an eclectic mix of distinctive surnames representing the diverse origins of the occupants – Devereux, Doyle, Murphy, O'Leary, Stafford, Furlong, Barker, Turner, Roberts, Broaders. Wexford's enduring medieval origin survives in placenames such as Kayser, Selskar, Castle Hill, Cornmarket, Westgate and John's Gate Street.

Wexford's character was shaped by its cramped environment on a steep incline, squeezed in between the seashore and high ground, with a marshy valley to the south. The principal streets flowed along the contours parallel to the sea, with steep laneways dropping off to the waterfront. The organic and incremental layout, dictated by the topography, creates a feeling of randomness with tightly packed houses ascending the slope. Unexpected, but welcome, glimpses of the harbour add to the town's appeal. Persistent reclamation from the harbour has been a constant factor in the evolution of the town.

Fig.1 This 1980s view of Wexford, on the cusp of unprecedented change, captures the charm of the town which had remained relatively unchanged for a century. The early morning perspective highlights Wexford's maritime personality and the symbiotic relationship between town and harbour.

JOHN DUFFY

Fig. 2   The keystones on Gandon's Dublin Custom House (1781–91) are carved as heads representing Ireland's river gods. The Slaney God is depicted with a crown of shellfish, representing the rich supply of seafood in the shallow estuary. The Slaney and its estuary were inextricably linked to Wexford's evolution.

PEOPLE AND PLACE

The shallow estuary was the reason for the town's existence and the origin of its name, but the 'barred haven' forced creative solutions. Necessity was the mother of maritime invention and stratagems emerged that were particular to Wexford. These were typified by the versatile Wexford cot, built to a vernacular design customised to cope with the vagaries of the fickle and deceptive harbour. For centuries, cots were used to fish the vast herring shoals that appeared off Wexford. The herring was so vital to the rhythm of life around the harbour that the size of the shoals dictated the economic prosperity of the town. The seasonal congregation of winter wildfowl on the mudflats spawned a specialist community of hunter/gatherers around the estuary. Indeed this essentially Mesolithic activity was undoubtedly the first in the Wexford area, although no evidence has yet surfaced from the constantly-shifting mud banks of the harbour. As well as providing abundant fish and fowl, which contributed to

the town's reputation as a gourmet centre, the harbour served as a routeway for communities on its shores. Travelling by cot across the harbour to buy supplies in Wexford town was much easier than making the circuitous journey by land. The seafaring community, based mostly in the self-contained southern suburb of the Faythe, created an exotic international dimension and their nautical terminology added a vivid element to everyday speech. The low thatched suburb on the edge of the town was as distinctive an element in Wexford as the Claddagh in Galway. By the seventeenth century, the skill of Wexford sailors was widely acknowledged and commented on by visitors to the town. Wexford's large fleet of small ships, specifically designed to cope with the difficult harbour, were supported by an array of related businesses, including dockyards, sail-makers, rope-walks, chandlers and ship carpenters.

Church organisation and infrastructure stamped a definite character on the early town and resonates down to the present day. The town and liberties was divided into eleven medieval parishes, each with its own church. These parishes continued in use until the seventeenth century and formed the template for the social and administrative structures in the town. Regional identity was evident

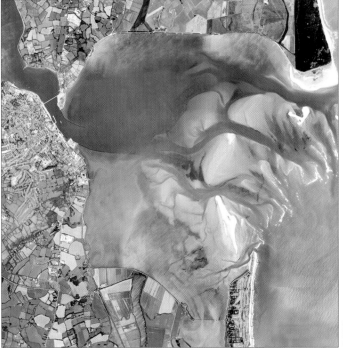

O. S. I.

Fig. 3   Seen from above, Wexford Harbour is a labyrinth of treacherous sandbanks and winding channels, created from silt deposited by the Slaney. Before the North and South Slobs were reclaimed in the mid nineteenth century, the estuary was much bigger. The main passage at the top has a barred approach. Until the 1920s, Rosslare Point, with the Fort at its tip, extended as far as the main channel. The nature of the harbour had a fundamental influence on Wexford's foundation and growth and ultimately led to the demise of the port.

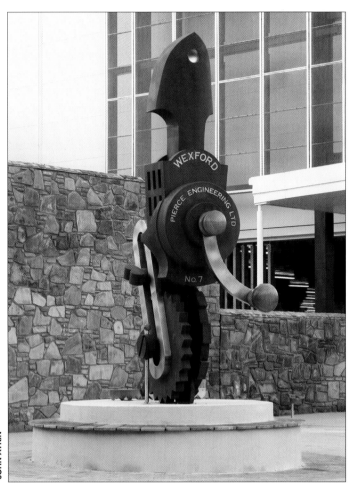

JOHN ATKIN

Fig. 4 Tesco's new premises at King Street is on the site of Pierce's Mill Road Iron Works. This sculpture by renowned artist John Atkin, commissioned by Tesco with the support of Wexford Borough Council, was installed in 2007 to commemorate the contribution made by Pierce's to the community and economy of Wexford and Ireland and its role in agricultural innovation. The finished sculpture, made from corten and stainless steel, with oak details, stands sixteen feet tall. Its form resonates of machinery and creates a shape and an identity that impressively represents Pierce's Foundry and its workers.

during the 1798 Rebellion, the siting of the twin churches and the catchment area for G. A. A. teams. The significance of the churches is shown by the use of twelve church dedications as street names. Following the Reformation, Wexford town remained staunchly Catholic, partly because of the ease of contact with Irish Colleges on the continent, to which local youths sailed for an otherwise prohibited education and then returned clandestinely as Counter-Reformation priests. The presence of a wealthy Catholic mercantile class fostered this pattern, and provided the bulk of the clerical recruits. The presence of the Franciscans, active in the town throughout the Penal Law period, was also a factor. This resilient Catholic ethos, and Wexford's advantageous location, was the reason why the town was chosen as the principal port of the Confederate Catholics during the war of the 1640s. This in turn precipitated the punitive devastation of the town by

Cromwell. Following confiscation and the introduction of New English settlers, some of the Catholic populace was allowed to filter back into the town, as 'hewers of wood and drawers of water'. Eventually Catholic merchants were permitted to resume business, as without their European contacts the port was moribund. For almost two centuries, politically the town was a monopoly of a Protestant minority, under the thumb of aristocratic politicians, more interested in maintaining oligarchic power than in promoting urban development. The absence of sustained municipal, mercantile or landed investment meant that the town had no urban set pieces, or major infrastructural investment in the eighteenth century, contrasting strongly with neighbouring Waterford, where a strongly mercantile Corporation and committed politicians invested massively in creating a flourishing port and landmark buildings. Although politically impotent, the Catholic mercantile elite grew increasingly prosperous and influential. Following Catholic

Fig. 5 The ubiquity of Pierce machinery is illustrated by the image of a Pierce turnip shredder (known as a mangle) on the cover of the American edition of Seamus Heaney's latest book, *District and Circle*. One of the poems in the collection is called 'The turnip snedder'.

ANN HENNESSY

Fig. 6 The construction of the quayfront in the early nineteenth century hastened the decay of the lanes that, for centuries, had provided access to individual jetties. Some of the laneways, like Oak's Lane shown here in a 1970s sketch, were arched over and enclosed with gates. Note the use of iron bollards to prevent damage from the wheels of carts.

Emancipation in 1829, this group of indigenous entrepreneurs – notably the Redmonds and Devereuxs – was able to stimulate the economic and social infrastructure of the town.

This regeneration promoted a host of activities and occupations as innovative ventures were established. Principal among these were shipbuilding, ironworks, distilling and malting, initiating a completely new industrial tradition in the town that endured until the middle of the twentieth century. The character of the town was altered considerably at the end of the eighteenth century by the construction of the first bridge across the Slaney, replacing the centuries-old ferry. Shortly afterwards, a uniform quayfront with a new service street replaced the irregular system of private jetties and associated approach lanes that had been in use since medieval times. This eventually led to the dereliction of the laneways, many of which had substantial populations, and the emergence of a proto-industrial district between the Main Street and the waterfront. It also created a bustling, integrated quay, where dockers and carters, with sailors of many nationalities, co-operated in the

demanding work of loading and unloading ships, and socialised in dockside taverns. The town's maritime past is remembered in placenames such as Oyster Lane, Fishers' Row, Paul Quay and Common Quay Street. In the mid twentieth-century, imaginative names with a nautical flavour were used for streets of a housing estate built in the fishing suburb of Maudlintown. These included Hantoon and Gulbar (sandbanks in the harbour) and Antelope (named after Wexford's last sailing ship).

As in the medieval period, the Church played a dominant role in Wexford's social and infrastructural growth during the nineteenth century. The whole-hearted support of wealthy and devout Catholic businessmen facilitated the construction of churches and schools, completely changing the town's physical and educational profile. For historical reasons, Catholic churches and institutions were built on spacious sites outside the town wall, with the Protestant churches remaining on cramped medieval plots in the core town. As in the rest of the country, the nineteenth-century Catholic revival created a highly structured devotional ethos in the town that lasted for more than a century. Lay people were encouraged to become members of church societies, some devoted to charitable work. On many summer occasions, professions

PADDY DONOVAN

Fig. 7 The slate cladding on these attractive town houses on Crescent Quay is a fine example of a traditional Wexford building technique.

Fig. 8 This elevated view from the new White's Hotel highlights the narrowness of the busy, winding Main Street which originated as a Viking thoroughfare. The tightly packed houses and angled profusion of rooftops reflect the organic growth of the town since medieval times.

Fig. 9   Wexford Arts Centre (currently undergoing major renovations) is the centre of year-round artistic activity in the town. This photograph shows 'Dúch Yesenin', an exhibition of paintings by Seán Ó Flaithearta, inspired by the people and environment of his native Aran Islands.

of faith were proclaimed by public processions (with participants rigidly segregated by gender) which wound along decorated routes through the streets. Periodically, groups of visiting priests conducted hellfire missions dedicated to reinforcing the town's overwhelmingly Catholic ethos.

Late in the nineteenth century, Wexford was changed irrevocably by the advent of the railway. The impact was exaggerated visually by running the rails along the waterfront, which, allied to the ever-increasing number of steamships in the harbour, emphasised the town's newly industrial character. The railway opened up communication and travel and in particular led to the growth of Rosslare as a holiday resort for Wexford town people, a custom that lasted for almost a century, creating the melancholic setting for *The Sea* (2005), Wexford writer John Banville's prize winning novel. In stark contrast to the buoyant nineteenth century, Wexford suffered stagnation and introspection during the first half of the twentieth century. As the town lost out to the bourgeoning port of Rosslare, traditional industries either closed or atrophied. Very little renewal took place, leading to deterioration in

the fabric of the town. This economically depressed period was a low point in Wexford's history and led to widespread unemployment and emigration. The atmosphere of the time is articulated in Billy Roche's novel, *Tumbling Down* (1986).

The morning frost tingled unthawed on the woodenworks. Far away a chapel bell donged out a funeral lament as a little procession of old men and women toddled home from ten mass. A bunch of men on the dole stood on the street corner debating the day's racing form while a uniformed postman glided effortlessly by on his bicycle, sweetly whistling 'Carolina Moon'. The smoke from the gasworks curled up in the shape of Scandinavia and disappeared into the atmosphere. Wexford, a topsy-turvy town that rose up and tumbled down into rows and rows of gardenless houses. Streets filled with people whose only ambition was to live until they died.

The second half of the century ushered in a modern era of expansion which, by the start of the new

Growing up in Wexford by Eoin Colfer

Wexford is the town where I grew up and where I still choose to live, which must say something for it. I have generally been happy here, and when I haven't it was my own fault though I tried to blame narrow Viking streets or the Gulf Stream.

It is a town of diversity. The medieval town wall runs above buried fibre-optic cables. Mussel boats are berthed on the quay alongside pleasure craft, and the famous twin-spire skyline is augmented by luxury hotels and state-of-the-art theatres.

There is diversity among Wexford's residents too. Some are transient. Tourists from London, Sydney or California, tracing back their ancestors' journeys; bringing with them centuries of emotional baggage, laden with sepia photographs and copied certificates.

Wexford attracts the cultural tourists too. Opera buffs, traditional music lovers, gourmands. Sun-worshippers flock here from the capital in the summer, consuming mountains of ice-cream and lakes of Lucozade. Arriving the colour of the former, departing the colour of the latter.

Our permanent residents come from all corners of the globe. Locals are in the majority, but our island's prosperity brought with it scores of immigrants, refugees and the return of Wexfordians who had never wanted to leave, adding layers of exoticism and newness, language, sights and smell. The whole world is here, every colour and creed.

So. A town of diversity. Of course, when you're a boy, you don't care about any of that. All you care about is experience.

My earliest memories of Wexford are more sensory splashes than events in their proper place or time. Colours, sounds and scents that were strange and wonderful. I remember triangular holes pecked by the birds in the silver tops of our milk bottles. The baker's van parked on the footpath, racks of loaves in the back, blurred by heat haze. The salt smell of Wexford quay when the tide was in, and the lush rotten smell when it was out. The Guillemot lightship, fire-engine red, tied to rusting bollards with ropes thicker than my arm. Its mast and bulb a turret that surely housed a princess or two. The grey imposing Arts Centre, with its arch-stones like teeth over the door, poised to snap shut, its walls dotted with squares of ART which could be recognisable as trees and houses but often were mysterious blobs. Crossing Wexford bridge in a car was an adventure, and seemed to take forever and yet not long enough. The rails blurred past as though they were moving and not we, and I hoped with each crossing, that this time we would land somewhere new and amazing.

The memories of Wexford that hold the most power for me are those of my adolescence. I remember the long hike downtown from our suburban estate to stroll the Main Street with the other peacocks. I was small and must have looked tiny flanked by my growth-spurted friends. Even to me the streets seemed narrow. It only took four of us, stretched like stars, touching fingertips, to span the road.

All this preening was for the girls, and I can still see them dressed in the styles of the day, which seems like yesterday, but is a bit more distant than that. Gypsy skirts, peasant blouses, big earrings, crayon strokes of mascara, long flicked hair. No volumising mousse then, just spray. The ozone layer recoiled

over Wexford every Friday night. We sat in electric clusters outside the junior disco, swagger, blush and smile. I don't think young people blush so much any more, though I have seen a few smile.

Juvenile things happened. A friend belly-slid down a mud mountain in his beloved Miami Vice white suit. Another fell down an open manhole and lost his front teeth. I danced with a shy girl at a céilí. My brother, best friend and I sat on the snow-covered rooftop outside my bedroom window looking down at the alien glow hovering above the town, wishing the days away until Friday came.

Similar things could have happened anywhere but they did not. Not to us. Wexford was as much a part of our exploits as the money in our pockets or the decorated denim jackets on our backs. This was our town and we inhabited it completely, absorbing morsels of useful information. We catalogued every garden and alley, where we could and could not venture. We kept track of the fluid inter-estate alliances so that we would not unwittingly breach an enemy's border. We knew to cross the road several times on the way to school, to avoid certain garden dogs. We trekked the Horse River and explored the Rocks, ate berries, spied on lovers, plagued shopkeepers, bought dozens of C90s and became experts at table soccer; had the odd fight, broke a few limbs, obsessed over sparse moustaches and grew up, grumpily ignorant of our own happiness. Those days seem mythic now. As though they were a lifetime away and a lifetime long.

After college I returned to Wexford to teach. After three years in Dublin, the town seemed smaller and I was not yet nostalgic for alleys and arcades. The town had other layers to be discovered. My friends were gone to London, Dublin and New York so I found new ones among the town's dramatic circles.

Wexford has a strong artistic culture. Almost everyone is in a drama group or choir, playing guitar on Thursdays or writing a novel. I was no different and spent my evenings working on a play and my nights in the rehearsal rooms of the Wexford Light Opera Society or Wexford Drama Group, depending on the season.

In my experience, Wexford is unique in its love of the stage. Theatre is embraced and attended by all and you are as likely to catch a performance of a modern classic such as Billy Roche's The Cavalcaders as you are to see a Gilbert and Sullivan standard.

My first complete effort was on a temporarily rigged stage in the Talbot Hotel. A one-act with a cast that included most of my friends and gave us a legitimate excuse to go out six nights. Several more plays followed before my wife and I decided to travel for a few years.

I have lived all over the world but still when the time came to settle down with my family, we unanimously chose Wexford. When I think of it, the house I live in now is remarkably similar to the one I grew up in. A semi-detached in a small estate, beside a school. I don't remember consciously choosing it for this reason, but perhaps I want the same surroundings for my boys as I myself had growing up.

I would love to think that they could explore the town as I did. They can swagger down the Main Street, cycle the hills cursing their steepness, learn to take comfort from the smell of the sea, absorb art accidentally, embrace diversity, explore the road less travelled, and grow up grumpily ignorant of their own happiness.

WEXFORD FESTIVAL OPERA

Wexford Festival Opera

The phenomenon that is Wexford Festival Opera had its origins in a 'Festival of Music and the Arts', organised by a group of music lovers in 1951. The organisers included Dr Tom Walsh who became the Festival's artistic director for sixteen years. The highlight was a production of nineteenth-century Irish composer Michael Balfe's *The Rose of Castille,* a little-known opera that was mentioned by James Joyce in *Ulysses.* In following years, guided by the Festival Council, a policy of staging obscure operas, at the end of October, was received enthusiastically by critics and audiences alike and the Festival grew from strength to strength. The amazing success was partly due to the dedicated support of the wider community, both onstage and behind the scenes. It became easier to attract leading opera talent as well as young professionals who would later become major stars. In late autumn, the presence of international performers and elegantly-dressed opera-goers adds an exotic air to the town. An emphasis on fringe events including art exhibitions, music, drama, shop-window displays and singing pubs, lends a carnival atmosphere and attracts thousands of visitors. An opening-night fireworks extravangza on the waterfront is a traditional and much-anticipated feature of the event. At present, the construction of a spectacular new Wexford Opera House (computer-generated image above and below right) on the footprint of the old Theatre Royal represents an ambitious and exciting future for the Festival and a major cultural centre for the south-east.

DEREK SPIERS

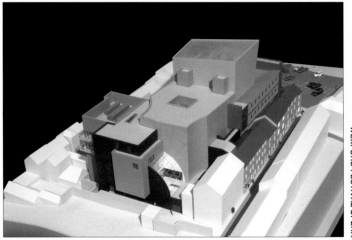

WEXFORD FESTIVAL OPERA

PADDY DONOVAN

Fig. 10   For Wexford people, and especially the younger generation, the opening of the Opera Festival is synonymous with a dramatic fireworks display over the harbour, which attracts a huge crowd from far and near to enjoy the spectacle from the waterfront and other vantage points.

millennium, culminated in unprecedented growth. This resurgence was unexpectedly heralded not by an industrial initiative but by an arts festival. In 1951, a production of Michael Balfe's little-known opera, *The Rose of Castile*, staged by a group of music enthusiasts in the Theatre Royal, marked the beginning of Wexford Festival Opera which won widespread critical acclaim.[1] Wexford, formerly of international significance in the realm of trade and commerce, was again placed centre-stage by an arts event. The Festival dramatically impacted on the town, not only from the economic contribution by thousands of visitors, but also because the fringe events of exhibitions, drama and music spurred a renaissance in other art forms. The Festival is given enthusiastic support locally as Wexford's personality is coloured by a pervasive interest in the arts. It has long been one of the best towns in Ireland for bookshops, for example. Involvement in music and drama accelerated due to the presence of army bands in the military barracks and visits by travelling troupes to the Theatre Royal. The town is renowned for its brass bands and Male Voice Choir, and has a thriving music school as well as a long-established Light Opera Society, Drama Group and Pantomime Society. In the 1970s, the revived arts profile of the town led to the

transformation of the old Town Hall in Cornmarket into the vibrant Wexford Arts Centre.

The level of artistic activity shaped the town's culture, and a remarkable number of writers of international stature has emerged in recent years, notably the distinguished novelist John Banville, the playwright Billy Roche (whose *Wexford Trilogy* was staged in London's

Fig. 11   Two of Wexford's foremost artists enjoying a coffee in Wexford Arts Centre. Singer-songwriter and entertainer, Pierce Turner (left), home from New York, the 'poetic champion of Celtic soul', and Billy Roche, musician, novelist and playwright, of *Wexford Triology* fame.

PADDY DONOVAN

Fig. 12 Apart from mussel farming, Wexford no longer has a commercial involvement in the sea. The legacy of the town's traditional maritime involvement finds expression in the leisure pursuits of fishing, sailing and other water-based activities. These activities are based around Wexford Boat Club but numbers of small boats are kept at different location around the harbour, including the new marina at Crescent Quay. This picture shows a small boat leaving the cot 'safe' at Maudlintown on an early morning fishing trip. Many of the surviving cots are kept in the 'safe', but unfortunately, their numbers are dwindling. It is vital that the skills and traditions involved in the building of these vernacular craft are not lost.

West End), and Eoin Colfer, author of the celebrated *Artemis Fowl* series for children. The town's creative ambience has been acknowledged by John Banville who observed that 'All the landscapes of my books are in some way imbued with wexfordness, even when they are supposed to be modern Greece, or medieval Prussia. When I needed to paint a picture of Copernicus's Torun or Kepler's Weilderstadt, it was Wexford that I conjured up'. Other prominent Wexford writers include Nicholas Furlong, Vincent Banville, Paul O'Brien, Larry Kirwan and Vonnie Banville. Larry Kirwan and Pierce Turner are internationally known singer-songwriters.

The town also has a distinguished sporting tradition and has produced such G. A. A. legends as Rich Reynolds, Willie Goodison, Ned Wheeler, Willie Murphy, Oliver (Hopper) McGrath, Ned Buggy, Liam Bennett and Larry O'Gorman. A longstanding sometimes friendly rivalry with the rural 'over the waters' (Castlebridge and points north as far as Buffers Alley), encouraged sporting excellence in the town.

The unprecedented developments of recent times have added an exciting new layer of infrastructure to Wexford's streetscape that demands a certain intellectual acceptance and appreciation. This adjustment is often successfully made but at times it is challenging to incorporate contemporary architecture in a medieval environment, particularly on infill sites. Modern hotels, apartment blocks and offices tower over narrow, winding streets and

laneways, marking another phase in the evolution of the town. After a long period of stagnation, these new buildings represent growth and prosperity, immigration instead of emigration. The recent influx of yet another wave of non-nationals to Wexford will in time add another distinctive trait to the town's cosmopolitan persona.

Current changes in Wexford are the latest in a millennium-long process. Collectively, these have created the modern town. Ultimately, the town's personality consists not only of its physical structure but also of its inhabitants. Many activities, such as the maritime involvement, are no longer relevant but still resonate in the town's subconscious memory. A highly specific blend of environment, human endeavour and historic events has coalesced over the past millennium to shape the distinctive character of the modern town and the resilient nature of its citizens. If the town's unique qualities are to be retained, it is vital that modern development acknowledges and respects the past, particularly the medieval layout and ambience, the vibrancy of the pedestrianised Main Street as the core shopping district, the distinctive atmosphere of the quayfront, and the cultural significance of the town wall that so strongly marks the imprint of the medieval town. If this can be done – and the portents are auspicious – Wexford's personality can become even more enriching and welcoming for residents and visitors alike. Long may it flourish.

APPENDIX 1: AN EXTRACT RELATING TO WEXFORD HARBOUR FROM *THE SEA-MIRROR* BY WILLIAM BLEAUW (AMSTERDAM, 1625)

For to sail out of the bay of Greenore towards Washford [Wexford] with a ship that draws little water, you may boldly run along the shore, and sail through betwixt the Haenmans path and the Soudre [Rosslare Point?], that is a channel where at high water and ordinary tides is eight foot [of] water; with a spring tide there is ten foot [of] water. The Haenmans path is a dry sand, which makes the south side of the channel of Washford, lying off the Soudre. The Soudre that is the south of the main land of Washford haven. But if your ship go deeper, then you must (sailing out of Greenbay) go further off from the shore, for to come without [outside] the sand that shoots off from Haenmans paths, yet you must also take heed not to go too far there-off, for if you come so far off in ten fathom, you shall come too near unto the bank that lies without, which is on the inner side very steep and needle too, therefore go no further off the shore than seven, eight or nine fathom, but coming somewhat more northerly about Haenmans paths, then you may well go off into ten or eleven fathom; also you may not come nearer Haenmans paths then in seven fathom.

If you desire to be upon the bar of Washford and to leave the showld [shoal/shallow] of Haenmans paths, to wit, to go to the northwards, then take heed unto these marks: at the north side of the channel of Washford lies a high hill with a round hommock, which is to be seen all over the foreland, and a little castle [Ardtramon] in the lowland, a little above the strand, against the land to look on. Bring that round hommock a little to the northwards of the castle, and sail so in, but bring not the hommock within, or to the southwards of the castle, for then you should be in danger of the sand of Haenmans paths, unless it were by need, and with a bare wind, then you might borrow so near to bring them one in another, and so sail in, but it is best to keep them somewhat out one of another, to wit, the little castle to the southwards of the hommock. If it should happen that you could not see these marks well, not discern them, then you may go about the sand of Haenmans paths by your lead in seven fathom without any danger.

For to know then when you are far enough sailed to the westwards, or are past Haenmans path, and are open before the channel, you shall see in the south land a little castle that stands about four leagues in the land within the strand, in the side of the high land of Washford, about southwest and by west from you. When that shall be upon

that point from you, and that it stands betwixt the two northernmost little sandhills, that are upon the foot strand of the Soudre (which is upon the south shore) then you are past Haenmans paths. Sail in then upon the marks of that little castle, and the little sandhills over the bar of the haven there is at high water about sixteen foot deep. As soon as you are past the outermost flat at the point of Haenmans paths, you shall go somewhat near to Haenmans paths, although it be very steep, that the tide does not bring you upon the tail of the north grounds, where the mast stands, that is a foremast of a ship that is there lost, and lies there sunken into the sand, by the foremast the north grounds are very steep and needle too, but without and within very flat going up.

In this channel and upon the bar, an east and west moon makes highest water: but the flood runs yet afterwards a half tide strong by the channel northwards: so that when it is highest water in the channel and upon the bar, yet runs the tide thwart [across] over the channel. Therefore a man must keep him so near to Haenmans paths, as is said, that is the cause that the tail of Haenmans paths is cast up still more and more to the northwards than it was wont to do, and yet hereafter it is like that it will stretch itself more to the northwards, so that the foresaid marks (by likelihood) will not continue certain always. Even as the flood after the highest water runs yet a half tide or three hours strong (in the channel) to the northwards. So also runs the ebb a half tide to the southwards after the lowest water, but not so strong as the flood.

Being over the showldest [shallowest] of the bar, you shall have three, three and a half, and four fathom, and in the channel betwixt the north grounds and Haenmans path, against the mast, five fathom depth. Run in by Haenmans paths, all along until you come to the foot strand, and then edge over to the north shore, for to avoid the grounds which lie to the westwards above the Soudre. You may borrow off the showld on the north side, by your lead into ten or eleven foot, according to the draught of your ship. In the right deep of this edging over, you shall have at high water fifteen foot deep.

The mark of this edging over is a white little castle that stands on the north side of the haven in the valley of the land. When that comes over the steep point of the innermost island of the two that lie by the north shore, and seems to be about a man's length high, then you may boldly run in north-west with it, until a little chapel within the land, and to the southwards of Washford (a little or about a cable's length to the northwards of that other forenamed little castle on the side of that ragged land, that has served for a mark to sail over the bar) comes over a black hommock that you may see upon the high land, a little to the southwards of the castle of Washford. When you have brought these marks one in the other, edge then over again to the south land upon the marks, for then you shall be above the sands of the Soudre. And with that course also shall not be in danger of the tail of the sand that shoots off from the point of Passage [Ferrybank], which is on the north side; but it is there broad and large, that a man may there turn to and again. It is altogether showld [shallow] water, of ten, and ten foot and a half at high water. Sailing up upon these foresaid marks, you shall come about the distance of a shot of a cast piece without the castle of Washford on the south shore. Sail then in along by it and keep the sounding of the shore until you come within the castle, there you may anchor and shall find there about three fathom water. For a man that is there unacquainted, it is best to anchor there, because before the town lie some sunken rocks. He that will lie before the town, must (right against the quay, or the head of the market) go a good way off the shore because of a sunken rock that lies thereabouts, and go right against the west end of the town, and anchor there in three fathom, or thereabouts.

ENDNOTES AND BIBLIOGRAPHY

The abbreviations listed here are used for sources that occur frequently: other sources are given in full.

A. F. M.	*Annals of the Four Masters*	**O. P. W.**	Office of Public Works
Arch. Ir.	*Archaeology Ireland*	**O. S. I.**	Ordnance Survey of Ireland
Cal. doc. Ire.	*Calendar of Documents relating to Ireland*	*R. I. A. Proc.*	*Proceedings of the Royal Irish Academy*
Cal. close rolls	*Calendar of Close Rolls*	*R. S. A. I. Jn.*	*Journal of the Royal Society of Antiquaries*
Cal. i. p. m.	*Calendar of Inquisitions Post Mortem*		*of Ireland*
D. K. P. R. I.	*Reports of the Deputy Keeper of the Public*	**T. C. D.**	Trinity College Dublin
	Records of Ireland	*Wex. Hist. Soc. Jn.*	*Journal of the Wexford Historical Society*
N. A. I.	National Archives of Ireland	*A. U.*	*Annals of Ulster*
N. L . I.	National Library of Ireland	**Hore, *Wexford***	*History of the town and county of Wexford*
N. H. I.	*New History of Ireland*	**S. P. C.**	St Peter's College, Wexford

WEXFORD TOWN: INTRODUCTION

1. Spenser, E., *The Faerie Queen* (1589), canto II, v. 41.

2. W. J. Smyth, 'Society and settlement in seventeenth-century Ireland' in W. J. Smyth and K. Whelan (eds), *Common ground* (Cork, 1988), p. 61.

3. E. Scallan, *Wexford boat club* (Wexford, 2006).

LOCATION AND ENVIRONMENT

1. J. Duffy, *River Slaney: from source to sea* (Tullow, 2006).

2. A. Smyth, *Celtic Leinster* (Dublin, 1982), p. 157.

3. H. F. Hore (ed.), 'Particulars relative to Wexford and the barony of Forth: by Colonel Solomon Richards, 1682, in *R. S. A. I. Jn.*, vi (1862), pp 89–90.

4. Geological information is extracted from D. Tietzsch-Tyler and A. G. Sleeman (eds), *Geology of south Wexford* (Dublin, 1994).

5. B. Colfer, *The Hook Peninsula* (Cork, 2004), pp 7–8.

6. An organism with a disk-shaped or globular body (such as the sea-lily), commonly anchored by a stem to the sea-floor.

7. For a detailed account of glacial activity in the region see E. Culleton, *The south Wexford landscape* (Dublin, 1980); R. Carter and J. Orford (eds), Irish Association for Quaternary Studies Field Guide No. 4, *The south and east coasts of Wexford* (Dublin, 1982).

8. Culleton, *South Wexford landscape*, pp 51–2.

9. Culleton, *South Wexford landscape*, p. 45; Jim Hurley, pers. comm.

10. M. J. Gardiner and P. Ryan, *Soils of county Wexford* (Dublin, 1964), *passim*; Culleton, *South Wexford landscape*, pp 26–9.

11. C. J. Wilson, 'The birds of Wexford slobs and harbour' in D. Rowe and C. J. Wilson (eds), *High skies–low lands* (Enniscorthy, 1996), pp 143–206.

12. Hore (ed.), 'Barony of Forth: Solomon Richards', pp 89–90.

13. D. Rowe, 'Punt gunning' in *High skies–low seas*, pp 129–36.

PRE-VIKING SETTLEMENT

1. N. Culleton, *Early man in county Wexford* (Dublin, 1984), pp 3–9.

2. G. Stout, 'Wexford in pre-history 5,000 B. C. to 300 A. D.' in K. Whelan (ed.), *Wexford: history and society* (Dublin, 1987), p. 4–6.

3. C. McLoughlin, 'Prehistoric remains at Kerlogue, Co. Wexford' in *Arch. Ire.*, xvi, 3 (Autumn, 2002), pp 16–19.

4. Stout, 'Wexford in pre-history', pp 15, 36; S. Lewis, *A topographical dictionary of Ireland*, 2 v (London, 1837), ii, p. 711.

5. McLoughlin, 'Prehistoric remains at Kerlogue', p. 19.

6. M. Cahill, 'Boxes, beads, bobbins and notions' in *Arch. Ire.*, viii, 1 (Spring, 1994), pp 21–3; 'Unspooling the mystery' in *Arch. Ireland* xv, 3 (Autumn, 2001), pp 8–15; 'Finding function in the late Bronze Age' in *Ancient gold technology: America and Europe* (Madrid, 2004), pp 349–58.

7. Stout, 'Wexford in pre-history', pp 23–4.

8. G. Stout and M. Stout, 'Early landscapes: from prehistory to plantation' in F. Aalen, K. Whelan and M. Stout (eds), *Atlas of the Irish rural landscape* (Cork, 1997), pp 41–3.

9. B. Raftery, *Pagan Celtic Ireland* (London, 1994), p. 204.

10. G. H. Orpen, 'Ptolemy's map of Ireland' in *R. S. A. I. Jn.*, xxiv (1894), pp 21–97; J. H. Andrews, *Shapes of Ireland* (Dublin, 1997), pp 26–9.

11. G. H. Orpen, 'Rathgall, Co. Wicklow, Dún Gallion and the dunum of Ptolemy' in *R. I. A. Proc.*, xxxiii (1913–16), pp 41–57.

12. Moore, *Archaeological inventory*, p. 26, nos. 225, 226, 228; T. J. Westropp, 'Five large earthworks in the barony of Shelburne, county Wexford' in *R. S. A. I. Jn.*, xlviii (1918), pp 1–18.

13. N. Culleton, *Celtic and Early Christian Wexford* (Dublin, 1999), pp 67–9.

14. E. Gwynn (ed.), *Metrical Dindshenchas*, 5 v (Dublin, 1913), v, pp 169–83.

15. M. Clinton, 'Settlement patterns in the early historic kingdom of Leinster' in A. P. Smyth (ed.), *Seanchas: studies in early and medieval Irish archaeology, history and literature in honour of F. J. Byrne* (Dublin, 2000), p. 277.

16. M. Stout, *The Irish ringfort* (Dublin, 1997), p. 32.

17. Stout and Stout, 'Early landscapes', pp 44–7; Stout, *The Irish ringfort*, p. 24.

18. F. J. Byrne, *Irish kings and high-kings* (London, 1973), p. 131.

19. D. Ó Corráin, *Ireland before the Normans* (Dublin, 1972), p. 27.

20. A. Smyth, *Celtic Leinster* (Dublin, 1982), p. 156; Byrne, *Irish kings*, p. 131; J. O'Donovan (ed.), *The topographical poems of Seán Ó Duibhagáin and Giolla na Naomh Ó hUidhrin* (Dublin, 1862), p. 93.

21. Moore, *Archaeological inventory*, pp 28–89.

22. Culleton, *Early Christian Wexford*, p. 61.

23. Culleton, *Early Christian Wexford*, p. 62.

24. Culleton, *Early Christian Wexford*, pp 81–96, 143–5.

25. Smyth, *Celtic Leinster*, p. 9.

26. M. Browne and C. Ó Clabaigh (eds), *The Irish Benedictines* (Dublin, 2005), pp 105–6.

27. Culleton, *Early Christian Wexford*, pp 203–5.

28. H. Clarke, 'The topographical development of early medieval Dublin' in *R. S. A. I. Jn.*, cvii (1977), pp 29–51.

29. A. Gwynn and R. Hadcock, *Medieval religious houses Ireland* (Dublin, 1970), p. 151.

30. W. Reeves, 'On the townland distribution of Ireland' in *R. I. A. Proc.*, vii (1857–61), pp 473–90.

31. B. Colfer, *Arrogant trespass: Anglo-Norman Wexford 1169–1400* (Enniscorthy, 2002), pp 94–6.

32. P. H. Hore, *History of the town and county of Wexford*, 6 v (London, 1900–11), v, p. 216.

URBAN ORIGINS: THE VIKING ERA

1. For a general background to the Vikings, see E. Roesdahl, *The Vikings* (London, 1991); P. H. Sawyer, *Kings and Vikings: Scandinavia and Europe AD 700–1100* (New York, 1994).

2. *A. F. M.*, i, p. 431.

3. M. Ní Dhonnchadha, 'Inis Teimle, between Uí Chennselaig and the Déissi' in *Peritia*, 16 (2002), pp 457–8.

4. J. Henthorn Todd (ed.), *Cogadh Gaedhel re Gallaibh* (London, 1867), pp xxxix, 824–5.

5. *A. U.*, i, p. 325.

6. *A. U.*, i, p 335; *A. F. M.*, i, p. 459.

7. For a general background, see Ó Corráin, *Ireland before the Normans*, pp 80–110.

8. *A.F.M.*, i, p. 543.

9. Ó Corráin, *Ireland before the Normans*, p. 105. For the recent discovery of a Viking settlement near Waterford, see R. O'Brien, P. Quinney and I. Russell, 'Preliminary report on the archaeological excavation and finds retrieval strategy of the Hiberno-Scandinavian site of Woodstown 6, County Waterford' in *Decies*, lxi (2005), pp 13–122.

10. A defended on-shore base.

11. John Bradley and Andrew Halpin, 'The topographical development of Scandinavian and Anglo-Norman Waterford' in W. Nolan and T. P. Power (eds), *Waterford: history and society* (Dublin, 1992), p. 106.

12. *A. F. M.*, ii, p. 631.

13. Hore, *Wexford*, v, p. 5.

14. M. Oftedal, 'Scandinavian place-names in Ireland' in B. Almquist and D. Greene (eds), *Proceedings of the seventh Viking congress* (Dublin, 1976), p. 133.

15. e.g. G. Orpen (ed.), *The song of Dermot and the earl* (Oxford, 1892), l. 484.

16. Hore, *Wexford*, v, p. 58.

17. H. Clarke, 'Proto-towns and towns in Ireland and Britain in the ninth and tenth centuries' in H. B. Clarke, M. Ní Mhaonaigh and R. Ó Floinn (eds), *Ireland and Scandinavia in the early Viking Age* (Dublin, 1998), pp 349–50.

18. J. Bradley, 'The topographical development of Scandinavian Dublin' in F. Aalen and K. Whelan (eds), *Dublin city and county: from prehistory to present* (Dublin, 1992), p. 43; Bradley and Halpin, 'Waterford', p. 105.

19. E. P. Kelly and E. O'Donovan, 'A Viking Longphort near Athlunkard, Co. Clare' in *Arch. Ire.*, xii, no. 4 (1998), pp 13–16.

20. H. Clarke, 'The topographical development of early medieval Dublin' in *R. S. A. I. Jn.*, cvii (1977), pp 29–51.

21. E. Bourke, 'Two early eleventh-century Viking houses from Bride Street, Wexford, and the layout of properties on the site' in *Wex. Hist. Soc. Jn.*, xii (1988–9), pp 50–61.

22. P. Wallace, 'Wexford town: Oyster Lane' in *Excavations* (1974), p. 28.

23. Bradley, 'Scandinavian Dublin', p. 48.

24. M. T. Flanagan, *Irish history, Anglo-Norman settlers, Angevin kingship* (Oxford, 1989), pp 28–32.

25. J. Bradley, 'Planned Anglo-Norman towns in Ireland' in H. Clarke and A. Simms (eds), *The comparative history of urban origins in non-Roman Europe* (Oxford, 1985), p. 445.

26. Hore, *Wexford*, v, p. 61; see also Wexford O. S. (1841), sheet 37.

27. For a discussion on the transition of Olaf to Tullock or Doologue, see R. Haworth, 'The site of St Olave's church, Dublin' in J. Bradley (ed.), *Society and settlement in medieval Ireland* (Kilkenny, 1988), pp 177–91. In seventeenth-century Wexford, the present South Main Street was known as Toolock's Street (Hore, *Wexford*, v, p. 338).

28. Bradley, 'Scandinavian Dublin', p. 49.

29. Bourke, 'Viking houses'.

30. Bradley, 'Scandinavian Dublin', p. 51.

31. G. Hadden, 'The origin and development of Wexford town' in *Old Wex. Soc. Jn.*, I (1968), p. 14. There was a Kayser Lane in all Norse towns in Ireland.

32. P. Harbison, 'Exotic ninth-to-tenth century cross-decorated stones from Clonmore, Co. Carlow and Begerin, Co. Wexford' in G. Mac Niocaill and P. Wallace (eds), *Keimelia: studies in medieval archaeology in memory of Tom Delaney* (Galway, 1988), p. 62.

33. Hore, *Wexford*, v, p. 60.

34. O. S. index to the townland survey of counties Wexford, Waterford and Dublin (1841).

35. Clarke and Simms, 'Urban origins', p. 685.

36. Hore, *Wexford*, v, p. 92.

37. M. Richards, 'Norse place-names in Wales' in B. Ó Cuív (ed.), *The impact of the Scandinavian invasions on the Celtic-speaking peoples c. 800–1100 AD* (Dublin, 1959), p. 57. Selskar could mean 'Seal Rock'. Seals were commonly called 'sels' on the south Wexford coast until quite recently. There is a Selskar rock just off-shore at Bannow. Tuskar Rock contains the same element.

38. *Faithche*, a green level space: P. Dineen, *Irish-English Dictionary* (Dublin, 1927). There was a *faithche* outside Dublin also; see Doherty, 'Exchange and trade', p. 83 where the *faithche* is described as an area of peace.

39. There were suburbs in 1169; see A. B. Scott and F. X. Martin (eds), *Expugnatio Hibernica, the conquest of Ireland by Giraldus Cambrensis* (Dublin, 1978), p. 33 where the 'entire suburbs' are mentioned.

40. Hore, *Wexford*, v, p. 84.

41. Bradley, 'Scandinavian Dublin', pp 50–1.

42. Ó Corráin, *Ireland before the Normans*, p. 105.

43. J. Bradley, 'The interpretation of Scandinavian settlement in Ireland' in Bradley (ed.), *Settlement and society*, pp 49–78.

44. Hore, *Wexford*, v, p. 93.

45. E. Curtis, 'The English and Ostmen in Ireland' in *English Historical Review*, xxiii (1908), p. 217.

46. A more comprehensive discussion of this topic can be found in Colfer, *Arrogant trespass*, pp 20–3.

47. Called Tingtown in the *Civil survey*, p. 300.

48. C. Doherty, 'The Vikings in Ireland' in Clarke, Ní Mhaonaigh and Ó Floinn (eds), *Ireland and Scandinavia*, pp 302–3.

49. D. Ó Corráin, 'Note' in *Peritia*, ii, p. 187.

50. Bradley, 'Scandinavian settlement', pp 57, 65.

51. For a discussion on *Dubhgall*, see B. Ó Cuív 'Personal names as an indicator of relations between native Irish and settlers in the Viking period' in Bradley (ed.), *Settlement and society*, p. 82.

52. *Expugnatio*, p. 35.

53. Ó Corráin, 'Nationality and kingship', p. 32.

54. Byrne, *Irish kings*, p. 271.

55. Flanagan, *Irish society*, p. 58.

56. D. Ó Corráin, 'The career of Diarmait Mac Máel na mBó king of Leinster' in *Old Wex. Soc. Jn.*, iii, (1970-1), p. 31.

57. For a general background to Diarmait Mac Murchada, see G. H. Orpen, *Ireland under the Normans*, 4 v (Oxford, 1911–20), i, pp 39–75; S. Duffy, *Ireland in the Middle Ages* (Dublin, 1997), pp 50–58.

58. *A. F. M.*, ii, p. 1057.

59. *A. F. M.*, ii, p. 1161.

60. Byrne, *Irish kings*, p. 272.

61. Orpen (ed.), *Song*, l. 140.

URBAN EXPANSION: THE ANGLO-NORMAN TOWN

1. F. Braudel, *Civilisation and capitalism: the structures of everyday life*, i (re-print, London, 1988), pp 479–509.

2. M. M. Postan, *The medieval economy and society* (London, 1972), pp 207–23.

3. C. Doherty, 'Exchange and trade in medieval Ireland' in *R. S. A. I. Jn.* cx (1980), pp 71, 81–2.

4. J. Otway-Ruthven, 'The character of Norman settlement in Ireland' in *Historical Studies*, v (1965), pp 75–84.

5. J. Bradley, 'Planned Anglo-Norman towns in Ireland' in Clarke and Simms (eds.), *Urban origins*, pp 410–21.

6. Orpen, *Ireland under the Normans*, i, pp 77–100. For a general background, see Colfer, *Arrogant trespass*, pp 23–35.

7. *Expugnatio*, p. 29; Orpen (ed.), *Song*, ll. 325–55.

8. *Expugnatio*, p. 31; Orpen (ed.), *Song*, ll. 375–400.

9. There was a distinctive Flemish colony in Pembroke. R. R. Davies, *Domination and conquest: the experience of Ireland, Scotland and Wales 1100–1300* (Cambridge, 1990), p. 11.

10. Orpen (ed.), *Song*, ll. 441–60; *Expugnatio*, p. 31.

11. *Expugnatio*, pp 31-5.

12. *Expugnatio.*, p. 51.

13. *Expugnatio*, p. 53; Orpen (ed.), *Song*, ll. 1395–7. For a description of the site, see I. Bennett, 'Preliminary archaeological excavations at Ferrycarrig ringwork, Newtown Td., Co. Wexford' in *Wex. Hist. Soc. Jn.*, x (1984–5), pp 25–43.

14. *Expugnatio*, pp 57–9; Orpen (ed.), *Song*, ll. 1404–8.

15. *Expugnatio*, pp 57, 59, 67; Orpen (ed.), *Song*, ll. 1526–31.

16. *Expugnatio*, pp 67, 75; Orpen (ed.), *Song*, ll. 1556–1731.

17. *Cal. doc. Ire.*, i, no. 10; *Expugnatio*, p. 71.

18. *Expugnatio*, pp 79, 85, 87.

19. *Expugnatio*, p. 93.

20. *Expugnatio*, p. 95.

21. During his stay in Wexford, his officials spent £40 on herrings to feed his retinue (*Cal. doc. Ire.*, i, no. 34).

22. *Expugnatio*, p. 105; *Song*, ll. 2738–68.

23. For early Anglo-Norman settlement in county Wexford, see Colfer, *Arrogant trespass*, pp 35–45.

24. *Expugnatio*, p. 105.

25. Orpen (ed.), *Song*, ll. 2902–3.

26. *Expugnatio*, p. 141; Orpen (ed.), *Song*, ll. 2994–3004.

27. *Expugnatio*, p. 171.

28. Bourke, 'Two early eleventh-century houses', p. 59.

29. D. Crouch, *William Marshal: court, career and chivalry in the Angevin empire 1147–1219* (London, 1990), p. 61.

30. Hore, *Wexford*, v, pp 118–9.

31. *Cal. doc. Ire.*, i, no. 85.

32. Hore, *Wexford*, ii, p. 19.

33. Bradley, 'Planned Anglo-Norman towns', pp 414–21.

34. Hore, *Wexford*, v, p. 112.

35. Hore, *Wexford*, v, pp 41–7, 139.

36. A county in which royal privileges were exercised by its earl or lord.

37. Hore, *Wexford*, v, p. 115–6.

38. E. Curtis, 'The English and Ostmen in Ireland' in *English Historical Review*, xxiii (1908), pp 217–10.; P. H. Hore 'The barony of Forth' in *The Past*, i (1920), p. 66; ii (1921), p. 64.

39. Hore, *Wexford*, v, p. 38.

40. *38th Rep. D. K. P. R. I.*, p. 41.

41. Hore, *Wexford*, v, p. 102.

42. *Cal. i. p. m.*, 18 Ed. II, p. 363.

43. Bradley, 'Anglo-Norman towns', p. 429.

44. O. S. Wexford 37 (1841).

45. *Cal. close rolls*, 18 Ed. II, p. 363.

46. Hore, *Wexford*, v, pp 173, 182.

47. *Cal. i. p. m.*, vi, p. 324.

48. Otway-Ruthven, 'Character of Norman settlement', p. 80.

49. J. Russell, 'Late thirteenth-century Ireland as a region' in *Demography*, iii (1966), p. 504.

50. *Expugnatio*, p. 33.

51. P. F. Wallace, 'Archaeology and the emergence of Dublin as the principal town of Ireland' in Bradley (ed.), *Settlement and society*, pp 130–5.

52. G. Mac Niocaill, *Na buirgéisí* (Baile Átha Cliath, 1964), p. 303.

53. Personal observation.

54. C. Sheehan, 'South Main St./North Main St., Wexford' in *Excavations* (1997), no. 608.

55. E. Bourke, 'Westgate etc.' in *Excavations* (1990), no. 121.

56. *Cal. close rolls*, 18 Ed. II, p. 363.

57. Hore, *Wexford*, v, p. 124.

MEDIEVAL CHURCHES

1. Bradley, 'Anglo-Norman towns', p. 445.

2. R. Johnson, *Viking age Dublin* (Dublin, 2004), pp 89–90.

3. M. Hurley, 'Topography and development' in *Late Viking Age and medieval Waterford* (Waterford, n. d.), p. 7.

4. Moore, *Archaeological inventory*, p. 162, no. 1482; Hore, *Wexford*, v, p. 76.

5. Moore, *Archaeological inventory*, p. 162, no. 1483.

6. P. Harbison, 'Barralet and Beranger's antiquarian sketching tour through Wicklow and Wexford in the autumn of 1780' in *R. I. A. Proc.*, 104, C, no. 6 (2004), pp 148–51.

7. C. Sheehan, 'Wexford' in *Excavations*, no. 229.

8. Colclough Papers, N. L. I., Ms 29, 755(4).

9. Hore, *Wexford*, v, p. 37.

10. *Calendar of the ancient deeds and muniments preserved in the Pembroke estate office, Dublin* (Dublin, 1891), pp 11–13.

11. *Cal. doc. Ire.*, i, no. 85. A mill-stone was uncovered during recent development work in this vicinity (personal observation).

12. F. Grannel, *The Franciscans in Wexford* (Wexford, n. d.).

13. A. Gwynn and R. Hadcock, *Medieval religious houses Ireland* (Dublin, 1970), p. 151.

14. Hore, *Wexford*, v. p. 153.

15. M. Archdall, *Monasticon Hibernicum* (London, 1786), p. 755.

16. Hore, *Wexford*, v, p. 38.

17. Moore, *Archaeological inventory*, p. 162, no. 1481.

18. H. Leask, *Irish churches and monastic buildings* 3 v (Dundalk, 1960, reprinted 1978), iii, p. 56.

19. *Dublin Penny Journal* (1834).

20. E. Murphy, 'The Semples and St Selskar's' in *Wex. Hist. Soc. Jn.*, xx (2004–5), pp 45–55.

21. *Papal registers* (London, 1897), 3 Innocent VI, Jan. 5, 1355, p. 565.

22. H. F. Berry (ed.), *Statute rolls of the parliament of Ireland 1–12 Ed. II* (Dublin, 1914), pp 124–5.

23. e.g. Hore, *Wexford,* v, p. 84.

24. Hore, *Wexford,* v, pp 153, 155; Archdall, *Monasticon Hibernicum,* pp 755–6.

25. A dam on a stream. Bolan's Lane was formerly called Well Lane so there may have been a stream in this area (N. Rossiter, 'Lost lanes and hidden treasures' in *Wex. Hist. Soc. Jn.,* 19 (2002–3), pp. 75–6).

26. Archdall, *Monasticon Hibernicum,* p. 757.

27. Hore, *Wexford,* v, p. 234.

28. O. S. Wexford 37 (1841)

29. O. S. Wexford (1882)

30. O. S. Wexford 37 (1903).

31. Hore, *Wexford,* vi, p. 266.

32. Hore, *Wexford,* v, pp 84, 154; H. F. Hore (ed.), 'A choreographic account of the southern part of county Wexford, written about 1684 by Robert Leigh, esq., of Rosegarland, in that county' in *R. S. A. I. Jn.,* v (1858–9), pp 451–67.

THE IRISH REVIVAL: THE COLONY UNDER PRESSURE

1. The Gaelic revival in county Wexford is discussed in Colfer, *Arrogant trespass,* pp 71–82.

2. Hore, *Wexford,* v, p. 101.

3. Hore, *Wexford,* v, p. 101.

4. J. Lydon, 'The impact of the Bruce invasion' in *New history of Ireland,* ii, pp 3–37.

5. Hore, *Wexford,* v, p. 105.

6. *Cal. i. p. m.,* vi, pp 324–7.

7. *Cal. i. p. m.,* vi, p. 110.

8. J. Otway-Ruthven, *A history of medieval Ireland* (London, 1980), p. 252.

9. Otway-Ruthven, *Medieval Ireland,* p. 112.

10. A. Gwynn, 'The Black Death in Ireland' in *Studies,* xxiv (1935), pp 25–42.

11. Hore, *Wexford,* v, p. 126.

12. Colfer, *Arrogant trespass,* pp 223–48.

13. K. Nicholls, 'Anglo-French Ireland and after' in *Peritia,* i (1982), p. 401.

14. Hore, *Wexford,* v, p. 129; Otway-Ruthven, *Medieval Ireland,* p. 362.

15. Leask, *Irish castles,* p. 76.

16. Hore, *Wexford,* v, pp 412–3.

17. Hore, *Wexford,* v, p. 139.

18. Hore, *Wexford,* v, pp 133, 175.

19. Hore, *Wexford,* v, p. 202.

20. T. W. Moody and F. X. Martin (eds), *The course of Irish history* (Cork, 1967), pp 174–82.

TOWN WALL AND CASTLE

1. Braudel, *Civilisation and capitalism,* pp 492–5.

2. *Expugnatio,* p. 33.

3. J. Wren, 'Wexford main drainage' in I. Bennett (ed.), *Excavations* (1995), no. 287.

4. Hore, *Wexford,* v, p. 60.

5. M. Ryan and M. Cahill, 'An investigation of the town wall at Abbey Street, Wexford' in *Old Wex. Hist. Soc. Jn.,* viii (1980–1), pp 56–64.

6. The battlements of this square tower were apparently restored, probably in the 1850s when one of Wexford's twin churches was built outside the wall at this point. A similar mural tower, located 100m to the south, was demolished at the same time with part of the town wall.

7. Hore, *Wexford,* v, p. 61.

8. C. Sheehan, 'South Main St./North Main Street., Wexford' in I. Bennett (ed.), *Excavations* (1997), no. 608.

9. J. Wren, 'Cornmarket, Wexford' in I. Bennett (ed.), *Excavations* (2000), no. 1070; D. Noonan and S. Elder, 'Cornmarket, Wexford' in I. Bennett (ed.), *Excavations* (2000), no. 1071.

10. Bradley, 'Anglo-Norman towns', p. 441.

11. Bradley, 'Anglo-Norman towns', p. 442.

12. Hore, *Wexford,* v, p. 60; Loftus Ms in Marsh's Library.

13. Hore, *Wexford,* v, p. 92.

14. Hore, *Wexford,* v, p. 132.

15. Hore, *Wexford,* v, p. 200.

16. Moore, *Archaeological survey,* pp 161–2.

17. Hore, *Wexford,* v, pp 107, 122, 141.

18. Hore, *Wexford,* v, p. 141.

19. The earthen rampart may date to the Cromwellian siege of the town in 1649.

20. Hore, *Wexford,* v, pp 176, 60.

21. Shown in a drawing in the Corporation archives.

22. Hore, *Wexford,* v, p. 232.

23. Hore, *Wexford,* v, p. 170.

24. Hore, *Wexford,* v, p. 60.

25. Hore, *Wexford,* v, p. 350

26. 'Wexford corporation's eighteenth-century leases' in *Wex. Hist. Soc. Jn.,* xiii (1990–1), pp 144–5.

27. A. Griffith, *Dublin magazine* (September, 1764).

28. Hore, *Wexford,* v, p. 159.

29. 1840 O. S. town plan (National Archives, O. S. 140 4/638/20).

30. *Griffith's Chronicles* (Enniscorthy, 1877), pp 27–8.

31. Wexford Corporation archives.

32. Hore, *Wexford,* v, p. 141.

33. Hore, *Wexford,* v, p. 247.

34. Hore, *Wexford,* v, p. 363.

35. Down Survey (1655), N. L. I., Ms 725.

36. J. Wren, 'Wexford' in I. Bennett (ed.), *Excavations* (1994), no. 229.

37. E. Bourke, 'Westgate, etc.' in I. Bennett (ed.), *Excavations* (1990), no. 121.

38. Otway-Ruthven, *Medieval Ireland,* p. 186.

39. *Cal. doc. Ire.,* i, no. 2900; For an analysis of the impact of the partition of Leinster on county Wexford, see Colfer, *Arrogant trespass,* pp 71–82.

40. Orpen, *Normans,* i, p. 373.

41. *Ormond deeds,* i, no. 7.

42. Hore, *Wexford,* v, p. 64.

43. *Cal. doc. Ire.,* i, nos. 1030, 1269.

44. *Cal. doc. Ire.,* i, no. 1872.

45. *Cal. doc. Ire.,* ii, no. 1950.

46. Orpen, *Normans,* i, p. 373.

47. Pers. comm. with Dr Ned Culleton, earth scientist.

48. J. Bradley, 'Planned Anglo-Norman towns', p. 444.

49. Hore, *Wexford,* v, p. 102.

50. Hore, *Wexford,* v, p. 104.

51. Leask, *Irish castles,* p. 47; T. McNeill, *Castles in Ireland* (London, 1997), p. 118.

52. Leask, *Irish castles,* p. 47.

53. K. O'Conor, 'The origins of Carlow Castle' in *Arch. Ire.,* no. 41 (Autumn, 1997), pp 13–16.

54. T. O'Keeffe and M. Coughlan, 'The chronology and formal affinities of Ferns donjon, Co. Wexford' in J. R. Kenyon and K. O'Conor (eds), *The medieval castle in Ireland and Wales* (Dublin, 2003), pp 133–48.

55. Down Survey Map (1655), N. L. I., Ms 725.

56. W. Blaeuw, *The sea-mirror: containing a brief instruction on the art of navigation* (Amsterdam, 1625)

57. Hore, *Wexford,* v, p. 104.

58. Hore, *Wexford,* v, p. 105.

59. Hore, *Wexford,* v, p. 122.

60. *39th Rep. D. K. P. R.I.,* p. 49; Hore, *Wexford,* v, p. 232.

61. Hore, *Wexford,* v, p. 113.

62. Hore, *Wexford,* v, p. 154.

63. Hore, *Wexford,* v, pp 154, 170, 183; vi, p. 391.

64. Hore, *Wexford,* v, pp 188–9.

65. Hore, *Wexford,* v, pp 216, 244, 238.

66. Hore, *Wexford,* v. p. 66.

67. P. Lenihan, *Confederate Catholics at war* (Cork, 2001), pp 156–7, 177, 212, 168.

68. J. Ohlmeyer, 'The Dunkirk of Ireland: Wexford privateers during the 1640s' in *Wex. Hist. Soc. Jn.,* xii (1988–89), pp 23–49.

69. Hore, *Wexford,* v, pp 285–91.

70. Hore, *Wexford,* v, pp 66, 337, 359.

71. Hore, *Wexford,* v, p. 68.

72. Hore, *Wexford,* v, p. 70.

TRADE AND TRIBULATION

1. Bourke, 'Two early eleventh-century Viking houses', pp 50–61.

2. *Cal. doc. Ire.,* i, no. 34.

3. *Ann. Loch Cé,* i, p. 256.

4. *Expugnatio,* p. 35.

5. *Cal. doc. Ire.,* ii, nos. 1117, 1902; Mac Niocaill, *Na buirgéisí,* pp 526, 528.

6. Hore, *Wexford,* v, p. 96.

7. W. Childs and T. O'Neill, 'Overseas trade' in *N. H. I.* (Oxford, 1993), pp 497, 508.

8. D. B. Quinn and K. W. Nicholls, 'Ireland in 1534' in T. W. Moody, F. X. Martin, F. J. Byrne (eds), *N. H. I.* (Oxford, 1976), p. 7.

9. A. K. Longfield, *Anglo-Irish trade in the sixteenth century* (London, 1929), p. 52.

10. John De Courcy Ireland, 'County Wexford in maritime history' in Whelan (ed.), *Wexford,* p. 493.

11. Hore, *Wexford,* v, pp 123–4.

12. Longfield, *Anglo-Irish trade,* p. 35.

13. Longfield, *Anglo-Irish trade,* p. 212.

14. De Courcy Ireland, 'Wexford in maritime history', p. 493.

15. De Courcy Ireland, 'Wexford in maritime history', p. 493; D. Taylor, The overseas trade of mid sixteenth-century Bridgewater (MA dissertation Bristol University, 2006); <http://www.bris.ac.uk/Depts/History/Maritime/Sources/2006taylor.pdf>

16. Longfield, *Anglo-Irish trade,* pp 170-1.

17. Hore, *Wexford,* v, pp 143, 241–3.

18. Hore, *Wexford,* v, p. 119.

19. H. Goff, 'English conquest of an Irish barony: the changing patterns of land ownership in the barony of Scarawalsh 1540–1640' in Whelan (ed.), *Wexford,* pp 122–49.

20. Hore, *Wexford,* v, p. 156.

21. Longfield, *Anglo-Irish trade,* p. 119.

22. Longfield, *Anglo-Irish trade,* p. 123.

23. Hore, *Wexford,* vi, p. 410; Hore, *Wexford,* v, p. 201.

24. H. Hore, 'Woods and fastnesses, and their denizens in ancient Leinster' in *R. S. A. I. Jn.,* iv (1856–7), p. 238.

25. Hore, *Wexford,* v, pp 201–2.

26. T. C. Barnard, 'An Anglo-Irish industrial enterprise: iron-making at Enniscorthy, Co. Wexford, 1657–92' in *R. I. A. Proc.,* 85, C (1985), pp 101–44.

27. De Courcy Ireland, 'Wexford in maritime history', p. 495.

28. Stanihurst, 'Description of Ireland' in Holinshed's *Chronicles* (1807–8), p. 30.

29. Stanihurst, 'Description of Ireland', p. 494.

30. Longfield, *Anglo-Irish trade,* p. 56.

31. Moody and Martin (eds), *Course of Irish history,* pp 174–82.

32. P. Corish, 'Reformation and Counter-Reformation (1500–1700)' in M. J. Berney (ed.), *Centenary record of Wexford's twin churches* (Wexford, 1958), p. 37.

33. P. Corish, 'Two centuries of Catholicism in county Wexford' in Whelan (ed.), *Wexford,* p. 225.

34. Corish, 'Two centuries of Catholicism', p. 225.

35. J. Lydon, *The making of Ireland* (London, 1998), pp 154–62.

36. Corish, 'Two centuries of Catholicism', p. 224.

37. Corish, 'Two centuries of Catholicism', p. 224.

38. Hore, *Wexford,* v, p. 200.

39. M. Berney (ed.), 'Wexford mass houses of the penal days' in *Centenary record*, p. 55.

40. F. Grannell, *The Franciscans in Wexford* (Wexford, n. d.), p. 17.

41. Corish, 'Two centuries of Catholicism', pp 226–28.

42. Hore, *Wexford*, v, p. 245.

43. Hore, *Wexford*, v, p. 248.

44. Corish, 'Reformation and Counter-Reformation', p. 45.

45. Hore, *Wexford*, v, p. 229.

46. A. Clarke, 'The Irish economy 1600–60' in *N. H. I.*, iii, p. 181.

47. Hore, *Wexford*, v, pp 240–3.

48. Hore, *Wexford*, v, pp 210–17.

49. Hore, *Wexford*, v, pp 237–8.

50. Hore, *Wexford*, v, p. 233. The design of the crest may have been based on the burning of a ship during the taking of the town by the Anglo-Normans in 1169.

51. P. Corish, *The Catholic community* (Dublin, 1981), p. 30.

52. Hore, *Wexford*, v, p. 203.

53. Hore, *Wexford*, v, pp 228–9.

54. For a case study see Goff, 'English conquest of an Irish barony'.

55. Comprehensive accounts of this period can be found in Lenihan, *Confederate Catholics*; M. Ó Siochrú, *Confederate Ireland 1642–1649: a constitutional and political analysis* (Dublin, 1999). For a concise overview, see J. Lydon, *The making of Ireland* (London, 1998), pp 163–96.

56. Hore, *Wexford*, v, pp 253–6.

57. *Griffith's Chronicles*, p. 382.

58. T. C. D., Ms F. 2. 11, 111; Extracts in Hore, *Wexford*, v, pp 254–5.

59. Boazio, 1599; see Andrews, *Shapes of Ireland*, p. 60.

60. *Griffith's Chronicles*, pp 29–30; Petty's map, 1685; the fort was still in existence in 1795 (Hore, *Wexford*, v, p. 54).

61. Hore, *Wexford*, v, pp 254–7.

62. Corish, 'Reformation and Counter-Reformation', pp 45–6; Hore, *Wexford*, v, p. 256.

63. Corish, 'Two centuries of Catholicism', p. 229.

64. Hore, *Wexford*, v, pp 266, 270; Lenihan, *Confederate Catholics*, pp 108, 123.

65. *Griffith's Chronicles*; Wexford town plan, 1840 (N. A. I., OS 140 4/638/20.

66. Hore, *Wexford*, v, p. 258.

67. W. Smyth, *Map-making, landscapes and memory: a geography of colonial and early modern Ireland* (Cork, 2006), p. 151.

68. Hore, *Wexford*, v, p. 259.

69. Ohlmeyer, 'The Dunkirk of Ireland' in *Wex. Hist. Soc. Jn.*, xii (1988–9), p. 23. The information on the Wexford privateers is based mostly on Ohlmeyer's paper.

70. Hore, *Wexford*, v, pp 270, 272.

71. J. Ohlmeyer, 'A failed revolution' in J. Ohlmeyer (ed.), *Ireland from independence to occupation* (Cambridge, 1995), p. 1; See also Lenihan, *Confederate Catholics*, pp 221–9.

72. Ohlmeyer, 'The Dunkirk of Ireland', pp 29–30.

73. Smyth, *Map-making, landscapes and memory*, pp 153–4.

74. N. Canny, 'Early modern Ireland c. 1500–1700' in R. Foster (ed.), *The Oxford illustrated history of Ireland* (Oxford, 1989), p. 146.

75. Ohlmeyer, 'The Dunkirk of Ireland', p. 29.

76. Hore, *Wexford*, v, pp 278–9.

77. Hore, *Wexford*, v, pp 285–7.

78. Hore, *Wexford*, v, p. 291.

79. Hore, *Wexford*, v, p. 294.

80. Hore, *Wexford*, v, p. 394.

81. The Bullring was referred to as the Market Place in an 1662 survey (Hore, v, *Wexford*, p. 347).

82. Details of the siege are taken from contemporary accounts printed in Hore, *Wexford*, v, pp 285–304.

83. Hore, *Wexford*, v, p. 299.

84. Hore, *Wexford*, v, p. 305.

CROMWELLIAN CONFISCATION AND COLONISATION

1. L. M. Cullen, *The emergence of modern Ireland* (London, 1981), p. 87.

2. Smyth, *Map-making, landscapes and memory*, p. 357.

3. Hore, *Wexford*, v, p. 315.

4. For an overview of this period, see Smyth, *Map-making, landscapes and memory*, pp 153–65.

5. Hore, *Wexford*, v, 395.

6. J. H. Andrews, 'The struggle for Ireland's public commons' in P. O'Flanagan, P. Ferguson and K. Whelan (eds) *Rural Ireland: modernisation and change 1600–1900* (Cork, 1987), p. 15.

7. Hore, *Wexford*, v, pp 308, 325.

8. Hore, *Wexford*, v, p. 306.

9. Smyth, *Map-making, landscapes and memory*, p. 161.

10. R. C. Simington (ed.), *The Civil Survey of the county of Wexford* (Dublin, 1953).

11. Down Survey maps (1655), N. L. I., Ms. 725.

12. Hore, *Wexford*, v, pp 310–13.

13. Hore, *Wexford*, v, p. 313.

14. Hore, *Wexford*, v, pp 313, 321, 325, 336, 352.

15. K. Whelan, 'Towns and villages' in Aalen, Whelan and Stout (eds), *Atlas of the Irish rural landscape*, p. 185.

16. H. F. Hore (ed.), 'An account of the barony of Forth, in the county of Wexford, written at the close of the seventeenth century' in *R. S. A. I. Jn.*, vi (1862), pp 66–7.

17. Hore, *Wexford*, v, pp 305, 308–9.

18. Grannell, *Franciscans in Wexford*, p. 31.

19. Hore, *Wexford*, v, pp 320, 314; *Griffith's Chronicles*, p. 29.

20. Hore, *Wexford*, v, pp 324, 326.

21. Hore, *Wexford*, v, pp 311, 318.

22. Hore, *Wexford*, v, pp 312, 360. Taverns were similarly targeted in eighteenth-century New York at times of civil unrest; P. Linebaugh and M. Rediker, *The many-headed hydra: the hidden history of the revolutionary Atlantic* (London, 2000), p. 207.

23. Hore, *Wexford*, v, pp 315–6.

24. Hore, *Wexford*, v, p. 326.

25. Celestine Rafferty, 'The Roman Catholic parish registers of Wexford town from c.1672: some considerations of their significance and use in historical research' in *Wex. Hist. Soc. Jn.*, no. xv (1994–5), pp 103, 108.

26. S. Pender (ed.), *A census of Ireland* (Dublin, 1939).

27. Hore, *Wexford*, v, pp 328, 329–31, 359, 360.

28. Hore, *Wexford*, v, pp 307–9, 320, 336.

29. Hore, *Wexford*, v, pp 311, 336–50.

30. Hore, *Wexford*, v, p. 362.

31. Hore, *Wexford*, v, pp 244, 313, 387.

32. Hore (ed.), 'An account of the barony of Forth', p. 83.

33. Hore, *Wexford*, v, pp 326–55.

34. Hore, *Wexford*, v, 336.

35. Hore, *Wexford*, v, pp 337–54. The origin of the street could date to the late fourteenth century as devotion to St George became popular at that time.

36. Hore (ed.), 'Particulars relative to Wexford 1682', p. 88.

37. Hore, *Wexford*, v, pp 361–2.

38. Rafferty, 'Parish registers', pp 103–4.

39. For an account of Wadding's life, see Celestine Rafferty, "Immensity confined": Luke Waddinge, Bishop of Ferns' in *Wex. Hist. Soc. Jn.*, 12 (1988–9), pp 5–22.

40. Corish, 'Reformation and Counter-Reformation', p. 48.

41. 'Wexford mass houses of the penal days' in Berney (ed.), *Centenary record*, p. 55.

42. Lydon, *The making of Ireland*, pp 204–5.

43. J. Ranson, 'The Kilmore carols' in *The Past*, v (1949), pp 61–102.

44. Hore, *Wexford*, v, p. 389.

45. Rafferty, 'Parish registers', pp 107–8.

46. Hore, *Wexford*, v, p. 385.

47. Hore (ed.), 'Particulars relative to Wexford', p. 88.

48. Hore, *Wexford*, v, pp 367–82.

49. For a general background to this period, see Lydon, *The making of Ireland*, pp 208–17; Corish, *The Catholic community*, p. 72.

50. Hore, *Wexford*, v, pp 385–7.

WEXFORD CHARTERS

1. *Cal. doc. Ire.* i, no. 39.

2. *Cal. doc. Ire.*, i, no. 85.

3. Hore, *Wexford*, v, pp 118–9.

4. Hore, *Wexford*, ii, p. 19.

5. Colfer, *Arrogant trespass*, pp 71–82.

6. *Griffith's Chronicles*, pp 290–1.

7. Hore, *Wexford*, v, pp 139; 188–94.

8. Hore, *Wexford*, v, pp 210–17; 365–82.

9. *Griffith's Chronicles*, pp 289–90.

EIGHTEENTH-CENTURY WEXFORD.

1. Corish, *Catholic community*, pp 73–6.

2. Smyth, *Map-making, landscapes and memory*, p. 370.

3. 'Report of the state of popery in Ireland, 1731' in *Archivium Hibernicum*, iv (1915), pp 166–71.

4. For a fuller account of this period, see N. Furlong, 'The times and life of Nicholas Sweetman, bishop of Ferns, (1744–86)' in *Wex. Hist. Soc. Jn.*, ix (1983–4), pp 1–19. For an account of the family, see J. Mannion, 'A transatlantic fishery: Richard Walsh of New Ross and the Sweetmans of Newbawn in Newfoundland 1734–1862' in Whelan (ed.) *Wexford*, pp 373–421.

5. Corish, *Catholic community*, p. 89.

6. Hore, *Wexford*, v, p. 394; *Griffith's Chronicles*, p. 288.

7. Wexford Corporation Minute Books c. 1708–1740s (Wexford County Library Archives).

8. Hore, *Wexford*, v, p. 70.

9. Hore, *Wexford*, v, p. 396.

10. S. O'Sullivan, 'Jonathan Swift and Wexford's spa' in *Wex. Hist. Soc. Jn.*, vi (1976–7), pp 63–8.

11. Hore, *Wexford*, v, pp 398–9.

12. Hore, *Wexford*, v, p. 86; M. T. Kehoe, *Wexford town—its streets and people* (Wexford, n. d.).

13. In 1757, out of twenty-three corn merchants, ten had Anglo-Norman surnames; the mayor, bailiffs and magistrates had Cromwellian settler names (Hore, *Wexford*, v, p. 399).

14. D. Goodall, 'The freemen of Wexford in 1776' in *The Irish Genealogist*, v, nos 1, pp 103–21; 2, pp 314–34; 3, 448–63; Hore, *Wexford*, v, pp 365–6.

15. For the political situation in county Wexford, see B. Cleary, 'Sowing the whirlwind' in *Wex. Hist. Soc. Jn.*, xiii, (1992–3), pp 9–79.

16. *Minutes of evidence taken before the select committee on the Wexford election petition* (London, 1830).

17. Amyas Griffiths in *Dublin Magazine*, August 1764; printed in Hore, *Wexford*, v, pp 400–1.

18. B. Browne, 'John Barry: the forgotten American hero' in *Wex. Hist. Soc. Jn.*, xv (1994–5), pp 43–51.

19. Corporation Minute Books, quoted in P. Reck, *Wexford – a municipal history* (Wexford, 1987), p. 169.

20. Hore, *Wexford*, v, pp 402–3.

21. Hore, *Wexford*, v, pp 403–4.

22. Corporation Minute Book, quoted in Reck, *Wexford*, p. 169.

23. De Courcy Ireland, 'Maritime history', p. 496.

24. *Wexford Herald*, 18 Dec. 1788.

25. K. Whelan, 'The Catholic community in eighteenth-century county Wexford' in T. Power and K. Whelan (eds), *Endurance and emergence. Catholics in Ireland in the*

eighteenth century (Dublin, 1990), pp 129–70.

26. Hore, *Wexford,* v, pp 403–4.

27. *Griffith's Chronicles,* p. 261.

28. Corporation Minute Book, quoted in Reck, *Wexford,* p. 171.

29. Hore, *Wexford,* v, p. 237.

30. Furlong, 'Wexford port', p. 169.

THE 1798 REBELLION: A WEXFORD TOWN PERSPECTIVE

1. For an analysis of eighteenth-century Ireland, see K. Whelan, *The tree of liberty* (Cork, 1996). The dispersal of Wexford families is mapped in K. Whelan, *Fellowship of freedom* (Cork, 1998), p. 18.

2. L. Cullen, *The emergence of modern Ireland 1600–1900* (Dublin, 1983), p. 251.

3. Whelan, *Fellowship of freedom,* p. 71.

4. The background to the rebellion is discussed in Cullen, *Modern Ireland,* pp 193–233. A narrative account is given in D. Gahan, *The people's rising* (Dublin, 1995).

5. B. Cleary, 'The Battle of Oulart Hill: context and strategy' in D. Keogh and N. Furlong (eds), *The mighty wave: The 1798 rebellion in Wexford* (Dublin, 1996), pp 79–96; N. Furlong, *Fr John Murphy of Boolavogue 1753–1798* (Dublin, 1991).

6. He was buried in nearby Carrig graveyard where his tombstone can still be seen. See Hilary Murphy (ed.), 'Memories of Colonel Jonas Watson' in *Wex. Hist. Soc. Jn.,* 15 (1994–5), pp 115–8.

7. Furlong, *Fr John Murphy,* pp 91–2.

8. Handcock's narrative of 1798, N. L. I., Ms 16,232, p. 122; See also James Gordon, *History of the rebellion in Ireland in the year 1798* (Dublin, 1801), p. 152.

9. The fullest (though cryptic) account is in Edward Hay, *History of the Insurrection of the county of Wexford, A.D. 1798* (Dublin, 1803), pp 128-33.

10. Whelan, *Fellowship of freedom,* pp 72–3.

11. Furlong, *Fr John Murphy,* pp 91–2.

12. Dixon went to county Meath with the northern division of the rebel army: see Eamon Doyle, *The Wexford insurgents of '98 and their march into Meath* (Enniscorthy, 1997). With his equally notorious wife, Madge, he later escaped to America. The Dixons' extremism can be attributed to the rape of Madge Dixon by soldiers. See Anna Kinsella, 'Women in folk memories and ballads' in D. Keogh and N. Furlong (eds), *The women of 1798* (Dublin, 1998), p. 189; Dáire Keogh 'The women of 1798; explaining the silence' in T. Bartlett, D. Dickson, D. Keogh and K. Whelan (eds), *1798: a bicentenary perspective* (Dublin, 2003), p. 513n.

13. *Griffith's Chronicles,* p. 261. For the role of Protestants in the Rebellion, see P. Comerford, 'Euseby Cleaver, Bishop of Ferns, and the clergy of the Church of Ireland in the 1798 Rising in Co. Wexford' in *Wex. Hist. Soc. Jn.,* xvi (1996–7), pp 66–94.

URBAN GROWTH: TRADE AND INDUSTRY

1. Whelan, *Tree of liberty,* p. 49.

2. P. Jupp. 'Urban politics in Ireland 1801–1831' in D. Harkness and M. O'Dowd (eds), *The town in Ireland* (Belfast, 1981), p. 109.

3. Lewis, *Topographical dictionary of Ireland,* ii, p. 701; G. H. Bassett, *Wexford county: guide and directory* (Dublin, 1885), p. 71.

4. P. Kerrigan, *Castles and fortifications in Ireland 1485–1945* (Cork, 1995), pp 161, 182–3; T. Lacy, *Sights and scenes in our fatherland* (London, 1863), p. 503.

5. *Griffith's Chronicles,* p. 272.

6. *Griffith's Chronicles,* p. 271; Hore, *Wexford,* v, p. 320.

7. *Griffith's Chronicles,* p. 295.

8. King Street is presumably named after John Kinge (or his descendants) who was granted extensive lands in this part of the town in 1608 (Hore, *Wexford,* v, p. 207).

9. For the background to emancipation, see J. Lydon, *The making of Ireland* (London, 1998), pp 283–9.

10. J. Glynn, 'The Catholic Church in Wexford town 1800–1858' in *The Past,* xv (1984), p. 24.

11. *Wexford Herald,* 20 Aug. 1806.

12. *Griffith's Chronicles,* p. 272.

13. The naming of part of the quay after the Duke of Wellington, the hero of Waterloo, would suggest a date c. 1820.

14. Lewis, *Topographical dictionary,* ii, p. 709.

15. *Griffith's Chronicles,* p. 305; Lewis, *Topographical dictionary,* i, p. 602.

16. *Wexford Herald,* October, 1792.

17. A. O'Sullivan, 'Castlebridge' in Rowe and Wilson (eds), *High skies–low lands,* pp 53–5.

18. *Irish Farmers Journal,* March 1814.

19. Lewis, *Topographical dictionary,* i, p. 280.

20. O'Sullivan, 'Castlebridge', pp 53–5.

21. Lewis, *Topographical dictionary,* ii, pp 700–11.

22. N. A. I., OS 140 4/638/20 (O. S. town plan 1840).

23. *Griffith's Chronicles,* pp 289–90.

24. 'Wexford Corporation's eighteenth-century leases' in *Wex. Hist. Soc. Jn.,* xiii (1990–1), pp 142–8.

25. *Parliamentary Gazetteer* (London, 1845).

26. Whelan, 'The modern landscape' in Aalen, Whelan and Stout (eds), *Atlas,* pp 87–92.

27. For an overview of the Famine, see Lydon, *The making of Ireland,* pp 301–5.

28. M. Gwinnell, 'The Famine years in Co. Wexford' in *Wex. Hist. Soc. Jn.,* viiii (1983–4), p. 52. For an account of the Famine in county Wexford, see A. Kinsella, *County Wexford in the Famine years* (Enniscorthy, 1995).

29. Tom and Teresa Wickham, 'The Wexford Union Workhouse' in *Taghmon Hist. Soc. Jn.,* part 1, no. 5, pp 80–98; part 2, no. 6, pp 78–99; E. Carthy, 'Wexford workhouse in Famine times' in *Wex. Hist. Soc. Jn.,* xvi (1996–7), pp 95–113.

30. Gwinnell, 'Famine years', p. 36.

31. *Wexford Independent,* 6 June 1846.

32. *Wexford Independent,* 28 February 1847.

33. Numbers are from Carty, 'Wexford workhouse'; Gwinnell, 'Famine years'.

34. Gwinnell, 'Famine years', p. 43.

35. M. Gwinnell, 'Economic life in county Wexford in the nineteenth century' in *Wex. Hist. Soc. Jn.,* x, p. 16.

36. *Griffith's Chronicles,* p. 456. The Nymph Bank (named after the ship from which it was discovered) was found in 1736, extending along the coasts of Wexford, Waterford and Cork at a distance of about thirty miles.

37. H. D. Inglis, 'A journey through Wexford in 1834' in *The Past,* vii (1964), p. 177.

38. Lewis, *Topographical dictionary,* ii, pp 700–11.

39. *Griffith's Chronicles,* pp 328, 296.

40. Lewis, *Topographical dictionary,* ii, p. 709.

41. N. Rossiter, *Wexford port – a history* (Wexford, 1989), pp 24–46; 'Wexford shipping' in *Centenary record,* p. 120.

42. Glynn, 'Wexford town', p. 26.

43. 'Wexford shipping' in *Centenary record,* p. 120.

44. Lacy, *Sights and scenes,* p. 408.

45. N. Furlong, 'The history of land reclamation in Wexford harbour' in *Wex. Hist. Soc. Jn.,* ii (1969), p. 71.

46. 'Wexford shipping' in *Centenary record,* pp 121–2.

47. Lacy, *Sights and scenes,* p. 408.

48. Bassett, *Directory,* p. 65.

49. 'Wexford shipping' in *Centenary record,* pp 122–3.

50. J. Ranson, *Songs of the Wexford coast* (Wexford, 1975), pp 21–3, 12.

51. *Griffith's Chronicles,* pp 384, 443.

52. *Griffith's Chronicles,* pp 376–7, 293.

53. B. Long, *Bright light, white water* (Dublin, 1993), pp 53–5.

54. De Courcey Ireland, 'Maritime history', p. 499.

55. O. S. town plan 1840. The stream is now culverted. A mill-stone was exposed in this locality during development work in the early 1990s.

56. D. Rowe, 'The Rowes of Spawell Road' in *Wex. Hist. Soc. Jn.,* 18 (2000–1), pp 125–31.

57. Hore, *Wexford,* v, p. 88.

58. *The sixth report of the Commissioners* (London, 1808).

59. Lewis, *Topographical dictionary,* ii, p. 708.

60. *Wexford Independent,* 29 November 1845; *Wexford Independent* 16 May 1868.

61. Glynn, 'Wexford town', p. 28.

62. Wexford Corporation Minute Books, 1852.

63. H. Murphy, 'When Wexford workers first united' in *Wex. Hist. Soc. Jn.,* xv (1994–5), p. 100.

64. O. S. town plan 1840.

65. J. G. Kohl, 'A journey through Wexford in 1842' in *The Past,* vii (1964), p. 191.

66. *Stretten's Dublin, Cork and south of Ireland* (Dublin, 1890), pp 306-15.

67. *Wexford Independent,* 6 May 1868.

68. A. O'Sullivan, 'Pierces of Wexford' in *Wex. Hist. Soc. Jn.* xvi (1996–7), pp 126–42.

69. M. Maume, 'The Selskar Iron Works' in *Wex. Hist. Soc. Jn.,* xviii (2000–1), pp 5–14.

70. I. Hearne, 'The Star Iron Works' in *Wex. Hist. Soc. Jn.,* xviiii (2002–3), pp 5–37.

71. Lewis, *Topographical dictionary,* ii, p. 497.

72. Hilary Murphy, 'The Drinagh cement works' in *Wex. Hist. Soc. Jn.,* vi (1976–7), pp 38–44.

73. N. L. I., P 770.

74. Furlong, 'Land reclamation in Wexford Harbour' in *Wex. Hist. Soc. Jn.,* vi (1969), pp 53–77.

75. Minutes of Wexford Harbour Board Commissioners.

76. C. Wilson, 'The Wexford wildfowl reserve' in Rowe and Wilson (eds), *High skies–low lands,* pp 245–7.

77. O. S. maps 1882 (Wexford County Library)

78. This section is based on E. Shepherd, 'The town of Wexford and the railways' in *Wex. Hist. Soc. Jn.,* xviii (2000–1), pp 59–93.

79. For a detailed account of Rosslare Harbour, see J. Maddock, *Rosslare Harbour: sea and ships* (Rosslare, 1996).

80. H. Murphy, 'A humiliating defeat for Richard J. Devereux' in *Wex. Hist. Soc. Jn.,* xiii (1992–93), pp 129–34.

81. For a general background, see Lydon, *The making of Ireland,* pp 319–55.

ECCLESIASTICAL EXPANSION

1. For a detailed analysis of the church in Wexford in the first half of nineteenth century, see Glynn, 'Wexford town', pp 5–53.

2. W. H. Grattan Flood, *History of the diocese of Ferns* (Waterford, 1916), p. 134.

3. *Griffith's Chronicles,* pp 274–7; 'St. Peter's College' in *Centenary record,* pp 134–42.

4. Lacy, *Sights and scenes,* p. 433; Lewis, *Topographical dictionary,* ii, p. 711.

5. Glynn, 'Wexford town', p. 9.

6. *Wexford Independent,* 4 Jan. 1832. The Lancastrian system of education, based on the use of senior students as monitors, was developed in London in the late eighteenth century and quickly gained popularity.

7. *Second report from the Commissioners of Irish Education Inquiry* (London, 1826–7), pp 800–35.

8. Grannell, *Franciscans in Wexford,* p. 43.

9. Glynn, 'Wexford town', p. 25.

10. Grannell, *Franciscans in Wexford,* p. 47.

11. É. Murphy, 'The Semples and St Selskar's' in *Wex. Hist. Soc. Jn.,* xx (2004–5), pp 45–55.

12. *Griffith's Chronicles,* p. 276; K. Spenser, 'Pugin and County Wexford' in *Wex. Hist. Soc. Jn.,* viii (1980–81), pp 77–90.

13. 'The Presentation Convent' in *Centenary record,* pp 145–6.

14. Glynn, 'Wexford town', p. 29; 'Convent of Mercy' in *Centenary record,* p. 147.

15. Glynn, 'Wexford town', p. 29; 'The Christian Brothers in Wexford' in *Centenary record,* pp 143–4.

16. *Centenary record*, pp 156, 149, 152,

17. Glynn, 'Wexford town', pp 41–6.

18. 'The beginning of a new era' in *Centenary record*, pp 77–8.

19. B. O'Leary, 'Richard Pierce: architect and acolyte of the Gothic revival' in *Wex. Hist. Soc. Jn.*, xx (2004–5), p. 87.

20. O. S. Town plan, 1840.

21. O. S. Town plan, 1840.

22. M. Berney, 'Finding the money' in *Centenary record*, pp 79–82.

23. For a description of the churches, see O'Leary, 'Richard Pierce', pp 87–91.

24. Grannell, *Franciscans in Wexford*, p. 44.

THE MODERN TOWN

1. *The Free Press* (1903–5, various dates).

2. G. Kehoe, 'Rosslare Fort and its people' in *Old Wex. Soc. Jn.*, v (1974–5), pp 44–6.

3. *The Free Press* (1903, various dates).

4. A. Kinsella, 'Who feared to speak in 1898' in *Wex. Hist. Soc. Jn.*, 17 (1998–9), pp 221–34; Hilary Murphy,

'Bullring monument was unveiled in 1905' in *A Wexford century: People newspapers souvenir millennium supplement*, p. 6.

5. Michael Enright, *Men of iron* (Wexford, 1987).

6. Lydon, *The making of Ireland*, p. 318.

7. J. J. Lee, *Ireland 1912–1985* (Cambridge, 1989), pp 17–8.

8. H. Murphy, 'World War One claimed many lives' in *A Wexford century*, p. 15.

9. De Courcy Ireland, 'Wexford in maritime history', pp 500–1.

10. Rowe, 'The Yankee slip' in *High skies–low lands*, p. 39.

11. Lee, *Ireland 1912–1985*, p. 28.

12. Corporation Minutes (cited in Reck, *Wexford*, p. 181).

13. H. Murphy, 'Enniscorthy's taste of war over Easter' in *A Wexford century*, p. 19.

14. Maume, 'The Selskar Iron Works', p. 11.

15. H. Murphy, 'Michael Collins addressed Treaty meeting in Wexford' in *A Wexford century*, p. 26.

16. De Courcey Ireland, 'Wexford in maritime history', pp 500–1.

17. Maddock, *Rosslare Harbour*, p. 99.

18. Rossiter, *Wexford port*, p. 48; De Courcey Ireland, 'Wexford in maritime history', p. 501.

19. Maddock, *Rosslare Harbour*, p. 99.

20. W. P. Creedon, *Exemplar Hiberniae: 100 years of Local Government in Co. Wexford* (Dublin, 1999), pp 7, 25, 121.

21. J. Jenkins, *The Tate School Wexford 1867–1949* (Wexford, n. d.)

22. Reck, *Wexford*, pp 148–9.

23. Rossiter, *Wexford port*, pp 50–5.

24. Hearn, 'The Star Iron Works', p. 34.

25. Eithne Scallan, *Clonard Wexford: the church of the Annunciation* (Wexford, 2007).

26. *Census 2006 socio-economic results: migration, birthplace, nationality, economic status, household composition: paper prepared for Wexford County Development Board* (2007).

27. T. Williams, *Fairways of the sea* (Rosslare, 2004).

28. *Wexford town and environs Development Plan, 2002*.

PERSONALITY

1. K. Daley, *Tom Walsh's opera: the history of the Wexford Festival 1951–2004* (Dublin, 2004).

FIGURE SOURCES AND ATTRIBUTIONS
Unless specifically attributed, all maps and diagrams in this volume are based on research by the author.

Fig. 3, p. 10 After D. Tietzsch-Tyler, and A. G. Sleeman (eds), *Geology of south Wexford* (Dublin, 1994).

Fig. 11, p. 15 After E. Culleton, *The south Wexford landscape* (Dublin, 1980), p. 51.

Fig. 12, p. 16 After Culleton, *South Wexford landscape*, p. 26.

Fig. 6, p. 22 After C. McLoughlin, 'Prehistoric remains at Kerlogue, Co. Wexford' in *Arch. Ire.*, xvi, 3 (Autumn, 2002), pp 17.

Fig. 16, p. 27 After F. Aalen, M. Stout and K. Whelan (eds), *Atlas of the Irish rural landscape* (Cork, 1997), p. 44.

Fig. 2, p. 31 After E. Roesdahl, *The Vikings* (London, 1987), pp xx–xxi.

Fig. 3B, p. 33 From E. Bourke, 'Two early eleventh-century Viking houses from Bride Street, Wexford and the layout of properties on the site' in *Wex. Hist. Soc. Jn.*, xii (1988–9), p. 55.

Fig. 7, p. 42 After I. Bennett, 'Preliminary archaeological excavations at Ferrycarrig ringwork, Newtown Td., Co. Wexford' in *Wex. Hist. Soc. Jn.*, x (1984–5), p. 34.

Fig. 17, p. 49 From *The invasions of England and Ireland with all their civill warrs since the conquest* (1601) in J. H. Andrews, *Shapes of Ireland* (Dublin, 1997), p. 92.

Fig. 7, p. 61 After Andrews, *Shapes of Ireland*, p. 34.

Fig. 2, p. 69 From *Les belles heures de Jean, Duc de Berry*, executed by the Limbourg brothers, c. 1408.

Fig. 3, p. 69 After Black Death web page <www.insecta-inspecta.com/fleas/bdeath/Black>.

Fig. 9, p. 62 After T. Jones Hughes, 'Town and baile in Irish place-names' in N. L. Stephens and R. Glasscock (eds), *Irish geographical studies* (Belfast, 1970), p. 248.

Fig. 10, p. 62 After W. Smyth, 'Society and settlement in seventeenth-century Ireland: the evidence of the '1659 census'' in Smyth and Whelan (eds), *Common ground*, p. 61.

Fig. 8, p. 84 Hore, *Wexford*, vi, p. 396.

Fig. 14, p. 88 After J. Silke 'The Irish abroad, 1534–1691' in *New history of Ireland*, iii, p. 616.

Fig. 3, p. 101 After J. Andrews, 'The struggle for Ireland's public commons' in P. O'Flanagan, P. Ferguson and K. Whelan (eds), *Rural Ireland: modernisation and change 1600–1900* (Cork, 1987), p. 15.

Fig. 21, p. 127 After Aalen, Whelan and Stout (eds), *Atlas*, fig. 17, p. 74.

Fig. 26B, p. 132 After T. Jones Hughes, 'Continuity and change in rural county Wexford in the nineteenth century' in K. Whelan (ed.), *Wexford: history and society*

(Dublin, 1987), p. 352.

Fig. 2. p. 135 From K. Whelan, *Fellowship of freedom* (Cork, 1998), p. 24.

Fig. 11, p. 140 From Whelan, *Fellowship of freedom*, p. 73.

Fig. 16, p. 144 After Hore, *Wexford*, v, p. 62.

Fig. 19, p. 147 From Whelan, *Fellowship of freedom*, p. 72.

Fig. 17, p. 166 Unpublished map courtesy of David Miller.

Fig. 42, p. 172 After *Report of the Railway Commissioners* (London, 1837).

Fig. 19, p. 181 Unpublished map courtesy of Kevin Whelan.

Fig. 20, p. 181 After David Miller, 'Mass attendance in Ireland in 1834' in S. Brown and D. Miller (eds.), *Piety and power in Ireland 1760–1960* (Notre Dame, 2000), p. 173

Fig. 17, p. 192 After *Sensmap subtidal summary report Wexford Harbour* by Ecological Consultancy Services Ltd. (Dublin, 2001).

Fig. 27, p. 197 After *Wexford town and environs development plan 2002*.

BIBLIOGRAPHY

Manuscript sources

Books of Survey and Distribution, vol. 12., N. A. I.

Colclough Papers, N. L. I., Ms 29, 755(4).

Depositions Trinity College, Dublin. T. C. D., Ms 818 Wexford, i; T. C. D., Ms 819, Wexford, ii.

Down Survey maps (1655), N. L. I., Ms. 725.

Thomas Handcock's narrative of 1798, N. L. I., Ms 16,232.

Tithe Applotment Books, N. A. I.

Wexford Corporation archives.

Wexford Town Plan, 1840: N. A. I., OS 140 4/638/20.

Printed primary sources

Annals of the kingdom of Ireland by the four masters (ed.), J. O'Donovan, 7 v (Dublin, 1848–51).

Calendar of Close Rolls (London, 1892–1963).

Calendar of the ancient deeds and muniments preserved in the Pembroke estate office, Dublin (Dublin, 1891).

Berry, H. F. (ed.), *Statute rolls of the parliament of Ireland 1–12 Ed. II* (Dublin, 1914).

Brooks, E. St John (ed.), *Knights' fees in counties Wexford, Carlow and Kilkenny* (Dublin, 1950).

Calendar of Inquisitions post mortem (London, 1904–74).

Commission of public instruction, Ireland (London, 1835).

Curtis, E. (ed.), *Calendar of Ormond deeds*, 6 v (Dublin, 1932–43).

Gwynn, A. and R. N. Hadcock, *Medieval religious houses Ireland* (Dublin, 1970).

Hore, H. F. (ed.), 'A choreographic account of the southern part of the county of Wexford, written anno 1684 by Robert Leigh, esq., of Rosegarland, in that county' in *R. S. A. I. Jn.*, v (1858–9), pp 451–67.

Hore, P. H., *History of the town and county of Wexford*, 6 v (London, 1900–11).

Lewis, S., *A topographical dictionary of Ireland*, 2 v (London, 1837).

Meadows, H. L., *Alphabetical index to the townlands and towns of the county of Wexford* (Dublin, 1861).

Minutes of evidence taken before the select committee on the Wexford election petition (London, 1830).

Moore, M., *Archaeological inventory of county Wexford* (Dublin, 1996).

O'Flanagan, M. (compiler), *Letters containing information relative to the antiquities of the county of Wexford collected during the progress of the Ordnance Survey in 1840*, 2 v (Bray, 1933).

Orpen, G. (ed.), *The song of Dermot and the earl* (Oxford, 1892).

'Report of the state of Popery in Ireland, 1731' in *Archivium Hibernicum*, iv (1915), pp 166–71.

Scott, A. B. and F. X. Martin (eds), *Expugnatio Hibernica, the conquest of Ireland, by Gerald de Barry* (Dublin, 1978).

Second Report from the Commissioners of Irish Education enquiry (London, 1826–7).

Simington, R. C. (ed.), *The Civil Survey of the county of Wexford* (Dublin, 1953).

Stout, G. *et al.*, *Sites and monument record, county Wexford* (Dublin, 1987).

Sweetman, H. S. (ed.), *Calendar of documents relating to Ireland*, 5 v (London, 1875–86).

White, N. B. (ed.), *Extents of Irish monastic possessions* 1540–1 (Dublin, 1943).

Secondary works

Aalen, F. (ed), *The future of the Irish landscape* (Dublin, 1985).

Aalen, F., 'Buildings' in Aalen, Whelan and Stout (eds), *Atlas*, pp 145–79.

Aalen, F., K. Whelan and M. Stout (eds), *Atlas of the Irish rural landscape* (Cork, 1997).

Andrews, J., *The Wexford Civil Survey as a source for historical geography* (private circulation, 1956).

Andrews, J., 'Land and people, c. 1780' in T. W. Moody and W. E. Vaughan (eds), *New history of Ireland iv, eighteenth century* (Oxford, 1986), pp 236–64.

Andrews, J., *Shapes of Ireland* (Dublin, 1997).

Andrews, J., 'Landmarks in early Wexford cartography' in Whelan (ed.), *Wexford*, pp 447–66.

Andrews, J., 'The struggle for Ireland's public commons' in P. O'Flanagan, P. Ferguson and K. Whelan (eds), *Rural Ireland: modernisation and change 1600–1900* (Cork, 1987), pp 1–23.

Anon., 'The Presentation Convent' in Berney (ed.), *Centenary record*, pp 145–6.

Anon., 'The Convent of Mercy' in Berney (ed.), *Centenary record*, pp 147–8.

Anon., 'The Christian Brothers in Wexford' in Berney (ed.), *Centenary record*, pp 143–4.

Anon., 'The beginning of a new era' in Berney (ed.), *Centenary record*, pp 77–8.

Anon., 'Wexford shipping' in Berney (ed.), *Centenary record*, pp 120–3.

Anon., 'Wexford mass-houses of the Penal days' in Berney (ed.), *Centenary record*, pp 54–7.

Archdall, M., *Monasticon Hibernicum* (London, 1786).

Barnard, T. C., 'An Anglo-Irish industrial enterprise: iron-making at Enniscorthy, Co. Wexford 1657–92' in *R. I. A. Proc.*, C, lxxxv (1985), pp 101–44.

Barrett, G. F., 'Recovering the hidden landscape' in Aalen, Stout and Whelan (eds), *Atlas*, pp 64–6.

Barry, T., *Medieval moated sites of south-east Ireland* (Oxford, 1977).

Barry, T., *The archaeology of medieval Ireland* (London, 1987).

Barry, T., R. M. Cleary and M. Hurley (eds), *Late Viking age and medieval Waterford* (Waterford, n. d.).

Bartlett, T., D. Dickson, D. Keogh and K. Whelan (eds), *1798: a bicentenary perspective* (Dublin, 2003).

Bassett, G., *Wexford county: guide and directory* (Dublin, 1885).

Bennett, I., 'The settlement pattern of ringforts in county Wexford,' in *R. S. A. I. Jn.*, cxix (1989), pp 50–61.

Bennett, I., 'Preliminary archaeological excavations at Ferrycarrig ringwork, Newtown Td., Co. Wexford' in *Wex. Hist. Soc. Jn.*, x (1984–5), pp 25–43.

Berney, M. J. (ed.), *Centenary record of Wexford's twin churches* (Wexford, 1958).

Berney, M., 'Finding the money' in Berney (ed.), *Centenary record*, pp 79–82.

Bourke, E., 'Two early eleventh-century Viking houses from Bride Street, Wexford and the layout of properties on the site' in *Wex. Hist. Soc. Jn.*, xii (1988–9), pp 50–61.

Bourke, E., 'Westgate, etc.,' in I. Bennett (ed.), *Excavations* (1990), no. 121.

Bradley, J. and H. King, *Urban archaeology survey, county Wexford* (Dublin, n. d.).

Bradley, J., 'Planned Anglo-Norman towns in Ireland' in H. Clarke and A. Simms (eds), *The comparative history of urban origins in non-Roman Europe* (Oxford, 1985), pp 411–67.

Bradley, J., (ed.), *Settlement and society in medieval Ireland* (Kilkenny, 1988).

Bradley, J., 'The interpretation of Scandinavian settlement in Ireland' in Bradley (ed.), *Settlement and society*, pp 49–78.

Bradley J. and A. Halpin, 'The topographical development of Scandinavian and Anglo-Norman Waterford' in W. Nolan and T. Power (eds), *Waterford: history and society* (Dublin, 1992), pp 105–30.

Bradley, J., 'The topographical development of Scandinavian Dublin' in F. Aalen and K. Whelan (eds), *Dublin city and county: from pre-history to present* (Dublin, 1992).

Braudel, F., *Civilisation and capitalism: the structures of everyday life* (London, 1988).

Brewer, J. N., *The beauties of Ireland, being original delineations, topographical, historical and biographical, of each county*, 2 v (London, 1826).

Browne, M. and C. Ó Clábaigh (eds), *The Irish Benedictines* (Dublin, 2005).

Byrne, F., *Irish kings and high kings* (London, 1987).

Browne, B., 'John Barry, the forgotten American hero' in *Wex. Hist. Soc. Jn.*, xv (1994–5), pp 43–51.

Browne, B., 'Lemuel Cox: an American bridge builder in Ireland' in *The Past*, 27 (2006), pp 106–12.

Browne, B. (ed.), *The Wexford Man: essays in honour of Nicky Furlong* (Dublin, 2007).

Bolger, D. (ed.), *Wexford through its writers* (Dublin, 1992).

Cahill, M., 'Boxes, beads, bobbins and notions' in *Arch. Ire.*, viii, 1 (Spring, 1994), pp 21–3.

Cahill, M., 'Unspooling the mystery' in *Arch. Ire.*, xv, 3 (Autumn, 2001), pp 8–15.

Cahill, M., 'Finding function in the late Bronze Age' in *Ancient gold technology: America and Europe* (Madrid, 2004), pp 349–58.

Canny, N., 'Early modern Ireland c. 1500–1700' in R. Foster (ed.), *The Oxford illustrated history of Ireland* (Oxford, 1989), pp 104–60.

Carter, R. and J. Orford (eds), Irish Association for Quaternary Studies Field Guide No. 4, *The south and east coasts of Wexford* (Dublin, 1982).

Carty, E., 'Wexford Workhouse in Famine times' in *Wex. Hist. Soc. Jn.*, xvi (1996–7), pp 95–113.

Childs, W. and T. O'Neill, 'Overseas trade' in A. Cosgrove (ed.), *A new history of Ireland,* ii (Oxford, 1993), pp 492–524.

Clarke, A., 'The Irish economy 1600–1660' in *New history of Ireland,* iii, pp 168-86.

Clarke, H., 'The topographical development of early medieval Dublin' in *R. S. A. I. Jn.,* cvii (1977), pp 29–51.

Clarke, H. and A. Simms (eds), *The comparative history of urban origins in non-Roman Europe* (Oxford, 1985).

Clarke, H., M. Ní Mhaonaigh and R. Ó Floinn (eds), *Ireland and Scandinavia in the early Viking age* (Dublin, 1998).

Clarke, H., 'Proto-towns and towns in Ireland and Britain in the ninth and tenth centuries' in Clarke, Ní Mhaonaigh and Ó Floinn (eds), *Ireland and Scandinavia,* pp 331–380.

Cleary, B., 'The Battle of Oulart Hill: context and strategy' in D. Keogh and N. Furlong (eds), *The mighty wave: the 1798 Rebellion in Wexford* (Dublin, 1996), pp 79–96.

Cleary, B., 'Sowing the whirlwind' in *Wex. Hist. Soc. Jn.,* xiii (1992–3), pp 9–79.

Clinton, M., 'Settlement patterns in the early historic kingdom of Leinster (seventh to mid twelfth century)' in A. P. Smyth (ed.), *Seanchas: studies in early and medieval archaeology, history and literature in honour of F. J. Byrne* (Dublin, 2000), pp 275–98.

Colfer, B., *The promontory of Hook* (Wexford, 1978).

Colfer, B., 'Anglo-Norman settlement in county Wexford' in Whelan (ed.), *Wexford,* pp 65–101.

Colfer, B., 'Medieval Wexford' in *Wex. Hist. Soc. Jn.,* xiii (1990–1), pp 5–29.

Colfer, B., 'The Hook, county Wexford' in Aalen, Whelan and Stout (eds.), *Atlas of the Irish rural landscape,* pp 262–76.

Colfer, B., *Arrogant trespass: Anglo-Norman Wexford 1169–1400* (Enniscorthy, 2002).

Colfer, B., *The Hook Peninsula* (Cork, 2004).

Comerford, P., 'Euseby Cleaver, Bishop of Ferns, and the clergy of the Church of Ireland in the 1798 Rising in Co. Wexford' in *Wex. Hist. Soc. Jn.,* xvi (1996–7), pp 66–94.

Corish, P., 'Reformation and Counter-Reformation (1500–1700)' in M. Berney (ed.), *Centenary Record* (Wexford, 1958), pp 35–49.

Corish, P., 'The diocese of Ferns in the Penal Days' in *The Past,* viii (1970), pp 5–17.

Corish, P., *The Catholic community in the seventeenth and eighteenth centuries* (Dublin, 1981).

Corish, P., 'Two centuries of Catholicism in county Wexford' in Whelan (ed.), *Wexford,* pp 222–47.

Corish, P., 'James Caulfield, Bishop of Ferns (1786–1814)' in *Wex. Hist. Soc. Jn.,* xvi (1996–7), pp 114–25.

Creedon, W. P. (compiled by), *Exemplar Hiberniae: 100 years of local government in county Wexford* (Dublin, 1999).

Croke, F. (ed.), *George Victor Du Noyer 1817–1869: Hidden landscapes* (Dublin, 1995).

Crouch, D., *William Marshal: court, career and chivalry in the Angevin empire 1147–1219* (London, 1990).

Cullen, L., *The emergence of modern Ireland 1600-1900* (Dublin, 1983).

Cullen, L., 'Economic development: 1691–1750' in Moody and Vaughan (eds), *New history of Ireland,* iv, pp 123–58.

Cullen, L., 'The 1798 rebellion in Wexford: United Irishman organisation, membership, leadership' in Whelan (ed.) *Wexford,* pp 248–95.

Cullen, L., 'Man, landscape and roads; the changing eighteenth-century landscape' in W. Nolan (ed.), *The shaping of Ireland* (Dublin, 1988), pp 123–36.

Culleton, E. (ed.), *The castles of county Wexford by W. H. Jeffrey* (typescript produced by Wexford Historical Society, 1979).

Culleton, E., *The south Wexford landscape* (Dublin, 1980).

Culleton, E., *Early man in county Wexford 5000 B. C. – 300 B. C.* (Dublin, 1984).

Culleton, E., (ed.), *Treasures of the landscape: county Wexford's rural heritage* (Wexford, 1994).

Culleton, E., *Celtic and Early Christian Wexford* (Dublin, 1999).

Curtis, E., 'The English and Ostmen in Ireland' in *English Historical Review,* xxiii (1908), pp 217–10.

Daley, K., *Tom Walsh's opera: the history of the Wexford Festival 1951–2004* (Dublin, 2004).

Davies, R. R., *Domination and conquest: the experience of Ireland, Scotland and Wales 1100–1300* (Cambridge, 1990).

De Courcy Ireland, J., 'County Wexford in maritime history' in Whelan (ed.), *Wexford,* pp 490–506.

De Paor, M. and L. De Paor, *Early Christian Ireland* (London, 1961).

Doherty, C., 'Exchange and trade in early medieval Ireland' in *R. S. A. I. Jn.,* cx (1980), pp 67–89.

Doherty, C., 'The Vikings in Ireland: a review' in Clarke, Ní Mhaonaigh and Ó Floinn (eds), *Ireland and Scandinavia,* pp 288–330.

Doyle, E., *The Wexford insurgents of '98 and their march into Meath* (Enniscorthy, 1997).

Doyle, E., 'The Wexford rebels of '98 in the folk memory of county Meath' in *Wex. Hist. Soc. Jn.,* xviiii (2002–3), pp 120–52.

Duffy, J., *River Slaney: from source to sea* (Tullow, 2006).

Duffy, S., *Ireland in the middle ages* (Dublin, 1997).

Edwards, N., *The archaeology of early medieval Ireland* (London, 1990).

Enright, M., *Men of iron* (Wexford, 1987).

Estyn Evans, E. *The personality of Ireland* (Belfast, 1981).

Falkiner, C. L., 'The Hospital of St John of Jerusalem in Ireland' in *R. I. A. Proc.,* C, xxvi (1907), pp 275–317.

Flanagan, M.-T., *Irish society, Anglo-Norman settlers, Angevin kingship* (Oxford, 1989).

Frame, R., *Ireland and Britain 1170-1450* (London, 1998).

Fraser, R., *A statistical survey of county Wexford* (Dublin, 1807).

Furlong, N., 'The history of land reclamation in Wexford Harbour' in *Wex. Hist. Soc. Jn.,* ii (1969), pp 53–77.

Furlong, N., *Dermot, king of Leinster and the foreigners* (Tralee, 1974).

Furlong, N., 'The times and life of Nicholas Sweetman, Bishop of Ferns (1744–86)' in *Wex. Hist. Soc. Jn.,* ix (1983–4), pp 1–19.

Furlong, N., *Fr John Murphy of Boolavogue 1753–1798* (Dublin, 1991).

Furlong, N., *A history of county Wexford* (Dublin, 2003).

Furlong, N. and J. Hayes, *County Wexford in the rare oul' times,* 4 v (Wexford, 1985–2005).

Furlong, N., *Diarmait, king of Leinster* (Cork, 2006).

Gahan, D., *The peoples' rising* (Dublin, 1995).

Gahan, J. V., *The secular priests of the diocese of Ferns* (Strasbourg, 2000).

Gardiner, M. J. and P. Ryan, *Soils of county Wexford* (Dublin, 1964).

Gaul, L., *Masters of Irish music* (Dublin, 2006).

Geoghegan, P. and D. Culligan, *Building sensitively in the landscapes of county Wexford* (Dublin, 1988).

Glynn, J., 'The Catholic Church in Wexford town 1800–1858' in *The Past,* xv (1984), pp 5–54.

Goff, H., 'English conquest of an Irish barony: the changing patterns of land ownership in the barony of Scarawalsh 1540–1640' in Whelan (ed.), *Wexford,* pp 122–49.

Goodall, D., 'The freemen of Wexford in 1776' in *The Irish Genealogist,* v (1973), no. 1, pp 103–21; no. 2, pp 314–34; no. 4, pp 448–63.

Goodall, D., 'All the cooking that could be used' – a county Wexford election in 1754' in *The Past,* xii (1978), pp 3–22.

Gordon, J., *History of the Rebellion in Ireland in the year 1798* (Dublin, 1803).

Graham, B., 'The towns of medieval Ireland' in R. A. Butlin (ed.), *The development of the Irish town* (London, 1977), pp 28–60.

Graham. B., 'The definition and classification of medieval Irish towns' in *Irish geog.,* xxi (1988), pp 20–32.

Grannel, F., *The Franciscans in Wexford* (Wexford, n. d.).

Grattan-Flood, W. H., *History of the diocese of Ferns* (Waterford, 1916).

Griffith, R., *General valuation of rateable property in Ireland: county Wexford* (Dublin, 1853).

Griffiths, G., *Chronicles of the county Wexford to 1877* (Enniscorthy, 1877).

Gwinnell, M., 'The Famine years in county Wexford' in *Wex. Hist. Soc. Jn.,* ix (1983–4), pp 36–54.

Gwinnell, M., 'Some aspects of the economic life of county Wexford in the nineteenth century' in *Wex. Hist. Soc. Jn.,* x (1984–5), pp 5–24.

Gwynn, E. (ed. and trans.), *The Metrical Dindshenchas,* 5 v (Dublin, 1924).

Gwynn, A. and R. Hadcock, *Medieval religious houses Ireland* (Dublin, 1970).

Gwynn, A., 'The Black Death in Ireland' in *Studies,* xxiv (1935), pp 25–42.

Hadden, G., 'The origin and development of Wexford town' in *Wex. Hist. Soc. Jn.,* parts 1 and 2, i (1968), pp 5–16; part 3, ii (1969), pp 3–12; part 4, iii (1970–1), pp 5–10.

Hadden, G., 'The Slaney Gab[b]ard' in *Wex. Hist. Soc. Jn,* ix (1983–1984), pp 74–7.

Harbison, P., *Guide to national and historic monuments of Ireland* (Dublin, 1992).

Harbison, P., 'Exotic ninth-to-tenth century cross-decorated stones from Clonmore, Co. Carlow and Begerin, Co. Wexford' in G. Mac Niocaill and P. Wallace (eds), *Keimelia: studies in memory of Tom Delaney* (Galway, 1988), pp 59–79.

Harbison, P., 'Barralet and Beranger's antiquarian sketching tour through Wicklow and Wexford in the autumn of 1780' in *R. I. A. Proc.,* 104, C, no. 6 (2004), pp 132–90.

Haren, M. (ed.), *Calendar of papal letters relating to Great Britain and Ireland,* xix (Dublin, 1978).

Haworth, R., 'The site of St Olave's church, Dublin' in Bradley (ed.), *Society and settlement,* pp 177–91.

Hay, E., *History of the Insurrection in the county of Wexford, A. D. 1798* (Dublin, 1803).

Hearne, I., 'The Star Iron Works' in *Wex. Hist. Soc. Jn.,* xviiii (2002–3), pp 5–37.

Henthorn Todd, J. (ed.), *Cogadh Gaedhel re Gallaibh* (London, 1867).

Holland, C. H., *The geology of Ireland* (Edinburgh, 2001).

Hore, H. F., 'Woods and fastnesses, and their denizens in ancient Leinster' in *R. S. A. I. Jn.,* iv (1856–7), pp 229–40.

Hore, H. F. (ed.), 'Particulars relative to Wexford and the barony of Forth by Solomon Richards, 1682' in *R. S. A. I. Jn.,* vi (1862), pp 89–90.

Hore, H. F. (ed.), 'An account of the barony of Forth, in the county of Wexford, written at the close of the seventeenth century' in *R. S. A. I. Jn.,* vi (1862), pp 66–7.

Hurley, J. *The South Wexford coast* (Kilmore, 1994).

Hurley, M., 'Topography and development' in Barry, Cleary and Hurley (eds), *Late Viking Age and medieval Waterford,* pp 7–10.

Inglis, H. D., 'A journey through Wexford in 1834' in *The Past,* vii (1964), pp 172–85.

Jenkins, J., *The Tate School, Wexford 1867–1949* (Wexford, n. d.).

Johnson, R., *Viking Age Dublin* (Dublin, 2004).

Jones Hughes, T., 'Town and baile in Irish place-names' in N. L. Stephens and R. Glasscock (eds), *Irish geographical studies* (Belfast, 1970), pp 244–58.

Jones Hughes, T., 'Continuity and change in rural county Wexford in the nineteenth century' in Whelan (ed.), *Wexford,* pp 342–72.

Joyce, P. W., *The origin and history of Irish names of places,* 3 v (Dublin, 1910–13).

Jupp, P., 'Urban politics in Ireland 1801–1831' in D. Harkness and M. O'Dowd (eds), *The town in Ireland* (Belfast, 1981), pp 103–24.

Kavanagh, A. and R. Murphy, *The Wexford gentry,* 2 v (Bunclody, 1994–6).

Kehoe, G., 'Rosslare Fort and its people' in *Old Wex. Soc. Jn.,* part 1, iv (1972–3), pp 43–52; part 2, v (1974–5), pp 35–45.

Kehoe, M. T., *Wexford town – its streets and people* (Wexford, n. d.).

Kelly, E. P. and E. O'Donovan, 'A Viking longphort near Athlunkard, county Clare' in *Arch. Ire.,* xii, no. 4 (1998), pp 13–16.

Keogh, D. and N. Furlong (eds), *The mighty wave: the 1798 rebellion in Wexford* (Dublin, 1996).

Keogh, D., 'The women of 1798; explaining the silence' in Bartlett, Dickson, Keogh and Whelan (eds), *1798,* pp 512–28.

Kerrigan, P., *Castles and fortifications in Ireland 1485–1945* (Cork, 1995).

Kinsella, A., *County Wexford in the Famine years 1845–49* (Enniscorthy, 1995).

Kinsella, A., 'Women in folk memory and ballads' in Keogh and Furlong (eds), *The women of 1798,* pp 187–99.

Kinsella, A., 'Who feared to speak in '98' in *Wex. Hist. Soc. Jn.,* xvii (1998–9), pp 221–34.

Kohl, J. C., 'A journey through Wexford in 1842' in *The Past,* viii (1964), pp 186–204.

Lacy, T. *Sights and scenes in our fatherland* (London, 1863).

Laffan, W. (ed.), *Painting Ireland: topographical views from Glin Castle* (Tralee, 2006).

Leask, H., *Irish castles and castellated houses* (Dundalk, 1941).

Leask, H., *Irish churches and monastic buildings,* 3 v (Dundalk, 1977).

Lee, J. J., *Ireland 1912–1985: politics and society* (Cambridge, 1989).

Lenihan, P., *Confederate Catholics at war* (Cork, 2001).

Leslie, J., *Ferns clergy and parishes* (Dublin, 1936).

Lewis, S., *Topographical dictionary of Ireland,* 2 v (London, 1837).

Linebaugh, P. and M. Rediker, *The many-headed hydra: the hidden history of the revolutionary Atlantic* (London, 2000).

Loeber, R., *The geography and practice of English colonisation in Ireland 1534–1609* (Athlone, 1991).

Long, B., *Bright light, blue water* (Dublin, 1993).

Longfield, A. K., *Anglo-Irish trade in the sixteenth century* (London, 1929).

Lydon, J. F., *The lordship of Ireland in the middle ages* (Dublin, 1972).

Lydon, J. F., *Ireland in the later middle ages* (Dublin, 1973).

Lydon, J. F., 'The impact of the Bruce invasion' in *New history of Ireland,* ii, pp 3–37.

Lydon, J. F., *The making of Ireland* (London, 1998).

Mac Niocaill, G., *Na buirgéisí* (Baile Átha Cliath, 1964).

McLoughlin, C., 'Prehistoric remains at Kerlogue, Co. Wexford' in *Arch.*

Ire., xvi, 3 (Autumn, 2002), pp 16–19.

Maddock, J., *Rosslare Harbour: sea and ships* (Rosslare, 1996).

Mannion, J., 'A transatlantic fishery: Richard Walsh of New Ross and the Sweetmans of Newbawn in Newfoundland 1734–1862' in Whelan (ed.), *Wexford,* pp 373–421.

Maume, M., 'The Selskar Iron Works' in *Wex. Hist. Soc. Jn.,* xviii (2002–3), pp 5–37.

Mitchell, F., *Shell guide to reading the Irish landscape* (Dublin, 1986).

Mitchell, F. and M. Ryan, *Reading the Irish landscape* (Dublin, 1997).

Moody, T. and F. X. Martin (eds), *The course of Irish history* (Cork, 1967).

Moore, M., *Archaeological inventory of county Wexford* (Dublin, 1996).

Moynihan, M., 'The administration of justice in Wexford' in *Wex. Hist. Soc. Jn.,* v (1974–5), pp 5–21.

Mullarney, K., L. Svensson, D. Zetterstrom and P. Grant, *Collins Bird Guide* (London, 1999).

Murphy, E., 'The Semples and St Selskar's' in *Wex. Hist. Soc. Jn.,* xx (2004–5), pp 45–55.

Murphy, H., 'The Drinagh cement works' in *Wex. Hist. Soc. Jn.,* vi (1976–7), pp 38–44.

Murphy, H., *Families of county Wexford* (Dublin, 1986).

Murphy, H., 'A humiliating defeat for Richard J. Devereux' in *Wex. Hist. Soc. Jn.,* xiii (1992–3), pp 129–34.

Murphy, H. (ed.), 'Memories of Colonel Jonas Watson' in *Wex. Hist. Soc. Jn.,* xv (1994–5), pp 115–18.

Murphy, H., 'When Wexford workers first united' in *Wex. Hist. Soc. Jn.,* xv (1994–5), pp 98–101.

Murphy, H., *A Wexford century: People newspapers souvenir millennium supplement* (2000).

Nicholls, K., *Gaelic and Gaelicised Ireland in the middle ages* (Dublin, 1972).

Nicholls, K., 'Anglo-French Ireland and after' in *Peritia,* i (1982), pp 370–403.

Ní Dhonnachadha, M., 'Inis Teimle, between Uí Chennselaig and the Déissi' in *Peritia,* 16 (2002), pp 457–8.

Nolan, W., *Tracing the past: sources for local studies in the Republic of Ireland* (Dublin, 1982).

Noonan, D. and S. Elder, 'Cornmarket, Wexford' in I. Bennett (ed.), *Excavations* (2000), no. 1071.

O'Brien, R., P. Quinney and I. Russell, 'Preliminary report on the archaeological excavation and finds strategy of the Hiberno-Scandinavian site of Woodstown 6, county Waterford' in *Decies,* lxi (2005), pp 13–122.

O'Callaghan, J., 'Fortified houses of the sixteenth century in south Wexford' in *Wex. Hist. Soc. Jn.,* viii (1980-1), pp 1–51.

O'Conor, K., 'The origins of Carlow Castle' in *Arch. Ire.,* no. 41 (Autumn, 1997), pp 13–16.

Ó Corráin, D., *Ireland before the Normans* (Dublin, 1972).

Ó Corráin, D., 'The Uí Chennselaig kingdom of Leinster 1072-1126' in *Wex. Hist. Soc. Jn.,* v (1974–5), pp 26–31.

Oftedal, M., 'Scandinavian place-names in Ireland' in B. Almquist and D. Greene (eds), *Proceedings of the seventh Viking congress* (Dublin, 1976).

Ohlmeyer, J., 'The Dunkirk of Ireland: Wexford privateers during the 1640s' in *Wex. Hist. Soc. Jn.,* xii (1988–89), pp 23–49.

Ohlmeyer, J., 'A failed revolution' in J. Ohlmeyer (ed.), *Ireland from independence to occupation* (Cambridge, 1995), pp 1–23..

O'Keeffe, T., *Medieval Ireland: an archaeology* (Charleston, 2000).

O'Keeffe, T. and M. Coughlan, 'The chronology and formal affinities of Ferns donjon, Co. Wexford' in J. R. Kenyon and K. O'Conor (eds), *The medieval castle in Ireland and Wales* (Dublin, 2003), pp 133–48.

O'Leary, B., 'Richard Pierce: architect and acolyte of the Gothic revival' in *Wex. Hist. Soc. Jn.,* xx (2004–5), pp 75–102.

Ó Muirithe, D., *The Wexford carols* (Mountrath, 1982).

Ó Muirithe, D. and D. Nuttall (eds), *The folklore of county Wexford* (Dublin, 1999).

O'Neill, T., *Merchants and mariners in medieval Ireland* (Dublin, 1987).

O'Reilly, W., 'Charles Vallancey and the military itinerary of Ireland' in *R. I. A. Proc.,* C, cvi (2006), pp 125–217.

Ó Riordáin, S., *Antiquities of the Irish countryside* (London, 1953).

Orpen, G. H., 'Ptolemy's map of Ireland' in *R. S. A. I. Jn.* xxiv (1894), pp 115–24.

Orpen, G. H., *Ireland under the Normans,* 4 v (Oxford, 1911–20).

Ó Siochrú, M., *Confederate Ireland 1642–1649: a constitutional and political analysis* (Dublin, 1999).

O'Sullivan, A., 'Castlebridge' in Rowe and Wilson (eds), *High skies – low lands,* pp 53–5.

O'Sullivan, A., 'Pierces of Wexford' in *Wex. Hist. Soc. Jn.*, xvi (1996–7), pp 126–42.

O'Sullivan, S., 'Jonathan Swift and Wexford's spa' in *Wex. Hist. Soc. Jn.*, vi (1976–7), pp 63–8.

Otway-Ruthven, J., 'The character of Norman settlement in Ireland' in *Historical Studies*, v (1965), pp 75–84.

Otway-Ruthven, J., *A history of medieval Ireland* (London, 1968).

Parle, J., 'Solving a wartime fuel crisis in Co. Wexford' in *Wex. Hist. Soc. Jn.*, xv (1994–5), pp 15–33.

Parle, J., *The mummers of Wexford* (Wexford, 2001).

Parliamentary Gazetteer (London, 1845).

Pender, S., (ed.), *A census of Ireland circa 1659 with supplementary material from the poll money ordinances 1660–61* (Dublin, 1939).

Quinn, D. B. and K. Nicholls, 'Ireland in 1534' in T. W. Moody, F. X. Martin and F. J. Byrne (eds), *A new history of Ireland*, iii (Oxford, 1976), pp 1–38.

Rafferty, C., ''Immensity confined': Luke Waddinge, Bishop of Ferns' in *Wex. Hist. Soc, Jn.*, xii (1988–9), pp 5–22.

Rafferty, C., 'The Roman Catholic parish registers of Wexford town from c. 1672: some considerations of their significance and use in historical research' in *Wex. Hist. Soc. Jn.*, xv (1994–5), pp 102–14.

Raftery, B., *Pagan Celtic Ireland* (London, 1994).

Ranson, J., 'The Kilmore Carols' in *The Past*, v (1949), pp 61–102.

Ranson, J., *Songs of the Wexford coast* (Wexford, 1975).

Reck, P., *Wexford – a municipal history* (Wexford, 1987).

Richards, M., 'Norse place-names in Wales' in B. Ó Cuív (ed.), *The impact of the Scandinavian invasions on the Celtic-speaking peoples c. 800–1100 A. D.* (Dublin, 1959).

Reeves, W., 'On the townland distribution of Ireland' in *R. I. A. Proc.*, vii (1857–61), pp 473–90.

Roche, B., *Tumbling down* (Dublin, 1986).

Roche, R., *The Norman invasion of Ireland* (Tralee, 1970).

Roche, R., *Tales of the Wexford coast* (Enniscorthy, 1993).

Roche, W., N. Rossiter, K. Hurley and T. Hayes, *Walk Wexford ways* (Wexford, 1988).

Roesdahl, E., *The Vikings* (London, 1991).

Rossiter, N., *Wexford Port – a history* (Wexford, 1989).

Rossiter, N., 'Lost laneways and hidden treasures' in *Wex. Hist. Soc. Jn.*, 19 (2002–3), pp 62–76.

Rowe, D. and C. Wilson (eds), *High skies – low lands: an anthology of the Wexford slobs and harbour* (Enniscorthy, 1996).

Rowe, D., 'Punt gunning' in Rowe and Wilson (eds), *High skies–low lands*, pp 129–36.

Rowe, D., 'The Yankee slip' in Rowe and Wilson (eds), *High skies – low lands*, p 39.

Rowe, D., 'The Rowes of Spawell Road' in *Wex. Hist. Soc. Jn.*, xviii (2000–1), pp 125–31.

Rowe, D. and E. Scallan, *Houses of Wexford* (Whitegate, 2004).

Russell, J. 'Late thirteenth-century Ireland as a region' in *Demography*, iii (1966), pp 500–12.

Ryan, M. and M. Cahill, 'An investigation of the town wall at Abbey Street, Wexford' in *Old Wex. Soc. Jn.*, viii (1980–1), pp 56–64.

Rynne, C., *Industrial Ireland 1750–1930: an archaeology* (Cork, 2006).

Sawyer, P. H., *Kings and Vikings: Scandinavia and Europe A. D. 700–1100* (New York, 1994).

Scallan, E., *Wexford Boat Club* (Wexford, 2004).

Scallan, E., *Clonard Church: the church of the Annunciation* (Wexford, 2007).

Sheehan, C., 'South Main Street/North Main Street, Wexford' in I. Bennett (ed.), *Excavations* (1997), no. 608.

Shepherd, E., 'The town of Wexford and the railways' in *Wex. Hist. Soc. Jn.*, xviii (2000–1), pp 59–93.

Simms, A., 'Core and periphery in medieval Europe: the Irish experience in a wider context' in Smyth and Whelan (eds), *Common ground*, pp 22–40.

Skrine, H., 'A glimpse of Bagenal Harvey' in *Wex. Hist. Soc. Jn.*, xiii (1992–93), pp 92–100.

Smyth, A. P., *Celtic Leinster: towards an historical geography of early Irish civilisation A. D. 500–1600* (Dublin, 1982).

Smyth, A. P. (ed.), *Seanchas: studies in early and medieval Irish archaeology, history and literature in honour of Francis J. Byrne* (Dublin, 2000).

Smyth, W., 'Society and settlement in seventeenth-century Ireland: the evidence of the '1659 census'' in Smyth and Whelan (eds), *Common ground*, pp 55–83.

Smyth, W., *Map-making, landscapes and memory: a geography of colonial and early modern Ireland* (Cork, 2006).

Spencer, K., 'Pugin and county Wexford' in *Wex. Hist. Soc. Jn.*, viii (1980–1), pp 77–90.

Stanihurst, R., 'Description of Ireland' in R. Holinshed, *Chronicles* (London, 1577).

Stout, G., *et al*, 'The sites and monument record for county Wexford, an introduction' in *Wex. Hist. Soc. Jn.*, xi (1986–7), pp 5–13.

Stout, G., 'Wexford in pre-history: 5,000 B. C. to 300 A. D.' in Whelan (ed.), *Wexford*, pp 1–39.

Stout, G., *Newgrange and the Bend of the Boyne* (Cork, 2002).

Stout, M., *The Irish ringfort* (Dublin, 1997).

Stout, G. and M. Stout, 'Early landscapes: from prehistory to plantation' in Aalen, Whelan and Stout (eds), *Atlas*, pp 31–63.

Swan, L., 'Enclosed ecclesiastical sites and their relevance to settlement patterns of the first millennium A. D.' in T. Reeves-Smyth and F. Hammond (eds), *Landscape archaeology in Ireland* (Oxford, 1983), pp 269–80.

Sweetman, D., *The medieval castles of Ireland* (Cork, 1999).

Sweetman, D., 'The fortified house in Ireland' in Smyth (ed.), *Seanchas*, pp 448–53.

Sweetman, D., 'The hall-house in Ireland' in Kenyon and O'Conor (eds), *The medieval castle in Ireland and Wales* (Dublin, 2003), pp 121–32.

Taylor, D., The overseas trade of mid sixteenth-century Bridgewater (MA Bristol University, 2006) <http://www.bris.ac.uk/Depts/History/Maritime/Sources/2006taylor.pdf>

Tietzsch-Tyler, D. and A. G. Sleeman (eds), *Geology of south Wexford* (Dublin, 1994).

The Free Press (Wexford, various dates).

Thomas, A., *The walled towns of Ireland* (Dublin, 1992).

Tobin, M., 'The population of county Wexford in the seventeenth century' in *The Past*, vi (1950), p. 134.

Wallace, P., 'Wexford town: Oyster Lane' in *Excavations* (1974), p. 28.

Wallace, P., 'Archaeology and the emergence of Dublin as the principal town of Ireland' in Bradley (ed.), *Settlement and society*, pp 123–60.

Walsh, D., *100 Wexford country houses* (Enniscorthy, 2001).

Watt, J., *The church in medieval Ireland* (Dublin, 1972).

'Wexford Corporation's eighteenth-century leases' in *Wex. Hist. Soc. Jn.*, xiii (1990–91), pp 144–5.

Wexford County Council and Wexford Town Council, *Wexford town development plan, 2002*.

Whelan, K., 'The Catholic church, the Catholic chapel and village development in Ireland' in *Irish Geog.*, xvi (1983), pp 1–15.

Whelan, K., 'The regional impact of Irish Catholicism 1700–1850' in Smyth and Whelan (eds), *Common ground*, pp 257–77.

Whelan, K., 'The modern landscape: from plantation to present' in Aalen, Whelan and Stout (eds), *Atlas*, pp 67–103.

Whelan, K. (ed.), *Wexford, history and society* (Dublin, 1987).

Whelan, K., 'A list of those from county Wexford implicated in the 1641 Rebellion' in *The Past*, xvii (1990), pp 24–54.

Whelan, K., 'The Catholic community in eighteenth-century county Wexford' in T. Power and K. Whelan (eds), *Endurance and emergence: Catholics in Ireland in the eighteenth century* (Dublin, 1990), pp 129–70.

Whelan, K., *The tree of liberty* (Cork, 1996).

Whelan, K., 'Towns and villages' in Aalen, Whelan and Stout (eds), *Atlas*, pp 180–96.

Whelan, K., *Fellowship of freedom* (Cork, 1998).

Wickham, T. and T., 'The Wexford Union Workhouse' in *Taghmon Hist. Soc. Jn.*, part 1, no. 5, pp 80–98; part 2, no. 6, pp 78–99.

Williams. T., *Fairways of the sea* (Rosslare, 2004).

Wilson, C. 'The Wexford Wildfowl Reserve' in Rowe and Wilson (eds), *High skies–low lands*, pp 245–7.

Wilson, C. J., 'The birds of Wexford Slobs and Harbour' in Rowe and Wilson (eds), *High skies–low lands*. pp 143–206.

Wren, J., 'Wexford' in I. Bennett (ed.), *Excavations* (1994), no. 229.

Wren, J., 'Cornmarket, Wexford' in I. Bennett (ed.), *Excavations* (2000), no. 1070.

INDEX